# CAPITOL
# GAMES

# CAPITOL GAMES

## *Clarence Thomas, Anita Hill, and the Story of a Supreme Court Nomination*

# Timothy M. Phelps

# Helen Winternitz

New York

Quotations from *The Economics and Politics of Race*
copyright 1983 by Thomas Sowell, Inc., are reprinted by permission
of William Morrow and Company, Inc.

Library of Congress Cataloging-in-Publication Data
Phelps, Timothy M.
    Capitol games : Clarence Thomas, Anita Hill, and the behind-the-
  scenes story of a Supreme Court nomination / Timothy M. Phelps and
  Helen Winternitz.—1st ed.
      p.   cm.
    Includes index.
    ISBN 1-56282-916-5
    1. Thomas, Clarence, 1948–   .  2. Hill, Anita.   3. United States
  Supreme Court.   4. Judges—United States—Selection and appointment.
  5. Sexual harassment of women—United States.   I. Winternitz,
  Helen.   II. Title.
  KF8745.T48P48   1992
  347.73′2634—dc20
  [347.3073534]                                            92-9168
                                                              CIP

Designed by Nina D'Amario
Levavi & Levavi

FIRST EDITION
10  9  8  7  6  5  4  3  2  1

*For Constance Miller Phelps*
*and*
*Madeleine Hill*

# Acknowledgments

Dawn Ceol, who ably covered the Thomas nomination for *The Washington Times*, did prodigious research for this book. Like the others mentioned here, she had no part in the writing of the book and no control over its point of view. But the book would not have been as well informed without her efforts.

James Workman, a young Washington writer and journalist, and Amy Dickinson, a veteran of television journalism, both did invaluable research as well.

Christine Merkle of the *Newsday* Washington Bureau was indispensable both in tracking down information and checking its accuracy.

The editors of *Newsday* are due special thanks for providing the time free of routine chores that made the Anita Hill story happen and this book possible. Michael Weber, Marie Cocco, Stephanie Saul, and intern Thom Kupper of the *Newsday* staff contributed important suggestions and information to the original reporting on the Thomas nomination. *Boston Globe* reporter Walter Robinson provided competition and an occasional helping hand.

Michael Millemann, a University of Maryland professor of law, explained the recent history of the Supreme Court with great patience. Henry J. Abraham, currently a University of Virginia professor of law, taught rigorous classes in constitutional law that provided the foundation of knowledge brought to bear on this book.

Robert Warren and Theodore B. Olson of the Gibson, Dunn & Crutcher law firm kept coauthor Phelps out of jail long enough to complete the book.

In the publishing world, we thank Lizzie Grossman, Peter Matson, and Philippa Brophy, of Sterling Lord Literistic. We also thank Pat Mulcahy, our editor at Hyperion.

There are others we would like to thank but cannot name, including those who recognized the importance of Anita Hill's story before the world knew of it.

# Authors' Note

This book was written by both of us. We shared the tasks that went into its research and writing. It is narrated, however, in the single voice of Timothy M. Phelps for the sake of clarity. The use of his voice also reflects the exceptional role he played in the tumultuous events that occurred in the process of Clarence Thomas's elevation to the Supreme Court.

# Contents

| | | | | |
|---|---|---|---|---|
| *Prologue* | **xiii** | | *Chapter 13* | **227** |
| *Chapter 1* | **1** | | *Chapter 14* | **247** |
| *Chapter 2* | **17** | | *Chapter 15* | **261** |
| *Chapter 3* | **31** | | *Chapter 16* | **277** |
| *Chapter 4* | **45** | | *Chapter 17* | **299** |
| *Chapter 5* | **61** | | *Chapter 18* | **331** |
| *Chapter 6* | **81** | | *Chapter 19* | **379** |
| *Chapter 7* | **93** | | *Chapter 20* | **391** |
| *Chapter 8* | **109** | | *Epilogue* | **417** |
| *Chapter 9* | **123** | | *Bibliographical Note* | **435** |
| *Chapter 10* | **149** | | *Index* | **439** |
| *Chapter 11* | **167** | | | |
| *Chapter 12* | **197** | | | |

# Prologue

The ceremony was performed in secret at high noon. It had been arranged only that morning, October 23, 1991. Chief Justice William H. Rehnquist, attended by Robb M. Jones, his administrative assistant, gave the oath.

"I, Clarence Thomas, do solemnly swear that I will administer justice without respect to persons, and do equal right to the poor and to the rich, and that I will faithfully and impartially discharge and perform all the duties incumbent on me as an associate justice of the Supreme Court of the United States according to the best of my abilities and understanding, agreeably to the Constitution and laws of the United States. So help me God."

Watching in the oak-paneled conference room, the court's inner sanctum, were only his wife, Virginia, and his very best man, U.S. Senator Jack Danforth. Senator Danforth took pictures with Mrs. Thomas's camera. Clarence Thomas had leaped aboard the court with the hounds of the the press nipping at his heels amid rumors about pornographic video tapes. And he had done so while Chief Justice Rehnquist was still in mourning for his wife.

Not since 1941, when Harlan Fiske Stone was confirmed as chief justice by the Senate while on vacation at Rocky Mountain National Park, Colorado, had any justice taken the oath in a private ceremony.

This unseemly ending to the nomination of Clarence Thomas to the United States Supreme Court scandalized the marble-encrusted institution as much as the testimony about pubic hairs and judicial penis size had two weeks earlier. Nan Rehnquist, the chief justice's beloved wife, had been buried just two days before. She had endured a long struggle with cancer. The loss saddened everyone in the little family that is the Supreme Court: the justices, their spouses, children and grandchildren, their secretaries and law clerks. The chief justice is well-liked; he is as warm to his colleagues as he is cold to the rights of the criminally accused.

Because of Mrs. Rehnquist's death, Clarence and "Ginny" Thomas were asked to postpone the oath that would marry them into the court family until November 1, a comfortable fifteen days after the Senate confirmed Thomas by the narrowest margin in this century.

But Washington was still jangling with rumors, and the media was working overtime. The White House did not want any more nerve-racking news. *Newsday,* which had catalyzed the controversy by printing the story about Professor Anita Hill's charges, as well as other influential papers such as *The New York Times* and *The Washington Post,* were all looking hard for more information.

In addition, I had unwittingly made everyone more nervous by asking Senator Arlen Specter a pointed question about the controversial nomination during a television forum aired by ABC's *Nightline:*

"Senator Specter, what would you do, what would happen, what would the Senate do if a month from now or a year from now, you were to learn to your complete satisfaction that Anita Hill's allegations were true?"

Specter, one of the members of the Judiciary Committee who had taken on the University of Oklahoma law professor with a no-holds-barred vengeance, was feeling politically penitent. Facing a serious challenge from the right wing of his own party in the 1992 primary election, the normally moderate Republican had been trying to flex his muscles by coming to the defense of the ultraconservative Thomas. In doing so, he had alienated some of the moderates—particularly women—whose support he needed to win the general election against a Democrat.

The senator tried to avoid the question but, when pressed, he surprised the national television audience by saying that he thought impeachment would be a possibility. Clarence Thomas had just been confirmed, and already there was talk, albeit hypothetical, of his removal. He would be much safer, though, once actually sworn onto the court.

The administration had taken steps already, refusing suggestions that a White House celebration of Thomas's confirmation be postponed because of Mrs. Rehnquist's imminent death. It had also announced that Thomas would take an oath of office—not the judicial oath he took in private later, but the federal oath of office sworn by all federal employees—at the celebration.

The insensitivity of Thomas and the White House had infuriated some, if not all, of the justices. Mrs. Rehnquist had died the day before the party. President George Bush had had to call the chief justice, impart his condolences, and ask his permission to proceed. Trying to make the best of a bad situation, the White House put out the word that it would have preferred a small reception. The problem was that Thomas had invited hundreds of guests even after being warned that the chief justice's wife was fast slipping toward death.

With Mrs. Rehnquist's burial pending, a thousand people assembled on the White House lawn for the festivities. Never in modern times had a justice been sworn in with so much hoopla. Music from the Marine band, positioned on the Truman balcony, spilled across the lawn and over the crowd. Thomas's family and friends were there, as well as a couple of the Catholic nuns who had been his teachers. Leola Williams, Thomas's mother, who had driven north with a group from Georgia, fainted from excitement. She was whisked off for minor medical care and missed most of the celebration, which had been perfect except for the fact that her first husband showed up. This was the man who had fathered Clarence Thomas and then abandoned him to a difficult childhood.

Mingling with smalltown folk from Thomas's home were celebrities Sylvester Stallone and Reggie Jackson. Pat Robertson, the fundamentalist preacher, also came to see Thomas and give thanks that the Supreme Court was getting in Thomas a potential believer in charismatic religion. Robertson's price of admission was the one million

dollars his organizations had spent to help Thomas along the rough
road to confirmation.

Also in attendance were staffers from the White House and Justice
Department who had worked so hard for Thomas, and, of course, the
politicians—many Republicans and some Democrats, like Dennis
DeConcini of Arizona—whose votes had won Thomas his confirmation.

Prominent in the crowd were the Thomas loyalists who testified for
him at the Hill hearings, propelling themselves to instant stardom in
some circles. Finally, Clarence and Ginny Thomas were surrounded
almost completely by adulatory faces. The critics were elsewhere.
Ginny Thomas spotted John Doggett III, the loquacious and audacious Texas lawyer who had critiqued Hill for the Judiciary Committee. Demonstrating a more than healthy male ego and a penchant for
homemade psychoanalysis, Doggett claimed that Hill had romantic
fantasies about him. To the Thomases, Doggett was a hero.

Substituting for the grieving Rehnquist, Justice Byron R.
"Whizzer" White gave the oath. Justice White is no liberal, but he was
a bit acerbic that day, expressing Rehnquist's sentiments as well as his
own. After pointedly referring to the death of the wife of the chief
justice, White told Thomas that he had not yet escaped the hounds.

"When at 10 o'clock on November 1, you take the judicial oath that
is required by statute, you will become the 106th justice to sit on the
Supreme Court, and we look forward to that day," he said with a chill
formality.

The Bush administration tried to sidestep the distinction that had
been drawn. Marlin Fitzwater, the White House press secretary, told
the media that Clarence Thomas was indeed a justice; the federal oath
was sufficient. Some journalists wrote or broadcast that Thomas was
a member of the court, and therefore immune from all but the most
heinous charges.

Apparently the White House and Thomas were not convinced by
their own ploy. While they were awaiting the arrival of November and
the swearing-in date, speculation rose that at least one newspaper was
readying another scandalous salvo. On October 23, Thomas requested
that he be sworn in immediately, that same day. The other Supreme
Court justices were not notified of the event, which normally they
would have attended. It would have been their official embrace of a

new colleague who would work closely with them in the years ahead, and argue at length with them in the innermost sanctum of the nation's highest court.

Only afterward was the news released via the Supreme Court spokeswoman, Toni House, with an explanation that the oath had been hurried up because Thomas was anxious to get his staff on the Supreme Court payroll and up to speed on their new job. It didn't quite make sense. A week's delay wouldn't have made a big difference for the staff, most of whom were already on the payroll at the United States Court of Appeals for the District of Columbia Circuit, where Thomas had been a judge for more than a year. Officials at the White House admitted privately that they wanted to get Thomas on the high court to forestall any further damaging disclosures.

On this unfortunate note the nomination of only the second black man to sit on the Supreme Court had ended after one hundred and fifteen days of agonizing revelations and pain for Thomas, the court, and for the nation, as well as for a young law professor at the University of Oklahoma.

# CAPITOL GAMES

# Chapter 1

Clayland Boyden Gray, legal adviser and close friend
to President George Bush, knew the man he wanted for the job of
retiring Supreme Court Justice Thurgood Marshall. And Gray knew
his opinion mattered, for he had uncommon influence in the normally
low-profile job of White House counsel. Gray, who in aristocratic
fashion shortens his first name to its initial, is a patrician with a
commanding nose and wispy white hair. He has much in common with
George Bush. C. Boyden Gray's father, who was national security
adviser to President Eisenhower, had been a golfing buddy of Senator
Prescott Bush of Connecticut, the President's father. The two had
moved in similar directions since boyhood, and when George Bush
rose to the vice presidency in 1981, he hired Gray as his counsel. Their
friendship flourished and Gray went with Bush to the White House.

Gray had come to be an arch conservative, with libertarian, free-
market leanings, and he dedicated himself to that ideology. He had not
just hired lawyers to help him do the President Bush's legal work, but
lawyers who were committed to the conservative movement, to the
reincarnation of politicians of the ilk of Barry Goldwater.

Now Gray was excited by the prospect of placing another conservative on the Supreme Court for a lifetime term. The Republicans had
been handed the chance to turn the course of judicial history further
to the right. The news of Thurgood Marshall's intention to retire had
arrived at lunchtime on June 27, 1991, brought in a letter to the White
House by the justice's secretary. The letter announced the departure
of the last liberal voice from the era when Earl Warren as chief justice
dominated a court that vastly expanded the legal meaning of civil

rights and civil liberties. The announcement was a surprise. Unusual for Washington, no rumors had been circulating. Even Marshall's close friend on the court, former justice William J. Brennan, Jr., had not been consulted much ahead of time. Although Marshall was eighty-two years old and ailing, he had vowed to stay on the bench so that the Republican administration would not have the opportunity to name his successor.

Gray had first learned of the man he wanted to fill Marshall's seat when he was heading up a project to rid business of what the Republicans thought was unduly restrictive government regulation. In that endeavor he had come across Clarence Thomas, an ambitious black lawyer who then chaired the Equal Employment Opportunity Commission (EEOC) and shared Gray's antipathy for affirmative action. They had encountered each other socially in conservative circles, but it was chance that brought them together at the crucial moment.

A few weeks before Marshall's announcement, both Gray and Thomas entered a ten-kilometer road race whose charitable purpose was to raise money to fight breast cancer. While running down a stretch of Pennsylvania Avenue, the two found themselves rubbing shoulders. In between breaths, they struck up a conversation about the wrangling that was going on between the White House and Congress over a major piece of civil rights legislation. Trying to balance the drift of an increasingly right-wing Supreme Court, the Democrats in Congress had launched a bill to give minority workers a better chance at suing their bosses for discrimination. The court had made such lawsuits more difficult.

President Bush had been locked in a bitter battle over this civil rights bill for more than a year. The President was fighting not only Democratic sponsors of the legislation, such as Senator Edward M. Kennedy of Massachusetts, but also respected moderates within his own party, such as John C. Danforth of Missouri. As White House counsel, Gray was the captain of that fight, uncompromising even in the face of allegations that the president was not being fair. Critics were charging that President Bush was playing to middle-class fears. The President, under Gray's tutelage, had artfully condemned the civil rights legislation as the Democrats' "quota bill," a label implying that minorities would be given automatic preference for jobs wanted by whites.

Gray and Thomas became so engrossed in the politically complicated topic during the race that they stopped running and walked
together for an hour.

By that time, Thomas had earned the confidence of the conservative
Republicans controlling the executive branch of the government and
had been promoted to a federal judgeship on the U.S. Court of Appeals for the District of Columbia Circuit. This seat on the appeals
court was a prime jumping-off position for the Supreme Court.

As he walked with Gray, Thomas told him exactly what he wanted
to hear. Thomas said that the legislation would only hurt his fellow
black Americans by encouraging them to look to the government for
help as had happened with quotas, rather than looking inside themselves for the will to work. It was this sort of talk that made Gray, an
heir to the R. J. Reynolds tobacco fortune born into the cream of
North Carolina society, realize he had an intellectual soulmate in
Thomas, a fatherless boy born in a ramshackle community at the edge
of a marsh in coastal Georgia.

Hence after receiving Thurgood Marshall's retirement message, Gray
went into action quickly. He called Thomas and asked him to come to a
meeting at 4:30 p.m. that same Thursday, June 27. It was a measure of
Gray's unusual influence that he took the initiative rather than the U.S.
attorney general, Richard Thornburgh. Traditionally, it would have
been the other way around, with the attorney general serving as the
president's key adviser on Supreme Court nominations.

John Sununu, the White House chief of staff, joined in: In the early
evening, he telephoned Tom Jipping, the point man on judicial appointments for the most right-wing lobbying groups in Washington.
Sununu wanted to know who Jipping and his consituency would prefer
on the high court. The call was out of the ordinary; in the recent past
the White House, at least nominally, had tried to keep the radical right
at arm's-length on such issues. Jipping acted fast. Later the same
evening, Sununu received the response by fax machine: their man was
Clarence Thomas. Jipping also talked up Thomas to Lee Liberman, an
assistant to Gray and a kindred spirit to Jipping, and Bill Kristol, Vice
President Dan Quayle's chief of staff.

"The entire *conservative movement not only supports him, but
believes* in him," Jipping wrote in his faxed memorandum to Sununu.
"No dissent is likely from anywhere in the movement. . . . The

movement will need little energizing and they will be willing to fight for him."

The next day before flying north for a weekend at his Maine retreat in Kennebunkport, President Bush brought together Gray, Thornburgh, Sununu, and Vice President Dan Quayle. They discussed Edith Jones, a super-conservative judge from Texas who had been the runnerup to David Souter the year before. But the very mention of her name brought up a hornet's nest of opposition from the left, and that June there was no stomach for that kind of confirmation battle. The president was eager to fill the newly vacant seat, possibly with Clarence Thomas. It was President Bush who had nominated Thomas to the Court of Appeals two years earlier. The president liked Thomas's philosophy espousing black self-help. And, despite his public criticism of the "quota bill," the president favored putting someone from a minority group in Marshall's seat.

Within the confines of the meeting, Thornburgh voiced some obvious worries about nominating Gray's choice. Thornburgh had spent nearly an hour interviewing Thomas, Friday, June 28, at the Justice Department, and came away impressed. But he warned the President that Thomas might have a tough time being confirmed by the Senate because his politics had inspired the enmity of civil rights organizations and because the American Bar Association was not likely to give him a strong recommendation.

Thomas, who had turned forty-three that week, did not have the usual profile of a Supreme Court nominee. He had been a judge for a scant fifteen months and had practiced law for only five years of his career. His few legal writings were provocative, but not of a scholarly nature. Thomas's resume couldn't compare—except for the fact that he was black—with the justice who had retired from his seat. Marshall was already a legend when he was nominated by Lyndon Johnson in 1967; he was the pioneering architect of the legal challenge to segregation, and he had served both as a federal judge and as U.S. solicitor general.

But youth, and even inexperience, had become virtues under the Republican administrations for judicial jobs that once called on some of the wisest or most seasoned people in the land. Conservative orthodoxy seemed to be replacing stature as the chief qualification. For presidents like Reagan and Bush who were determined to bring about a conservative counterrevolution in the federal courts, youth ensured the judicial longevity of those they chose. A careful culling of candidates for judgeships also ensured their ideological purity. The overarching idea was to create conservative courts that would carry into the next generation, no matter who controlled the White House. Inexperience also meant the lack of a record on which the Senate could challenge a presidential appointee. There was, of course, the risk of eroding the stature of the judiciary. But some on the political right thought that the Supreme Court, in particular, could do with some trimming of its power.

At the White House meeting, Thornburgh and Sununu pushed hard for consideration of a Hispanic nominee, arguing that President Bush was much more likely to reap political rewards from the burgeoning Hispanic population than from blacks, who always voted solidly for the Democrats. Bush was swayed enough to order a review of potential Hispanic candidates. The question of what sort of minority to choose remained up in the air.

Gray, meanwhile, argued forcefully for Thomas. He was backed up by Quayle, who had already begun the political spadework to deal with Thornburgh's objections. Before the meeting, the vice president had called Senator Danforth to find out if the senator was willing to go all the way for his protégé. Back in 1974, when Danforth had been Missouri's attorney general, he had hired Thomas fresh out of Yale Law School and when elected to the Senate had brought young Thomas to Washington as a legislative assistant.

But Danforth was not on the best of terms with the White House. He was engaged on the other side of the increasingly acrimonious battle over the the civil rights bill. The moderate senator had forged a compromise bill to replace one already vetoed by President Bush. But Gray, backed by the president, had refused the compromise. At the time, Danforth had every reason not to be cooperative with the wishes of the White House.

On the other hand, Danforth genuinely admired Thomas. And, having helped Thomas into the arena of national politics, the senator had a stake in the matter. In any case, he was not the kind of man to hold a grudge.

"Will you really take the lead on this nomination? Will you put yourself on the line?" Quayle asked him.

"Absolutely. I'll do everything I can," Danforth assured him.

To political insiders, Danforth's willingness to go to the mat for Thomas meant everything. Few senators, perhaps none, were more respected by their colleagues, Republicans and Democrats alike. As an ordained Episcopalian minister, he has earned a reputation for being principled and had added credibility at that moment because he was standing on a piece of moral high ground as a Republican supporting the civil rights bill.

One of the remaining questions—a crucial one—was how strong the opposition to Thomas would be. If it were unified, it could spell trouble for the White House. But the nomination of Thomas to fill Marshall's seat might prove to be a brilliant tactic. Thomas was black and conservative, a rare combination that violated the political standard. The move could throw the the old-line leaders of the national civil rights organizations into a quandary, which in turn could fracture any unity on the left wing of the political establishment. Would the civil rights leaders embrace Thomas because he was black, or denounce him for his politics? Or would they wobble somewhere in between? What were the decison-makers of the all-important National Association for the Advancement of Colored People (NAACP) going to do?

The White House knew that the man who would have the most influence over that decision was Benjamin L. Hooks. Now sixty-six, Hooks had been executive director of the NAACP for fourteen years, and a champion of the very ideas that so much disturbed George Bush and Clarence Thomas. But Hooks was thought to be more pragmatic and less ideological than some in the civil rights movement. He was a lawyer and a Baptist minister, and had also been a savings-and-loan executive and a county judge in his hometown of Memphis. He arrived on the national scene when President Richard Nixon appointed him to the Federal Communications Commission. The question was how to approach Hooks. The answer came from an unexpected quarter— Washington journalist Arch Parsons.

Parsons, a veteran black reporter in the Washington bureau of *The Baltimore Sun,* had been writing about civil rights for years. With connections all over the city and throughout the civil rights establishment, he was in a unique position to help Thomas get the Supreme Court seat. He was a good friend of Hooks and also an admirer of

Thomas, whom he had watched rise through the conservative ranks from the EEOC to the federal bench. Parsons thought he might be able to bridge the gap between this maverick black Republican and the civil rights establishment. For Parsons, the crucial issue was having a black on the Supreme Court. He believed that Thomas, even with his right-wing views, would serve his race better than most other candidates that the Bush administration might field.

"I do know this," Parsons said later. "There is a hell of a difference between a black conservative and a white conservative."

Arch Parsons is not a one-track kind of man. He is a veteran reporter, having been one of the first blacks to break down the racial barriers of the New York city newspapers. He went on to work as a United Nations correspondent, covering the Suez War in the Middle East, among other things, for *The New York Herald Tribune.* His lengthy career has also included doing research on the gaseous diffusion of uranium for the Manhattan Project, working in West Africa for the Ford Foundation, and holding down a number of government jobs in Washington in health and housing departments. Parsons likes being involved in the political life of the capital, where he moves easily in both white and black circles. He knows Thomas and considers him a friend.

Parsons decided to step out of his role as a Washington journalist, as many others had done before him, and onto the stage of Washington politics. *The Baltimore Sun* knew nothing of the story unfolding beneath its very nose.

Parsons quickly sought out Clint Bolick, a quirky but respected lawyer with a philosophy that puts him on the conservative edge of civil rights policies. Bolick is now vice president of the Institute for Justice, a law firm that pushes a conservative, libertarian agenda. He also has a history of having worked happily for Thomas at the EEOC, and maintains good connections at the White House.

Parsons had one basic question for Bolick. Would it help if he could assure the White House, through Bolick, that the civil rights community would lay off Thomas? Bolick said yes, absolutely. The two men, Parsons and Bolick, went to work. They went over Thomas's record as chairman of the EEOC, which had handled a multitude of charges of unfairness at the workplace brought by minorities, women, the elderly, and the handicapped. The complicated decisions concerning job discrimination could be interpreted in varying ways. A case, albeit a fairly thin one, could be made that Thomas's conservative policies had not grossly hindered minorities. This positive-sounding information was funneled to Hooks at the NAACP headquarters in Baltimore.

The White House was briefed about the development. Bolick telephoned, connecting with Lee Liberman, whom Bolick knew well as the zealously conservative assistant to White House counsel Gray. Liberman was enthusiastic about this political windfall, although it wasn't yet clear how Hooks would respond.

Events were moving at a fast pace in the office of the White House counsel. The final obstacle that Gray needed to clear for Thomas was the powerful political argument in favor of a Hispanic person.

President Bush's advisers reviewed the possibilities. The strongest Hispanic candidate with a satisfactorily right-wing ideology appeared to be Emilio M. Garza, a little-known judge on a federal court of appeals in Texas. There were other Hispanic judges who had more judicial experience and who were also Republicans, but none who could be counted on to be pro-life and universally conservative.

Gray had been furious with Thornburgh on Friday for even suggesting that Bush consider anyone but Thomas. He stormed back to his office after the meeting, complaining bitterly that the attorney general had derailed his plan to have Thomas named that very same day. But the president had agreed that they should at least look into a Hispanic candidate.

Anxious to make a decision, Thornburgh and the others advising Bush on the Supreme Court asked Garza to get on the next possible airplane and fly up to Washington. After interviewing him, the presidential advisers came to the conclusion that Garza was too green. The same age as Thomas, Garza had served a brief two years on a federal district court before being elevated to the appeals court. He had been on the higher court only two months before Marshall's announced retirement. Before his judgeships, he had practiced law privately; his specialty was representing defendants against malpractice and product-liability suits, a low-profile area without great public appeal.

The White House had to be certain, though, about Thomas's character. Gray telephoned Evan Kemp, who had taken over the chairmanship of the EEOC from Thomas. Kemp had come to know Thomas well. In addition, Kemp was a stalwart right-winger whom Gray trusted completely. The two had been friends for twenty-five years and were allies in a common cause against liberalism. At the EEOC, Kemp was as strict as Thomas on workers who petitioned the agency with complaints about discrimination on the job. Kemp, after all, had succeeded, even though he himself was crippled and confined to a wheelchair. Like Clarence Thomas, Kemp felt that people should challenge adversity rather than ask the government for help. Gray asked Kemp a lot of personal questions about Thomas. Everything sounded right; it was becoming obvious that Thomas had the inside track.

After Bush played golf in Maine Saturday morning, Gray and Thornburgh tried to call the President from Washington. But they could not get the call through due to the thorough security system. Finally, they reached Bush and Sununu in the Maine White House to discuss the nomination.

While they all but settled on Thomas, the decision was made subject to some last-minute checks. These may have included a review of Thomas's 1984 divorce. Rumors in Republican legal circles had it that Kathy Grace Thomas had divorced her husband on bitter terms. But this talk was not borne out by the legal documents, which showed a no-fault divorce that resulted in Thomas keeping custody of his son.

This last-minute foot-dragging about his favorite candidate was too much for Gray. Furious with Thornburgh that the decision had been postponed, he shouted at the attorney general, "You're fouling up the whole plan." Gray, who seemed to the others to be fanatic about nominating Thomas, feared that any delay might derail his momentum with the President.

As the process moved inexorably in Thomas's direction that weekend, Ronald A. Klain sat in his Capitol Hill home reading some of Thomas's speeches. Klain, chief counsel to the Senate Judiciary Committee, was an important figure in any Supreme Court nomination. He knew Thomas, had a good impression of him, and was doing some research in case he was nominated. Klain found in a 1987 speech Thomas had delivered at Claremont College in California a passage quoting and lauding Barry Goldwater's notorious words twenty-seven years earlier: "Extremism in the defense of liberty is no vice . . . moderation in the pursuit of liberty is no virtue." These words had helped cost Goldwater the presidency. Klain said later that Thomas's resurrection of them "just blew me away. That was what set off my alarm bells. I didn't think anyone left in America still believed in that, so I was a Thomas skeptic from the start."

For those engaged in the nitty-gritty of politics, Sunday mornings in Washington are given over not to sermons or meditations but to the dialogues on the major network talk shows. Administration officials and politicans are the familiar faces. The issues of the week are debated and hints are made about political decisions in the offing. This Sunday was no different.

Attorney General Thornburgh made headlines with a hopelessly bold assertion about how the next Supreme Court justice was being chosen. On *Meet the Press* he insisted that the nominee of the Bush administration would *not* be selected according to his views on abortion or any other issue. "Nobody's going to give a multiple choice test to a prospective nominee on any question, let alone a question about which there's such political difference," Thornburgh said.

He also intimated that the decision had already been made, that Bush would appoint someone from a minority group. The way he put it, however, made the endeavor sound a little like a trip to a county fair freak show. The prospective nominees included "qualified women, blacks, Hispanics, persons with disabilities and the like," he told the national television audience. "Certainly, the President wants a court—Supreme Court and other courts that reflect the diversity of our society."

Thornburgh's assertion, repeated later by Bush, that there was no litmus test on the abortion issue was at best disingenuous. Was it by accident that the four justices appointed by the Reagan and Bush administrations were all, to some extent at least, at odds with the Supreme Court's 1973 landmark decision in the case of *Roe* v. *Wade*, which established a woman's constitutional right to have an abortion?

Thomas was not likely to be an exception to the trend. The Republicans in the White House, and the conservative lobbyists who did their best to influence judicial nominations, were sure that President Bush would never name a justice who wholeheartedly endorsed the abortion-rights decision. The only problem was that the issue was so politically explosive that potential justices shied away from any discussion of it, no matter what their thoughts.

There were a few strong indications of where Thomas stood, though. For starters, Thomas had been raised as a thoroughgoing Catholic. The White House undoubtedly was also aware that Thomas had moved on from Catholicism to an extreme branch of Episcopalianism that condemned abortions.

Appearing on the same television program that Sunday was Senator Patrick J. Leahy of Vermont, a Democrat and member of the Senate's judiciary committee, which passes on nominees for judgeships. Leahy voiced a rather plaintive plea for a nominee who would provide "a moderating influence" to the Supreme Court, someone who would balance a court in danger of becoming rampantly right wing.

Over the past two decades, the Republicans in the White House had managed to create a court dominated by conservatives. The turning point had come in 1990 with the retirement of Justice Brennan. The departure of Marshall from the court was an unexpected bonus for the conservatives. From Marshall's point of view, there was little point in hanging on, since his adversaries definitely had the upper hand. Had he only known that George Bush's popularity, then soaring as a result of the Persian Gulf War, would soon dive because of the economy, he might have decided differently.

Senator Leahy was not to go unchallenged with his request. A sharp-tongued conservative from Utah, Senator Orrin G. Hatch, was also on the television program. Hatch was a colleague of Leahy's on the judiciary committee and he was ready to argue. Senator Hatch believed that the conservatives had every right to weight the court their way, if only because the liberals had enjoyed years at justice's helm. It was going to be tit for tat as far as Senator Hatch was concerned.

"This question of balance never came up during the Warren years. There wasn't much argument for balance back then," Hatch said.

On the surface, the senator's reply to his colleague sounded fair. But, the history of how the Warren court, whose rulings so appalled the conservative wing of American politics, came into being was not as straightforward as Hatch implied. In fact, the two key players in the Warren court's leftward odyssey were appointed by the Republican President Dwight D. Eisenhower. The President had named Warren to the position of chief justice and elevated Brennan to the court, not foreseeing the legal upheaval the two would catalyze. In those days, the views of nominees were not thoroughly vetted as they would be by the time of the Bush administration.

As Sunday morning, June 30, progressed in Washington, the White House got some good news about what kind of battle Clarence Thomas might face. It might not be as tough as feared. The NAACP's Ben Hooks had said he wouldn't draw the line against Thomas. He wanted a black man on the court, even if it was a black conservative. This highly valuable and highly secret information was passed to Parsons, who gave it to Bolick who passed it in turn to Lee Liberman in the White House counsel's office. The NAACP members, if they had known, would have been in an uproar. But Liberman and Gray were instantly relieved. Hooks had said that he himself would remain neutral if Thomas was nominated, and that he might even try to be of some help. He said he would try to steer the powerful NAACP away from opposing Thomas.

This news meant that Thomas most likely would not be facing the sort of dangerous trial that Judge Robert Bork had undergone. In 1987, the civil rights community and an array of liberal groups banded together to defeat the nomination of Bork to the Supreme Court. The defeat had been a blow to conservatives who saw in Bork a finely honed, intellectual exemplar of their ideology.

"The information we gave the White House was that the civil rights establishment, which had been completely unified in the Bork nomination, would not be unified," Clint Bolick recalled. "And if it did turn out to be unified, it would not be highly energized in opposing Clarence Thomas." What Bolick called "the monolithic, liberal, special interest opposition" would not be marching lockstep into the fray this time around.

By midday, President Bush had been briefed. He telephoned Thomas, telling him he was the frontrunner for the Supreme Court nomination. He asked Thomas to travel to Kennebunkport on Monday. The president liked to surprise the nation with his appointments, a habit that had gotten him into trouble before. Even as plans were being made for the President to announce the nomination of Thomas at a press conference in Maine on Monday, the White House put out the word that the announcement would probably be made after Bush returned to Washington.

Although both stunned and exuberant, Thomas kept his silence. He did not even confide in his wife, Virginia Thomas. The next morning, Thomas was in an Air Force jet taking him, Gray, and Thornburgh to Pease Air National Guard Base in New Hampshire. From there a van whisked them over the border to Maine and they slipped unnoticed by the press into the president's eight-acre ocean-front estate.

They arrived shortly after noon, Monday, July 1. When he was introduced to Barbara Bush, the first lady greeted him with a happy "Congratulations!" This salutation was slightly awkward, since Thomas still had not been officially offered the the nomination.

For the sake of privacy, Thomas was escorted to meet President Bush in a second-floor bedroom. The whole Bush clan had gathered at the house on Walker's Point for the ninetieth birthday of the President's mother, Dorothy Walker Bush. The bedroom was the best place to talk in peace. Having told Thomas that he was indeed the choice for the Supreme Court, President Bush made him promise that he would carry through with the nomination process, no matter how rough it got. He also gave him some some avuncular-sounding advice: "Do like the umpire—call them as you see them."

President Bush brought Thomas out to the porch where a seafood salad was being served to the top officials. They were greeted with applause. Thomas took a minute out from lunch to call Virginia from a telephone extension and tell her, with everyone else listening, to turn on the television. She had not been invited to Kennebunkport because it was thought that her sudden disappearance from her legal job at the Department of Labor would tip off the press. After lunch, Bush and Thomas sneaked around the house to the guest house, from where they stepped outside to the waiting microphones. Bush put his arm around Thomas's shoulders and introduced Thurgood Marshall's replacement to the world.

The timing of Thomas's nomination, on a Monday afternoon of a short week before a long Fourth of July weekend, was perfect. There was no time for reporters to do much more than write the obvious story about Thomas's character, which was spoonfed them by the White House. The national press corps was briefed on Thomas's extraordinary life, his rise from poverty to power. The next day, the newspapers and networks rushed reporters to Pin Point, the Georgia backwater where Thomas was born. They produced features on Pin Point, or articles on how important Americans were reacting to the nomination. Before much serious reporting on the man's past or beliefs could be done, the nation was off eating hot dogs.

And there seemed little not to like in the Clarence Thomas whom Americans had met on their television screens and in their newspapers. His story seemed so appealing, an affirmation, as Thomas said in Kennebunkport, of the American dream. From a Georgia shack, the story went, Thomas had pulled himself up by the bootstraps to reach the very pinnacle of respectability.

Thomas offered something to many different groups. He was a religious man who had studied for the priesthood. Thomas was someone whom black Americans could look to with an instant pride that transcended politics. And conservatives could look to his outspoken record opposing racial quotas and championing the likes of Oliver North. In addition, Thomas had an affable manner and a big laugh.

Little was written about the complex journey that Thomas had taken from boyhood to manhood, or the pendulum swing his philosophy had taken from a militant embrace of Malcolm X to a prosperous alliance with white Republicans. He could not have been more unlike Thurgood Marshall. These complexities, of course, were not the side of Clarence Thomas that the American public saw in Kennebunkport.

"Only in America could this have been possible," said Thomas when he took his place in front of the microphones. He recalled that "as a child, I could not dare dream that I would ever see the Supreme Court—not to mention be nominated to it."

He came close to tears when he recalled the grandparents who raised him. He choked up when he mentioned the nuns who had taught him when he was growing up. (This gave the reporters in my own office a moment's pause as they thought back to their days in parochial schools and the regular ruler-on-the-knuckles punishment.) The President stood stoically behind Thomas, looking straight ahead.

From this point on, the White House referred to Clarence Thomas as the man who had struggled against poverty, segregation and adversity, and won. In the "talking points" handed out to key supporters to guide them in their dealings with the press, this was the first point listed. The tone of the nomination had been set. Because he really didn't have much legal experience, Thomas was being sold on his character.

Despite Thomas's controversial views on racial issues and his decidedly right-wing ideology, the nominee seemed to have a lot going for him. Gray could only have chuckled to himself at how fortunate a find he had made. With Thomas, he had flummoxed the civil rights opposition, using one of their own against them. Gray could feel the assurance of knowing he had Senator Danforth and the NAACP's Hooks on board. He could not lose, unless something went wrong. And the White House had been very careful about that.

"We spent a lot of time checking out Thomas," one Bush administration official assured a reporter. "Due diligence was spent."

Everything was going swimmingly until President Bush made a blunder while talking to the press corps about Thomas's race. The nominee was adamant that he be judged on his merit not his skin color, an idea that had come to form an important part of his philosophy.

But the White House had already made it clear to reporters that Bush wanted to appoint a black or some other minority member to replace Marshall. Asked if Thomas's nomination was not in contradiction with his vehement opposition to quotas, to promoting individuals because of their minority status, President Bush responded that race had absolutely nothing to do with the choice of Thomas.

"I don't even see an appearance of inconsistency, because what I did is look for the best man," the president insisted. "The fact that he is black and a minority had nothing to do with this in the sense that he is the best qualified at this time."

The reporters persisted, and Bush dug himself in deeper.

"Was race a factor whatsoever, sir, in the selection?" he was queried.

"I don't see it at all" was Bush's response. "I don't feel he's a quota," Bush said, perhaps rendered inarticulate by the corner he was in. "I don't feel that I had to nominate a black American at this time for the court. . . . I would reiterate, I think he's the best man. And if credit accrues to him for coming up through a tough life as a minority in this county, so much the better. So much the better."

There at Kennebunkport, Thomas was drawn into the humiliating brouhaha.

"What do you say to critics who say the only reason you're being picked is because you're black?" he was asked.

"I think a lot worse things have been said," he replied, tensing up.

"I disagree with that, but I'll have to live with it."

President Bush's statement that Thomas was the best qualified man for the job—the president corrected himself and said person—was patently untrue. Equally untrue was his statement that race was not a factor. Thousands of American lawyers had better qualifications. Thomas was not even the best qualified black jurist, or black Republican jurist. Not by a long shot. But he was, in C. Boyden Gray's judgment at least, the best qualified black, conservative, anti-abortion candidate.

The small but transparent lie the President made under mild pressure may have set the tone for what came later, when the Thomas nomination was under real pressure. President Bush's sidestepping of the truth did not provoke a controversy, but it did offend a few of the purists among the conservatives.

William Schneider, a resident fellow at the conservative American Enterprise Institute, called the nomination a "worse than tokenism choice."

"It is an effort to divide the black community, and I imagine that blacks will close ranks against him," he told the privately owned White House Bulletin. "The cynicism of this choice—the white man's Negro—may be transparent. It could backfire. Liberals will once again argue that the President is using race for political advantage and that he is not really committed to a civil rights agenda."

Schneider, of course, was wrong about the black community, as the White House knew ahead of time. He also gave too much credit to the liberals, who were struggling over what to say about a conservative black nominee, over how to attack the philosophy without attacking the man.

Bush's final comment on Clarence Thomas in Kennebunkport was prescient. Asked about the method he used to make his choice, Bush said, "As I thought of any hypothetical things that could go wrong, I couldn't think of any."

# Chapter 2

Like a self-appointed army, hundreds of reporters and dozens of Washington lobbyists immediately started searching through Clarence Thomas's life. They marched, uninvited, into his garage, where he kept the overflow from his large collection of books. They questioned his neighbors and his son and hunted down his ex-wife and his former in-laws. The unilluminating seven-minute tape of his divorce proceedings became an instant hit at the County Courthouse in Rockville, Maryland.

Thomas had not left Kennebunkport before computer banks started churning out thousands of pages of speeches he had made, statements he had written, and interviews he had given. Reporters were looking for information and they wanted it fast, before someone else found it. A journalist could make a career coup by sinking a Supreme Court nominee. A lobbying group could reap publicity and prestige by coming up with some negative item about the man the White House was touting with such confidence.

It is not contradictory to say that the groups were motivated most of all by their real concerns for the fate of the Supreme Court and the reporters by their professional duty to find the truth. Whatever the motives of this volunteer militia of investigators, all would agree that Supreme Court justices should be beyond reproach. Anyone nominated for the job of shaping American justice should be as clean and unbiased as is humanly possible. Once confirmed, Thomas might well spend the rest of his lifetime on the court, making decisions for as long as forty years that would affect every man, woman and child in the United States.

Thomas was going to have to withstand the scrutiny of every phase of his personal life and of every phase of his political life. His ability as a judge would be examined. Everything that he had said would be interpreted. The words he had set to paper would be read and then read again between the lines. His position on civil rights would be the source of endless debate, as would his possible approach to abortion, the most volatile legal issue in the country.

The first breakthrough came before dawn the day after the nomination. Three lawyers for The National Abortion Rights Action League (NARAL) had stayed up all night reading through hundreds of pages of Thomas's documents. Their eyes had grown bleary by the time they came across something worth exclaiming about. It was a speech Thomas had made in which he praised an essay by a conservative writer that condemned the historic *Roe* v. *Wade* decision legalizing abortion. Even though Thomas was attacking abortion only indirectly, the NARAL lawyers thought that their discovery was dramatic. It was enough to start rallying those women across the country who favored the right to choose abortions.

Kate Michelman, the group's leader, announced the beginning of a "campaign" to defeat Thomas. Unlike the leaders of the civil right groups, Michelman was not conflicted. She wanted to act fast to counter the positive images of Thomas being portrayed in the press. Michelman's call for an immediate press conference to be held that afternoon was so rushed that many Washington news organizations didn't know about it.

"We wanted to interject some sobering information about this man and the danger he posed to the rights of Americans before this Pin Point, Georgia, story became indelibly marked in the minds and the consciousness of the American public," Michelman said later. "We wanted to contribute to some balance in the reporting on this man. Everyone focused on his personal story."

Michelman, one of the most articulate and forceful of the liberal lobbyists in Washington, was not motivated by fame or funds as much as by her own life story.

Shortly after being abandoned by her husband with three young children to care for, Michelman discovered she was pregnant a fourth time. She had no job, no credit, no money, not even a car. She had to go on welfare amid worries that she wouldn't be able to keep her family together. Finally, despite her Catholic upbringing, Michelman made what she describes as an agonized decision to have an abortion.

This was in 1970, three years before the Supreme court ruled on *Roe* v. *Wade*. While Michelman lived in Pennsylvania, a state that allowed abortions, she was required to proceed through a series of difficult steps. First she had to appear before a hospital review board of four men, all of them strangers, who questioned her in intimate detail. The experience, she recalled, was utterly degrading.

"I was an adult woman, a mother of three, and yet I had to win their permission to make a decision about my family, my life, and my future," she later told the Senate.

Michelman was admitted to the hospital to prepare for the abortion; *then* she was informed that she still needed the written approval of the man who had deserted her. She left the hospital, found him, and begged his cooperation. Michelman would always remember how she had been humiliated and dehumanized.

There was a sense of desperation in the women's rights movement when Clarence Thomas was nominated. The Supreme Court was on the verge of overturning *Roe* v. *Wade*, if not explicitly, then by chipping incrementally at the protections the pro-choice ruling afforded to women who wanted abortions.

Only a month before the Thomas nomination, the Supreme Court had outraged advocates of abortion rights by circumscribing discussions within clinics that provided advice on family-planning. The ruling applied to all family-planning clinics that received federal funds. It upheld a federal regulation that prohibited any discussion of abortion at these clinics. Critics called the regulation "the gag rule" because it meant that a doctor could not inform a woman about the abortion option.

Any proof as to where Thomas might stand on the abortion issue was of the utmost importance. In the tortured politics of modern-day

Supreme Court nominations, a would-be justice had to be against the *Roe* v. *Wade* decision and for the right of a fetus to live. In other words, a nominee had to be pro-life to get the nod, but not outspokenly so. If the nominee was clearly against abortion, he would face a furious grilling by the Democrats who controlled the Senate.

The speech that excited NARAL's attention was one given by Thomas to the Heritage Foundation, a thinktank in Washington that had been founded by savvy conservatives. In the speech, Thomas spoke mostly about matters pertaining to civil rights, but one line delivered late in the speech touched on the abortion issue.

Thomas obliquely praised an essay by Heritage trustee Lewis E. Lehrman that had appeared in the *American Spectator* magazine in June 1987. When the NARAL lawyers tracked down the article, they found an argument that the Declaration of Independence itself prohibits abortion. The Declaration's "unalienable rights," Lehrman wrote, "with which all men are endowed by their Creator" includes the "right to life" of the unborn. Lehrman's article described the *Roe* v. *Wade* decision as "a spurious right born exclusively of judicial supremacy with not a single trace of lawful authority" and called the results of the decision a "holocaust."

NARAL thought it had found enough evidence to upset the Thomas nomination. But Thomas's "Lehrman speech," as it came to be inappropriately known, was not all that solid as evidence. The reference to Lehrman was little more than a throwaway line. The article was, however, one whose ideas Thomas could well have endorsed since, like Lehrman, he had a great interest in the notion of God-given rights mentioned in the Declaration. But Thomas's speech, when read carefully, did not laud the Lehrman article as "splendid," as his opponents said later. Thomas described the article rather as "a splendid *example* of applying natural law."

In reality, it was reasonable to assume from Thomas's legal philosophy as well as his background that he would come down squarely on the side of the conservative justices on the court. And it was clear that NARAL was willing to try to use anything on point to establish its suspicions about Thomas. Other groups advocating women's rights had the same worries, and the same goal of derailing the nomination.

By the end of the July 4 week the outspokenly feminist National Organization for Women (NOW) had joined the cause. One of the leaders of NOW, Flo Kennedy, emphasized the group's staunch opposition to Thomas. But, in doing so, she offered a remark that touched a raw nerve with conservatives and made the point that this nomination would be treated by many as a struggle over ideologies. It might get as nasty as that of Bork, whose defeat left liberals joyous, conservatives in anguish, and Washington convinced that politics were no longer separable from the decision of who would be on the Supreme Court.

"We don't need to ask a lot of questions before we Bork this guy," Kennedy said, using a verb coined in political circles. Her words confirmed the fears of conservatives about the fairness with which Thomas would be treated.

When Clarence Thomas showed up at a White House gate on the same day as Michelman's press conference, the guard didn't recognize him, and demanded to see his driver's license. It would probably be the last time in his life that he would have any difficulty being admitted into the halls of power. When he left, he rode in a chauffeur-driven limousine, having been through the first of many strategy and briefing sessions to prepare him for hearings scheduled in two months before the Senate's Judiciary Committee.

The Judiciary Committee is the political point where the three branches of the American government periodically converge, sometimes amicably and sometimes extremely contentiously. The idea behind the whole process is laid out in a few phrases in the Constitution of the United States. The President, according to Article II, Section 2, of the Constitution, "shall nominate, and by and with the advice and consent of the Senate, shall appoint . . . judges of the Supreme Court." The phrases are simple, but the reality is not.

Nowadays, the Judiciary Committee of fourteen senators has the first crack at the would-be justices picked by the White House. If the atmosphere is politically contentious or the person chosen is outspoken, the nominee can expect to be grilled. The Senate has the power to give the "thumbs up" or the "thumbs down" to the White House's nominee. The Senate's conduct during these decisions about the Supreme Court can enlighten or sour the mood of the entire government.

In Thomas's case, the White House wanted to be prepared for a political fray, if it came to that. Kenneth Duberstein, a former White House chief of staff under President Reagan, had been brought in to manage, or, as he put it, "quarterback" the White House campaign for Thomas. The exhausting effort was to be performed without charge, although Washington insiders smiled at the mock nobility of such a thought. Duberstein's consulting business would be enhanced by this further demonstration of his continuing closeness to the White House. The year before, Duberstein had handled the nomination of Justice David Souter to the Supreme Court, an effort that had proceeded smoothly from beginning to end.

Justice Souter's case, though, had been a relatively simple one to quarterback. He was a mild-mannered, conservative judge from New Hampshire who had never engaged in national politics. Thomas, in contrast, was a complicated figure, who had served as the chairman of the controversial Equal Employment Opportunity Commission. He had come to elicit the admiration of the right and the antipathy of the left.

Duberstein was going to have a real task in selling Thomas to the Senate and protecting him from the offensives of "the coalition" of liberals that included groups like NARAL. The job was to create a positive image of the new nominee, to make Thomas a well-known and well-liked personality. Duberstein was an expert craftsman at this sort of political portraiture, as were many others in the capital, where image vies with substance in importance. An effective lobbyist knows how to groom a political player for the Washington showring. Image-making is one of Washington's most important industries.

Clarence Thomas did not fit the standard image of what Americans thought judges were supposed to be like. He also did not always fit the image of Clarence Thomas being painted by the White House. He drove a new black Corvette, purchased with borrowed money for roughly $35,000 just four months before his nomination. (This was a man who had paid off $10,000 in student loans only months earlier.) He smoked big cigars and kept his muscles thick with a regimen of heavy-duty weightlifting. He enjoyed reading the works of both Winston Churchill and Ayn Rand, one a brilliant statesman and the other a philosopher-author of the ultimate self-help novel, *The Fountainhead*. Thomas loved the westerns of Louis L'Amour.

Thomas was a religious man, but the religions he had followed were various. He had been born a Baptist, raised a Roman Catholic, and sent to a seminary to study for the priesthood. His first marriage to a black woman was performed in an Episcopal church, his second to a white woman in a Methodist church. He would eventually start attending a fundamentalist Episcopalian church in the Washington suburbs. He named the son he had with his first wife Jamal Adeen Thomas, in the fashion of Black Muslims. His second wife, Virginia Thomas, had a straitlaced middle-class background and had worked as a lobbyist for the Chamber of Commerce. She fondly called him Batman because of the way he appeared in his low-slung, curvaceous and powerful sports car.

Although Thomas had lived in both the black world and the white world, he could have been alienated from both. His world view seemed fractured. He was a member of the generation of blacks that owed what success it had to the civil rights movement. But he had denounced the reasoning of the Supreme Court's all-important *Brown* v. *Board of Education* decision outlawing segregation in public schools. He described the decision as "dubious social engineering." He reacted to court-mandated school busing to achieve integration by demanding that white judges leave blacks alone.

And after vowing never to work in civil rights, Thomas devoted himself to ending what he saw as the social experiments by white America to ease its guilt for its history of slavery and bigotry. He opposed affirmative action as a method for bettering the black underclass, but, as EEOC chairman, he set out to pursue individual cases of discrimination to the ends of the earth.

Thomas had a great sense of humor but he also was an angry man, who chafed against reality. Although he willingly worked for Republican administrations, he labeled some of his political colleagues "racists."

This was the raw material with which Duberstein had to work. His first move was to brief Thomas on the art of not talking, of not trying to explain anything difficult. The Supreme Court nominee would benefit by lowering his profile. The first problem to deal with was NARAL's inflammatory accusation about abortion.

The White House's response, which it repeated over and over like a mantra whenever the issue came up, was to answer tersely.

"Judge Thomas has not stated a public position on abortion. There

will be efforts to assign him a position, such as this attempt, but we will
not comment on these kinds of speculation."

Thomas's own response, as dictated by the White House strategy,
was to say nothing at all. Thomas ceased to exist as a thinking,
speaking individual the minute he was nominated. The press and the
public could not ask him any questions, could not ask him to address
the many contradictions in all that he had said over the years.

"I'm dying to answer your questions, but I'm under wraps,"
Thomas told reporters as he made a round of courtesy calls to the
offices of senators on Capitol Hill who would be deciding his fate in a
few months. Shepherding Thomas from office to office was Frederick
D. McClure, the White House's liaison to Congress. McClure made
sure that Thomas didn't get into any exchanges with the press corps.

The White House, despite all the advantages that seemed to ensure
Thomas's confirmation, was not taking anything for granted. Just as
Michelman and her allies talked of mounting a campaign, the White
House was already implementing one. It was to be concentrated on
what insiders, who were working on Thomas's nomination at both the
White House and the Justice Department, called the "Pin Point
strategy." The idea was to emphasize Thomas's character and the fact
that he had risen "up from poverty" in Georgia, as one Justice Department official put it. The White House was also developing the somewhat related "southern strategy." This idea concentrated on winning
support for Thomas from conservative southern Democrats, who were
sensitive to the power of black voters among their constituencies.

For both the pro-Thomas and the anti-Thomas camps, the nomination was akin to a political campaign. It would be covered as such in
the press. Who was winning became the story, more so than the deeper
question of who Clarence Thomas was, and what effect he would have
on the Supreme Court and the nation.

The coalition of groups in opposition to Thomas had its work cut out
for it. By the time they got together for their first meeting, a full week
after the nomination, public attention had moved on to other matters,
and an admiring view of Thomas's life was hardening in the public's
mind, like a message drawn in cement. The first polls taken by the
media showed that the American public favored Thomas's confirmation by a margin of two to one.

The coalition is what is left, in the 1990s, of the liberal political forces of the 1960s—civil rights, women's and labor groups, a variety of public interest groups, some professional organizations, and lobbyists for the disadvantaged and defenders of the environment. These various groups number about two hundred, but only a few dozen of them gear into action on Supreme Court nominations. On this issue, the lead was taken by a group called the Alliance for Justice.

Aggravated Republicans like to brand the liberal groups as slick, big-money organizations bent on distorting the public will. But the Alliance for Justice, at least, hardly fits that description. It would be more accurately described as a horse and buggy type operation. It is run by a director and a staffer whose task is to monitor judicial nominations, look for information useful in defeating conservative candidates, and pass on the research to others. The director, Nan Aron, is a lawyer and longtime liberal known for her intelligence and her dedication to her cause.

The somewhat disheveled Alliance offices are shared for reasons of economy with organizations like the Center for Ecology and Social Justice, the Cuban American Research and Education Fund, and other small-time outfits. The Alliance is a place where sincerity rather than money greases the wheels. It also is a place that has earned a reputation over the years.

It was in the mid-1980s that Aron started a project to try and block confirmation of some of the most extreme of the right-wing appointees to the federal bench. While Supreme Court seats got most of the public's attention, the real action unfolds at lower levels of the federal judiciary. There are 850 judges on the U.S. district courts and the U.S. courts of appeals, where most federal law is decided.

When President Ronald Reagan began his second term in 1985, the Republican White House decided that an effective way to implement its agenda could be through the federal judiciary. If conservative federal judges could be installed across the country some of the basic goals of the movement—such as outlawing abortion, reinvigorating the death penalty, getting rid of affirmative action programs—could be quietly accomplished. Conservative judges would make conservative rulings. The Reagan administration started a screening process so that hundreds of judicial candidates were chosen, listed, and nominated on the basis of their commitment to right-wing ideology.

Aron's project served as a call-to-arms of the liberal public-interest community to target judicial nominees whose records showed particular hostility to civil rights and women's rights. The project was largely unsuccessful, though, in its first two years. Even Daniel Manion, the poorly qualified son and philosophical heir of the founder of the John Birch Society, made it onto the bench. In reality, with the Republicans in control of the Senate, the liberals had no good way to block judicial appointments. The Senate's Judiciary Committee was chaired by Senator Strom Thurmond, the extremely devout conservative from South Carolina.

When President Reagan elevated William H. Rehnquist to be the Supreme Court's chief justice in 1986, the Alliance and its allies drew the line in the sand, and were pulled right over it. Rehnquist was on the conservative extreme of the court and promised to lead it further rightward. Despite an all-out effort, Aron's Alliance for Justice and its allied groups lost the fight. Rehnquist was easily approved by a two-thirds vote of the Senate. Then, a more extreme Antonin Scalia slipped onto the court. Rehnquist, once alone on the far right, was now outflanked there. The Republicans were becoming increasingly confident about the future of the court, and the liberals increasingly concerned.

In 1987 when the Republicans nominated the controversial Judge Robert H. Bork, a battle was raised that would alter the nomination process from then on. A fierce struggle was waged before the Judiciary Committee.

By then the political landscape of the Senate had changed dramatically. The Democrats had gained the majority. Senator Joseph Biden of Delaware, not Strom Thurmond, chaired the Judiciary Committee. The Democrats of the Senate were ready when Bork came along as a symbol of the right wing's judicial and social agenda.

Bork was a brilliant theorist, a Yale Law School professor emminently qualified to be on the Supreme Court. But he was a legal fundamentalist whose literal interpretation of the Constitution was, to the liberals, not unlike the Ayatollah Khomeini's fundamentalist approach to the Koran. And contrary to American legal tradition of all stripes, he was a majoritarian, which meant that he believed in subordinating the rights of the individual. Even the conservative but libertarian Cato Institute balked at supporting him.

By 1987, the liberal groups were also stronger. The Alliance's work on judicial nominations was being supplemented by a group called People for the American Way, an organization with a broad membership of individual donors. It was founded by Norman Lear, the Hollywoood producer who contributed Archie Bunker to American culture.

Bork's nomination had been anticipated, and the response was immediate. A few minutes after President Reagan announced the nomination, Senator Edward M. Kennedy verbally eviscerated Bork on the Senate floor with a speech that had been prepared in advance. It was meant as a chilling warning about what Bork would do to Americans.

"Women would be forced into back alley abortions, blacks would sit at segregated lunch counters, rogue police could break down citizens' doors in midnight raids, school children could not be taught about evolution . . ." Kennedy asserted, twisting Bork's already extreme ideology into something Kafkaesque. He exaggerated, but he succeeded in making that nomination seem like a threat to ordinary Americans. His broadside rallied the troops to battle. Kennedy personally organized a grassroots campaign against Bork in key states.

The campaign against Bork was aided by eighty-six television spots featuring Gregory Peck, dreamed up and paid for by Lear and his organization. Labor unions threw in their people and muscle, and civil rights groups made sure that southern Senators knew the blacks in their states were opposed to Bork. The judge didn't help himself by playing an arrogant role before the Senate and eschewing White House advice.

Bork's nomination was soundly defeated and the process of judging nominees for the Supreme Court was fundamentally changed. Both conservatives and liberals had learned that politics could play the deciding part.

Four years later, when Clarence Thomas was nominated, the liberals of the coalition could not immediately muster the same unity as had been enjoyed during the Bork nomination. For starters, they had a problem because Thomas was black. If they opposed and defeated him, would the Bush administration come back with a white conservative? That was a daunting possibility.

Furthermore, the liberals had lost their best voice. Senator Kennedy had been silenced by his own indiscretions. The newspapers that summer were full of stories about the senator's bar hopping and a bottomless romp around the family estate in Palm Beach on the night of his nephew's infamous sexual encounter. Although William Kennedy Smith eventually was acquitted of the charge, his uncle's reputation had received yet another layer of tarnish. Senator Kennedy was in no position to be passing judgment on others.

In addition, liberals generally had had a hard time. President Bush had managed to damage their image. In his handy defeat of Michael Dukakis in 1988, he had played to whites' racial fears by running television commercials of black rapist Willie Horton. Bush had continued to beat the Democrats about the head with the issue in the fight over the civil rights legislation. Democrats were terrified by racial politics, a fear that would grow as the economy worsened and competition increased for jobs. The time for cheerfully championing quotas for minorities was gone.

The civil rights community was already troubled when Thomas was nominated. Affirmative action programs, not just quotas, were becoming politically suspect. The nomination of a black man from the southern heartland, who was also a conservative, sent it reeling.

The leaders of the NAACP, who normally took a leading place in the black political world, didn't know what to do. They had always championed the cause of helping blacks make it to high positions. Could they now stand in the way of one of their own? To oppose Thomas meant maneuvering against currents of support for Thomas in black neighborhoods across the country. At the same time, Thomas stood against everything for which the NAACP had fought. What's more, he had attacked its hero Thurgood Marshall and challenged its claims to leadership of the black community. The NAACP was a thing of the past, Thomas had argued, saying that it was now time for new people and new agendas to lead the black cause. Another complication was the undisclosed assurances on Thomas's behalf that Ben Hooks, the executive director, had passed on to the White House.

Coincidentally, a spotlight of political attention was immediately thrown on the NAACP because its national convention was scheduled in Texas a week after President Bush announced the Supreme Court nomination. As more than five thousand NAACP delegates converged at the convention center in Houston, members of the organization's board of directors gathered separately. About two-thirds of the sixty-four board members met at a hotel for a rump session on the Thomas nomination.

The meeting was tense. Outsiders were kept away so that the board members could wrangle privately over their decision. Some talked about getting telephone calls from black officials in the Bush administration, urging them to support Thomas or at least hold off any opposition. Thomas was a fellow black, they were needlessly reminded. Keeping to his word, Hooks argued against rushing to judgment. Hooks indicated he would prefer not to take any stand, at least until after the September Judiciary Committee hearings. By then the NAACP's position on Thomas would be moot, since Thomas's fate would have been decided. If the organization was going to have an effect, it had to act without delay. And that was the majority sentiment, to come out quickly and cleanly against Thomas.

As Congressman Craig Washington of Texas told the convened delegates later to cheers and applause, most of the board members felt that "Clarence Thomas is not fit to shine the shoes of Thurgood Marshall." His choice of this image, the racial stereotype of the subservient black shoeshine boy, was typical of the disdain with which the civil rights community had for years dismissed Thomas. It was a disdain that had embittered him and driven him further into the arms of the conservatives. At the meeting no one, not even Hooks, dared suggest that the organization endorse Thomas.

But Hooks had an ace up his sleeve. The executive director told the members of the board about a time-consuming recommendation made by Wade Henderson of the organization's Washington office. He wanted to perform a study of Thomas's record before jumping to a conclusion. Henderson was a smart lawyer with liberal credentials who had been hired away from the American Civil Liberties Union (ACLU) five months earlier. He was respected within the NAACP and viewed by some as a potential successor to Hooks, speculation that was a source of tension between the two men. Although Henderson disliked Thomas's politics, he argued that it would be reckless to move too quickly. He didn't want to leave the organization open to criticism that it was reacting against Thomas with kneejerk ideology. He wanted to evaluate the nominee as calmly as possible.

The board members realized a vote then in Houston would likely split the organization. They were too far from unanimity. They agreed to have Henderson conduct his study with a completion date in mid-August. A few days later the date was amended to the last day in July, in order to provide more time for a campaign if the organization did indeed oppose Thomas.

The NAACP's inaction at the time of the convention meant there would be little or no concerted opposition to Thomas in the crucial first month after his nomination. The liberal groups would not have a common front, while the public, with the help of the Bush administration, began making up its mind.

"The NAACP would have provided cover for a number of organizations," said one liberal working for a coaliton group. "It would have given organizations a leg up on timing to circulate their reports, it would have allowed women's groups to get out. Plus it would have been a signal to a lot of white liberals that it was okay to oppose this guy even though he's black. A lot were pussyfooting around. If Hooks had announced his decision it would have freed up the whole debate."

To further complicate the situation, Hazel Dukes, president of the NAACP board, suggested that a meeting be held with Thomas. Such a meeting would be virtually unprecedented in modern times, for it was thought undignified, even unseemly, for Supreme Court nominees to go around to partisan groups to plead for support. The Supreme Court had a high reputation to maintain, one that kept it at a distance from the mundane and sometimes dirty methods of regular politics. No immediate decision was made on this matter, either.

Such a meeting could have been useful to Thomas, since he would have been able to explain himself to the civil rights leaders. He might not have espoused their politics but he could have told them where he was coming from, although that was by no means a simple story. He had followed twisting paths to get from the marshlands of the segregated South to the peaks of national power.

# Chapter

# 3

In June 1948, just before the worst of the summer heat clamped down on the little enclave of Pin Point, Georgia, Clarence Thomas was born to a teenage mother who had trouble fending for herself in the world and a father who was not above philandering. A midwife attended Leola Thomas as she gave birth to her second child in a rotting wooden house that was hardly more than a shanty. It had dirt floors and was without electricity or plumbing. Newspapers served as wallpaper. The house belonged to an aunt with whom the family lived. Before Clarence Thomas reached his second birthday, his father abandoned his mother, who would soon have three children.

"Clarence and Emma Mae had been born and I was pregnant with Myers," recounted Leola Williams, who has remarried now for the fourth time, but has never forgiven her first husband. "What happened was that he had a problem. My husband had another woman pregnant and so he went off to Philadelphia."

Aunt Annie Graham continued to shelter the young mother and her three children. They were as poor as anybody in Pin Point, a community of several hundred blacks close to Savannah; it clings to a marshy peninsula where two rivers meet at a sharp angle, hence the town's

name. The people of Pin Point survive by doing menial labor, serving
as maids and gardeners in the houses of wealthy whites in nearby
Savannah, or working in "the crab factory" that stood on the bank of
one of the rivers. The factory, if the cluster of sheds in the marsh grass
could be given so grand a description, was run by a white entrepreneur
who paid low wages for the tedious job of picking the meat from crabs
and shucking oysters. Aunt Annie's house was situated at the water's
edge and looked out over the factory.

"For crabs, I got five cents a pound. I also did maid's work," Leola
Thomas said in an interview.

Through child's eyes, Clarence Thomas watched as his mother and
other Pin Point women lined up to catch the early morning bus to
town, standing in the dark, the cold and the rain. He remembered how
in the evenings, the women "stood on solitary corners with their
shopping bags in the heat and humidity waiting for the bus where they
would crowd in the back, with no air-conditioning." When his mother
got home after working long hours in the big kitchens, her feet and
hands ached.

If things went well, she could bring home ten to fifteen dollars a
week, enough for living, but for nothing extra. The Thomas family ate
crabs and grits, cornflakes and watered-down Pet condensed milk.
Sometimes, Thomas's mother brought home the crusts trimmed from
bread used for hors d'oeuvres at her employers' parties. Sometimes
they had eggs and fried catfish. They dressed in secondhand clothes
collected by the Sweet Field of Eden Baptist Church, a modest edifice
at the other end of the enclave from the seafood factory. In between
there was a hodgepodge of simple houses and shacks, shadowed by oak
trees whose thick limbs were draped with Spanish moss. When
Thomas was a boy, a loose web of dirt lanes and byways connected the
community of closeknit relatives.

He played with his cousins and other boys, inventing games from
scratch. Under the cool gloom of the oak trees, the small gang of Pin
Point youngsters would chase after bicycle tire rims that they balanced
with bent coat hangers. They wrestled in the soft dirt. They tied
together strings of tin cans and ran about, trying to raise as much
clatter and dust as possible. They took castoff stockings and stuffed
them with moss to make balls for games, pretending to dribble the
unbounceable balls.

Thomas, though, was always different from the others. Often he ignored the cajoling of his peers and stayed inside by himself, thinking or reading.

"We used to go and try to get Clarence out of the house and sometimes he just wouldn't come. He was always reading a book," recalled Abraham Framble, a distant cousin. "I think about that now and I think about all those times he wouldn't come out and play. He was inside pumping information into his brains."

Thomas read hand-me-down books that an uncle obtained from the white family he worked for. If Clarence couldn't understand them, he thumbed through them, anyway. He also studied the newspapers on the walls at home, according to his mother, trying to make sense of words still beyond his grasp.

But Thomas's days in Pin Point ended abruptly. When Thomas was six years old and his mother was on her way to work for a white family, Aunt Annie's house went up in flames. One of the boys had set a curtain on fire and the house, with its rotting lumber, burnt down. It happened so quickly that a telephone message about the house's demise was waiting for Leola when she reached town.

Leola took the three children to Savannah and rented a cheap tenement room. With three other families they shared a kitchen and a filthy toilet that leaked sewage into the backyard. She put the two oldest children—Emma Mae and Clarence—in an all-black public school.

This was the year Thurgood Marshall won his case, *Brown* v. *Board of Education*, before the Supreme Court that made segregated schools unlawful, but decisions far away in Washington had no immediate effect on the blacks living in East Savannah under the burden of bigotry.

Leola was having trouble managing; she went to the office of the Red Cross and beseeched those in charge. Their answer was firm: Leola's father was alive and earning money. If she needed help, that was the direction from which it must come. But the situation was more complicated than it appeared on the surface.

Her father, Myers Anderson, was in Savannah, too, doggedly building a business delivering fuel oil to residences. Although he was the grandfather of her three children, Anderson was reluctant to come to the rescue. He had always felt estranged from Leola because he had

never married her mother, whom he'd met when they both lived in the
hinterlands of Liberty County well outside Savannah. Leola's mother
took refuge in Pin Point, living with her sister, caring for the baby girl
who had no official father. Myers Anderson, meanwhile, married another woman and shunted Leola and her mother over to Pin Point
where Aunt Annie's care was available. He moved to Savannah with
his wife Christine Anderson.

The official Mrs. Anderson never bore a child. She was a kind
woman, though, and her heart went out to her husband's grandchildren. She quietly asked Anderson to take them under his wing. Leola
was not providing well for the children and, besides, she was com-
plicating her life with another man, who was not interested in the
children, but whom she would soon marry. Meanwhile, a friend of
Anderson's told him that Leola was unable to pay her grocery bills,
and urged him to act. Anderson decided to leave Emma Mae with
Leola, but to raise the two boys. Myers Anderson seemed to have a will
made of steel, and an anger that could cut like a whiplash. He was
going to show the boys how to succeed the hard way, just as he had
done.

When Myers Anderson came into town as a young man from Liberty
County, he was already hardened to work. He had come from Sunbury, a rural hamlet some forty miles from Savannah, originally
founded as a seaport by wandering New England Puritans who
brought their slaves with them. So pious were these Puritans that no
mixed-race children were born to their slaves. Anderson's grandmother was nine years old when freed from slavery, and she stayed on
in Sunbury on a small farm. It was there that Anderson learned to toil.

When he arrived in Savannah as a young man with a third-grade
education and a wife to support, he started his first business, buying
ice from a wholesale company and trundling it around to households
where he could resell it at a small profit for the old-fashioned iceboxes
of the time. He soon added wood to his delivery business. Then,
branching out, he bought a machine to make cement cinderblocks,
and built himself three stout little houses in a modest neighborhood
in black East Savannah—one to live in, the others to rent.

Anderson also teamed up with a man named Sam Williams, who
would become his closest friend, to open a nightclub where blacks

could enjoy themselves, eating, drinking and dancing. The establishment prospered until the landlord of the place took over the business for himself. Anderson then turned his energies to another enterprise, delivering fuel oil for household heaters. He bought a tank truck and expanded his business until he had customers all over Savannah, east and west, black and white. Anderson was unstinting. He rose at three-thirty in the morning and worked until his wife had dinner on the table at night.

But he also had a streak of kindness in him. "If someone didn't have money for wood or fuel or, even if he never expected to get the money, he'd give it to them because he didn't want them to go cold," remembered Sam Williams.

It was this same friend who converted Clarence Thomas's grandfather from a Baptist to a staunch Catholic. Williams also taught Anderson how to read, and to figure simple sums. When he arrived from the country, Anderson had been taxed to write his own name; but, as in all things, he persisted. Progressing to the Bible by poring over it with his index finger, moving from word to word, Anderson achieved a literacy that enabled him to vote. Armed with that privilege in an era when blacks were deterred from voting, he never missed a chance to cast his ballot.

Anderson joined the increasingly powerful local NAACP that was challenging Savannah's white elite. Although covered by a veneer of civility, bigotry flourished as viciously in Savannah as elsewhere.

Myers Anderson had felt the prejudice personally. Thomas recalled the day that a wealthy white woman drove up in a fancy car and summoned Anderson with the belittling call of "boy." Anderson's two grandsons witnessed the scene, which shamed him in their presence.

Anderson also suffered economically, no matter how hard he worked; he had trouble getting licenses that would have enabled him to participate in the building boom after World War II. Black builders, unable to obtain electricians' licenses, had to hire highly paid white workers to make their wiring jobs legal.

Although Savannah had been founded in 1733 as a utopian colonial community in which slavery was prohibited, the founders' idealism was short-lived. By 1750, the possession of slaves was legal, and the coastal town soon became a hub for the trade in blacks whose labor created the wealth of the Southern cotton plantations.

Savannah was still very much a Jim Crow society in the 1950s when Anderson began taking his grandsons along to the weekly NAACP meetings. Blacks were second-class citizens, legally, socially, and economically. They were not seen in most white neighborhoods unless they were wearing chauffeur's caps or maid's aprons. The segregation went far beyond schools. Blacks couldn't swim at Savannah's beaches. In public places, they were relegated to separate bathrooms and drank from separate water fountains. The courthouse even insisted on keeping a separate book for their tax records. The newspaper never mentioned the results of black schools' sports events. Blacks were expected, always, to treat whites with humility.

"It was 'nigger' this and 'nigger' that. And if a white man wanted a job, there wasn't a chance for a black man to get it," said W.W. Law, a veteran civil rights leader who headed the Savannah branch of the NAACP for more than a quarter of a century. "So it was men like Myers Anderson, who employed themselves and who didn't have to be frightened of a white boss firing them, who were part of the backbone of our NAACP."

Anderson and Thad Harris, a friend who worked for himself as a carpenter, made forays out into the Savannah business world to get information for the NAACP. For example, if they found a grocery store with black customers, but no black cashiers, they would recommend a boycott. The pressure from blacks kept mounting, as the NAACP began sit-ins at all-white counters in downtown cafeterias and department stores. When demonstrators were arrested, the NAACP called a boycott against all the stores on Savannah's main white business street. Unlike other southern cities, though, Savannah avoided serious violence. The city's business elite capitulated relatively early on—in 1963, when Thomas was a teenager—and the once segregated restaurants, theaters, hotels, and other public places were opened to blacks. Racism was coming to an end officially, if not unofficially.

A rare photograph of Myers Anderson shows a tall man with muscular arms hanging loose at his sides, and eyes that jump out of the black-and-white image. His hands were large, toughened by work. When the Thomas brothers came to live in the Anderson household, Clarence was seven, and he learned immediately that his "granddaddy"—or his "daddy" as the boys sometimes called him—was not to be trifled with.

Misbehavior would bring an immediate whipping, either by Anderson's tongue or by his thick leather belt. But he also provided them with comfortable lodgings in his six-room house, which had a clean indoor toilet, and his wife fed them three hearty meals a day.

One of the first things Anderson did with his new charges was to put down the money to enroll the boys in a private Catholic school, St. Benedict the Moor. It was run by white Franciscan nuns, who saw it as their duty to venture into the South and bring decent education to black children. The nuns stuck with their charges, riding in the rear of buses with the black students and ignoring the taunts of racist whites who called them "the nigger sisters." Clarence Thomas entered the nuns' tutelage in the second grade with the words of Anderson ringing in his ears.

"Boy, you are going to school today. You're goin' do better than I'm doing."

The nuns, many of whom had come from Ireland, wore brown habits and brooked no discourtesy or slovenliness. They lived in a convent across the street from the sturdy brick school building. The students wore ties and white shirts, blue sweaters, and blue pants. When one of the sisters entered a class, the boys stood and chorused, "Good morning" or "Good afternoon." No one uttered another word unless spoken to. The use of the word "ain't" and all other grammar that fell short of acceptable English was outlawed. The nuns forced their charges to learn the rules not only for grammar, but also for success. The students were disciplined at school and laden with homework; they would love their teachers for it later.

"I have nothing but warmth and honor now for those nuns, but at the time I can assure you I was afraid of them," said Floyd Adams, a boyhood friend of Thomas who runs Savannah's black newspaper and is a Savannah alderman. Adams, a huge man with an imposing presence, nonetheless looks sideways around his office when speaking of the nuns to make sure one of them is not lingering, somehow.

"Whatever the nuns said was gospel. They evoked fear and you respected them. If you did something out of line or if you didn't do your work, you knew you were in for discipline. You'd hold out your hand. Sometimes they used rulers and sometimes they used those flagpoles, those slender kind the American flag came on for the schoolroom. Whatever it was, you feared that hit, that pain.

"At times, they lost their tempers. They had that Irish blood. They'd grab a person and hit him and you always had the idea that this could happen to you. The nuns, they also could stare you in the face and bully you down that way. A seasoned police officer couldn't do better."

One incident that stuck in Adams's memory was the day that a petite nun made a two hundred-pound teenaged student kneel in front of the class, then slapped him in the face with all her might.

Clarence Thomas fared well in the Franciscan system of education, where the highest status a student could achieve was that of altarboy. That meant learning to recite the entire Catholic mass in Latin, a drill that began in third grade. The parish priest coached the altarboys and Thomas was soon one of them, performing his Sunday duties at church in a long white cassock. His path had already taken quite a turn from its origin in Pin Point; he had adopted his grandfather's exacting values with a vengeance.

At home, the regimen under Anderson was strict: Thomas and his brother worked in the winter afternoons on Anderson's truck, leaping out to haul the heavy fuel hose around to the tanks at the back of customers' homes. Young Thomas didn't relish the shivering hours he spent after school riding in the oil truck. But he learned from the time he spent under the domination of his grandfather, whom he remembers as "tough as nails," and filled with homegrown wisdom.

Granddaddy Anderson was given to bits of crusty advice, such as: "Old Man Can't is dead. I helped bury him."

Religious to his core, Anderson also passed on the idea that human beings had rights that came from God, not man. The segregation of the time, then sanctioned by the federal government, was at odds with Anderson's perception of divine law. This was one reason he'd become so involved in the civil rights movement. Anderson was forcing Thomas to both work and think.

After dinner, the boys did homework. If they overslept in the mornings, Anderson would blister their ears with accusations that laziness was okay for the rich but certainly not for a penniless pair of boys.

On Saturday mornings, when the boys slept past seven, Grandfather Anderson would come by the open window of their bedroom and shout, "Y'all think yua'll are rich?" This was sufficient, Thomas remembered, to make them spring from their beds.

If Anderson heard from neighbors or friends that the boys had done anything wrong, they could expect punishment, ranging from beatings to banishment to a lonely room. An infraction could be as minor as dropping a candy wrapper on the ground, or failing to greet an adult with the proper respect.

Thomas recalled the impossibility of even thinking of playing hooky or faking illness. "In his deep, resonanant, and all powerful voice, [Anderson] would often say, 'If you die, I'll take you to school for two days to make sure you're not faking.' I often wondered if the other students would object to a dead person being in the classroom."

Anderson's wife, the step-grandmother whom the boys affectionately called "Tina," would sometimes intervene to protect them from their grandfather's wrath.

"Sometimes she'd whip them light, not really hit them at all, for something they'd done, so that when granddaddy got home, they'd be safe," said Leola Williams, who visited her sons sporadically.

The boys' mother had soon returned to the sanctuary of Aunt Annie's house in Pin Point. While working as a servant, she was able to take them on occasional outings to movies or fairs, along with the white children she was being paid to tend.

"My daddy was a very hard person," Leola went on. "He could love but never show it. Sometimes you just wanted somebody to put their arms around you, but he wasn't the one to do it. Tina would tell me not to worry, that he cared for me anyway. That he was a kind man and you could tell by seeing how generous he was with helping out the neighbors.

"But all he'd have to do is look at me and I'd start crying. He criticized Clarence and Myers, but they didn't cry. They took it better, I guess."

Clarence and Myers worked out in Liberty County, too, rehabilitating the old farm. They began the task on a winter holiday in 1957 when most children were more carefree.

"I remember one Christmas," Thomas said, in one of many speeches he would later make as an adult, "when all the other kids were running up and down the road and enjoying their toys, shooting firecrackers, and generally having a great time. My grandfather came up to me and my brother . . . and said that he had work for us to do. So, as usual, we piled into the 1951 Pontiac and rode. He took us to a field that had lain fallow for years and had grown up. He drove down the remnants of an old road. We made our way across the field to an old oak tree. He looked at it, surveyed it, paced pensively and announced that we could build a house there. . . . Five months later we were finishing the steps to the house that we built."

In the summers, Anderson took the boys back out to the farm. First, they grew vegetables. Later, with the help of some cousins and the two boys Anderson cleared and fenced in seventy-two acres. It was a back-breaking job. First Myers Anderson acquired cows, then he cultivated corn, watermelons, greens, collards, and rice. The boys did everything from picking beans to driving the tractor their grandfather eventually bought.

"Myers Anderson always said he was going to make a man out of each of those boys," Jack Fuller, a cousin of Anderson, commented. "There was no question that Myers and Tina were the real parents who made those boys into something."

Years later, Clarence Thomas often raised the memory of his grandfather, who died in 1983, in his speeches. Anderson became the exemplar for success in Thomas's world view.

"I grew up under state-enforced segregation, which is as close to totalitarianism as I would like to get. My household . . . was strong, stable, and conservative. In fact, it was far more conservative than many who fashion themselves conservatives today. God was central. School, discipline, hard work, and knowing right from wrong were of the highest priority. Crime, welfare, slothfulness, and alcohol were enemies. But these were not issues to be debated by keen intellectuals, bellowed about by rousing orators or dissected by pollsters and researchers. They were a way of life: they marked the path of survival and the escape route from squalor.

"Of course, I thought my grandparents were too rigid, and their expectations were too high. I also thought they were mean at times. But one of their often-stated goals was to raise us so that we could 'do for ourselves,' so that we could stand on 'our own two feet.' This was not their social policy, it was their family policy—for their family, not those nameless families that politicians love to whine about. The most compassionate thing they did for us was to teach us to fend for ourselves, and to do that in an openly hostile environment. In fact, the hostility made learning the lesson that much more urgent. It meant the difference between freedom and incarceration, life and death, alcoholism and sobriety.

"We were raised to survive in spite of the dark, oppressive cloud of governmentally sanctioned bigotry. Self-sufficiency and spiritual and emotional security were our tools to carve out and secure freedom. Those who attempt to capture the daily counseling, oversight, common sense, and vision of my grandparents in a governmental program, are engaging in sheer folly."

No matter what Clarence Thomas did, though, he was never able to fit in with the society around him.

"He caught it from both sides. The whites didn't accept him, of course. But the blacks didn't accept him, either," said a Savannah woman who grew up with Thomas and attended Catholic schools for black girls. "He didn't fit in with blacks because he was darker than most, and had nappy hair."

With his tightly curled hair, broad features, and dark skin, Thomas epitomized the black stereotype at a time before racial pride would ease such stigmas.

Thomas remembered being teased for his looks. In an interview in 1987 for *The Atlantic*, he said his peers would call him "ABC," a jeering acronym for "America's blackest child."

Being Catholic, which meant wearing uniforms and refusing meat on Friday and carrying around whole texts of Latin in his head, also set Thomas apart.

White Savannah offered even less acceptance. "If you were black, there were a whole series of 'do's' and 'don't's'. An example of this is that if you were standing in a department store, assuming they served blacks at all in that store, and a white person came afterwards, he or she could always move ahead of the black customer," Thomas recalled in a speech.

"Another example is that in certain stores, if you were black and tried on an article of clothing or a pair of shoes, you had to buy it whether it fit or not. In essence . . . a Negro had no rights which the white man was bound to respect."

Thomas did have some pleasant memories, though, of buying goodies to eat at black stores on East and West Broad streets, which edged downtown white Savannah. These streets had many captive black customers, who feared trying to patronize white businesses. He remembered going to the movies and not minding an occasional rat scurrying in the corner.

But Thomas always did well in school; he read a great deal. When he couldn't be found, his grandparents would dispatch somebody to the local library, one for blacks that had been built by the Carnegies.

"I used to run to the library to flip through the pages and dream," he said. "I just remember *The New Yorker*. You know, what did I know about New York? But I said, One day, I'm going to be sophisticated enough to deal with these kinds of things."

Thomas was developing a powerful intellect; he was determined to get ahead.

In 1964, the year the Civil Rights Act was signed into law, Clarence Thomas left familiar struggles to begin a new trial—he was going to be at the cutting edge of integration. His grandfather pulled him out of an all-black parochial high school and enrolled him in an all-white Catholic boarding school, the St. John Vianney Minor Seminary. Anderson had hopes that his grandson would go on to become a priest. Thomas did well at the school but, being terribly lonely, he hated it. He was an oddity and the subject of racism. There were no other black faces to turn to for aid.

In the dormitory, after the lights were switched out, the white junior seminarians would entertain themselves by yelling, "Smile, Clarence, so we can see you." No one ever spoke up in his defense.

He would comfort himself, as he always had, by escaping into the pages of books. He tried to sneak into the lighted bathroom to read, but his fellow students snitched to the seminary teachers. He was forbidden to break the rules, and was forced to lie in his lonely bed until he came up with a new tactic: he persuaded his mother to bring him a flashlight so that he could read clandestinely, huddled under his blankets. Thomas's black friends, whom he saw during vacations, called St. John's the Cemetery.

One of young Thomas's favorite authors was Richard Wright, whose novels about black anger at the shallow pieties of American culture struck a chord. Wright's characters lashed out destructively and self-destructively at the world. In one of Wright's best-known novels, *Native Son*, the whole of the American racist society is entered into evidence in the trial of a misfit black man who murdered a white woman, stuffing the corpse into a furnace, and then killed a black woman, stuffing that body down a ventilator shaft.

He would say later in another speech that this was one of Wright's books that "really woke me up." For Thomas, Wright "captured a lot of the feelings that I have inside that you learn how to suppress."

In the summer at the Savannah library, he read accounts of lynchings that had occurred over the previous century. "As I read, I seethed with anger and simmered with bitterness," Thomas remembered.

But Thomas turned his anger and pain inward, and kept on the laborious path his grandfather had prescribed. He protected himself with the decision that, if nothing else, he had to earn dignity in the world.

He had plenty of disrespect to struggle against. In one incident he would never forget a white seminarian scrawled a crude note in Thomas's yearbook: "Keep on trying Clarence, one day you'll be as good as us." Thomas's reaction was to decide "then and there at the ripe old age of sixteen that it was better to be respected than liked. Popularity is unpredictable and vacillating. Respect is a constant."

Outwardly, Thomas did well. He made excellent marks and quarterbacked the football team. His grandfather was so proud of him that he would drag out young Thomas's report cards at the NAACP meetings and boast that this was proof that blacks could succeed.

Thomas was paraded around the black parochial schools as an example to emulate. He was encouraged to recruit other black students for the seminary. Lester Johnson, a parochial school student who would later become a friend of Thomas, remembers Clarence suggesting to him that he think about turning to the seminary.

"I might be able to take all the whites," he told Thomas, "but what about having a life with no girls. Now, that's a serious problem."

Thomas shrugged off the dilemma by saying: "That may be a disadvantage, but there are a couple of big advantages. It's a good education and it's free." Thomas was accustomed to repressing his urges, having had little chance to socialize with the opposite sex.

When Thomas graduated from St. John Vianney, Anderson sent him to attend the Immaculate Conception Seminary in the cornfields of a northwest corner of Missouri, where he was one of a handful of blacks. Racism hadn't been left behind in the South. In the spring of 1968, Thomas was walking up the stairs to his dormitory and someone who had been watching television shouted that an assassin's bullet had brought down Martin Luther King. A fellow seminarian, a young white man, who was on the stairs ahead of Thomas and unaware of his presence, yelled back: "That's good. I hope the S.O.B. dies."

Thomas never forgot that moment; it distilled the essence of his years at the seminaries. Despite strong opposition from his grandfather, he left, angry at the church, an institution whose preachings about brotherly love amounted to hypocrisy for him. Thomas would not become a priest. He left confused, too, about integration, a policy that had destined him to environments in which he was deeply wounded.

It was Dr. King's assassination that propelled Clarence Thomas into political activity. He marched in mass demonstrations in the late sixties in which young people of all races protested against the war in Vietnam and the political establishment. His inner anger matched the outer anger he was finding around him.

# Chapter 4

The assassination of Dr. King did open another door for Thomas, though, as a wave of guilt swept over white America. The death of the nation's greatest civil rights leader would help Thomas gain admission to Holy Cross College, the elite Catholic school in Worcester, Massachusetts. The school's officials decided they would try to compensate for the tragedy by recruiting black students. Thomas was benefiting from the very sort of affirmative action plan—one which assuaged guilt by promoting blacks—that would come to offend him deeply in the long run.

Thomas entered the Jesuit campus of Holy Cross in 1968, troubled by his experiences and looking for answers to the ills of racism. He arrived when universities across the country were in turmoil over the Vietnam War and the established values of American society were under attack.

Black students were standing up and protesting that colleges were not teaching African-American culture and history. The Black Panthers were militantly demanding a right to power.

This was the first time that Thomas had been exposed to radicalism, to the ideas of Malcolm X and the Black Panthers. And he embraced the student militancy, at least on the surface. He grew a goatee and let his hair spring out into an Afro. He took to wearing fatigues and army boots, characterizing himself as one among the many thousands of symbolic foot soldiers setting out to revolutionize American society.

Underneath this image, Thomas wasn't all that certain who he was. Notes he made about that period give a hint of the contradictory impulses in the mind of the young man who had started out in Pin Point:

"Turn 20 summer of 1968 . . . MLK shot previous spring . . . Bobby Kennedy assassinated . . . depressing, scared, serious, angry, confused . . . years of rage."

Despite the militancy of the time, there was much that had not changed at Holy Cross. There were only five other blacks in his class, a few dozen total at the college. Racism hadn't died. In at least one case, a white student insisted he was in the wrong room when he was introduced to the black student who had been assigned quarters with him. A poll taken of the student body when Thomas was at Holy Cross showed that although more than 90 percent of his classmates agreed that American society discriminated against blacks, nearly half felt that "Negroes tend to have less ambition" than whites.

Thomas soon joined up with the other blacks at Holy Cross and helped found the college's Black Student Union. He was the secretary-treasurer. The union pushed Holy Cross to do more for blacks—to hire more black professors, to provide more financial aid for blacks, to start more courses in black studies. Thomas was never at the political vanguard, but he was intense about the issues of the 1960s.

Thomas, like others enamored of social revolution, volunteered time in the poor areas of town, tutoring black children and helping with a free breakfast program whose purpose was to properly nourish the underprivileged. With his black friends, he took part in all-night "rap sessions" in which young men smoked marijuana and argued about what was on their minds—the racism around them on the campus, the war in Vietnam, the horrors of apartheid in South Africa, President Nixon and his mistaken policies. Thomas loved to debate and would often play devil's advocate just to keep the ideas raging. He tested out various political postures, advocating the hardline doctrine of Malcolm X one day and the old-fashioned self-help remedies of Booker T. Washington the next.

Thomas's friends all knew him by the nickname "Cooz," because he loved to imitate the elaborately skillful moves of Bob Cousy, the Boston Celtics' basketball star. He played intramural basketball and football and ran as a sprinter on the track team. He was short, five feet nine inches tall, but powerful from working out with weights—able to bench press 275 pounds. His friends all knew him for his deep, resonating laugh.

Thomas was always something of a maverick; when members of the Black Student Union voted to live together as a way of maintaining solidarity within the college, he dissented. He made the point that they were at Holy Cross to learn the ways of the white world, not to retreat to their own corner. He argued that voluntary segregation wasn't an answer to anything. But when the college administration consented and designated a "Black Corridor" in Healey dormitory, which had been named for a black Roman Catholic bishop, Thomas went with the others. To prove his point, though, he insisted on bringing along his white roommate, John Siraco, an easygoing student who eventually went on to become a pediatrician. In their almost militarily neat room, Siraco tacked up a poster of Julie Christie and Thomas balanced that with one of Malcolm X.

As he had done all his life, Thomas read and studied. He was often holed up in the library, and made very good grades. Stubborn about improving himself, he picked English as a major in part because it was painfully difficult for him, harder than other fields at the liberal arts college. He also felt that he needed to further perfect his English in order to succeed in a society where the oddities of black southern speech were frowned upon. For Thomas, the English of officialdom seemed foreign, like a second language, that necessitated immense study.

He would admonish the other black students to remember why they were there. College wasn't for fun and games, Thomas maintained. He enjoyed spending holidays on campus, rather than making the long journey back to Savannah, because he could make good use of the time studying. He also worked as a waiter in the college dining hall to help make fiscal ends meet. He wasn't much of a partygoer and wasn't adept, like some of his friends, at charming the women. Instead, he often felt awkward.

Thomas wanted rules about how the college men should act around women. He persuaded the Black Student Union to implement guidelines for instances when women came into the dormitory. With women present, Thomas wanted students to avoid the use of foul language, dress politely, and be careful about the embarrassing issue of shared bathrooms.

"Cooz never liked to socialize," recounted Lester Johnson, the friend of Thomas's from Catholic school days who also attended Holy Cross, and now has a law practice in Savannah. "He'd like to come around the dormitory and talk, but usually he'd stay on campus when we'd party. He was always about business.

"The guys from Savannah would tease him, too, when he wouldn't party. They'd say, 'What woman would want this man anyway. He's got boots on, he's got nappy hair, he's into books and Black Power.' Thomas had the sense of humor to take the teasing but it didn't change him. He was just straitlaced underneath. All the guys had several girlfriends, except Thomas." His desire to achieve overshadowed almost everything.

Thomas, though, was one of the first to marry. He met his wife, Kathy Ambush, by chance, according to Johnson. Ambush, the daughter of a dental technician in Worcester, attended nearby Anna Maria College, a black Catholic school for women.

"Kathy and some of her friends came over to Holy Cross for a dance of some kind but when they got there, they found that all the cool black guys were off at another women's college. So the women went on up to the Black Corridor to see where everyone was. There were only a few guys there, one who was into karate and martial arts, plus a couple of radical guys against the war who wouldn't go to any parties because they were too serious. Cooz was there, too, reading his books and trying to get ahead. That's how they met."

In the winter of 1969 when antiwar protests were becoming epidemic, Thomas got caught up in the angry tenor of the time. A mass of Holy Cross students, blacks and whites, tried to obstruct a recruiter from General Electric, a company that held military contracts. About fifty students barred the way and after the confrontation, sixteen of them were suspended, a disproportionate number of them black. The members of Black Student Union met in outrage and decided to stage a mass walkout. Thomas was in on it. After rallying and flinging down their student identification cards, all but a few of the blacks at Holy

Cross hefted their suitcases into cars and drove off. They didn't know if their act of rebellion would result in permanent exile from academia. But the college administration capitulated, all the suspensions were lifted, and the blacks returned to their corridor.

It had been the most radical action of Thomas's life; he had risked his precious education for principle, an act of "liberation" of blacks "from their historic shackles," as he described it to friends. But he cooled off during his final years at Holy Cross and began to consider a career as a lawyer, a profession that could grant him respect and a platform from which to vent his ideas and his pent-up opinions. Thomas remembered his motivation when he made this career decision.

"At that age, you think you actually can go out and change the world. I wanted to right some wrongs that I saw in Savannah, some specific wrongs with respect to my grandfather and what he was able to do with his life, as well as the overall wrongs that I saw as a child there," Thomas said later.

In 1971, Thomas graduated with honors, ninth in his class, and a day later he married Kathy Ambush at an Episcopal Church in Worcester.

Thomas had been admitted to several top law schools. From them he chose Yale, which offered him badly needed financial aid. Thomas offered Yale a qualified student who was also black. Yale law school had implemented an aggressive affirmative action plan whose goal was to have blacks or other minorities comprise 10 percent of each class. Of the some 170 students in Thomas's first-year class, 12 were black.

Although Thomas in all likelihood had benefited again from affirmative action, he was growing to resent it. He was moving through the privileged halls of Yale, but he couldn't know for certain whether he was walking on his own merit or on a social plan of white university officials.

"Clarence did not like what he felt was the stigma of affirmative action," said Henry Cornelius Terry, a fellow black student at the law school. "He felt that people would assume that we were not as good as others."

Thomas remembered years later how the quandary infuriated him. "You had to prove yourself every day because the presumption was that you were dumb and didn't deserve to be there on merit. Every time you walked into a law class at Yale, it was like having a monkey jump down on your back from the Gothic arches."

As had been his lot before, Thomas was angry, and he looked for a way to survive. For starters, he dropped a lot of the Holy Cross militancy and went about the huge task of learning the law—everything from the sweeping meaning of the U.S. Constitution to the minute details of legal contracts. For the most part, he lived quietly off campus with his wife. In his classes, he preferred not to draw attention to himself. Few professors have sharp recollections of Thomas.

He liked to sit in the back of the class, do his work, and avoid being judged. Above all, he didn't want to be judged as a black. And he avoided taking on civil rights as a specialty because he didn't want to be categorized.

"It was typical Clarence in a way," said Lester Johnson from Savannah. "He would say, 'I don't want to be pigeonholed.' His perception was that whites don't think we are intellectually equal and if we are doing civil rights law, it is because we can't put our minds to anything else. Clarence wanted to show them that a black person can compete with them in other areas of the law, in corporate law and in tax law. He resented it when people thought he automatically was going to go into civil rights."

Thomas had not sorted out his internal contradictions, though. He worked with other black law students to pressure the school to recruit qualified minority students and professors. He worked at a New Haven legal-aid storefront, providing free services to poor people on welfare. He spent one summer back in Savannah working at Georgia's first integrated law firm on civil rights cases. At school, he dressed in overalls, a way of identifying politically with the masses.

Thomas also began to move toward the right, making fast friends with Harry Singleton, a black student who defined himself as a conservative among the mostly liberal student body at the mostly liberal law school. Like Thomas, Singleton came from a poor family—his father was employed as a janitor. They felt a bond that set them apart from other minority students who had come from plusher backgrounds and whom they labeled the black elite. They saw themselves, unlike others, as having to climb out of a deep pit. It was during his years at Yale that Thomas's views began making a pendulum swing from left to right.

"Clarence Thomas was never one to go along with the crowd," said Singleton, who now practices in Washington, D.C. "At Yale, his philosophy was evolving. We were about to enter the world as trained lawyers. It was sobering and it caused him to start looking at things differently."

In 1973, Kathy Thomas gave birth to a son. His parents named him Jamal, a Muslim name that was to linger as a reminder of the days of Thomas's more radical politics.

That same year, the Supreme Court handed down its decision in the case of *Roe* v. *Wade*. This legalizing of abortion was, from the beginning, one of the court's most controversial decisions. But years later in the Senate hearings that would be the final step in his rise to the Supreme Court, Thomas denied that he had ever discussed his own opinion of the decision at Yale. Thomas's position, or lack of position, on the abortion law has been made into a sensitive issue. Many of his classmates and professors were later questioned on the topic. Some remembered that *Roe* v. *Wade* was a hot topic at the time Thomas was at Yale.

"It was the central case of the time," one of the law school teachers, Professor Harry Wellington, recalled. "Everyone was talking about it and I find it inconceivable that he was not part of the discussion. Inconceivable."

Another issue that would rise to plague Thomas at the hearings was the question of whether or not he had a penchant for pornography. One of his classmates remembered that Thomas was a regular viewer of pornographic films.

Leaving his wife at their apartment, Thomas would go off weekly to one of New Haven's pornographic movie houses, according to Henry Terry, who now practices law in Boston. Terry said Thomas was not at all shy about making visits to the local theater that showed hard-core pornographic movies, as opposed to the more artful erotic movies popular with students of the 1960s.

"Clarence Thomas was an habituator of porn films," Terry said in an interview. "Clarence used to talk about going to see these movies. He and another guy in his class would go once a week, whenever a new film came in, and come back roaring with laughter about what they had seen."

The theater was off-campus, in a slightly seedy neighborhood of New Haven. It "advertised its movies as XX[-rated], triple X, quadruple X," Terry recalled. "And so I take those to be porn films."

Thomas liked to talk about the movies, according to Terry, who said his fellow student was not at all secretive about his interests. Thomas seems to have abandoned the sort of propriety that he had wanted to implement at his Holy Cross dormitory. Terry remembered Thomas at a party joking about films like *Deep Throat* and *The Devil in Miss Jones*.

"They were not making any secret of it. And others found it amusing that he liked these films so much," Terry recalled.

Another fellow Yale law student, Lovida Coleman, also remembered Thomas enjoying pornographic films. She and Thomas were part of a group of law students who met regularly for breakfast. Thomas liked to regale his fellow students with details from the films he had seen, making jokes, for instance, about the plot of a popular pornographic movie of the time called *Behind the Green Door*.

A pornographic fantasy, the movie shows in graphic detail the sexual adventure of an uptight woman who is abducted and introduced to the pleasures of a bizarre but friendly exhibitionist orgy. The woman's abductors escort her behind a green door onto a stage, where she has most kinds of imaginable sex with several partners, exciting the audience, which is made up of a pair of transvestites as well as male and female, black and white heterosexuals. The film culminates with the actors on stage and in the audience—which also includes an obese woman—stripping down and participating in multiple scenes of group sex.

"He could make us all laugh hysterically," Coleman said, remembering Thomas's accounts of pornography he had seen. "I remember another classmate tried to rival Clarence with a story of how he had tried to make a home porno movie as an undergraduate."

Coleman, knowing nothing about Thomas's trips to the more hardcore Crown Theater, argued that there was nothing odd about Thomas's behavior. She said X-rated movies were part of the student culture at the time and were shown by mainstream organizations like the law school's film society.

Whatever his extracurricular activities, Thomas always remained diligent about his law school studies. He graduated from Yale in 1974 in the broad middle of the class. He had won no academic honors but had made it through.

During his last semester at Yale, Thomas had a frustrating time deciding where his future lay. He wanted to go back home to Georgia to practice law. Although he had not distinguished himself at Yale, he had not done badly. And Yale was, some felt, the best law school in the country. He should have no trouble finding a job.

But the big firms in Atlanta seemed clearly prejudiced. He was asked all sorts of irrelevant questions about his past before being rejected. Thomas recalled being interviewed by a partner in one of the firms, who had graduated from an obscure law school and whose office was full of Confederate artifacts, asking him about his grades in grammar school. Other well-established firms offered him, perhaps as a lure, a chance to spend some of his time doing lawyering that was pro bono, work for the public good. This meant aiding the poor and the underprivileged. At that point Thomas would head for the door.

"I went to law school to be a lawyer, not a social worker," he later told *The Atlantic*. "If I want to be a social worker I'll do it on my own time."

Or, as he put it in another interview, "I wasn't going to soothe anyone else's guilt."

Instead, his spirit "bent but not broken" by the rejections, he took a job with John Danforth, who had yet to take his political career to Washington. Danforth was then Missouri's attorney general. A Yale law alumnus himself, Danforth promised to treat Thomas equally— just as respectfully and just as harshly as any of the other lawyers who assisted him. He offered to assign Thomas to the area of tax law, as tedious a field as a young Yale lawyer could find. Tax law, to its advantage from Thomas's point of view, had nothing to do with the civil rights stereotype of black lawyers.

First, Thomas had to pass the Missouri bar exam. That summer after law school he lived in the St. Louis home of Margaret Bush Wilson, who was about to become the chairman of the NAACP. Wilson found him to be a disciplined, agreeable young man of twenty-six. He was already sounding like a conservative, she recalled later, but was persuasive and had an open mind.

Burdened with student loans, Thomas had to support his wife and baby on the $10,800-a-year salary of an assistant attorney general. They lived in rural Jefferson City, in an apartment overlooking the penitentiary, while Kathy Thomas worked for a degree at Lincoln University.

Thomas could not afford any luxuries. But having been always fascinated with expensive cars he decorated his office with a picture of a Rolls-Royce as well as what many visitors took to be the Confederate flag. It was in fact the state flag of Georgia, which not accidentally greatly resembled the Confederate flag. This was exactly the point that Thomas was trying to make.

While working for the attorney general, Thomas switched his party allegiance to that of his boss, registering to vote as a Republican. With this act, Thomas stepped off the political path that his grandfather, the NAACP stalwart, had always followed. At his grandfather's insistence, Thomas had registered to vote at the age of eighteen, as a Democrat. While a student at Yale, he had voted for George McGovern's presidential bid in 1972.

After seven months of arguing routine criminal appeals, Thomas was allowed to do tax work. Colleagues at Danforth's office characterized Thomas as likable, hardworking, and ambitious, a person looking for a position of prominence. John Ashcroft, who shared an office with Thomas, and went on to become governor of Missouri, described him as a "candid, frank individual, who was a very hard worker."

Thomas's biggest victory over the next two years was the winning of a legal decision that upheld the state's right to abolish "vanity" license plates. Local bigshots would no longer be able to enjoy the special low-numbered license plates that distinguished them from the masses. This was a clean shot at the establishment that Thomas clearly relished.

In the isolation of a midwestern state capital, Thomas found the time and the space to think and read. At that point, Thomas had not aligned himself with any lasting philosophy.

His world view had twisted as often as his experiences, beginning with the worship of a Baptist God in a humble Georgia church, switching toward the Catholic priesthood, moving on to black militancy, adapting to the law of the Ivy League. It seemed he was always groping for an absolute that would explain the fractured episodes of his life as he rose from segregated poverty to success in the white man's world. He needed a philosophy that would mesh his unflagging desire for an ostentatious automobile with his anger at an American society that had so mistreated people of the black race. How could he justify being rewarded as a rising professional in a white government by the same society that had economically handcuffed his grandfather and the rest of black Savannah?

His years at Yale had pushed him toward the right, and Danforth's example had led him into the Republican fold. From that point, he would eventually come to reinterpret the teachings of his grandfather, finding in his upbringing not the lessons of civil rights but the seeds of conservatism.

It took Thomas Sowell, a black economist with unorthodox ideas, to make those seeds sprout.

"A friend of mine, I'll never forget it, called me up and said, 'Clarence, there's another black guy out here who is as crazy as you are,'" Thomas told an interviewer later. "'He has the same ideas that you have. There are *two* of you!'"

Sowell, a protégé of right-wing economist Milton Friedman, now an academic at the conservative Hoover Institute at Stanford University, attacks his fellow blacks in the civil rights leadership on racial and class lines, dismissing the concept of affirmative action as a scheme of the black elite to enrich itself. There is a sharp racial antagonism toward lighter skinned blacks in his writings, a theme that Thomas, derided himself by fellow blacks for his dark color, could identify with.

Once Thomas picked up his first book by Sowell, he became a permanent devotee of the economist's philosophy. To read Thomas Sowell is to better understand Clarence Thomas.

Sowell scoffs at the idea that racial inequities are so desperate a problem.

"All that is unique about our times is the extent to which we ignore earlier times, and regard our racial or ethnic differences as unprecedented. In reality, today's intergroup differences are not only smaller

than in the past, but are continuing to narrow," Sowell writes in the
book *The Economics and Politics of Race*, a work Clarence Thomas
has specifically praised.

In the same book, Sowell questions whether the civil rights movement still has a purpose: "There are powerful incentives to continue
the political crusades of the past, even after their beneficial effects are
exhausted. Part of the reason is inertia. A large civil rights establishment, inside and outside government, has to find work to do, and must
convince itself and others that this work is vitally important. More
generally, there is a fatal fascination with the prospect of morally
regenerating other people or (failing that) smiting the wicked.
Whether that will in fact advance the economically disadvantaged is
another question entirely."

Sowell goes after the NAACP, impugning the motives of its leadership and belittling its desegregation strategy: "Ironically, it is precisely the same [northern] mulatto elite that excluded other blacks
which launched a nationwide attack on white exclusions of blacks,
marked by the founding of the National Association for the Advancement of Colored People in 1909. The NAACP's continued dominance
by the mulatto elite cause some other blacks to call it the National
Association for the Advancement of Certain People. The NAACP
agenda reflected the priorities of the elite—equal access to white
institutions and white neighborhoods, enabling them to escape the
black masses. Given the poverty of the black masses, who at this point
could not afford to buy homes in any neighborhood, or to attend any
colleges or theaters, or to stay at hotels or go to concerts, it is difficult
to understand the emphasis of the NAACP during this era on public
accommodations and restrictive covenants without understanding the
class composition of the people who ran it."

Affirmative action gets similar treatment: "[I]n the name of the
poor and the disadvantaged, those who were already well off were made
still better off—while the ostensible beneficiaries were either neglected
or made worse off."

Sowell, in the same work, has an explanation of the female place in
society that reads like a red flag to those espousing women's rights:
"How then, can women as a group be so far behind men as a group,
in both incomes and occupations? Because most women become wives
and mothers—and the economic results are totally different from a

man's becoming a husband and father. However parallel these roles may be verbally, they are vastly different in behavioral consequences. There are reasons why there are no homes for unwed fathers."

"Women," Sowell also wrote to explain why women have lesser professional roles, "have historically specialized in fields that they could leave and re-enter some years later, without large losses from obsolescence. Someone who is a good editor, teacher, or librarian is likely to be good in these occupations again in five or six years."

Thomas had an epiphany. He said that reading Sowell "was like pouring half a glass of water on the desert. I just soaked it up." Thomas eventually managed to meet Sowell and became a missionary for the economist's philosophy, giving mini-lectures to his colleagues.

After Danforth ran for the U.S. Senate and won in 1976, Thomas resigned at the end of that year from the Missouri attorney general's office. His mentor was gone and, in addition, he wanted to make some money and pay off his college loans.

Thomas doubled his pay working for Monsanto, the giant chemical company. His job in the company's St. Louis office, which Danforth had helped arrange, consisted of registering herbicides with the Environmental Protection Agency (EPA) and working on problems of disposal of hazardous products. He played softball on the company team. At Monsanto, as at Yale, Thomas did well without becoming a standout. But after two and a half years, when Danforth called and offered him a job in the nation's capital, Thomas jumped for it.

Once in Washington, Thomas rose quickly from the rank of Danforth's congressional aide to officialdom within the Reagan administration. He would rise quickly to the pinnacle of the judiciary, a favorite of the conservative Republicans who had laid claim to the executive branch the entirety of the 1980's and into the 1990's.

Clarence Thomas had come a long way down strange and lonely paths from his birthplace in Georgia. While he was transforming himself from one step upward to the next, the people he left behind stayed pretty much the same.

Pin Point has grown in size, of course, but it has retained its folksy, friendly ways. Any stranger who ventures into the enclave by the marshy river instantly gets directions and advice from a boy on a bicycle or an old woman walking along the edge of the main road. The narrow road is now paved, making a sort of tunnel through the live oak trees Running water, indoor plumbing, and electricity service the homes, which had only woodstoves and kerosene lanterns when Thomas was a boy. The old crab factory, which has long been defunct, is slowly sinking into the marsh. If you glance inside a window, you can see the empty wooden tables, worn smooth by the hands of women like Thomas's mother and sister, who picked crabs and shucked oysters.

The only outstanding features of Pin Point are brand-new, bright blue signs that boast to all comers: WELCOME TO PIN POINT, BIRTH PLACE OF SUPREME COURT JUSTICE CLARENCE THOMAS 1991. The people are proud of Thomas, for regardless of his politics he has put himself and Pin Point on the map. As part of a support-Thomas effort organized by a local politician, a busload of his old acquaintances rode to Washington during the controversial Supreme Court hearings in the fall. Thomas did not reciprocate with any immediate visit to his birthplace where his sister, Emma Mae Martin, still lives.

Her house, which is on the shore a hundred yards from where she and her two brothers were born, is probably the poorest in Pin Point. Consisting of three small rooms and a kitchen, it shelters six people who include Emma Mae's two daughters, her son, his wife and child. Emma Mae, a plump and generous woman, has at times had as many as nine people under her roof.

Outside, the paint is chipping off the wooden sides of the tiny house and the screens are ripped on the porch that looks out over an assortment of junk, including old tires and a derelict automobile on blocks. Inside, the house is cluttered with blankets, foldout couch-beds, pillows, cots, empty glasses and cups, magazines, and baby bottles. A large-screen color television blares constantly in one corner of the claustrophic living room that doubles as a bedroom.

But, for Martin, life has stabilized. She now works as a cook in the kitchen of the same Savannah hospital where her mother is employed as a nursing assistant. The pay isn't high but she works seven days a week and is able to support herself.

For more than a dozen years, Martin had to depend on welfare. Her husband had turned out to be a gambler who could not care for his family, she said, recounting a story much like that of her own mother. Although she worked sometimes in the crab factory and at other minimum-wage work, she was forced to depend upon government handouts to make ends meet. Her burden increased when the elderly Auntie Graham, who had done so much to provide for Martin and her brothers, suffered a stroke. With both her brothers long gone— Thomas was in Washington by then—Martin assumed full care of her debilitated aunt.

Thomas visited her occasionally over the years. When he was of college age, the two would celebrate by buying moonshine at twenty-five cents a bottle. In later years, he would just bring her favorite, a twelve-pack of Bud, said Martin, who doesn't regret her status in life. She holds no grudges against her brother for his prosperity, which is enormous compared with her poverty.

"I chose to do what I wanted," Martin said. "He chose to do what he wanted. He picked up on a lot of those ideas that Granddaddy Anderson used to lay down."

Sam Williams, the Savannah friend of Myers Anderson who converted the Baptist to Catholicism, has a completely different reaction to the current Clarence Thomas. Williams now runs a small moving business.

"Clarence betrayed all of us. He could have helped us out from those high positions he got. Up in Washington, we had nobody in our corner and Clarence didn't even make a gesture in our direction. The only thing black about him is his skin," concludes Williams, who said he saw Thomas disappoint and eventually alienate his grandfather.

"Myers was a Democrat for life. He felt the Republicans didn't have nothing to offer. His attitude was that he had a problem with anybody who would go for Reagan," said Williams, who remembered an incident that revealed Anderson's feelings.

Thomas, once he was earning good money, promised to buy his grandfather a car. But he never came through on the promise and Anderson didn't forgive him.

"I'd see Myers two or three times a week," Williams said. "And I can tell you that after Clarence got everything he wanted, he didn't come around. Myers could see this happening. Myers was a man who would do all he could for you, but if you didn't reciprocate, he fell off with you and that was it. That's what happened with Clarence."

Williams grimaces at Thomas's conservative attitude toward government programs to help pull blacks out of poverty.

"How you going to pull yourself up by your bootstraps when you don't have any boots," Williams said. "Clarence didn't bring himself up, his grandfather did. Myers made those boots for Clarence."

Sam Williams and W.W. Law, Savannah's veteran NAACP leader, were both praised in speeches Thomas made about the Savannah civil rights movement. Law also knew Anderson well, and watched Thomas grow up.

Law, who is now retired from his job as a postman, is quietly furious about Thomas's political conduct. Law has a rugged face and, when he talks about the past, he puts his hand on his forehead, closing his eyes and surveying in his mind the decades he has worked in the civil rights movement.

"Clarence would not even have been considered for the Supreme Court without the things the NAACP did," said Law, who has developed a harsh theory about Thomas's politics.

"During the greater portion of his formative years, in terms of his final intellect, he was a minority among whites. And so what happened was that he wanted to make his views palatable. Then once you find out you can benefit, you have a motivation, whether or not you are aware of it yourself. It is a weird and strange situation for a black to be comfortable with the likes of Reagan and Bush. There is little or no evidence that Clarence did anything but enhance his own rights. I would rather wait for a proper justice to fill Marshall's seat, not someone who has compromised."

Thomas would most certainly argue with these characterizations. Since his nomination to the Supreme Court, though, he has declined interviews with the press or writers of any kind. Publicity, as the White House coached him, was not something he needed to seek out. The less said, the better his chances of being confirmed and beginning an unruffled tenure on the court.

# Chapter 5

Supreme Court nominations were once dignified affairs. The nominees—who were usually professors of law or experienced judges or senior political figures—were well known and respected. Sometimes, of course, they were part of a political deal or strategy. But before the mid-1950s, most nominees never appeared before the Senate's judiciary committee, so tussles between the legislative and executive branches over the judiciary were less public.

With a few exceptions the practice of questioning, and even grilling, the nominees started with William J. Brennan, Jr.'s, nomination in 1956. Although appointed by the Republican President Eisenhower, Brennan was a Democrat. But Brennan, a New Jersey judge with a considerable legal reputation, appealed to the President's political instincts. He was was an affable and popular Roman Catholic with an Irish working-class background. But he was too liberal for the infamous Senator Joseph McCarthy. The Communist-baiting and liberal-hating McCarthy still had enough influence over the Senate to delay Brennan's confirmation for five months. What Brennan put up with, though, was mild compared to what was in store for later nominees.

Now, with the White House giving as much weight to the ideology as to the qualifications of a nominee, the selection of a Supreme Court justice can be compared to a boxing match. The Republican White House manages its nominee in one corner of the ring. In the other corner are the opposition liberal groups, like the Alliance for Justice, and the Democrats, who are always searching for the right punch. From the Republican corner, the opposition seems to be attacking below-the-belt. But this is not always the case. These liberal groups received unsolicited and unverified information about the private sexual habits of one conservative nominee now on the court that might have scuttled the nomination, but decided not to check into it because it was thought to be irrelevant.

In the event of the Thomas nomination, the Bush administration seemed to score a near knockout in the first round. Not only had it presented a seemingly unbruisable nominee protected by his strength of character, it had shaken up the opposition by neutralizing the NAACP and splintering the civil rights community, at least temporarily. Thomas's antagonistic approach to affirmative action was not likely to be a problem for the White House. Although the Democrats controlled the Senate, they were on the defensive about quotas and other parts of their once respected civil rights agenda. Thomas also had the fervent support of Senator Danforth, who was capable of ushering Thomas into the offices of both Republicans and Democrats.

In the succeeding weeks, however, the opposition gained ground. Kate Michelman's scrap of information about Thomas and abortion worried the nominee's Republican handlers. The issue of abortion and the power of the women's movement created political dangers that the Republicans feared.

"In a thing like this, where it's close, everything takes on a higher velocity of importance," said one of Thomas's advisers, who like the opposition discussed the nomination as though it were a political fight rather than a matter for careful evaluation. "Everything he did or said takes on a bigger meaning. If it builds a head of steam, it becomes very important and in a close race, you've got problems."

After the Fourth of July holiday there was one disclosure after another about Clarence Thomas. None was big enough in itself to derail the nomination, but discomfited Republicans started wondering if the White House had done its homework.

The punching began with a little-noticed news article in *The Boston*

*Globe* about Thomas's having managed to get a medical deferment from the draft during the Vietnam War. Back in 1971, upon graduation from Holy Cross, Thomas had lost his automatic undergraduate student deferment. He already had been classified 1-A, prime material for service in southeast Asia. His number in the military lottery—which determined the order in which young men were drafted—was a low 109. But three months later, Thomas apparently failed the military medical exam and was reclassified as 4-F. Thomas continued to play exuberant intramural football matches. The records giving the medical reason for the deferment had been destroyed, as is routine. The only explanation—offered by the White House once Thomas was nominated for the Supreme Court—was that he suffered curvature of the spine.

But more difficult times for Thomas, and for Judy Smith, the deputy White House spokeswoman, began a week and a half after the nomination. Smith, Thomas's designated mouthpiece, was a savvy African-American who had worked in the U.S. Attorney's office in Washington and knew the players on both sides.

*The Washington Post* reported on July 10 that Thomas had "taken several puffs" of marijuana in college and "perhaps once" in law school.

Marijuana had recently ruined the Supreme Court chance for Douglas H. Ginsburg, who had been nominated to replace Justice Lewis Powell after Robert Bork had been rejected. Ginsburg was forced to withdraw after news reports indicated that he had smoked marijuana with frequency while a law school professor. The revelation about Thomas at first seemed significant, but he insisted he had experimented only lightly with the drug.

It was hard for the liberal opposition to wax indignant about what was described as a few joints. The White House, which was horrified by Ginsburg's drug use, was a lot more savvy four years later. It cast the whole revelation as a minor piece of information, chalking it up to a youthful indiscretion on the part of Thomas. It pointed out that a whole generation would be barred from public service if marijuana use in college was a disqualifier. Thomas himself, it turned out, had disclosed the information when he had been nominated to the Court of Appeals in 1989. The information was contained in the usual confidential FBI report sent to the senators on the Judiciary Committee.

The senators, who rely on their legislative aides to do much of their reading for them, had apparently never read the For Your Eyes Only report.

The most interesting aspect of the marijuana episode was that it was the result of a White House tactic: It was later revealed that the White House had leaked the story to *The Washington Post*. Realizing the information would get out eventually, the administration's tacticians wanted it out on their terms. The ploy worked; the story died quickly. The leaked information came from a confidential FBI report, a matter of some irony considering the Republicans' outrage about subsequent leaks.

On the same day, July 10, that the marijuana story went public, *Newsday* ran an article about a bit of trouble Thomas had had with the Internal Revenue Service (IRS). It reported that Thomas had been slapped with a federal tax lien in 1984 for failure to pay all of his 1982 income taxes. The amount of money involved—$2,150.59—was not large, and was eventually paid, but for a time Thomas had apparently ignored the repeated notices from the IRS to pay up.

The White House press office again sprang to the defense, explaining that Thomas had made a mathematical mistake on a somewhat complex income-averaging tax form and also had not been aware of the lien. How Thomas was able not to notice the IRS notices was never fully explained.

Later, I discovered that this was not the only run-in that Thomas had had with the tax authorities. In 1986, two years after the first incident, the state of Maryland filed a lien against Thomas for $1,031 in unpaid state taxes. By then, he was making a comfortable salary as the chairman of the EEOC. Although Thomas had filed his tax return, he had not been able to pay all that was due. He did make good on the debt within a month after the lien was filed, paying in two installments.

While the White House was trying to cope with dozens of press calls on these disclosures about marijuana and taxes, more news was hitting from another angle. *The Nation*, a weekly magazine that has long been one of liberalism's bastions, reported that Thomas had connections with the *Lincoln Review*, a quarterly magazine whose politics lie somewhere on the far edge of the right wing.

*The Nation* disclosed that Thomas had for ten years been listed as a member of the *Review*'s editorial advisory board. Thomas's own writing had thrice appeared in the magazine, which also featured pieces decrying the move to impose sanctions against South Africa, calling for the outlawing of abortion, and demanding the repeal of the minimum wage.

Thomas did not disclose his association with the *Lincoln Review* in forms requesting information about any of his affiliations that he had filled out for the Senate at the time of his Court of Appeals nomination. And his name had appeared in the magazine well after he had joined that court, a clear impropriety for a sitting judge.

The White House's Judy Smith, in her damage-control-for-Thomas mode, said his position on the magazine's board was merely honorary, which meant that he had never actively participated in editorial decisons. Also according to the White House, Thomas had requested his name be removed from the magazine when he was elevated to the bench. As proof, the White House produced a letter of apology from the magazine's editor for failing to comply speedily with Thomas's wish. The apology was late, though, having been written *after* the whole issue was raised. The White House could provide no copies of any correspondence from Thomas to the magazine, requesting the removal of his name. There was no written proof that Thomas had indeed made the request.

Thomas's connection to the far-right *Review* did not make much of a splash in the media. Something new, and strange, had been revealed about the thinking of the Supreme Court nominee, and it seemed to suggest that he might be on the very fringe of the American polity. But newspapers and television news programs were not, for the most part, prepared to translate this sort of discovery into easily digestible news. More would come of it, though.

Another interesting story that most of the media found difficult to handle was about Thomas's current religion. He was no longer a regular Catholic, far from it. *The Los Angeles Times* reported that Thomas and his second wife, Virginia, had been attending the Truro Episcopal Church in the Virginia suburbs of Washington for the preceding years. The congregation of the Truro church practices a charismatic religion. During services, its members occasionally "speak in tongues," uttering guttural, inarticulate sounds in the belief that the Holy Spirit is giving voice through them. The church is also the national center of the Episcopalian antiabortion movement. As important a clue as this story was to Thomas and his beliefs, most newspapers shied away from it. Most Americans never learned about it.

About the same time that these disclosures were being made, Thomas took a body blow from the Congressional Black Caucus. The black members of Congress, who comprise the Caucus, voted overwhelmingly to oppose Thomas. They were highly critical of the nominee's politics, particularly his stand on civil rights, and thought him unsuitable for a seat on the Supreme Court, particularly that of Thurgood Marshall.

The Caucus was the first major black political group to come out against Thomas. This put pressure on the NAACP and its reluctant executive director, Benjamin Hooks, to do the same. This also was "the wake up call for the [Bush] administration that this was going to be a tough battle," in the words of one official at the Department of Justice. There was to be opposition from the black community after all.

Not two weeks had passed since the nomination and the list of difficulties facing the White House kept growing. For the Bush administration, this summer might be wearing.

The next problem came in a report by *The Dallas Times Herald* that in 1983 Thomas, when he was heading the EEOC, had prepared two speeches in which he praised the Rev. Louis Farrakhan, a Black Muslim leader and outspoken anti-Semite. The White House recoiled.

Thomas had said in the speeches that Farrakhan was "a man I have admired for more than a decade." He ended both of the speeches, according to the prepared texts, with the following quotation from Farrakhan: "We the poor, we the oppressed, we the blacks, we the Hispanics, we the disinherited, we the rejected and most despised, we will overcome and then together we will be able to say in the words of Dr. Martin Luther King: Free at last, free at last, thank God Almighty, we have united and made freedom a reality at last."

Jewish leaders jumped angrily on this piece of news, saying that Farrakhan, their nemesis, had been making intolerable anti-Semitic remarks since the early 1970s. For years, Farrakhan's anti-Semitism had not become widely known to Americans other than blacks who listened to his preaching, and Jews, who despised him. It was not until

1984, the year after Thomas's speeches, when Farrakhan was quoted as saying Judaism was a "dirty religion" and Hitler was "wickedly great," that he became a terrible figure of national controversy. Now, Thomas's citations of Farrakhan were a serious matter. The Jewish leaders wanted an explanation, and they wanted it quickly.

Whereas in the other controversies the White House had spoken for Thomas, this time it was recognized that the implications were so serious that Thomas would have to respond personally. If the politically potent Jewish groups were roused into joining the opposition to Thomas, his nomination might be in jeopardy.

Thomas responded speedily with a statement. "I cannot leave standing any suggestion that I am anti-Semitic," he said. "I am, and have always been, unalterably and adamantly opposed to anti-Semitism and bigotry of any kind, including by Louis Farrakhan."

Thomas explained that Farrakhan's attraction had absolutely nothing to do with remarks about Jews. Farrakhan preached the concept of economic self-help, and this aspect of his philosophy is what Thomas had found appealing. Thomas winnowed the good from the evil. Thomas's statement was soothing but it did not completely placate Jewish leaders like Abraham Foxman of the Anti-Defamation League. Foxman argued that Thomas should have denounced Farrakhan, not just his anti-Semitic ravings. Although no Jewish organization moved to officially oppose Thomas, no guarantees were given the Republican strategists trying to keep Thomas's nomination out of trouble.

Clarence Thomas was taken aback and left reeling by this flurry of negative news stories. "On Monday I was an anti-Semite, on Tuesday I was a pothead, and on Wednesday I was a scofflaw," he told a friend.

Meanwhile, *Newsday* kept after the disclosure about Thomas being on the board of the *Lincoln Review*. This magazine was the only organization, other than his college alma mater, to which Clarence Thomas had lent his name. I worked on the story out of *Newsday*'s Washington bureau while Michael Webber, an investigative reporter, covered it from New York.

We found out that although the review was a black periodical— edited by blacks and written for blacks—it was very cozy with the white apartheid government of South Africa. Thomas, too, had made a gesture of friendship in that direction, as *Newsday* reported two weeks after the nomination. Back in 1987, long before South Africa was reconsidering its official racism, Thomas attended a dinner for the government's ambassador. The affair for the South African dignitary was arranged by Jay Parker and a business partner, both editors of the *Lincoln Review*. The two were also highly paid foreign agents for the South African government and its interests. Thomas, at the time, was chairman of the EEOC. Other black officials in the Republican administration also paid their political dues by attending the dinner honoring a man whose job was to represent apartheid.

"The purpose of the dinner was to give the ambassador an opportunity to meet with several prominent black Americans who have great interest in South Africa," Parker's firm wrote in requisite disclosure forms provided to the Justice Department under the Foreign Agents Registration Act.

This information had the potential to seriously hurt Thomas. With the NAACP still sitting on the fence in a state of indecision and black voters key to how the Senate would vote on the nomination, any link between Thomas and South Africa, even a tenuous one, could be very damaging. At the White House, Judy Smith uncharacteristically refused to comment. Parker, who had proudly discussed his relationship with Thomas in the days immediately after the nomination, went underground. His secretary fended off inquiring reporters and an answering machine turned away callers. Parker, it would turn out, knew a lot about Thomas and his thinking.

As July progressed and summer days in Washington grew oppressively humid, the rumors about Thomas were thriving in the cool of air-conditioned offices across the city. Some were ugly, some unfair and some possibly true. They spoke as much about the media as they did about the nominee.

Questions about Thomas's divorce of seven years earlier, a proceeding whose slim legal record had been examined by dozens of reporters, refused to go away. There was a rumor that something nasty had happened between the judge and his ex-wife, though there was absolutely nothing to substantiate it. The rumor had been unwittingly fueled by *The Wall Street Journal*, which had championed Thomas on its editorial pages. In its initial news story about the nomination, the newspaper had mentioned, but not explained, the existence of some concern in Republican circles about the divorce affecting the nomination. The *Journal* had said too much and too little, thus setting off the sort of manic speculation that happens all the time behind the often pretentious façade of the media. Reporters staked out the house of Kathy Thomas, who had moved to Boston, hoping to waylay her and wrest out every truth of her personal life. But she eluded the media. All that could be confirmed was that she was working at the respected Milton Academy, a private preparatory school. Her ability to stay out of sight made the rumor into mystery.

There was also a rumor that Thomas had harassed at least one of the women working for him at the offices of the EEOC, Anita Hill. The rumor or unconfirmed report came from former employees of the commission, or from others close to Hill. People working for the liberal groups had made some calls. I made some calls, as well. But there was no solid information, certainly nothing that could be printed. I had other leads for news stories that seemed more promising, so I did not pursue the matter aggressively at first.

Rumors are not pleasant to deal with, but I have no apologies for the the press's pursuit of them, particularly in the case of a Supreme Court nomination. And I don't have apologies for scrutinizing a Supreme Court nominee's private life. Presidents, senators and congressman can all be voted out of office, cabinet secretaries can be fired, but a Supreme Court appointment is for life. The court, with only nine members, is a coequal branch of the government. Character can be as important as a nominee's official record or judicial expertise. It is legitimate to ask, for example, whether we want to give a potentially deciding vote on the issue of separation of church and state to a man who attends a fundamentalist church. It is entirely legitimate for women's groups to ask whether Thomas would throw out what they consider to be a basic right to choose an abortion. It is similarly legitimate for pro-life groups to try to quiz the nominee about whether he is truly against abortion. And it is proper for the nominee not to answer sweeping questions about his philosophy.

Thomas's confirmation, although by no means in significant trouble, seemed less than assured by the middle of July. The opposition had scored a couple of unexpected hits, and the White House couldn't predict what might be in store during the remainder of the fight, which would culminate, of course, at the Senate hearings.

The White House, in the meantime, was doing all it could. President Bush himself had weighed in, making telephone calls to black leaders and urging them to consider Thomas seriously. The White House knew that even for blacks with politics diametrically opposed to Thomas, it would not be easy to turn a deaf ear to the President personally asking for help. Black officials in Bush's administration were recruited to use whatever influence they could over a wide variety of black organizations and institutions, such as the presidents of black colleges, and pastors of Baptist churches with black congregants. Black lawyers who worked in government departments were asked to spread the word for Thomas with other black lawyers gathering at a national convention.

After the lesson of the Bork nomination, this campaign by the White House was highly organized and motivated. Thomas's backers didn't want to leave anything to chance.

"The general White House atmosphere concerning this nomination is that we were pumped, everybody was really excited," said Leigh Ann Metzger, a special assistant to the President in the White House Office of Public Liaison. Metzger is a native of Atlanta, who by the age of twenty-nine had risen in right-wing circles. She keeps not only *Time* on her office coffee table but also *Liberty*, which describes itself as "a magazine of religious freedom."

"Souter had been almost too easy for us," Metzger recalled. "We were still in the glow of the Persian Gulf [war], so everyone was feeling a little high about it. We were thinking we would ride that same tide into the nomination."

Two or three times a week, the Thomas team of a dozen principal players from the White House and the Justice Department would meet at 9 A.M. on the second floor of the West Wing of the White House for strategy sessions. This was the office of Frederick McClure, the man in charge of liaison with Congress. Ken Duberstein, the former chief of staff brought back to manage Thomas, chaired the meetings.

This list of who came to these sessions made it clear how serious the White House was taking this nomination. In attendance were Judy Smith; McClure; Lee Liberman and Mark Paoletta from Boyden

Gray's office; Bill Kristol, chief of staff for Vice President Dan Quayle; Metzger; Deborah Amend, the director of media relations; David F. Demarest, Jr., head of the office of communications; Dorrance C. Smith, head of the office of public affairs; Ron Kaufman, head of the office of political affairs. Also present was Mike Luttig from Justice, now a Court of Appeals judge, but then serving as a kind of aide-de-camp to Thomas.

It was no accident, of course, that the group was so heavily weighted toward public relations. With Thomas, as with the President, the image was of paramount concern.

They were monitoring the nomination campaign. That meant keeping track of the NAACP and keeping a scorecard of senators' potential votes. It meant thinking of grassroots efforts in each state to build up support for Thomas and find sympathizers who could twist senatorial arms. It meant revving up the pro-Thomas themes and arranging for influential people to write opinion pieces for key newspapers.

It also meant thinking up ways to put out the brushfires that kept bursting into flame in July. Dorrance Smith, a former top official of ABC News and producer of its *Nightline* program, ran a sophisticated media operation for the group. He operated a state-by-state effort aimed at the regional press. Each day he distributed to the Thomas team clippings on the nominee that came in from newspapers and magazines around the country. He helped draft opinion articles on Thomas that would appear in the media under the names of important figures inside or outside the government.

Thomas did not come to these White House meetings, at least not at first. He did not seem to trust the strategy group. For one thing, it was clear from early on that someone among the group was talking to reporters. Thomas preferred to meet with a smaller strategy team in Luttig's office on the fifth floor of the Justice Department building. These meetings had a tendency to last late into the night as the participants traded ideas and information. Among the regulars were Luttig, John P. Mackey from the deputy attorney general's office, Paoletta, Kristol and Virginia Thomas. The nominee's wife could help with her in-depth knowledge of the Senate, which she had learned from her lobbying on behalf of the Chamber of Commerce and, later, the Department of Labor. This group advised Thomas on what they called his private strategy, his self-designed plan to split the black community as well as to mobilize the hardline conservative groups associated with Tom Jipping.

There was a clash between Thomas's two overlapping groups of advisers. The White House group, led by Duberstein, wanted a low-key, pragmatic approach modeled on the very successful nomination of David Souter the year before. This was also Senator Danforth's preference. With that strategy Duberstein and Danforth thought they could pick up the votes of Senate moderates.

"Duberstein wanted very much to get along with everyone, to keep everything calm," said a source in the White House. "He thought he could win this one the way he won Souter—to slide through."

As they prepared for the Senate hearings, Duberstein and Danforth were giving Thomas the same advice. They wanted him to duck volatile issues and go with crafting the image of a man who had pulled himself up by his bootstraps from Pin Point, Georgia.

The team that held its huddles at the Justice Department, generally representing the hardline conservatives in the administration, wanted a harder-edged campaign that did not shy away from Thomas's conservative ideology.

"Their main strategy was very much an outside-the-[Washington] Beltway game to split the black community, get public pressure, particularly on the Southern Democrats, and not worry if they have to take on the liberal Democrats," the White House source said.

Both strategies, in fact, were implemented. Officially, Duberstein and Danforth won out; it was their vision of Thomas that was presented to the senators. The hardline strategy also was put into play, although not publicly, aided by the cooperation of the well-funded radical right.

Over on Capitol Hill, Senator Danforth had jumped into action. He joined Fred McClure in the task of selling Thomas to the Senate. It was customary for a Supreme Court nominee to pay courtesy calls to Senate leaders and members of the crucial Judiciary Committee in their private offices. But after this round, Thomas, reinforced by Senator Danforth, kept going through the Senate roll. The idea was simple—it's harder to vote against a person who has met you face-to-face, shaken your hand and been as charming as possible. Thomas could present himself graciously, and the widely respected Senator Danforth could burnish the image. Their persistence seemed to be paying off. Even a few Senate liberals started whispering to each other that they might just have to vote for this guy, conservative though he was.

One of Thomas's early visits had been with Senator Strom Thurmond of South Carolina, the Judiciary Committee member and arch-segregationist who had reformed his racist attitudes, at least publicly, with the changing times. At the stop at Senator Thurmond's office, of all places, Thomas made a carefully scripted gesture to the civil rights community.

"I, of course, have benefited greatly from the civil rights movement, from the justice whom I'm nominated to succeed," Thomas said, referring to Thurgood Marshall. He didn't mention he had attacked Justice Marshall quite caustically on previous occasions.

The message was aimed at Ben Hooks, at the civil rights community, as well as at the dozens of black groups being lobbied by the White House. This was where the real battle of Clarence Thomas's nomination was being fought, in the black community.

By keeping the NAACP on the fence, the Bush administration had already succeeded in neutralizing Ralph Neas and the Leadership Conference on Civil Rights. Neas was executive director of the Leadership Conference, an umbrella organization for some 180 groups representing the nation's underprivileged—from racial and religious minorities to the disabled and the elderly—and possessing a lot of both moral and political clout. The Leadership Conference and its director had taken the lead role in knocking off Robert Bork. Neas, a liberal Republican who long worked on Capitol Hill, has political connections, influence, and organizing capabilities that others in the anti-Thomas coalition did not. The Leadership Conference had played a part in all the modern civil rights legislation. Although Neas did eventually work with Nan Aron of the Alliance for Justice in hiring a handful of grassroots organizers to drum up opposition to Thomas, he was essentially stymied. He could not take up any public role without a decision from his board of directors. The board, in turn, was waiting on one of the Leadership Conference's key members to take a stand—the NAACP. And, of course, the fact that Benjamin Hooks was that year the chairman of the board of the Leadership Conference, in addition to his position as executive director of the NAACP, made any action impossible for the time being.

But there was another, even more important goal in the White House campaign: the Democrats from the South. The Democratic party had a 57 to 43 edge in the Senate and an eight to six advantage on the Judiciary Committee. No Republican nominee could survive a strictly partisan vote. And in a close call there were several moderate Republicans who might vote with the Democrats, as they did on Robert Bork.

In order to get Thomas through the Senate, it was necessary to have support from the dozen somewhat conservative Democrats from the South. Many of their constituents were quite pleased with what the Republican administration was doing on the Supreme Court, but not all. Increased voter registration of blacks in the South had finally had an effect. While listening to their conservative constituents with one ear, the southern Democrats had to listen to their black constituents with the other. During the fight over the Bork nomination, Southern blacks, who were organized by Neas as well as the NAACP, made it clear that a vote for that nominee would cost these senators their votes.

With the Thomas nomination, though, the situation was very different. Public opinion polls showed that southern blacks *favored* Thomas. This could only be changed, if at all, by a strong showing of opposition from black organizations. Without that, there was seemingly no way to stop Thomas from being confirmed. The anti-Thomas forces were losing on this front.

And the pro-Thomas forces were receiving aid from Hooks, who had not stopped with his own NAACP. He had given the White House, through the same Parsons-Bolick-Liberman route employed earlier, names of black leaders who were potentially sympathetic to Thomas. This helped the White House decide whom to target. Among the names were those of John E. Jacob, president of the National Urban League, and the Rev. Joseph Lowery, head of the Southern Christian Leadership Conference.

On July 21, these efforts paid off. The Urban League announced that it was neutral on Thomas. It would not support him, but it would not oppose him. The Urban League members tended to be upper middle-class and were not exactly the black *vox populi*. But it was the first organization with a black membership to announce a decision on

Thomas. The Black Caucus negative vote was made by politicians not the voting public. The White House was overjoyed. In this situation, a pass was virtually as good as a nod.

The timing was perfect for the White House's purposes. The Urban League's decision would serve to take some of the sting out of the NAACP's next move. Hooks had sent word that he could hold back the NAACP no longer. Its board of directors had been scheduled to meet at the end of the month in Washington, and Hooks said it was clear that it would vote to oppose Thomas. Aware of the impending decision, the other groups in the anti-Thomas coalition planned to make their announcements the following week.

And Hooks continued to sound off in public about Thomas in ways that infuriated his own board members. Even as the NAACP's Washington office was putting together its promised report, which would blast Thomas's record, Hooks was communicating some very soothing things at a press conference in Iowa. Hooks said that Thomas "was not completely without some good points," and that there "ought to be a black on the Supreme Court."

Then, in words that reflected the information being fed to him by the conservative Bolick, Hooks praised Thomas's vigor: "If a black or woman has been individually discriminated against or mistreated he'll go to the ends of the earth to correct it." The idea behind this was that Thomas would pursue cases of individual prejudice, while eschewing far-reaching social action. The trick was in stating only one piece of the nominee's philosophy.

If the NAACP ever had a chance to turn around black public opinion, it was probably lost with those words. Hooks's statement was picked up by conservative groups and used effectively in advertising for Thomas.

For his part Thomas had done his best to meet his old enemies half way. Breaking with judicial formality, he decided to meet with the NAACP. Near the end of the third week in July, Thomas joined five NAACP officials at a private house in Washington. It was like a battlefield truce, with the opposing generals stopping to share a brandy before the killing. In addition to Hooks, representing the organization were Wade Henderson, head of the Washington office, and Hazel Dukes, president of the board of directors. The chairman and vice chairman of the NAACP's board also were there. Facing the five, Thomas was able to convince them that he had not forgotten his roots.

"He came across as being a brother," said one Washington insider familiar with what was said at this unusual meeting. This much was no small accomplishment for a person of Thomas's views.

But when the NAACP leaders tried to draw Thomas out on his opinions of specific legal issues, the nominee demurred. He maintained that he could not discuss issues that might come before him on the Supreme Court. Thomas asked the others to judge him on his character, his merits and not what they perceived as his ideology. But given Thomas's past criticisms of the court's decisions on civil rights, there was nothing said that could allay the fears of Henderson and the officials of the board. Hooks kept the details of his opinion and his behind-the-scenes dealing with the White House to himself. A detailed set of minutes of the meeting with Thomas was prepared to be read to the board of directors.

The NAACP meeting was not the only one Thomas had with black groups that summer. Thomas was conducting an unprecedented lobbying campaign for his own nomination, one that broke the unwritten rules of judicial aloofness.

Thomas also met in July with Algenita Scott-Davis, the president of the National Bar Association, the black lawyers' group, who wanted assurances that he appreciated what the civil rights movement had accomplished both for him and for minorities in general. Although Thomas wouldn't answer those queries directly, he referred the president of the association to another lawyer in Savannah, his old friend Lester Johnson. After being briefed by Thomas on how to convey his views in an uncontroversial way, Johnson wrote a careful response to the group.

After its meeting with Thomas, the NAACP got moving. Its Washington office hurriedly finished its evaluation of Thomas. It wanted the report ready for the end of the month, when the organization's board of directors was to meet in the capital.

"This is what Clarence Thomas wanted," said one board member, who clearly was not fond of the nominee's politics and was in no mood to mince words about Thomas. "He wanted to be evaluated on the fucking merits. We said fine, we'll take a look."

While the report was clearly going to be negative, it was not going to make any specific recommendation to the board. To point the way, though, Henderson asked John Hope Franklin, an eminent professor of the civil rights movement at Duke University, to contribute an epilogue.

Franklin went after Thomas hard, boldly attacking the nominee on one of his seeming strong points, his espousal of a self-help philosophy. Thomas's longtime advocacy of black self-reliance, instead of relying on government programs and racial quotas, was becoming increasingly popular. Franklin critiqued Thomas against the background of American history. The professor compared Thomas to Booker T. Washington, the black leader who almost a century before had urged blacks to concentrate on their own economic advancement rather than on their civil rights.

"The self-help syndrome has created and perpetuated a myth regarding advancement up the ladder of success in the United States," Franklin wrote. "While Washington was calling on African-Americans to rely on the quite commendable effort of self-reliance, the United States gave away a half-billion acres of public land to speculators and monopolists, making a mockery of the very notion of free land for poverty-stricken settlers. While Judge Thomas and his handlers praised the admirable concept of self-help and urged it as worthy of emulation, Chrysler, Lockheed, and the savings and loan industry, to name a few enterprising groups, were helping themselves at the public trough as the hungry, the homeless, and those in need of health care could merely shake their heads in disbelief.

"Self-help is admirable so long as it encourages initiative and achievement in a society that gives all of its members an opportunity to develop in a manner best suited to their talents. It must not be confused with or used as a substitute for society's obligation to deal equitably with all its members, and to assume the responsibility for promoting their general well-being. This surely involves equal educational, economic, and political opportunity regardless of age, gender, or race. Judge Thomas, in failing in his utterances and policies to subscribe to this basic principle, has placed himself in the unseemly position of denying to others the very opportunities and the kind of assistance from public and private quarters that have placed him where he is today."

This addition of the Franklin essay infuriated Hooks. But the report, finished only at the last minute, had already been sent to board members as they prepared to come to Washington. The media had also been used to safeguard the anti-Thomas report. The day before the board meeting, the secret report was leaked to *The New York Times*, an apparent attempt to head off any move by Hooks to squelch it.

As the end of July neared, the struggle over Thomas intensified. Other groups in the liberal coalition had orchestrated their announcements of opposition to Thomas in the week before the NAACP was set to declare its stand. The White House, meanwhile, was not idle. The Bush administration strategists had shadowed the coalition's moves. For nearly every announcement against Thomas, they cooked up a pro-Thomas event to counterbalance it. On the day that two major liberal groups, People for the American Way and the Women's Legal Defense Fund, scheduled press conferences to announce their opposition to Thomas, the White House had readied a response. A previously unknown group of women, many of them connected with the administration and called Women For Judge Thomas, scheduled a press conference as well. News organizations pliantly fell into the trap by giving both sides equal play, even though the pro-Thomas group was manufactured and minuscule.

A larger effort was orchestrated for the day of the NAACP announcment. At the request of the White House, conservatives organized a definite media attraction. A bus was chartered to carry relatives, friends and supporters of Thomas from Savannah to Washington. People from Pin Point and from the farmland of Liberty County, people who had gone to Catholic schools in Savannah—a load of ordinary folk who knew Thomas well or not so well—were delivered to the capital. They enjoyed a much publicized breakfast with the nominee on the same morning that the NAACP board members gathered at the Washington Court Hotel nearby.

After all the anguish that the NAACP had been through on the issue of Clarence Thomas, caused by the seemingly terrible question of having to judge him either as a black or a conservative, the final decision was so easy as to be anticlimactic. The report from Wade Henderson's office in Washington went over well.

Particularly persuasive was a long section that recalled an episode sixty-one years earlier, when the NAACP brashly opposed John J. Parker, a North Carolina federal appeals court judge whom Herbert

Hoover had nominated to the Supreme Court. As a candidate for governor of North Carolina, Parker had approved of literacy and poll taxes that kept blacks off the voting rolls, and had asserted that "the Negro . . . has not yet reached that stage in his development when he can share the burdens and responsibilities of government." Southern senators, the report recalled, were incensed that a black organization would dare to speak up to oppose the nomination of a federal judge to the Supreme Court. Parker lost in the Senate by a single vote, a victory for the NAACP that helped to establish it as a political force in the country.

What Henderson did not point out in his report was that the person nominated and confirmed in Parker's stead, Philadelphia lawyer Owen Roberts, was an even stauncher conservative who voted against civil rights and New Deal legislation at every opportunity. This was exactly the scenario that Hooks feared if Thomas was rejected. President Bush might well nominate a white person just as conservative as Thomas, maybe more so. And such a nominee could not bring to the court the experience of having grown up as a poor black in the segregated South, something that Thomas would never lose no matter what his politics.

With Henderson's report spurring them on, the members of the NAACP's board of directors voted 50 to 1 to oppose Thomas. It was a defining moment for the senior civil rights organization. The lone hold out was not Hooks, who had the political acumen to stick with the vast majority, but a board member who was a friend of Thomas. Hooks and William F. Gibson, a dentist from South Carolina who was chairman of the board, held a forceful press conference afterwards outlining their reasons for opposition. Gibson, who took the lead, dismissed suggestions that Thomas might change once he joined the court. "I guess I'm not a gambler," Gibson said. "I don't go to Las Vegas and I don't go to Atlantic City. . . . This is too big a gamble, too big a risk for us to take."

Hooks said the board voted "to move full-court press on opposition to this nomination." Gibson said the NAACP's stand would be "a lightning rod for others to join." Indeed, the giant of labor, the AFL-CIO, followed suit about two hours after hearing the NAACP's decision. The question for these groups now was whether they would be able to make much of a difference. Time was short and Washington was heading into its summer doldrums.

With the swampy heat of August in the offing, the senators adjourned for their summer recess. A solid majority was still inclined to vote in favor of Thomas.

The day before the adjournment, I had asked Senator Kennedy his feelings about Thomas. Snapping at me as he got on the miniature subway that ferries people back and forth from the Senate itself to the Senate office buildings, the senator said only that he couldn't tell how he felt before the hearings. Was this the same man who had risen to oppose Bork minutes after that nomination was announced? Eighty-eight-year-old Strom Thurmond, on the other hand, told me he had no doubts Thomas would win as he *walked* to his office rather than taking the trolley. Thomas's opposition was weak, while his support was robust.

But the senators were somewhat apprehensive about what effect the flurry of opposition would have on their constituents back home. That, they knew, would depend on how hard the NAACP, the labor unions, the women's groups and the others who so vehemently opposed Thomas worked the grassroots.

For the White House, the recess promised a spell of relief. All seemed to be going fairly well. Thomas had finished with his round of courtesy calls, having visited a full sixty of the one hundred senators. The media, too, seemed to be in a sort of recess. The negative disclosures about Thomas had stopped. There might not be anything remaining for the press corps to rant or rave about; but the course of national politics was unpredictable. As one Republican insider said about the quiet interlude, "You worry about the dog that didn't bark. You wonder what's happening. You never know what happens in August. You wake up one morning and. . . . "

# Chapter 6

Clarence Thomas was only thirty-one when he came to what he derisively called "the land of Oz, the land of make-believe." He had a low-paying job with modest prestige on Capitol Hill as one of Danforth's legislative aides. He worked in a Senate office building and lived with his wife and six-year-old son in a low-rent apartment for transient bureaucrats in suburban Maryland. But Thomas knew what he wanted, and he was not modest about it. He wanted, he told a startled reporter from the St. Louis *Post-Dispatch* over lunch, a seat on the United States Supreme Court. And he wanted to get rich, he told another reporter several years later. Not ordinary rich, but more than hundreds-of-thousands-of-dollars-a-year rich.

When Ronald Reagan vanquished Jimmy Carter to win the presidency in 1980, Thomas's plans no longer seemed so outlandish. A year after Thomas's arrival in Washington, the conservatives were suddenly in the White House, and they wanted to drastically restyle the government. In order to dismantle welfare and affirmative action programs, to stop busing, to reconfigure the social structure built by the Democrats, they needed people like Thomas. To carry out their plans they needed blacks who agreed with them, and there were not many such candidates around.

Organizing the transition team for the incoming Republicans was Ed Meese, who had established his political credentials by supervising the arrest of 750 student protesters at Berkeley back when Reagan was the governor of California. Meese's task was to recruit the crew that would run the new Reagan administration and set its agenda. To take a hard look at the EEOC, the federal agency in charge of protecting workers of all sorts from on-the-job discrimination, Meese found Jay Parker. When Meese made him chairman of the EEOC transition team in November 1980, nothing was made public about the connections Parker had with South Africa, or the bizarre right-wing groups with whom he consorted.

Until then, Parker had been laboring in shadows of national power as a somewhat obscure public relations man with a fervent but little noticed ideological crusade. The *Lincoln Review*, his magazine, had a small circulation. But Meese gave Parker the broad mandate of recommending policy and personnel changes at the EEOC, an agency whose social advocacy conservatives wanted to curb. To help him deal with the EEOC, Parker enlisted his own group, including two colleagues from his magazine. He plucked Thomas from the Senate building.

The assignment, with its exposure to the larger Reagan transition team, was just right for Thomas. It was easy to get lost in the ranks while working on the Hill with more than fifteen thousand other aides, secretaries, drivers, and others who served the senators and representatives. Thomas needed a higher profile, and the new Reagan administration needed him. And it had happened because of Parker, whom Thomas had first sought out as a political mentor. Senator Danforth had brought Thomas to Washington. But Jay Parker, who would become a close friend as well as a political ally, opened the way to the White House as Thomas made his way toward the top.

Thomas had come across Parker the same way he found Sowell, the economist who became his ideological mentor. One day while Thomas was working away in Senator Danforth's office, another legislative aide handed him a copy of the *Lincoln Review*. Within minutes, Thomas was on the telephone with the magazine's editor. He told Parker: "I like what you've got to say." It was a marriage of minds that would mellow into a long friendship.

Parker was the original black conservative, a supporter of Barry Goldwater for president from the late 1950s. Like so many people who join what is perceived to be an enemy camp, Parker was a zealot, a radical in the conservative cause. He fervently believed that no level of government, from the federal to the state to the local, had any business providing food, clothing or housing to anyone, no matter how poor or desperate. Private charitable groups should do that work, he said, and to his credit his own resume boasted a long list of such endeavors. He was also dead-set against affirmative action.

Parker, in the early 1970's, had been involved in two controversial enterprises of the far right. He served as president of the Friends of the FBI, formed to support J. Edgar Hoover when he was under attack for illegally spying on American citizens. Efrem Zimbalist, Jr., who then played an FBI agent on television, contributed his acting to a televison appeal for funds. But when the actor discovered that most of the money was going to the organizers of the group, he cried foul and disassociated himself from it. Although the bad publicity all but derailed the effort, Parker maintained the organization from the office he had opened in Washington.

Parker was the first black to serve on the national board of the hardline Young Americans for Freedom, which stridently backed the Vietnam War. He also was active in the American affiliate of the World Anti-Communist League, an international group that includes Nazis, neo-Nazis, and right-wing death squads in Central America.

In 1977, Parker took a step that would appall virtually all black Americans. Parker went to work for the South Africans, doing public relations and lobbying for a black "homeland" called Transkei. This was part of the grand apartheid plan to unequally divide the land of South Africa into wealthy white regions and poor black homelands. At that time, the South African government was spending tens of millions of dollars worldwide in a secret campaign to reverse the increasingly hostile view of their country. It was using the money to spread disinformation, buy interests in foreign publications, and subsidize interest groups sympathetic to its cause.

A year later Parker and two of his associates from his ultraright groups, the World Anti-Communist League and Friends of the FBI, founded the Lincoln Institute. They established it as a tax-exempt foundation, whose chief function was to publish the *Lincoln Review* magazine. Parker and two editors of the little magazine were on the South African payroll, through the Transkei homeland, at the time the magazine was begun. Not surprisingly, the magazine took a vociferous pro–South African stand.

It was clear from Parker's political history that he wouldn't go easy on the EEOC. It soon became clear that Thomas would happily agree. Thomas's first memorandum to Parker about the EEOC asserted that the agency had overstepped its authority under the Civil Rights Act of 1964. Thomas wrote that the EEOC had pushed employers to increase their hiring of women and minorities by using statistics rather than living proof of discrimination that favored white males. Thomas urged that efforts at equality based on numbers alone be stopped. He was attacking the principal method that social activists had been using to make companies employ the country's historically underprivileged people.

Thomas's connections with Jay Parker were not something the White House wanted to advertise. Thomas's memo about the EEOC for Parker might have drawn attention to the bond between the two. The memo was one of tens of thousands of pieces of paper from Thomas's speeches, writings, and interviews that the White House had been asked to supply the Senators during the summer. In the copy given to the committee, the name of the man to whom the memo was addressed was obscured. But the original shows the name very clearly—Jay Parker.

In another memorandum to Parker about the EEOC that was never publicly discussed, Thomas attacked the agency's guidelines on sexual harassment that had just been issued, just before the demise of the Carter administration. The guidelines, which were to become critical new weapons used by women to defend themselves in the workplace, would hold bosses responsible for harassment that occurred under their purview. Thomas recommended that the guidelines be reexamined and that employers be made less vulnerable, that bosses not be held liable for sexually harassing an employee unless they condoned or participated in it. Later on in the nomination process, when the issue of sexual harassment was suddenly critical, and Thomas's defenders were describing him as a champion of women's rights, this memorandum would have been of great interest had it been public.

While Thomas was critiquing the EEOC, he took a weekend off to

fly to San Francisco for a conference of black conservatives. It was a
rare chance for him to be among those whom he considered his true
brethren. One hundred of them gathered at the Fairmont Hotel to peer
into their futures. As Thomas later hinted with distaste, the gathering
was something of a job fair with some very eager participants. But it
was also a defining moment for the small movement, and it attracted
considerable attention from the press.

Speaking for the Republican administration, Meese assured the
black conservatives that they were welcome in the capital. The new
government would be glad to hire them in their areas of expertise, he
assured them, not just in civil rights where they might feel typecast.

Thomas got a big boost afterwards when prominently profiled in
*The Washington Post*, the showcase publication of the capital. The
*Post* touted Thomas as one of the black conservatives "on the center
stage of American politics." The man presented in that piece had no
ambivalence about conservatism. It was only several years since
Thomas had become a Republican, but he was described as a longtime
supporter of Reagan, and he seemed to fit the conservative mold
perfectly. The profile exemplified him as an opponent of everything
conservatives disliked—the minimum wage, rent control, busing programs to achieve racial balance in schools, and affirmative action
programs.

Thomas also criticized the welfare system by using a stunningly
personal example. In a discussion with a reporter, he excoriated his
own sister, Emma Mae Martin, who had stayed home in Pin Point
caring for her children and her aunt, and working at lowly jobs.
Thomas's portrait of his sister was less than charitable.

"She gets mad when the mailman is late with her welfare check, that
is how dependent she is," Thomas said. "What's worse is that now her
kids feel entitled to the check too. They have no motivation for doing
better or getting out of that situation." (In fact, Thomas cruelly
underestimated his sister. By the time of his nomination, Martin was
able to support herself without luxury but without government aid.)

And then, in characteristically strong words that he would just as
characteristically eat just a few months later, Thomas said that he had
refused and would continue to refuse to work on any "black" issues,
meaning areas concerned with discrimination. If he did so, he felt the
situation would be as it was in college and law school—the world

would assume he had gotten the job because of his race.

"If I ever went to work for the EEOC or did anything directly connected with blacks, my career would be irreparably ruined. The monkey would be on my back again to prove that I didn't have the job because I'm black. People meeting me for the first time would automatically dismiss my thinking as second-rate," he said.

With Parker's help and the piece in *The Washington Post*, Thomas had made it into the national limelight. It took the new Republican administration only two months, the *Post* reported later, to offer Thomas a low-profile job on the White House policy staff working on energy and environmental issues. He turned it down. He was then offered a more prominent position as Assistant Secretary for Civil Rights in the Department of Education, in charge of enforcing the civil rights laws as they applied to schools and universities.

This was "black work," the kind of job Thomas had forsworn. He would say later he was insulted by the offer, but he did accept it, creating yet another contradictory note in his rise toward power. At the age of thirty-two, Thomas had received a presidential appointment and was running a critical office with a staff of some fifty people.

It was at about that time, in the winter of 1981, that Clarence Thomas and Kathy Thomas, his wife of ten years, separated. The most that was ever made public about the reason for the marriage breakdown was the comment of friends who blamed it on "a mismatch of ambition." The two did reconcile for a few months, then called it quits for good that summer.

Thomas, in tough economic straits because of the separation, camped out for a while with his good friend, Gil Hardy. It was Hardy who recommended to Thomas that he bring to the civil rights office a lawyer and fellow Yale law graduate with whom Hardy was working in private practice in Washington. Thomas hired the young woman, whose name was Anita Hill, for his personal staff.

Thomas was not prepared for his public debut in Washington. He was taken aback, stung, by the immediate negative reaction to his politics. The piece in The Washington *Post* and his subsequent teaming up with the Reagan administration made him, as he put it, a "pariah, an outcast," in the black community. Never before had he been held so accountable for his views. Thomas, after all, had a penchant for debating, for taking any side of an argument just for the fun of it. But in Washington, at a time when the Reaganites were disposing of long-cherished principles, there was no such give or take. For taking part in the Reagan revolution, Thomas was ridiculed and socially ostra-cized.

"I never ran for office, I rarely raised my hand in college and suddenly my name is in the paper," Thomas said, sounding bewildered even years later by the reaction.

But Clarence Thomas had important things to say to the black community about its problems. He also had plenty to say about the black community to the nation. Despite the criticism, he continued. He set forth his ideas in speeches delivered from the beginning of his work in the administration to the end.

His ideas were not original, or popular. Had the black leaders of the civil rights community taken him seriously, had the nation listened, perhaps some progress could have been made in the 1980s toward remedying the calamity of the black ghettoes of America's inner cities. Certainly, one thoughtful black man might not have gone over so completely to the conservative side. Instead the right and the left deadlocked in disagreement, while the Reagan administration moved ahead with its plans to lessen federal power and federal regulation.

By the end of the Republican-dominated decade, Thomas's ideas had gained some acceptance, though. His emphasis on self-reliance didn't sound so outlandish. His challenges to forced integration and to welfare programs, his discomfort with affirmative action plans had gained some acceptance. Though his speeches to white audiences vacillated widely, Thomas was remarkably consistent in what he said to blacks for over a decade.

At an early speech at Clark College, a historically black school in Atlanta, he said that the problems of blacks should be attacked in different ways than in the past. With his federal job, he now had a platform from which he could start to sound out his philosophy.

"Today, we must recognize that, while discrimination continues as a pervasive barrier, many problems of blacks are socio-economic," he said.

He went on to recite some shocking statistics about black America. Functional illiteracy among youth was running as high as 40 percent, the number of unwed mothers had climbed to more than 48 percent of those giving birth, and more than 40 percent of black children were on welfare sometime in their youth.

In Thomas's message there was an urgent suggestion that the leaders of Rome, the civil rights leaders in this case, were busy fiddling on old instruments while their city burned.

"These problems cannot be solved by the law—even civil rights laws—but they can be solved by new ideas," he said.

While acknowledging "a great debt to the leaders who opened the doors of opportunity," Thomas asserted that "we must also look to ourselves admitting there are problems which antidiscrimination laws will not cure." Thomas argued for moving beyond the "orthodoxy" of having all blacks "saying the same things, adhering to the same party, believing in the same solutions. We fought too long and too hard to stop others from saying we all looked alike. We cannot now accept people acting as if we all think alike. This is far more dangerous." Sounding at the end of his speech like a true Republican, Thomas pointed out that "massive federal involvement still left us at the bottom rung of the economic ladder. Clearly then, the answer does not lie in more government intervention."

Thomas, who had been taught self-reliance by his grandfather, returned constantly to this theme in the context of civil rights and black society. Several years after the Clark College speech, he told another black audience that "today, it seems all too often that we look at our distant past as an indictment . . .

"Somehow, we have permitted ourselves to be trapped in a rhetorical discussion of our race that is shamelessly negative, a discussion that ultimately leads to the conclusion that we have no control over our fate—that others, bigots, friends, enemies and politicians have more to say about us than we do. To the extent that they do, we should retrieve and reassert our control but there is so much control that we do have. For example, we control the values that our kids have. I am raising a young teenager so I know how difficult and critical this is. When I was a kid . . . it was bad to say blacks are dumb but then it became all right to say we could not perform as well as whites because of something beyond our control. What's the difference?"

At his office within the education department, Thomas began shaping his image. He started dressing like a conservative in dark, expensive suits. And, predictably, he got into political fights with members of his staff who thought he was not enforcing civil rights laws in the nation's schools.

But Thomas stayed only a year at the civil rights office and mostly kept himself out of the public eye. He did, however, begin his fight with the civil rights community. Thomas objected to the government's policy of doing away with the historically black colleges in the South. The government was working to unify the black and white institutions. Thomas believed that the black colleges needn't be meddled with. After all, he had gotten a good education at his segregated Catholic schools in Savannah. He didn't think that blacks had to sit next to whites in order to learn. This certainly may have been true for Thomas, but some of the old-guard civil rights leaders felt that the result of Thomas's stance was exactly what white segregationists wanted.

On the face of it, though, nothing astounding happened during Thomas's brief term in the civil rights office. Anita Hill was working for him, and would later have much to say about his conduct, but she seemed quiet and calm as she went about her day-to-day legal business. Thomas was rarely seen in public paying attention to Hill, other than to occasionally ask her along with other women staffers to have a casual drink after work.

Much more clearcut was Thomas's relationship with Jay Parker, with whom he had grown closer. Parker had helped put Thomas on the federal government's map. And in the summer of his first year as a federal official, Thomas gave Parker permission to put his name on the masthead of the *Lincoln Review* as a member of the editorial advisory board. It was the first and the only time Thomas would lend his name to any such outside enterprise, though the arrangement would continue for a decade.

Parker had just resumed his lobbying on behalf of South Africa, this time with a deal to speak on behalf of Venda, another of the black homelands created under the scheme of grand apartheid. Parker was paid $3,000 a month, plus $900 a month in expenses. Judging from the reports he filed with the foreign agents registration section at the Department of Justice, his main task was to pay occasional visits to journalists and public officials—such as Thomas—to talk about the supposed virtues of Venda. The Venda deal was nothing, however, compared to what Parker and another *Lincoln Review* editor would get from the South Africans later.

Thomas had given his name to what was essentially propaganda for white South Africa, at the same time that he was in charge of ridding American schools of the injuries of racial prejudice. As with other times in his life, Clarence Thomas seemed in contradiction with himself.

In the meantime, over at the White House, the Republicans were having trouble finding blacks to fill other posts. Many qualified blacks were just not interested in joining the Reagan administration's dismantling of social policies that the civil rights movement had toiled years to establish. In June 1981, just after Thomas joined the administration, the president had nominated William M. Bell, an obscure black businessman from Detroit, to head the important EEOC. But the nomination had proved an embarassment.

Bell was billed as the head of an executive placement firm. But the company was not listed in the telephone book and had not placed any clients in jobs for a year. Bell was the only employee. He was not a lawyer, as all other EEOC chairmen had been. He was being adamantly opposed by civil rights groups who said he was unqualified.

The White House admitted that it had been struggling to come up with a black candidate to take the job. "We offered it to ten or twelve other blacks, and nobody wanted to take it," a White House aide told *Newsweek*. The philosophy behind this approach was exactly what Meese had promised it wouldn't be—hiring blacks to do "black work." Another illustration of the desperation with which Reagan had sought out black conservatives to help dismantle programs set up largely for blacks was its tapping Reverend B. Sam Hart to head the Civil Rights Commission, a national advisory panel on issues of race and prejudice. Reverend Hart was a black Philadelphia radio evangelist who was against busing and against homosexuality, good qualifications as far as the Reagan administration was concerned. But his nomination got into trouble with reports that he owed back taxes and rent in connection with his radio station. He also had not registered to vote in Philadelphia until late in 1981, about the time of his nomination, which quickly failed.

In February 1982, Bell's nomination also failed, after even Dan Quayle, then a conservative Republican senator from Indiana, announced he would oppose it. The two nominations were withdrawn. The White House then decided to fill Bell's spot with Thomas.

Before winter's end, Thomas, who had specifically vowed never to work at the EEOC, agreed to become its chairman. He was easily confirmed by the Senate after he promised to support at least some use of the affirmative action techniques he had been so critical of in 1980. He decided to take with him to the EEOC several of his assistants from the civil rights office at the Education Department, including Anita Hill.

When Thomas took over the chairmanship of the Equal Employment Opportunity Commission on May 17, 1982, there was no chair in his office, no pencils or pads, some files were covered with mold. The guard at the door of the agency's headquarters office initially refused to let Thomas enter because he lacked an agency identification card. On the same day the General Accounting Office (GAO), the investigatory arm of Congress, issued a report describing devastating financial mismanagement at the agency, which Thomas was suddenly responsible for fixing.

The report recounted how one employee had falsified her own time records to get an extra $4,000 and then was allowed to continue her work after a thirty-day suspension. The same woman later was given a cash award for what would seem in most government bueaucracies a rather unremarkable achievement—persuading the various EEOC offices to provide their telephone numbers to a new agency telephone directory, something they had previously been unwilling to do. And far more seriously, the agency was trying to deal with an annual caseload of sixty thousand complaints with just two malfunctioning computers. Not surprisingly, it had a backlog of cases.

Thomas was thirty-three, and until the year before had had no experience in management. He now was in charge of an agency of more than three thousand employees with nearly fifty offices around the country. Furthermore, the EEOC was a controversial agency with a legally and socially complicated mandate.

Created by the Civil Rights Act of 1964, the agency's purpose is to enforce the laws against discrimination in the workplace, from steel mills to corporate suites. It handles complaints from workers charging discrimination because of race, ethnicity, sex, age, or disability. Sexual discrimination includes sexual harassment.

The EEOC investigates employees' complaints, resolves them or files lawsuits against employers if necessary. The EEOC, in other words, is charged with remedying the racial and sexual discimination and other sorts of bias that still exist in many of the country's workplaces. The agency affects the jobs of millions of Americans and the companies that employ them.

Under the Carter administration, the agency, however poorly managed, was at the forefront of civil rights issues—the federal government's leading advocate for minorities and other historically dispossessed people. The Reagan administration wanted to put an end to this. Thomas was to be the Republican's agent at the EEOC, where he would eventually develop his ultraconservative philosophy and establish the political record by which he would be judged when he ascended to the Supreme Court.

Videos of Thomas's early speeches show an ungainly young man going through a kind of professional adolescence. He would read his speeches awkwardly, without polish, his language stiff. Despite his properly Washingtonian dark suits, he still looked like the radical he briefly had been in his college years. His beard was still fashioned into a goatee, and he wore thick-framed glasses.

This unconfident young man also had to contend with the fact that his constituency was hostile, a problem that he'd thought he would not mind. He had grown politically distant from the days in Savannah when he attended NAACP meetings with his grandfather.

"There were no trumpets or grand parties," Thomas said. "The civil rights community did not hail me as a champion of their cause. But that was good."

Thomas, however, did not reckon with the ruthlessness of the Reagan administration, which intended to hack down federal regulations and cut back on federal social programs. Thomas had qualms about the way in which the EEOC's mandate should be carried out, but he found himself facing an administration that was hostile to just about any sort of civil rights enforcemnt. The job, Thomas admitted later, was more than he had bargained for. There was little comfortable middle ground between civil rights demands and Reagan administration deeds.

Thomas had been forewarned of possible trouble by one of Reagan's actions a few months earlier. Reagan had given what many saw as proof of his racist bias by backing tax-exempt status for a South Carolina Christian college, Bob Jones University, that refused to admit blacks. Thomas was appalled at the message the administration was sending to black people and publicly called it a fiasco. The decision, he said, eliminated any shred of credibility for black members of the administration in an already hostile civil rights community. Still, Thomas took the promotion to the chairmanship.

He rationalized the situation by pointing out that every American government has had racists. "So what," he brashly said, "if there may be more here now. They may be more out front. I don't care. I prefer dealing with an out-and-out racist anyway to one who is racist behind your back."

Thomas was a black man in a white man's government, struggling to escape the orthodoxy of the civil rights movement. He was caught on shifting ground between two establishments at war about what government should do regarding bigotry and its legacy.

The Republicans believed that it was time to end the era of class-action suits, affirmative action programs and hiring quotas, while the civil rights leaders felt that such measures needed more time to effectively counterbalance the centuries of discrimination that had left black Americans at the bottom of society and the bottom of the workplace. Thomas came down on both sides of the issue. Because of the twists and turns he had taken in his life, Thomas embodied the very conflicts he was supposed to resolve. He hated racism and he despised the standard remedies.

Affirmative action, Thomas said, "was a narcotic of dependency" on which black people were hooked. They had come to expect help rather than earn their way upward. Over and over again, he complained about civil rights actions being taken on the basis of group characteristics, such as race or sex. He felt that people should be judged as individuals. Thomas himself was still angry inside about the uneradicable question mark left hanging on his own education and career by affirmative action and quotas. Would he have been admitted to Holy Cross or Yale if he were not black? He also knew, though, that working hard, earning an education, making a career, were things that the government could not have handed him for free. He had been helped, but he had also helped himself.

Similarly, Thomas believed that civil rights grievances should be handled on an individual, case-by-case basis. He opposed class-action lawsuits, which had been the vehicle of many major civil rights victories. He also adopted the hostility of Thomas Sowell, his ideological mentor, to statistical analysis of civil rights problems. According to the view of Thomas, the fact that blacks, or women, were underrepresented in a given workplace did not prove discrimination was the cause; the situation may have arisen from social or economic factors having nothing to do with prejudice. He felt that such presumptions of discrimination, which were common, should be scrapped, requiring every person to prove a job opportunity had been lost because of race, sex, or some other bias.

Moreover, Thomas believed that quotas, a standard remedy for statistical imbalances, were useless. They often were applied to professional, middle-class jobs. Americans weren't clamoring to be streetsweepers or dishwashers.

"If quotas help you, fine. If they make your life wonderful, fine. If they get you a BMW or a Mercedes, say that is why you want quotas. Man, quotas are for the black middle class," Thomas said. "But look at what's happening to the masses. They are just where they were before any of these policies."

Thomas was scoffing at the methods of fighting discrimination. He was all for battling the evil, but in a fashion that eschewed the larger social issues.

Once he had obtained an office chair and gotten a grip on the muddled EEOC bureaucracy, Thomas began putting his philosophy into practice. He decided the agency had to pursue every individual case of discrimination to the fullest, ending a practice of disposing of complaints as quickly as possible. Each complaint of merit was to be prosecuted. He wanted bosses guilty of clearcut cases of discrimination, which were not burdened by statistics or group theories, to be punished. He went so far in this direction as to complain that the civil rights laws ought to have criminal sanctions to bring against the worst offenders. He never made such a proposal formally, but he was clear about his disgust with simple bigotry.

But Thomas's overall position as chairman was not so simple. For all his conservative philosophy, he began his tenure at the EEOC with a generally moderate agenda and tone.

Thomas spent as much effort during his early years at the agency fighting eager right-wing officials in the Reagan administration as he did fighting the staunch civil rights leaders. Although he had vilified the idea of affirmative action, he resisted pressure to do away with it wholesale. He argued, for instance, that it was appropriate for the EEOC to intervene against companies with proven records of discrimination by slapping them with goals for minority hiring. He was willing to push for affirmative action in the most grievously segregated workplaces.

Thomas stood behind a crucial set of guidelines that required employers to factor race and sex into hiring criteria. The Reagan administraton was pressuring him to rewrite these Uniform Guidelines on Employee Selection Procedure, which were used as a national standard. But Thomas wouldn't budge on this issue at the outset of his chairmanship. Although the guidelines depended upon the sort of hiring statistics that Thomas found so abhorrent, he also saw their importance to workers who were not white males.

"We are not dealing with zoning ordinances here," he said of the guidelines. "Whole classes of people in this country have come to rely on the vital protection offered by measures such as these."

At times, usually in speeches before black audiences, Thomas could sound like a firebrand for civil rights, contradicting the very caution that he seemed to be injecting into the agency. He publicly criticized the conservatives breathing down his back for a more drastic reining in of the agency.

"There are some who would criticize present enforcement policies as immoral," Thomas said early on in his tenure at the agency, in one of the myriad speeches that would record his evolving, sometimes vacillating, philosophy. "But I say to you what is more immoral than the enslavement of an entire race? What is more immoral than the vicious cancer of racial discrimination? What is more immoral than the fabrication of a legal and political system which excludes, demeans and degrades an entire race? Those who seek to invoke morality today, must first address the pervasive and persistent immorality of yesterday."

He challenged the Reagan administration's dreamy idea that America could be easily transformed into a color-blind society, one in which race would no longer play a role. Social or economic disadvantages imbedded in the history of racial prejudice would somehow correct themselves, according to the Reaganite theory:

"It makes no sense to talk about rights, unless we intend to protect them. Unless we have the means and the will to aggressively protect individual rights, it is meaningless (if not fraudulent) to cry for a color blind society after this country has seen color for so long."

At times, Thomas took public positions that clashed with each other in a confusing sea of philosophical verbiage. He contradicted not only the administration's principles, but his own belief that discrimination should be corrected through individual cases rather than mass compensation for history's wrongs:

"Experience has taught us all that apparently neutral employment systems can still produce highly discriminatory effects. They can also perpetuate the effects of past discrimination."

And in another speech he doubled back on himself by declaring that "discrimination often affects whole classes of persons rather than merely individuals. The remedies must then address this broad group while making sure that, in protecting the rights of some, we do not wind up abridging the rights of others. At the same time, we must provide redress for past harm, not only the removal of barriers to true equality of opportunity in the job place."

Thomas's first full year in charge of the EEOC was 1983 and as it progressed, he found himself embattled on all fronts. He was trying to sort out the issues and also stand up to the zealots in the Reagan administration, particularly William Bradford Reynolds, the assistant attorney general for civil rights in the Justice Department. Some

Republican officials "looked at me as you would at a terminally ill relative or a friend destined for certain disaster," Thomas said.

"The hounds were snapping at [my] heels," he continued. "Some people appeared to want to change every policy which they found objectionable overnight, if not sooner. Others wanted me to proclaim my opposition to quotas loudly, using the strongest rhetoric."

At the same time, he was dismissed out of hand by the civil rights groups, particularly his fellow blacks. This kind of harsh treatment from both sides made Thomas, in his words, "boil inside."

In the spring of the year, Thomas had given strong public support to an affirmative action plan for the New Orleans Police Department. The plan called for promoting equal numbers of black and white policemen until half of the officers at every rank were black. The goal was a perfectly integrated police force.

The Justice Department hated the plan, which represented the sort of social engineering the Reaganites wanted to end. They took their objections to the federal appeals court level. Thomas tried to be reasonable. He argued that the position of the Justice Department in the case would "invalidate innumerable conciliation agreements, consent decrees, and adjudicated decrees to which the commission is a party, as well as the commission's own published guidelines regarding appropriate affirmative action."

Basically, Thomas felt that old, settled cases—old wounds, in essence—should not be reopened. The EEOC had prepared a brief making this argument, but it was never filed in the case. Thomas backed down after he was summoned to the White House, where he was told that "the government would speak with one voice." To make his humiliation complete, the news of this dressing-down was made public by a spokesman from the Justice Department.

Thomas was trying to stand up to Reynolds, the assistant attorney general who wanted to take the stuffing out of the EEOC. In August, the two men appeared together for a panel discussion on civil rights sponsored by the Urban League in New Orleans, the site of their previous disagreement. They remained in disagreement.

Reynolds said the Reagan administration's enforcement of civil rights had been "vigorous and uncompromising," a statement which sounded like political rhetoric.

Thomas countered by pointing out that the administration needed to do more to hire minorities and by objecting to Reynolds's statement.

"The issues we face are clearly too complex to be tossed around as oversimplified campaign slogans which inflame more than inform," he said.

The atmosphere in the Reagan administration remained hostile to the civil rights movement and its goal of getting disadvantaged people hired both outside and inside government. Perhaps the outstanding example of this hostility was a remark made in October by James Watt, the controversial Secretary of the Interior. Describing the members of his new coal advisory commission, Watt said nastily, "I have a black, I have a woman, two Jews and a cripple."

The brouhaha caused by this remark forced the controversial secretary to resign. But he had articulated, if grotesquely, something of the Reagan administration's attitude. It was an attitude that pained civil rights leaders and jaundiced their opinion of anyone who would work for such a government.

Had civil rights leaders not shunned Clarence Thomas during this period, things might have turned out differently. If they had acknowledged him as an ally, albeit with his own ideas, they would have had a chance to influence both his ideas, and their own. They all might have come out stronger. But by rejecting Thomas intellectually, politically and most of all personally, the civil rights leaders pushed this man, who was thoughtfully grappling with huge issues, further toward the right.

In the meantime, over on Capitol Hill, the Democrats on various congressional committees were howling about Thomas's activities, or lack of activities, at the EEOC. They had noticed a significant drop in the number of lawsuits filed by the agency on behalf of workers victimized by discrimination. This, the congressmen concluded, indicated that the EEOC was falling down on enforcing the antidiscrimination laws. The chairman of the agency was hauled over to the Hill to explain.

Thomas tried to be conciliatory. At one hearing, he promised the EEOC would continue to advocate affirmative action plans, including "race-conscious relief." That meant he wouldn't prohibit the sort of overarching remedies that he found distasteful. Thomas promised everything he could, and more. He assured the congressmen that "as long as I am chairman we will aggressively pursue all remedies available to us whether I like them or not."

Thomas was under pressure, from Capitol Hill, from the White House, from the Justice Department, and from the civil rights community. The only part of his job that he seemed to enjoy was the more mechanical task of organizing the disarrayed bureaucracy he had inherited and that the General Accounting Office had so sternly criticized.

"When Clarence Thomas went up to the Hill, no one was for him. The Republicans hated us because we were the EEOC and the Democrats hated us because we were the Reagan administration. Everybody looked on him as though he were some kind of Uncle Tom, monster, charlatan. It was dreadfully unfair. That's what Clarence dealt with almost the whole eight years that he was at the EEOC," recalled Ricky Silberman, his vice-chairman at the EEOC.

Under his tenure, many of the criticisms of the original GAO report were resolved. He set about computerizing the agency, making its bureaucracy function more smoothly and straightening out its finances. He made a habit of standing outside the front door of the EEOC's headquarters office in Washington every morning, with a characteristic Diet Coke in his hand, watching to see who came in late.

During his early years at the agency, Thomas was as hard on some of his own employees as the political world was hard on him. For instance, he went after Frank Quinn, the longtime head of the agency's San Francisco office, shortly after Quinn had spoken critically of the agency's management in public. To punish Quinn, who was about to retire, Thomas wanted to have him transferred to the warm Siberia of Alabama. The transfer never happened, but it gave others in the agency an idea of how unreasonably Thomas could act. On occasion, Thomas was said to have fired employees, including public relations person Angela Wright, by taping notes to their chairs.

EEOC employees said that Thomas in his early years at the agency was very different from the confident man whom President Bush presented to the nation in Kennebunkport. The early Thomas was insecure, sometimes unpleasant, and short-tempered. He was often uncomfortable with the agency's staff officials whom he assumed, not always correctly, were hostile. He was capable of firing or demoting middle-level career staffers who made presentations with which he did not agree.

"In the early years he was very ill at ease with career people," said one longtime employee of the agency. "He didn't like face to face meetings with people. [But] over the years as he got comfortable with the job and got his own people in positions of trust, he always seemed to be at ease with people, joking, friendly."

Thomas, under more pressure than he had ever imagined possible at work, was also under pressure at home. He was short on cash, enough so that he had trouble paying his income taxes. Kathy, his estranged wife, asked him to take over care of their son, Jamal, who was then ten. Thomas became a single parent, with all the accompanying stress.

And it was during his first full year chairing the EEOC that his grandfather, the man who had substituted for his father and given him his identity, died. Several weeks later, his grandmother died. Thomas cried in public for the first time in his life. He hinted later that he considered quitting the EEOC in failure.

"I had been thrust into highly visible and controversial positions, and for the first time in my life found myself embroiled in controversy," he said in a church homily. "I had been asked by then President Reagan to run a difficult agency, and found it to be much more than I had been warned about, and far more than I had bargained for. And just as the criticism poured in and the problems of the agency overwhelmed me, my grandfather died. I had taken the criticism and faced up to the problems. But somehow when the person who fed you, sheltered you, cared for you, raised you—somehow when that person dies it's hard to handle."

It was about this time that Anita Hill was deciding to leave her job at the EEOC, where she aided Clarence Thomas with a panoply of legal tasks; she was giving up the career she had always thought she wanted in the nation's capital. She told friends that the reason she resolved to leave the agency was because the chairman was persistently harassing her sexually. She left in 1983, to go back home to the quieter life of Oklahoma. She had found a job teaching as an assistant professor at the modest and highly religious law school at Oral Roberts University.

By late 1984, when it looked inevitable that Ronald Reagan would win reelection by a landslide, Clarence Thomas began straightening out the zigzags in his unsteady course on the issue of civil rights. The word around Washington had been that the Republican administration was fed up; the Reaganites were thinking of forcing him to resign or of not reappointing him when his term as EEOC chairman came up for renewal in 1986. Thomas responded by taking the rightward track, joining with Reynolds, who was leading the attack against expansive civil rights from his post in the Justice Department.

Reynolds was making great use of a new Supreme Court decision in a case involving a black fireman, Captain Carl Stotts, who argued that because of past discrimination he should not be laid off the job before others hired before him. The Court's decision held that union seniority took precedence over affirmative action goals when it came to laying off personnel. Reynolds and other Reaganites in the Justice Department jumped on the decision as proof that the high court opposed affirmative action programs of all kinds. This hugely stretched interpretation of the decison was at variance with what most careful legal readers thought. It provided Reynolds with a weapon, even though a shoddily crafted one, to attack affirmative action. Thomas did not argue with the message.

Over at the EEOC, Clarence Thomas was finally abiding by the Reagan game plan. Using his position as chairman of the EEOC's five commissioners, he initiated a review of the Uniform Guidelines on employer hiring. These were the same ones that he had insisted on maintaining a couple of years before. Now he said the guidelines had become "too rigid." His move shocked the the civil rights community, which feared the possibility of losing one of its most effective tools for levering companies into hiring more minorities. (By the time Thomas left the EEOC, the agency had yet to take action on the guidelines.)

And the man who had been so insistent that he not be typecast as a token black, appeared at Reagan-Bush campaign rallies for black groups. His message was that Reagan's first term had actually been a boon for blacks. He even talked up the administration's proposals for enterprise zones that theoretically would induce businesses to set up shop in the inner city. He later referred to the idea as a cheap gadget that insulted black intelligence.

Within a week of Reagan's reelection, Thomas suggested that the EEOC might abandon the use of affirmative action goals and timetables. In earlier years, he had said he would continue to use these methods of promoting the disadvantaged even if he had qualms about them. Thomas also reversed himself on the idea of a color-blind social policy. He agreed with the Reaganite proposal that American law could be color blind, that justice could be accomplished without making any special exceptions for the country's legacy of racial discrimination.

Although he would never feel at ease with his white government colleagues, Thomas stopped trying to reconcile his views with those of the mainstream black leaders, those in the civil rights movement and those in party politics who had given him the cold shoulder. Black leaders, he complained, were "sitting there watching the destruction of our race while arguing about Ronald Reagan." Instead of trying to work constructively with him and other Reagan administration officials, the leaders of his race had gone to the press to "bitch bitch bitch, moan and moan, whine and whine."

The response was equally acerbic. "Clarence is like a 1960s student who's filled with anger and not really directed anywhere. He's a very complicated, conflicted individual," one civil rights activist told the *Legal Times*, a respected Washington weekly.

Thomas seemed not to dispute that assessment, particularly when it came to his life in Washington.

"I don't fit in with whites, and I don't fit in with blacks. We're in a mixed-up generation, those of us who were sent out to integrate society. . . . If it were not for the few friends I have who do not give a damn about this stuff, this place could drive me insane."

In an interview with the *Legal Times*, Thomas said that even though it was the 1980s, he felt uncomfortable being a black man in some of Washington's better restaurants. He would go to church any day but Sunday. "I don't like people that much," he said. "God is all right. It's the people I don't like."

His choice of a football team points to the same antisocial iconoclasm. In a town that is fanatic about the Washington Redskins, he decided he liked their archenemy, the Dallas Cowboys. "I love unpopular causes," he admitted. He said he also liked the Los Angeles Raiders "because everybody hates them."

Thomas, his views now more acceptable to the Reagan administration, survived a government shakeup as the reelected president prepared for his second term in January 1985. The Reaganites wanted to consolidate the conservative gains they had made in the previous term.

The Justice Department soon started pressuring specific cities, states, and counties across the country to drop hiring agreements that included racial quotas. The department cited as its legal authority the Supreme Court's decision in the *Stotts* case the year before, even though most federal courts were interpreting it differently.

The Republicans were intent on turning the federal courts around by getting conservatives appointed all the way up to the Supreme Court. For this task, Reagan had at his side Ed Meese, who had been confirmed as attorney general despite ethical questions about financial problems that included unreported loans. They made it clear that anyone with aspirations for a federal judgeship had better toe the line—the hardline—politically.

Thomas seemed to make up his mind in opposition to affirmative action, calling the setting of hiring goals and timetables for employers "a fundamentally flawed approach." The EEOC commissioners voted against these affirmative action methods, after one switched sides and gave Thomas a majority. Word was sent out the same day to all EEOC offices not to include these standard methods in proposed settlements of complaints.

EEOC insiders said that it had been only this lack of a majority among the commissioners that had held Thomas back previously, that he felt a very strong duty to represent the agency's views, not just his own. But Thomas held enormous power over the agency's operations nonetheless.

His conservative resolve was strengthened by two of the key aides he had acquired. His chief of staff, Jeffrey Zuckerman, who had taken that position in late 1984, was an unflinching conservative and a White House ally. (Zuckerman raised a controversy when he admitted saying in private that blacks and women could beat job discrimination by offering to work for lower pay than white men.) Zuckerman and Ricky Silberman, the agency's vice chairman, were credited by outside observers as being the chief architects of Thomas's increasing conservatism.

He also rejected the notion of comparable worth, the idea that women should be paid as much as men for jobs entailing equal difficulty or expertise. He said that pay disparities alone between men and women proved nothing. This was enough to earn him the permanent enmity of women's rights groups.

Thomas went on to collaborate with Attorney General Meese on efforts to modify an executive order requiring that a portion of all federal jobs go to minorities.

Upset by these changes, senators and representatives began a new round of queries that would be rough on the EEOC chairman. It was the beginning of a new period that would embitter Clarence Thomas even more. Now he would add Congress to the long list of those who had tormented him. He spent much of the next three years in hearings up on the Hill "being taken to the woodshed," as he put it, by congressmen displeased with what he was doing or not doing.

In early May 1986, a few weeks after the U.S. bombing of Libya, Thomas was renominated for a second term. Thomas said later that he wanted to stay on because of his anger at the civil rights groups, to show them he could not be run out of town. But it was not immediately clear whether his path to confirmation would be blocked by congressional unhappiness with his policies.

Thomas's nomination was complicated further when the Supreme Court ruled that affirmative action was in fact a valid remedy for past job discrimination. The EEOC had joined the Justice Department the year before in asking the high court to reject a ruling that required a metal workers' union to increase its minority membership. The Supreme Court approved the ruling, destroying the Justice Department's and the EEOC's position that affirmative action was illegal.

So what was Thomas going to say now about affirmative action goals and timetables, having already flip-flopped on the issue in the past? At his confirmation hearings in July he flip-flopped again, assuring the committee that the commission would resume the use of such affirmative action methods in some cases. With those promises, Thomas was confirmed again.

The next month Ed Meese, Bradford Reynolds and Senator Strom Thurmond—three of the most conservative conservatives in the Republican administration—visited the EEOC offices briefly for Thomas's swearing in. It must have been an odd scene—the black chairman of the civil rights agency politely chatting with three white men of utterly different backgrounds. Thurmond had initiated his political career as a segregationist. And it was Thurmond who reportedly gave Thomas some advice that he thought might help his political profile: find a wife.

In fact, Thomas had already confided to friends that he was in love with someone he met that spring. She was Virginia Lamp, a white woman from Nebraska with very conservative politics who worked as a lawyer and lobbyist for the Chamber of Commerce.

Reynolds, Thomas's friendly nemesis, offered a few words of encouragement to Thomas at the swearing in.

"It's a proud moment for me to stand here, because Clarence Thomas is the epitome of the right kind of affirmative action working the right way," Reynolds said.

Thomas looked away in disgust. Those words contradicted everything he had tried to build for himself, particularly a reputation separate from his race. The incident illustrated how little the Republicans understood about him, or his principles. But there was a certain awful truth in what Reynolds had said.

Clarence Thomas kept moving to the political right,
until he was outstripping the average Republican. Within three short
years he was transformed from a moderate to a conservative to a
member of the radical right. By 1987, he was ranting and raving about
liberals in Congress, in the Supreme Court, in the media. He was
delivering key speeches to very conservative audiences to whom he
extolled the virtues of right-wing heroes like Ayn Rand, Oliver North,
and Robert Bork. They were fiery words, like those of a man on the
stump.

As Thomas grew more conservative, he became more strident and
more impatient with the moderate positions he himself had espoused
just a couple of years before. At the suggestion of Jeffrey Zuckerman,
his chief aide, he had hired two young speechwriters who would give
the EEOC chairman a new political vocabulary. The two were protégés
of Harry Jaffa, a California guru of esoteric new right jurisprudence.
In his earlier years, Jaffa had written for Barry Goldwater the famous
"Extremism in the defense of liberty is no vice," speech. The young
speechwriters imported Jaffa's ideas into the EEOC, and Thomas even

began quoting that same phrase of Goldwater's.

Thomas was sounding as if he had been born again in a political sense. Thomas's speeches were spattered with one of those imported ideas in particular, the concept of natural law. This was the idea that there existed a higher, or God-given law that superseded all laws of man. The same idea was used implicitly earlier in this century to strike down New Deal legislation regulating business, since violations of property rights were said to be violations of the natural law. But such arguments made many conservatives as well as liberals nervous because it could be used to justify just about anything. One man's natural right to property was another woman's natural right to privacy, and abortion.

If Thomas came to this concept through his speechwriters, it suited him well. It would become a keystone in his developing legal philosophy and a big issue by the time he was striving for confirmation to the Supreme Court.

In the natural-law concept, he first found an answer for a question that had long been burning inside him. Superpatriot that he had become, how could Thomas overcome the legal dilemma for blacks inherent in the American Constitution? The dilemma was made explicit by Thurgood Marshall, whose legal philosophy was so at variance with that of Thomas's, at the time of the 1987 bicentennial celebrations of the ratification of the U.S. Constitution. The iconoclastic Marshall said that there was little for blacks to celebrate about the document.

The country's founders had purposely ignored the divisive issue of slavery, except to say that for purposes of population counts a black man would be tallied as three-fifths of a white man. Thomas, who believed so fervently in the American system, needed a rationale to explain that disgraceful aspect of the country's legal birth. He found it in the Declaration of Independence, with which the concept of natural law meshed nicely.

"We hold these truths to be self-evident," the declaration said, "that all men are created equal, that they are endowed by their Creator with certain unalienable rights, that among these are life, liberty and the pursuit of happiness." The declaration also said that the people of America were assuming the "station to which the laws of nature and of nature's God entitle them."

Here, Thomas argued, was the real principle upon which the country was founded, that all men—whether black or white—were created equal. Even if it would take time and a civil war to develop this principle, it was inherent in the words of the Declaration of Independence, if not the Constitution.

Thomas didn't stop with this elegant principle, though. He emphasized the idea that men were subject ultimately to the abstract laws of "nature's God" and took that idea to an extreme. Ethereal though it was, Thomas used the concept to rationalize not only the foundation of the country but also the justification of conservatism.

In his speeches, Thomas insisted that natural law means that government could not take away a man's property. It allows for the "liberation of commerce," or "the common sense of the free market, the natural right to eat the bread [one] earns with [one's] own hands." Though tempered by an asserted belief in judicial restraint, Thomas's interpretation of natural law could mean the scrapping of federal regulations on business, freeing corporations from oversight, and leaving the wealthy with their riches. Ironically, it was the idea of an unfettered right of property that was used by the early Supreme Court to justify the holding of slaves.

But the Declaration of Independence and its mention of a higher law is not a part of the Constitution. Whatever its moral weight, it has no legal force. Or does it?

Thomas, taking a legally radical position, argued that the declaration and its potential natural-law principle are simply incorporated into any interpretation of the Constitution.

"The Constitution must always be understood in light of the ends set forth in the declaration," Thomas explained bluntly to a chapter of the Federalist Society in a speech he delivered at the University of Virginia in 1988. This society, which believes in the wholesale transfer of authority from the federal government to the states as well as in a reassertion of the paramount right to property, was founded by a group including Lee Liberman, the zealously conservative aide to C. Boyden Gray who was a key figure in deciding who got judicial nominations. Federalist Society chapters, based primarily at law schools across the country, became favored audiences for Thomas's speeches.

Thomas was so certain of his natural law theory that he contemptuously dismissed Oliver Wendell Holmes, perhaps the greatest Supreme Court justice of all time. All that Thomas then knew of Holmes, he admitted later, was that the justice had not been enamored of the theory of natural law, describing it as that "brooding omnipresence in the sky."

Even Thomas's grandparents, whose virtues were trotted out to enlighten most of the hundreds of audiences Thomas addressed, became devotees of natural law, posthumously. It was not such a strange application for Thomas to make of his theory. The hard-working, very religious couple "knew that they were inherently equal and that the daily contradictions were obstacles first to be overcome and then changed," he told the libertarian Cato Institute. Despite society's "negative treatment," they rose to human equality "according to God's higher law."

Thomas's theory of natural law was important because it became one of the cornerstones in the foundation of his philosophy. It also would be the subject of controversial debate as he passed the final obstacle, the Senate, on his way to the Supreme Court. But while in Thomas's view people could look to God or nature for their rights, they ought not look to government for any help at all. It was an extreme adaptation of his grandfather's philosophy of self-reliance, and the lack of personal compassion that a tough man had shown to his grandchildren.

"I for one, do not see how the government can be compassionate," Thomas told the Heritage Foundation. "Only people can be compassionate, and then only with their own money, their own property, or their own effort, not that of others."

It was this impatience with governmental sentimentality that shaped his opposition to the most sacred legal creed among blacks of his lifetime, the *Brown* v. *Board of Education* school desegregation case argued by Thurgood Marshall. While not quarreling with the bottom line, that the existing "separate but equal" school systems were unconstitutional, Thomas did not agree with how the court got there. Chief Justice Earl Warren's opinion in the case had emphasized the psychological effect of segregation on black children.

"The main problem with the Court's opinions in the area of race is that it never had an adequate principle in the great *Brown* precedent to proceed from. Psychological evidence, compassion, and a failure to connect segregation with the evil of slavery prevented the court from ending segregation as a matter of simple justice," Thomas said.

But for Thomas the real problem was the desegregation rulings that followed *Brown*. "We discovered that *Brown* not only ended segregation but required school integration. And then began a disastrous series of cases requiring busing and other policies that were irrelevant to parents' concern for a decent education. The [Supreme] Court appeared in these and many other cases to be more concerned with meeting the demands of groups than with protecting the rights of individuals."

As if he had never expressed any doubts in the matter, Thomas went on to attack all the basic Supreme Court decisions upholding affirmative action. He equated these plans to retribution, for he believed that they stole jobs from the deserving to compensate for social inequity. These moves, he liked to say, were the equivalent of a policeman taking your neighbor's television set to replace the one stolen from you by a thief.

"Retribution isn't justice, no matter how good it may make some feel," he said in a speech to the Cato Institute. "By permitting social engineering in the workplace, the court is fostering an ugly situation, the very racial clarification and strife that the 1964 Civil Rights Act sought to ameliorate."

In this new line of speechmaking, Thomas did not stick to his intellectually provocative ideas about racial inequality and what *not* to do about it. He took to warning, in the second half of the Reagan administration of all times, that the United States was becoming a totalitarian state.

"Maximization of rights is perfectly compatible with total government and regulation. Unbounded by notions of obligation and justice, the desire to protect rights simply plays into the hands of those who advocate a total state. The rhetoric of freedom (license, really) encourages the expansion of bureaucratic government."

Oliver North became one of Thomas's heros, an example of patriotic conservatism, respect for freedom, and limits on government. This was the same national-security officer who had lied to Congress about Irangate, destroyed documents sought by Congress and used his government power to misappropriate millions.

Quoting former Treasury Secretary William E. Simon, Thomas said that America was "careening with frightening speed toward collectivism and away from free individual sovereignty, toward coercive centralized planning, and away from free individual choices, toward a statist-dictatorial system and away from a nation in which individual liberty is sacred."

It is not easy to explain Thomas's transformation. Signs had appeared before of his deep conservatism. It had perhaps been repressed during his moderate phase by a desire, typical enough of any rising political bureaucrat, to get along and be accepted. But he found little encouragement for his moderation from the civil rights community. At the same time, it was clear to this very ambitious young man that political survival meant the adoption of the hardline Republicanism that ruled Washington.

In addition, Thomas was an impressionable person, a man who imbibed new ideas and spouted them out again with great fervor before moving on to something else. In his later years at the EEOC, he was surrounded by conservatives who showed him the way to greater power and prestige. Thomas's new far-right speechwriters were clever enough to find the right words to match the rage that had built up inside him over the years. They gave expression to his anger at the injustice of a racist society, white and black, which had rejected him because of the darkness of his skin and the curliness of his hair. Thomas undoubtedly carried a more personal anger from his boyhood, when his parents had essentially abandoned him, and his grandfather had taught him not to expect compassion. In the conservative atmosphere of Washington, Thomas's indignation blended easily with his ambition.

Thomas's anger was to be expressed through the ideas of the radical right rather than those of the radical left; this suited his taste for challenging society, and also his honest distrust of the liberal establishment. It was Silberman, the EEOC vice chairman, who pointed him away from professional equal-opportunity audiences and sent him into the mouth of the conservative whale—the Heritage Foundation, the Cato Institute, the Federalist societies—armed with the words of his new speechwriters.

Since Thomas's speeches, like those of any politician, had always reflected to some extent the views of the audience he addressed, it is not surprising that his opinions changed as his audiences changed. He must also have known that these people of the conservative movement had been given tremendous power over judicial appointments. They would have influence in the decision of whether Thomas would ever make it to the job he had so brashly set his sights on when he got to Washington—the Supreme Court. Which is not to say that his courting of them was completely disingenuous: the more he told them what they wanted to hear, the more he liked what he had to say.

Of course, one of the new conservatives in his life at the time of his turn to the far right was Virginia Lamp. She was the daughter of a prominent civil engineer, who had been head of his own firm in Omaha. Her mother was active in Republican politics. Thomas had met her in 1986 at a conference in New York City and had immediately fallen for her. He was thirty-seven, she not yet thirty. He was very black, she the palest white. They were married within half a year.

Thomas had been lonely following his divorce. Although he was on the most-eligible list of Washington's Republicans, who kept trying to pair him up with other prominent blacks, Thomas was not enjoying himself. He was no expert at either dining or dancing. His conversation tended to be more political than romantic. So although he did not approve of interracial marriage, Thomas had no doubts about remaking his life with Lamp.

"I know what it's like to be unhappy. This is someone I'm happy with," he told a friend about Lamp.

Politically, Lamp was akin to Thomas—being identified as a traitor to her sex, as he was to his race. Then a Chamber of Commerce lawyer, she lobbied Congress against ideas that would boost women's pay in the workforce or expand women's rights. Lamp, in the words of one of her liberal opponents, was friendly and hardworking, but politically was "to the right of Attila the Hun."

Lamp also had shown signs of being impressionable. The biggest known crisis of her adult life had been her entanglement in Lifespring, a self-help course that some called a cult. It took a strong grip on some of the participants' minds. The program emphasized deep emotional introspection in group settings that sometimes pushed the limits of normalcy.

After she had fled the program, Lamp recounted that in one session her group stripped down to bathing suits to the sound of bawdy music. The participants then pelted each other with sexual questions. Lamp became obsessed with Lifespring and had great difficulty breaking away. In 1985 she freed herself, and swinging the pendulum in the other direction, joined Cult Awareness Network, itself a controversial group that has been accused of connections with "deprogrammers" who kidnap members of cults in order to force them back into reality. She has continued to be active in the anticult group.

Back in Nebraska, Lamp's relatives admitted to reporters that they were startled that she was marrying a black man.

"He was so nice, we forgot he was black," her Aunt Opal Knop told the Washington *Post*, "and he treated her so well, all of his other qualities made up for his being black."

But some of Thomas's black opponents in the civil rights community took his choice of a white wife as a further rejection of the black community.

Thomas and Lamp were married in St. Paul's United Methodist Church on May 30, 1987, in Omaha, Nebraska. Jamal served as best man for his father. Thomas moved out of his rented home in the racially mixed county of Prince Georges County in Maryland across Washington to its lily-white Virginia suburbs. His wife sold her $90,-000 condominium there and they bought a $202,000 house, which was modest for the Washington suburbs. The two-story, three-bedroom house was part of a "new community" with grass, gardens, and sidewalks carved out of what used to be Virginia horse country. It was his new wife who eventually brought him into the Truro Church, where charismatic Episcopalians spoke in tongues and crusaded against abortion.

During this period, Thomas was also influenced by Jay Parker. The two were becoming the best of friends. They had plenty of time to hash out their thoughts on civil rights and other political and economic issues. Parker was so at odds with the American civil rights community that he bitterly opposed, in vain, the designation of Martin Luther King's birthday as a federal holiday.

Parker also was more involved than ever with the white South African government, which was fighting an increasingly powerful sanctions movement in the United States. Parker had been put directly on the South African payroll and given a tremendous pay raise. Parker lives now in the wealthiest of the Virginia suburbs of the capital in a spacious house whose front and side yards boast flagpoles flying oversize American flags.

Parker and another editor at the *Lincoln Review*, who was also a friend of Thomas, were splitting fees of almost $400,000 a year from the South African deal. Parker was also taking nearly $200,000 a year—almost a quarter of its income—in salary and expenses from donations to the little institute that published the *Lincoln Review*.

The masthead of Parker's magazine still included Thomas's name. And Thomas's involvement went further than that. His work appeared in the magazine three times, sometimes alongside pieces opposing sanctions against South Africa or otherwise bolstering the white regime against its critics. Thomas went out of his way to praise Parker in his speeches, saying how much he admired him and lauding his courage and strength.

As Thomas was working out his political philosophy, he developed his penchant for the author Ayn Rand. He liked Rand's book *The Fountainhead* so much that he would invite people to lunch in his EEOC office where he would show them the film version.

*The Fountainhead* is a philosophical tract rendered in the form of an easy-to-read novel. Its message is simple enough: if you pursue your own aims above all else, then the benefits you gain will also benefit society. In short, selfishness is good for everyone. Rand espouses an individualism so extreme that it denigrates that most fundamental of human values, compassion.

The protagonist of *The Fountainhead* is an idealized man who tolerates no weakness and makes no mistakes. He is cast as a modern architect in love with his own ego. His character is strange in that he is both serene and violent at once; he never loses his composure, whether he is dynamiting an empty, multistory housing project that doesn't measure up to his impeccable standards, or raping the woman he loves.

By mid-1988, Clarence Thomas had become engaged on another political battlefront. Congress, he declared, "conducts its business with little deliberation and even less wisdom." Thomas's attack was not too surprising, since Congress already had declared war on him as chairman of the EEOC.

Worst of all, it was not just his policies that the congressmen were criticizing, but his management. Thomas had often bragged, and rightly so, that he had whipped into shape the agency that he had inherited in a state of bureaucratic disrepair. He had lived up to his pledge to vigorously pursue individual cases of discrimination.

Thomas was able to demonstrate that he had been sharply increasing the number of lawsuits filed by the agency against employers, from 241 a year when he took over to 640 when he left. However, these were mostly individual suits, since he had discontinued the filing of most large-scale class actions. Overall, the amount of money being won by the agency for victims of dicrimination had stayed about the same. In other words, more lawsuits were being filed, but their scope was narrower.

During his seven and a half years as chairman of the EEOC Thomas had succeeded in retooling the agency to match his philosophy and that of the Reagan administration under which he had loyally served. The EEOC no longer used the weapons that had been developed in the heyday of civil rights, the class-action suits and affirmative action methods like quotas, hiring goals, or timetables to force companies to hire minorities. Under Thomas, the EEOC had stopped being an agency that sought to broadly alter society. Instead, it had become the defender of individuals who, one-by-one, had suffered discrimination and could prove it.

But Thomas had let one province of his agency—and a significant one—slip out of control. The criticism this time was coming not from the usual civil rights groups, the angry women and minorities who wanted larger action, but from the careful, normally middle-of-the-road lobby for senior citizens. The American Association of Retired Persons (AARP), was one of the most powerful lobbying groups in the capital. The retirees' lobby felt that Thomas had failed to enforce the laws against discrimination against older Americans. The reason, they suspected, was that the EEOC chairman had come to favor business interests because of his belief in unfettered capitalism. His relationship with big business was friendly.

One good example of that relationship was Thomas's reluctance, despite intervention by the courts and Congress, to change EEOC regulations to stop an abuse in the area of pensions. Retirees lost an estimated $450 million in pension benefits before the abuse was corrected. Businesses were freezing the pension accounts of persons who worked into their late sixties or longer. When these stalwart workers did eventually retire, their companies would calculate their pensions only for the years they worked until they had turned sixty-five. After that, never mind.

One of the victims of this EEOC inaction was Richard H. Bamford, who worked as marketing manager for an electrical cable company until he was sixty-eight. Because the company cut off his pension credits at sixty-five, Bamford stood to lose as much as $50,000 depending on how long he lived.

"I'm one of Thomas's victims," said Bamford, whose opinion of Thomas is understandably low. "I think the man is an opportunist. He figured out there's very few black conservatives so why not be one. He doesn't give a damn for the law."

Judge Harold H. Greene of federal district court in Washington sharply rebuked the EEOC for its tardiness in dealing with the problem. Deciding a lawsuit, he ruled in favor of the retired workers, calling the delay entirely unjustified and unlawful. Though the judge was later overturned on the legal issues, he infuriated Thomas by saying the agency's handling of the issue as "at best . . . slothful" and "at worst deceptive to the public."

But this issue was not Thomas's biggest problem. Congress discovered that the EEOC was failing to handle complaints about bosses discriminating against older workers. In fact, the agency was allowing the complaints to lapse. Thomas responded by acknowledging his agency had allowed nine hundred such cases to expire and forthrightly took responsibility.

The situation, Thomas said, "disgraces the agency . . . we deserve harsh criticism for this occurrence. It will not happen again."

Then, in June, Thomas admitted that there were as many as 7,456 lapsed complaints. In the meantime, the Senate's subcommittee on aging had concluded a year-long investigation and produced a critical report. It said that Thomas had misled Congress on the number of lapsed age-discrimination cases and that the agency's enforcement of antidiscrimination laws "had seriously deteriorated over the last five years." Although the report was never officially published, it was leaked to the press.

But the more the liberals attacked Thomas, the more popular he was with the White House. In the spring of 1989, the beleaguered Thomas got the news he had been hoping to hear. He was going to be named to the federal judiciary, placed in a prime spot to make the next step to the Supreme Court. President Bush would nominate him for the seat left vacant by Robert Bork on the U.S. Court of Appeals in Washington.

As with all nominees to the federal bench, Thomas needed the Senate's imprimatur. In February 1990, for the first time, he appeared before the Senate Judiciary Committee to undergo questions. This session with the committee was relatively easy, though. A federal appellate judge makes rulings that are important but that do not carry the absolute significance of a Supreme Court justice's decisions. The senators on the committee did hear, though, from disgruntled representatives of older people, women and blacks.

Thomas had not solved the difficulty with the complaints of older workers. One of the senators established that the agency had continued to let age discrimination cases lapse, after Congress had given them new life by extending the legal deadline. The number of such cases was now said to be thirteen thousand, or more. A second extension was required.

The association of retired persons had never before taken a position on a judicial nomination, and it was not going to take one now. But it sent a voluminous, furious letter to Senator Joseph Biden, the committee chairman, saying that Thomas had repeatedly misstated the facts about his "malfeasance" in office. The letter said Thomas had made "misstatements throughout," and that his testimony could not have been based on misinformation because the issues had been so thoroughly gone over before. The accusation was backed up by Senator David H. Pryor, an Arkansas Democrat, who said Thomas was guilty of "several erroneous statements" about the age discrimination cases in his testimony.

This was all just a polite way of saying that Thomas was lying.

Thomas had also antagonized women's groups—not just feminist groups, but organizations that represented working women.

Nancy Kreiter, research director of Women Employed, a national group based in Chicago, testified strongly against Thomas's confirmation. Her opposition to Thomas had grown over the years.

"In the beginning years, we really weren't sure about Clarence

Thomas," she said. "I don't think anyone expected the demise of the agency in the way it took place in the next eight years under his command. We think the bottom line performance profile was dreadful. There was a steady decline in settlements, a building backlog of cases. When he left we were hard pressed to to tell anybody that they should take their case there."

In Thomas's final year the agency had only filed in court seven equal pay for women cases, she said, whereas there were over one hundred in the two previous years.

Civil rights, the issue that dominated Thomas's thinking during his years as EEOC chairman, was hardly raised. The NAACP, although disgruntled by Thomas's politics, did not contest his confirmation. The late Althea Simmons, then the respected chief of the organization's Washington office, was mortally ill. Though Thomas always railed against the civil rights community, at critical moments in his career it stood aside and let him pass.

There were in fact mixed feelings about Thomas in that community. Barry Goldstein, a former staff member of the NAACP Legal Defense Fund, told reporters later that "Thomas was a very hard and conscientious worker" who was "sincerely committed to dealing with problems of discrimination in this country. On the other hand, he has not recognized the importance of affirmative action to overcome the history of discrimination."

Thomas, Goldstein said, had "changed his tune" after Reagan's reelection. "One possibility is that he was being opportunistic—perish the thought that that should happen in Washington—and that he decided to dance to the tune of the person who brung him."

# Chapter 9

Despite criticism of his record, Clarence Thomas was confirmed easily to the appellate court in the spring of 1990. This was the jumping-off point for his Supreme Court nomination sixteen months later. In the sweltering heat of the nation's capital, it seemed Thomas might be able to enjoy a relatively low-key beginning for his September confirmation hearings. He had not been dragged down by the liberal groups sniffing along his lengthy paper trail. The media had taken several nips at him that had left only minor wounds. The civil rights community had not been able to rally effective resistance.

All in all, the White House and the conservative groups were gaining confidence, although they were still wary. Thomas had not taken a vacation, but instead had spent his summer drilling for the hearings with his chief coach, Kenneth Duberstein, and other Republican tacticians. But they couldn't prepare for the unexpected: As one Republican insider had put it, there might have been a dog out there that hadn't yet barked. When it did, the liberals would hear it first.

The Alliance for Justice, the organization with the mission of blocking the appointment of conservatives to the federal judiciary, had heard about a woman professor of law now in Oklahoma who might have some devastating things to say about President Bush's nominee. The first, unconfirmed news about Anita Hill was provided to the Alliance by one of the law professor's woman classmates at Yale, who has remained anonymous. She recounted stories Hill had told her about the painful time she'd had working in Washington, about being sexually harassed by Thomas, who was then her boss. The liberal organization had also heard rumors about another possible victim of Thomas's harassment, but did not immediately contact either woman.

In August, the Alliance for Justice passed on the little bit it knew about Anita Hill—hardly more than a rumor—to the Senate, telling selected members of the staffs of Senator Howard Metzenbaum and Senator Ted Kennedy. Both senators were on the Judiciary Committee, which was scheduled to hold the critical hearings on Thomas the following month. No one working for the Senate rushed to try and verify the snippet of news about Hill: sexual harassment was a difficult issue. The charges being leveled at Thomas, even if they were true, would be hard to prove beyond a shadow of a doubt. In addition, the senators on the Judiciary Committee were all men who—whether Democrats or Republicans—did not, for the most part, comprehend how serious these charges were. They were not expert on the sexual problems suffered by women in the American workplace. The politics of the situation were complex.

At another time, Senator Kennedy would have been a natural person to take the lead in following up on this information. He was a veteran liberal, a champion of equal justice for blacks and women, and had led the successful campaign against Judge Bork. And recently the Massachusetts senator had hired Ricki Seidman, a woman lawyer known as one of the most persistent detectives in the microcosm of Washington politics. On his staff, she was now the investigator. Seidman, although young, knew what she was doing when it came to judicial nominations. She had been legal director of People for the American Way, one of the groups that had played a key role in defeating the Bork nomination. Seidman had the obvious advantage of being a woman and someone who could sympathize with victims of sexual abuse. She was the right person to make the delicate approach to Anita Hill.

But Senator Kennedy and his top legislative aides did not want to touch the issue. The senator didn't feel he was in any position to deal with another man's possible sexual improprieties. Kennedy had been embarrassed by a night of drinking and cavorting at the Kennedy compound in Palm Beach that ended with a woman alleging that his nephew had raped her. Senator Kennedy feared that he would be ridiculed trying to bring up charges of sexual harassment. With the trial of his nephew, William Kennedy Smith, imminent, the senator decided to keep his profile as low as possible.

The staff of Senator Metzenbaum were initially more receptive to the information. Just as liberal as Kennedy, Metzenbaum is known for speaking his mind. He was no friend of Thomas. He had spoken up loudly about Thomas's management of the EEOC and voted against him when he was up for his first judicial nomination. But the senator's staff moved cautiously and slowly on what little was known about Hill and her charges. Most people holding office on Capitol Hill, or even working there, are skittish about making use of personal information. It can backfire, and come across as dirty tricks. Moreover, Senator Kennedy was not the only politician who had been publicly chagrined about his own private conduct.

Senator Metzenbaum, a millionaire businessman, had learned the hard way. After he helped push through a special prosecutor's investigation of Ed Meese, who was attorney general designate at the time, the senator got into trouble himself. Meese had been taking hefty loans from people who later got government jobs; but it soon came out that Senator Metzenbaum also had a problem with his personal financial dealings. He had taken a $250,000 finder's fee for facilitating the sale of a Washington hotel, and was forced by bad publicity to return the money, while denying he had committed any impropriety.

Another factor slowing any senatorial investigation of Hill's allegations was the sheer volume of work that had yet to be done on Thomas. The staff of every senator on the Judiciary Committee was swamped. There were hundreds of Thomas's speeches to be read and digested so that senators could be provided a firm base of information from which to argue for or against the nominee. And there was the usual flurry of nasty rumors that occurs whenever a controversial figure appears under the Washington political spotlight. Those had to be sorted out. Hill's allegations might be just one of these flurries; no one knew for certain at this point.

The legislative aides who deal with judicial nominations for Senator

Metzenbaum, William Corr and Christopher J. Harvie, decided not to tackle the sensitive issue of Anita Hill themselves. Instead, they passed the task to Gail Laster, a young black lawyer on the staff of the senator's subcommittee who handled issues of the elderly. Laster, being both black and female, might be better qualified than anyone else to get a response from Hill.

Journalists like me who worked on the Thomas nomination through the summer were inundated with both paper and rumors. Overburdened was a good description of my desk in the Washington bureau of *Newsday,* an office whose location on Pennsylvania Avenue placed it literally in the middle of the political maneuvering over Thomas. Catercorner to the Justice Department and right next to FBI headquarters, I was about halfway between the White House and the senators' office buildings on Capitol Hill. The desk was covered with stacks of the nominee's speeches, piles of information about the EEOC, and heaps of other documents about Thomas, the Supreme Court and the Senate. The files I had started on various aspects of Thomas's life, career, philosophy, and political connections were mushrooming daily, spilling out of the file drawers. Anita Hill was one bit of information among many others that I set out to investigate.

In the meantime, bitter memories about the death of the Bork nomination were rallying the conservative movement. The highly politicized campaign against the ultraconservative judge, including the unprecedented series of anti-Bork television advertisements run by People for the American Way, had changed the judicial confirmation process fundamentally—and not for the better. The distinguished third branch of government, heretofore at least a step away from the political fray, had been dragged down to the level of the political campaign and the sound bite.

The Republicans in the White House and others in the conservative movement had been caught flatfooted by the concerted attacks on Bork, not all of them accurate or fair. It would not happen again. Bork had been their champion, the embodiment of a passionate belief in the evils of activist judges imposing their liberal social agenda on the country. They knew no one more qualified than Judge Bork, in terms of legal credentials and intelligence, to sit on the Supreme Court. They blamed his failed nomination on politics, and dirty politics at that.

It was, in fact, politics that motivated the opposition to Judge Bork—Republican politics. President Reagan had nominated Judge Bork as part of an effort to pack the Supreme Court with conservatives of the far right. This is what catalyzed the fight. Many senators, in recent decades, had come to believe that they owed the president deference in judicial nominations, and should vote against his choices only when a terrible error in judgment had been made. But given President Reagan's political move with Judge Bork in 1987, the Senate reasserted its constitutional responsibility to "advise and consent" on Supreme Court nominees. If the senators withheld their collective consent, a nominee wouldn't make it.

The Constitution provides ample legal coverage for anyone who wanted to do more than simply review a nominee's resume. In fact, the framers of the Constitution originally had drafted a plan to give the Senate the power of judicial appointment, then altered it to give a say to both the president and the senators. This, of course, left the system open to confrontation over judicial nominations, particularly those for the Supreme Court. In the last century, before the senators began to shy away from such confrontations, they rejected roughly one out of every four names sent up by the president for the high court.

Thomas was no Bork. He certainly was no constitutional scholar and his political philosophy had not been stable, comparable rather to the weight at the end of a pendulum swinging from the far left to the extreme right. By the time he was nominated, Thomas had swung further right than most people knew, or even imagined.

In the record of his speeches, it was possible to follow his philosophy rightward. He addressed establishment groups of right-wing activists and won them over. He had also made unpublicized visits to more controversial groups that, had they been discovered the summer of the nomination, certainly would have subjected him to an intense round of questioning from the Senate Judiciary Committee.

While Thomas was still chairman of the EEOC, he paid a private visit to a closed meeting at the national headquarters of the radical, religious New Right. The headquarters, which houses various coalitions, was run by Paul Weyrich, a former journalist well-known around the capital for unswerving dedication to the cause. He had helped found the Heritage Foundation and given the Moral Majority its name. Weyrich, a master political strategist, had adopted the organizational tactics he had observed being used by the left back in its political heyday. He had organized coalitions of New Right groups that brought together the *crème de la crème* of the conservative extremist movement.

Weyrich called his first coalition the Kingston Group. From there, he branched out, creating other coalitions with more specific interests like Library Court, which specialized in social issues, and the Stanton Group, which consisted of organizations interested in foreign policy. Thomas, in meetings both before and after he joined the Supreme Court, was to develop a special relationship with these organizations.

The one common denominator among most of the groups focusing on social policy was their opposition to abortion. Among them were the National Right to Life Committee, and the most extreme of the anti-abortion groups, the American Life Lobby, which considers abortion to be murder in every instance. The group allows no exceptions, whether it be to save the life of the mother, or the psychic life of a rape or incest victim. The leader of American Life Lobby, Judie Brown, is opposed additionally to birth control.

The groups in Weyrich's coalitions also crusade for prayer in the schools and against gay rights, women's rights and pornography; the members tend to be fundamentalist or evangelical Christians. Weyrich's tactical skills are evident in his uniting of these religious conservatives, though they are of opposing denominations, even teaming Baptists with Catholics.

These are not traditional conservatives, content with the current order, letting the power and perquisites of the upper classes dominate the social economy; rather these are radicals, intent on imposing conservative social values on the rest of the country through political warfare.

Back in 1980, Weyrich described the then emerging far-right campaign as "a war of ideology, . . . a war of ideas, and . . . a war about our way of life. We are different from previous generations of conservatives. We are no longer working to preserve the status quo. We are radicals, working to overturn the present power structures of this country."

For the Washington jobs concerning domestic policy that the Republican White House allocated to the New Right, the support of Weyrich's coalitions was essential. For example, when William Bennett was seeking the nomination as secretary of education in 1984, he submitted to what newspaper accounts called an ideological screening at Library Court, named after the address near the the Library of Congress where representatives of the coalition originally held biweekly meetings.

Thomas engaged in a similar process when he was still hoping for his first promotion out of the morass he found himself in at the EEOC. At the first of three meetings with Weyrich's pro-life groups, Thomas provided the assurances they wanted.

"Our people felt that they knew him and he was one of us," said Tom Jipping, who handles the tactics of judicial appointments for the right-wing. Jipping, one of Weyrich's chief aides, had backed Thomas from the time of his 1989 nomination to the court of appeals. In Jipping's opinion, neither Bork, a man from the aloof world of academia, nor Souter, from the mountains of New Hampshire, was "one of us" in the same sense that Thomas was.

Weyrich's coalitions had pushed the White House hard to have Thomas named to his first judgeship and then went to work to make sure he was confirmed to the appellate court. Jipping and others had expected another Bork-like battle at the time; it never materialized because the civil rights groups backed off. Jipping had had the opportunity to get to know Thomas well during that first confirmation process.

"I found him to be a very frank person," Jipping said of Thomas in an interview. Jipping is a man of thirty, who dresses in conservative blue suits, and keeps his hair neatly trimmed and papers neatly stacked in a cramped office lined with law books in a new building near the railroad tracks of Union Station. He speaks with passion about Clarence Thomas.

"He's somebody who has learned a great deal from his experiences in life," Jipping said. "He has a strong religious faith and lives his life on the basis of that faith. But he came to that appreciation of his faith through a very difficult life. He is a very inquisitive person, who desires to learn about everything. He is not caught up in the particular denomination he belongs to. He would identify himself as a Christian before he'd identify himself as a Catholic or an Episcopalian because he's come to his beliefs through his own searching and through prayer and studying the Bible himself."

In a major breach of judicial propriety, Judge Thomas returned to Library Court for a meeting several months after his confirmation to the appellate court to personally thank the members of the group for their support. It was a political appearance by a judge in front of a group with an ambitious legal agenda he would surely be called to rule on. (Thomas showed no more deference to propriety once he gained his seat on the Supreme Court, meeting again with the group).

The courting of Library Court had paid off for Thomas; not only did the right-wing coalition again provide the backing to get the big nomination when Thurgood Marshall resigned, its groups provided the funds, the people, and the energy to conduct a grassroots political campaign aimed at getting him confirmed. The left had shown the way with its campaign against Bork; the right would follow it with a campaign for Thomas involving conservatives who ran the gamut from White House officials to members of groups far removed from the norms of the American polity.

To coordinate support for Clarence Thomas, these New Right organizations—almost all of them members of Library Court—held weekly meetings at the Pennsylvania Avenue offices of the Family Research Council. The purpose of these meetings was to coordinate the efforts of each individual group. Thomas and his wife, Virginia, had dropped in for a tour of the offices when the council first moved there in 1989. This had been another gesture by Thomas toward the radical right groups who increasingly held the balance of power in judicial appointments.

The Family Research Council is a conservative think tank and lobbying group that focuses on opposition to abortion as well as efforts to improve child care and eliminate pornography. It is headed by Gary L. Bauer, who served in the Reagan administration, ultimately as the domestic policy adviser.

The strategy sessions for the Thomas nomination were attended by an array of groups on the political fringe, the best known of which was Phyllis Schlafly's Eagle Forum. This organization centered itself around a crusade against the Equal Rights Amendment for women, and spun off from there.

Schlafly once said the atom bomb was "a marvelous gift given to our country by a wise God" and maintained that sexual harassment was not a real problem because "men hardly ever ask sexual favors of women from whom the certain answer is no." The group is against sex education in the schools and sends out literature warning about "The ERA-Gay-AIDS Connection." Its writing labeled the ERA as a "gay rights amendment for homosexuals" and fulminated that the ERA would leave citizens unprotected from the "gay plague." The Eagle Forum went as far as to attack a public school education program on the Holocaust as child abuse in the classroom because it upset the students.

But Schlafly's group was tamer than that of Beverly LaHaye, a minister's wife who organized hundreds of thousands of housewives to fight the feminists. LaHaye's Concerned Women for America was another regular participant in the pro-Thomas meetings. LaHaye believed that "the woman who is truly Spirit-filled will want to be totally submissive to her husband. . . . This is a truly liberated woman. Submission is God's design for women."

LaHaye, who has been described as "the born-again alternative to Phyllis Schlafly," does not accept the constitutionally ordered separation of church and state. "Yes, religion and politics do mix," she said. "America is a nation based on biblical principles. Christian values should dominate our government. The test of those values is the Bible. Politicians who do not use the Bible to guide their public and private lives do not belong in office."

Not all the participants were women's groups. The Rev. Louis Sheldon's Coalition for Traditional Values was also represented at the strategy meetings. Sheldon, known as the California Jerry Falwell, is a creationist who fights abortion and gay rights.

These strategy sessions on the Thomas nomination were also regularly attended by two officials from the White House—Leigh Ann Metzger and Lee Liberman.

Metzger is a special assistant to the President in the Office of Public Liaison, the official contact person in the White House for conservative and religious groups. Liberman, who had been a key player in the Thomas nomination, is a shy intellectual lawyer who made sure she was unknown to the public and most of the press. Just thirty-five years old, she'd risen meteorically to a position where she was one of a handful of people shaping the nation's legal agenda.

Liberman never submits to interviews; she is a shadowy but potent figure. Under White House counsel Boyden Gray, Liberman has become the in-house expert on selecting judicial nominees. She pursues the task with a singlemindedness admired by most of those with whom she works. Liberman is a libertarian, someone who subscribes to a philosophy valuing individual rights above all else.

Utterly devoted to her job in the counsel's office, Liberman dispenses advice to her boss not only on judiciary but also on legislative issues like civil rights. She opposes affirmative action programs with a vehemence. Her liberal opponents have described her as a "right-wing Rasputin" bent on pushing the White House ever more toward the far edge of conservatism.

Liberman has conservative intellectual roots. She studied at the University of Chicago under Antonin Scalia and later worked for the conservative academic when he became an appellate court judge and then a Supreme Court justice, serving twice as one of his law clerks. This was a job that would cement their philosophical ties. Justice Scalia also was a philosophical hero of Clarence Thomas, who often praised him as he moved rightward. It was, therefore, no surprise that Thomas made Liberman's list. What was surprising was that the radical right had become so involved in the Thomas nomination, that White House officials were participating in an essentially political campaign by fringe groups to confirm a nominee to the high court.

But the loss of Bork had changed the rules. In some very real ways the right-wing campaign for Clarence Thomas's confirmation had begun in early 1989, a few months after Bork's defeat and before Thomas's nomination to the Court of Appeals. Activists across the conservative spectrum were talking about getting ready by finding Supreme Court candidates like Thomas, getting to know them, and preparing strategies for a politicized fight.

"Conservatives said after Bork, 'never again,' " Jipping said. "If we're going to lose again it is going to be after we gave it everything that we could. We're not going to repeat the too little, too late strategy."

"I had been in the Reagan White House during the Bork fiasco," recalled Bauer, who still sports a Reagan tie clip, "and I remember at the time thinking to myself, 'If I ever have a chance to do something about it, I'll never let something like this happen to another good nominee.' I'm a conservative who believes in tradition in the larger sense of that word. I think it's a real shame that Supreme Court nominations have come to this. But I think it would be an even greater tragedy if one side used one set of rules—that is, if the liberals approached Supreme Court nominations as if they were election battles—while conservatives sat around dotting i's and crossing t's and acting like it was an eighteenth century exercise in civility."

That Bauer did not do. He launched his own Citizens' Committee to Confirm Clarence Thomas campaign, which raised half a million dollars. Much of that money was spent on television advertising attacking Bauer's liberal counterparts for mudslinging. The ads literally showed mud being thrown at the face of Clarence Thomas. They ran mostly in Alabama, Georgia, Mississippi, North Carolina, and Louisiana, with the aim of putting pressure on the crucial Southern Democrats. Bauer kept the White House informed of what he was doing, but informally outside working hours; the White House did not want to be publicly identified with these far-right efforts for Thomas.

Bauer also supported an organization that called itself the African-American Freedom Alliance. It took out newspaper advertisements in black newspapers all through the South. The full-page ads asked: "We marched for freedom. So why don't we have the freedom to march to a different beat?" This group twisted the well-known rhetoric of the civil rights movement to favor Thomas, its greatest black critic. "Like Bull Connor, they [the liberal groups] are siccing the dogs on an innocent man [Thomas]," the ads proclaimed. The fact that Bauer's lily-white organization had provided $100,000 cash and the office space for this organization was not noted in its literature appealing to black solidarity.

The campaign to push the Thomas nomination, when all the behind-the-scenes efforts were tallied, was far more significant than anything that the opposition was able to muster. None of the liberal groups on the other side—People for the American Way, Alliance for Justice or the Leadership Conference on Civil Rights—could match the pro-Thomas effort. The biggest spender for Thomas was not one of the more traditional conservative groups, or even the passionate Bauer: it was a group whose involvement was practically unknown at the time—the Christian Coalition, a new organization based in Virginia Beach, Virginia, started by fundamentalist preacher Pat Robertson.

Robertson, renowned for his nationwide and worldwide network of charismatic Christians, had ties to Thomas's church in Virginia. Robertson was extremely enthusiastic about the prospect of Thomas joining the Supreme Court and ruling on the nation's constitutional issues, he said in an interview. Thomas, if his choice of a church was any guide, was a fellow charismatic.

Robertson spent more than one million dollars on Thomas's behalf, according to the figuring of Tom Jipping, who assisted the minister with his pro-Thomas campaign. This was several times the outlay of all the liberal groups. With this money, Robertson's Christian Coalition produced a television commercial, which literally surrounded Thomas with an image of the American flag. Jipping said it generated more than one hundred thousand letters, telephone calls, and telegrams to the Senate from Americans who liked the superpatriot image.

By 1991, members of the liberal coalition—the unions, the civil rights groups, the public-interest lobbying groups—had begun to look inward. Was busing a good thing after all? Was it true that only racists oppose it? Was welfare creating a dependent class? Was it dangerous to alienate the white middle-class by bumping its members from jobs for lesser qualified blacks? Was black society being hurt by that process?

"In '87, when Bork came up, we had been paved over by Reagan and we were convinced we were right," said a lawyer working for the anti-Thomas coalition. He compared the Bork and Thomas nominations. "Now, when we talk about race and issues related to it, we are less confident we have the answers. Also this time, we didn't have Kennedy making a speech as he did on Bork. The intensity of ideological opposition to Thomas wasn't there."

While the conservative groups were spending hundreds of thousands of dollars on ads and grassroots efforts for Thomas, in August 1991 the coalition was struggling to mount a campaign with a few thousands dollars here and there. People For the American Way, which had spent $684,000 on advertising against Bork, had no money for ads in 1991, a reflection in part of liberalism's loss of appeal. But it also reflected confusion and dissent within the coalition over how to oppose a conservative black man.

"Thomas is articulate, he has an extreme ideology—but not everything Thomas articulates on racial issues is wrong," John Gomperts, a lawyer working for People for The American Way, said. "The liberals were a little flummoxed. Thomas never said one line that was so hideous that the liberals could coalesce around it."

In fact there was sharp disagreement within the liberal camp about which issues to focus on. There were a lot of important questions about Thomas, but a campaign against him needed a theme. Thomas's opposition to affirmative action—a key reason why some of the groups opposed him—was a nonstarter because it would not sell politically. One obvious issue was Thomas's lack of qualifications; he had only practiced law for five years. But civil rights groups had always campaigned against establishing qualifications for jobs that black people could not meet. The NAACP, for instance, had no appetite for using the issue against Thomas, even though it was by then in offical opposition to the nomination.

Perhaps the strongest political issue against Thomas was his apparent position against abortion. Here, too, the black groups demurred. Many of the ministers active in the NAACP were fervently opposed to abortion, an issue on which the organization had taken no stand. As a whole, the liberal coalition was not about to spring into a battle led by women's groups under the banner of abortion.

Another issue—one with middle-class, middle-of-the-road appeal, unlike the others—was Thomas's failure while EEOC chairman to enforce the age-discrimination laws. But the White House got there first. It had lobbied the board of directors of the powerful American Association of Retired Persons (AARP), which was on record already as being unhappy with Thomas's performance at the equal employment agency.

The White House was anxious about the retirees' association taking a position against Thomas, not only because of its political omnipresence—it has constituents everywhere there are old people—but also because it had unusual influence over one particular senator on the Judiciary Committee. Dennis DeConcini, the conservative Democrat from Arizona, whose vote on Thomas was unpredictable and potentially crucial if the committee was closely divided when it came time to vote. Humidity-free and sunshine-filled Arizona is a mecca for retirees. The White House made full use of its best ally on the association board, a black who according to a White House source was very pro-Thomas. The Bush administration also recalled and dusted off

Thomas's old ties to the Catholic community to try to put pressure on the association's executive director, Horace Deets, who had been a priest.

The staff of AARP, which has tremendous clout on Capitol Hill, hated Thomas's politics and pushed the board to oppose him. Members of the staff believed that Thomas had betrayed his responsibilities to older Americans by letting thousands of their discrimination cases expire. But the staff could not fight the conservative tendency of the association's vast membership. Furthermore, the association could not easily afford to alienate Thomas's avid supporter, Senator Danforth, a politican who was crucial to passage of legislation benefiting the elderly. Given this and the common wisdom through the summer that Thomas would probably win confirmation, the association decided to pass on the issue. Had it done otherwise, Thomas might have been defeated. As it was, the anti-Thomas coalition kept casting about for a unifying issue with which to contrive a potent message.

"We were not coherent. There was no message management," said one of the liberal strategists. "It's hard because you have all these groups with their senior people involved all in it for different reasons. The dirty truth is that to some degree or another we compete a little bit. We compete for dollars, we compete for notoriety, we compete for respect."

"It was a central failing on our part," agreed Nan Aron, of the Alliance for Justice. "There was no overriding theme that united our opposition. The White House had its spin of his history and struggle over poverty, that he would bring a special perspective to the Supreme Court. We never put forth a competing group of ideas."

In the Bork campaign, Aron said, the women's groups were willing to melt in with the others. But in the Thomas campaign, with the fear that *Roe* v. *Wade* was in imminent danger of being overturned, the pro-choice groups felt their concerns were paramount. Initially anyway, they did not coordinate well this time around with black groups, which were headed by men.

Aron continued a lengthy analysis: "The country was not the same in 1991 as it was in 1987, with quotas and affirmative action being confusing and negative issues for segments of the population. Civil rights did not have the same cachet. You had Willie Horton and a constant barrage from the White House of criticism of civil rights. The civil rights community was embattled when Thomas was nominated. Issues like civil rights were a death knell. Affirmative action was a death knell. Women's rights had more impact. You had the economy. It was a whole different climate. With Bork, the enthusiasm was there from day one from the national groups.

"With Thomas, people's immediate reaction was to like him, to feel sympathetic, to admire him. We were dealing with a totally different symbol. It made organizing much more difficult. Because of the White House campaign, we were approaching people who felt favorably toward the nominee. There was a constant barrage of pr from the White House or Danforth. The NAACP, if you had gotten that machine oiled up from the beginning, might have made the difference. There wasn't that much interest in the black community, but the NAACP could have gotten the unions and women's groups interested, and people in the South. The Southern Democrats are the ones who are basically undecided on controversial social issues like judgeships—they are critical to forming a majority in the Senate and they are the ones who are hardest to get for us."

Eventually the groups did coalesce around a combination of women's rights, civil rights, privacy rights, and the right to choose abortions. NAACP officials even teamed up with women's groups to appear with anti-Thomas arguments before newspaper editorial boards. But the NAACP never put on the "full-court press" that Hooks had promised at the press conference in Washington earlier in the summer.

The NAACP has an extensive network of local chapters, including many in the South where the organization's influence, in the Thomas case, was most crucial. But this grassroots potential wasn't used. Wade Henderson's carefully crafted report, which had so angered Hooks, wasn't even distributed among the chapters.

In the end, the organization bumbled into helping Thomas with a public disagreement over his nomination. The quarrel began when the NAACP officers of a branch in Compton, California, endorsed Thomas in defiance of the national board's decision, whereupon a middle-level official at the organization's national headquarters in Baltimore threatened to suspend the errant officers unless they rescinded their endorsement. Several days of bad publicity for the NAACP and good publicity for Thomas ensued before a compromise was reached.

The liberal group that mounted the strongest lobbying effort was the National Abortion Rights Action League (NARAL). The organization's members knew that Thomas on the Supreme Court might well mean an end to federal support for abortion. NARAL spent more than $100,000 on television commercials featuring the gathering legal attack on abortion rights—but not mentioning Thomas by name. It took out newspaper advertisements against Thomas and sent postcards to five hundred thousand of its members to fill out for delivery to their senators.

While NARAL's efforts were extensive and started immediately upon Thomas's nomination, most other liberal efforts were relatively paltry or belated, beginning only in late August. People for the American Way used only its existing staff in five small national offices to try and drum up opposition. The Alliance for Justice and the Leadership Conference on Civil Rights together hired half a dozen grassroots organizers with the hope of turning public opinion across the country against Thomas. They put them in key states—most of them states with senators who were undecided members of the Judiciary Committee. They contacted local liberal groups, organized press conferences denouncing Thomas, and asked people close to the targeted senators to use their persuasion. As for the unions, only the American Federation of State, County and Municipal Employes and the United Auto Workers were engaged at all in the move to keep Thomas off the high court. The mighty AFL-CIO seemed to have geared its tactics to the ultimately trivial issue of securing a prominent spot in the upcoming hearings for the testimony of its president, Lane Kirkland.

On the other side of the struggle over Thomas's nomination, the conservatives had an invaluable asset, the President of the country. That summer Thomas was the frequent beneficiary of praise in the speeches of President Bush. Early in August, the President recycled a charge that the liberal coalition had used four years earlier against Bork, when they maintained that the nominee's philosophy was outside the mainstream of American public opinion. By 1991, the President was able to claim that the opposite was true about the newest conservative nominee:

"Judge Thomas has tremendous support from a broad section, a cross section, of America. And that across-the-board support includes

minority communities, overwhelmingly supported in minority communities, I might add, and it's now manifesting itself in measurable ways. So when you hear about opposition to Judge Thomas from one [Washington] group or another, it's clear that they are simply out of touch with mainstream America."

If the early polls on Thomas were a valid indicator, Bush was right. Blacks as well as whites supported Thomas. Or they supported the man presented to them so skillfully by the White House. The question the liberal coalition wanted John Q. Citizen to ask was, was Clarence Thomas really that man?

But Bush clearly had the liberals on the defensive. Affirmative action, which to white liberals and established black leaders was synonymous with civil rights and political morality, was now a political albatross. It had been hung around the necks of liberals by Jesse Helms and George Bush. It had been hung around the necks of black leaders by Clarence Thomas; his very popularity in the black community seemed proof that his self-help, no-special-treatment message had a new appeal.

President Bush had become accomplished at playing the politics of race, making his stands one way or another, depending upon the political context. During the summer of the Thomas nomination, the President followed the advice of Boyden Gray and rejected a compromise on the new civil rights legislation that Senator Danforth had put together. President Bush objected to a provision outlawing educational requirements for employment in jobs where education was not needed—a practice frequently used to keep out blacks. But the rationale the President used was ludicrous—the provision he found objectionable would undermine the nation's schools by deemphasizing education in hiring, he claimed. Even the mild-tempered Danforth ridiculed the President's argument, saying at a press conference that it could only be valid "if you believe that an employer on his own is going to further educational policy by shutting out fifty-year-old people who never got a high school diploma."

During the whole of his political career, George Bush had had a mixed and conflicting record on civil rights. During his moderate phase, Bush at first opposed but then voted for the 1966 open-housing bill. Running for the Senate in Texas in 1970, he campaigned for the black vote on a platform that included a plan to make companies and

unions with government contracts set up goals and timetables for hiring minorities. Upon his nomination as vice president in 1980, he reverted to the racial politics he had used when he first ran for the Senate in 1964, when Barry Goldwater was his party's standard bearer. Then Bush had energetically opposed the landmark civil rights bill, which included a ban on segregation in public places, such as restaurants and bathrooms. In the wake of the March on Washington headed by Martin Luther King, Bush was yelling in campaign speeches about "extremist groups" like the NAACP. He also railed against "militants" like Dr. King.

This all came from the same George Bush, a man who sometimes played politics first and worried about integrity later. He was the presidential candidate who had cynically benefited from the racial fears raised by the Willie Horton television ad. Bush was the president who nominated a black man to the Supreme Court and then insisted he had not paid attention to his skin color when making the choice. He also had spoken disingenuously when he declared his nominee the best qualified candidate for the job: this was one presidential claim that was investigated properly.

At the end of August, the American Bar Association reported on Thomas as part of its standard practice; through a committee of its members, it reviews and rates the qualifications of all judicial nominations, usually in cooperation with whatever administration is in the White House. The bar association's rating is highly regarded. Clarence Thomas received what was arguably the worst rating ever given to a Supreme Court nominee.

The bar association has three ratings: well qualified, qualified, and unqualified. It has never rated anyone nominated for the Supreme Court unqualified. Almost always, the association's committee has rated Supreme Court nominees as well qualified, usually unanimously so.

The ABA committee nevertheless rated Thomas as only qualified, with two of the fifteen members voting for not qualified and one not participating. Members of additional reading committees asked to evaluate Thomas's legal writing found it "disappointing." Not one of the members of the committee said that Thomas was well qualified.

Thomas's rating might have been even worse if the committee had

not felt itself under pressure to avoid the kind of controversy it had suffered during the Bork nomination. Judge Bork had received the well-qualified rating from a majority of the committee. But four of the bar association members on his rating committee had voted him not qualified, saying his ideological fervor was not compatible with the judicial temperment required of a Supreme Court justice. A fifth voted not opposed. The split verdict created a furor that fueled the opposition to Bork and alienated the Bush administration, which said the bar association had let politics muddy its rating. For a time, the White House suspended cooperation with the association.

It was—or should have been—a stunning blow to Thomas. Even G. Harrold Carswell, the unsuccessful Nixon nominee whose defenders were reduced to asserting the value of mediocrity, had received a unanimous qualified rating. But the White House handled Thomas's rating beautifully. Instead of fuming with indignation, as it had over Bork's much better rating, it asserted that it was pleased that the bar association had found Thomas qualified. "We are very pleased that the ABA's Standing Committee on the Federal Judiciary has found Judge Thomas qualified to be an Associate Justice of the United States Supreme Court," said Marlin Fitzwater, the president's spokesman, at the summer White House in Kennebunkport. "As the president stated here two months ago, Judge Thomas has excelled in everything he has attempted, and the President is confident that Judge Thomas will serve on the Court with distinction."

Without a fuss from the White House, the media didn't make a major point out of Thomas's relatively unsatisfactory rating. The bar association's language also made it difficult to tell the story. How could it be explained within the straitjacket confines of daily journalism, that when the ABA said qualified, it really meant barely acceptable. To most people, qualified sounds like an endorsement.

What did rate media attention—a week before the start of the all-important Judiciary Committee hearings—was a political advertisement produced by Floyd Brown, the creator of the notorious Willie Horton commercial, a man who describes himself as a conservative's version of Jesse Jackson. Brown reassembled the same team that put together the ad on Horton that derailed Michael Dukakis's presidential bid in 1988. When he called Tony Fabrizio, a consultant in suburban Alexandria, he found his former collaborator ready.

In a subsequent and very telling memo, Fabrizio warned Brown not to fight for Thomas based on his record:

"I am convinced that if we fight this battle on Judge Thomas's alleged positions on specific issues, we open ourselves to an unwinnable battle. I recommend that our message define the argument in terms of President Bush and Judge Thomas versus the liberal hypocrites who will judge Clarence Thomas's fitness to serve on the Supreme Court."

Brown and his conservative collaborators had been waiting for the next big ideological struggle after the defeat of Judge Bork. They had been raising money through direct-mail solicitations, and had it waiting to be funneled into a right-wing cause. Thomas was the cause.

Brown's television ad promoted Thomas by bashing his most obvious potential opponents in the Senate. The ad first appeared on Labor Day weekend, after it was purposely leaked in advance to garner extra attention. The recipient of the leak was a conservative journalist, Fred Barnes, who had news of the ad in time for his appearance on a Sunday television talk show that all of political Washington would follow.

The television spot attacked Senator Kennedy, dredging up the old embarrassments about his suspension from Harvard for cheating and his departure from the scene of an accident on Martha's Vineyard where a young woman died in his car. It threw in the latest scandal at Palm Beach as well, flashing a shot of the cover of a newspaper tabloid headlined TEDDY'S SEXY ROMP. Brown could not have known that, at the moment this ad was being designed, Senator Kennedy had in his hands a lead to Anita Hill.

The ad also targeted Senator Joseph Biden, the Judiciary Committee chairman, and Alan Cranston, a liberal Democrat from California who was not a member of the Judiciary Committee. Senator Cranston had been vilified for his involvement in the savings-and-loan scandal. Senator Biden was criticized for a humiliating episode of plagiarism that had forced him to withdraw three years before from a bid for the presidency. The television spot said little about Thomas, but was meant to be "a shot across the bow" of the liberals to get them to lay off of Thomas.

Despite later denials, Brown said the White House knew about the ad before it was aired. It was produced at the facilities of the Republican party's National Republican Congressional Committee, cutting costs on production that allowed more of the $80,000 budget to be spent on airtime.

But the broadcasting of the ad genuinely horrified Thomas's main handlers, Senator Danforth and Kenneth Duberstein. Senator Biden had been cooperative up until then, and they figured there was a good chance of getting his vote. The ad also created a partisan atmosphere—conservatives against liberals, Republicans against Democrats—at a time when the two men were intent on building bipartisan support for Thomas. Both President Bush and Thomas disavowed the ad, but the episode raised in senators' minds the question of why Thomas was enjoying so much support from the radical right.

Not everyone at the White House agreed with Duberstein, who was already being criticized in conservative Republican circles for being too conciliatory to the Democrats. But the White House announced that Bush had ordered John Sununu, his chief of staff, to call Brown and his fellow sponsor, Brent Bozell, to ask for a halt in the broadcasting of the derogatory ad. But Sununu made it perfectly clear in the conversation that the discussion was simply for the record.

"Sununu called Brent up and said, 'Brent, we understand that you have a job and I hope you understand that I have a job and my job is to let you know that the President wants you to pull these ads. So, I'm glad you know what your job is. I have my job.' I think Sununu loved our ads," Brown said.

Brown and Bozell refused. Why should they stop when they were getting so much free publicity for their cause, themselves and their organizations. The ad was airing only in local programs, but the gist of it was picked up on national network news shows.

"We like being attacked, because when we're being attacked by the establishment, our donors like it, they send us more money. We're having impact and we're doing what we wanted to do from the very beginning, which is to pull the spectrum right," Brown declared.

In the midst of the various efforts to keep Thomas off or get him on the high court, the nominee ignored judicial protocol and pursued his own campaign. It was almost unprecedented and certainly unseemly

for a Supreme Court nominee to lobby. But Thomas took on the black
community, particularly the black civil rights people he had so often
criticized.

Thomas "was his own best strategist and he was his own chief
strategist," said a well-placed source in the White House. "His idea of
strategy was to mobilize the grassroots, split the black community, get
out his story and mobilize outside groups into support."

One of the main focuses of Thomas's attention, and everyone else's,
was Alabama. This was so largely because that state's senior senator,
Howell Heflin, a Judiciary Committee member, might vote either way.
Another key vote in the full Senate—if the nomination came down to
a struggle on the Senate floor—was Heflin's Alabama protégé, Senator
Richard Shelby.

A few weeks before the Judiciary Committee hearings, Thomas
met in Washington with a delegation of black Democrats from Alabama. There were eight people in that delegation, but the only one
who really mattered was Joe Reed, the kingpin of black politics in
Alabama. Reed was close to Heflin, and had helped elect Shelby, the
junior senator. While other black groups in Alabama had almost all
come out against Thomas, Reed's Alabama Democratic Caucus had
not yet said a word.

At the time of that meeting both Clarence Thomas and the White
House were in a potential position to help Joe Reed on an issue close
to his heart and political soul. Reed's power base was Alabama State
University, an all-black college in Montgomery. The college had been
established after the slaves were freed so that Alabama whites would
not have to go to school with blacks. Reed was the chairman of the
college's board and controlled its hiring.

But by 1991, far into the era of integration, the school was under
pressure. Its facilities and teaching staff were inferior to the state's
white colleges, and some even thought it should close. Reed wanted to
keep his power base at the college, and he needed all the help he could
muster in Washington. The Supreme Court was scheduled to hear a
case later in the year that would decide the future of the historically
black colleges, the prime vestiges of the "separate but equal" system.
The Justice Department had taken a stand against the black schools,
and Reed wanted that position changed. He also knew that Thomas
had taken a strong stand in favor of perpetuating the black schools

when he was at the civil rights office in the Department of Education.

The meeting between the nominee and his fellow Southerners was held at the Washington headquarters of a black sorority, Delta Sigma Theta. The Alabama group was served lunch at the sorority and came downstairs to the conference room when Thomas arrived. There were no whites in the meeting, which appeared to make Thomas nervous.

"Clarence was *really* nervous," said Bobbie McDowell, an Alabama state representative. "He was so still, almost statue-like. Like terrified. But the longer we talked and asked questions, the more he loosened up. You see, he knew the brothers and the sisters were going to give him a hard time. The idea of his humble beginnings wasn't going to cut it so much with us."

McDowell wanted to ask Thomas about what he had said about welfare and his sister, Emma Mae Martin, eleven years earlier.

"I wanted him to respond about the harsh criticism he had made of his sister," she said. "Clarence didn't answer questions so much as tell stories. He said he had been horrified when the story broke. He called his family and his sister to apologize."

McDowell also wanted to get a grip on Thomas's politics. "What we wanted to know is, 'Are you good for black folks? Can we depend on you when you get to the court? Have you forgotten your blackness?' "

Thomas responded by talking about Myers Anderson and how the oil business of his grandfather, tough as he was, was dependent on white people for its license. Thomas told the delegation that he had decided back then he would work in the public arena to help people like his grandfather.

"He said, 'I'm a black man. I'm under no illusions about that. I'm a black man. Someone once said, if I get on the Court, I'd follow other justices, but I'm my own man,' " remembers Jerome Grey, another of the delegation members.

At one point during the meeting, Thomas grew angry when asked about a commonplace speculation, that once on the Supreme Court, he would be sucked under the influence of the intellectually powerful Justice Scalia.

"Scalia is a man like any other man, and I bow to no man," Thomas declared.

Several among the delegation were curious as to why Thomas had not brought his wife, Virginia, but none dared ask. Thomas's marriage to a white woman had drawn resentment from the black community, particularly from black women.

The session lasted well over the scheduled hour, and ended with a photo session of the Alabamans with the nominee. Many, although not all of the delegation members, came away impressed with Thomas. Joe Reed never did take a position on the nomination, which was exactly what Thomas and the White House wanted.

Meanwhile, Gail Laster, the lawyer on Metzenbaum's staff, had finally telephoned Anita Hill. She hit it off well with the Oklahoma law professor, finding out that they had friends in common. But when Laster managed to work the conversation around to asking about sexual harassment and Clarence Thomas, Hill was not forthcoming. The law professor said that she didn't know anything, but that sexual harassment was worth looking into. Her response was ambiguous. Given so little encouragement, Metzenbaum's staff decided there were more important things to do.

About the same time, Ricki Seidman on Senator Kennedy's staff also reached Hill and similarly asked her about the sexual harassment rumor. Seidman made more progress with Hill. She told Seidman she wanted more time to think and promised to call the Kennedy aide back.

As I was pursuing my own work on the Thomas nomination, I also spoke with Anita Hill. However, I did not immediately bring up anything about the sexual harassment issue with her; because of complex discussions going on about this sensitive topic, I had agreed to avoid it, at least temporarily. I also knew that my newspaper, like most responsible journals, was not likely to print such allegations from someone not willing to be named. Other people were planning to talk further to Hill about Thomas.

When I telephoned Hill, I interviewed her about Jay Parker, the lobbyist for South Africa who was Thomas's secret mentor. Having worked for several years as an aide to Thomas, she was familiar with his political life.

"My impression was he [Thomas] really looked up to him and he looked to him for political advice and used him as his political connection to the Reagan administration," Hill told me. "They were very close. He was an adviser practically to Thomas."

As the hearings approached, the liberal lobbying groups were scrutinizing the final reams of Thomas's documents from the EEOC, formally released in response to requests made under the Freedom of Information Act. One of the most ambitious requests for documents from the EEOC was made by People for the American Way, which eventually went into federal court to compel the agency to comply with the law. This group was looking for gaffes of this kind, including the rumored "chicken speech."

In an unintended parody of the desperate efforts of the liberals to find something, anything to block Thomas, lawyers for the liberal group spent hour after hour watching videotapes of Thomas's speeches as EEOC chairman. Most of the speeches were exceedingly boring. The lawyers had their eyes out for a video of Thomas speaking to agency employees, urging them in a humorous way to contribute to the combined federal campaign fund. In one of these speeches, rumor had it, Thomas had imitated a mentally ill person who thought she was a chicken. The "chicken speech" video, if it existed, was never found.

Although a chicken pantomime might not have done the trick, the liberals wanted to uncover something to keep Thomas off the high court. Although no one could predict with certainty what sort of justice Clarence Thomas would make, they feared that he would tilt the Supreme Court further to the right than they wanted to imagine.

# Chapter 10

EQUAL JUSTICE UNDER LAW: These are the four words inscribed in capital letters above the majestic columns at the front entrance to the Supreme Court the top of a wide flight of white marble steps flanked by a pair of sculpted figures of superhuman proportions—a woman representing the contemplation of justice, and a man representing the authority of law. This façade, in all its Greek Corinthian splendor, leaves no doubt as to the purpose of the institution—to elevate the law above the foibles of everyday humanity, to comprehend the highest justice and enforce it for all.

That is the ideal. The reality of the institution is not so uniformly splendid, being created by nine justices of human proportions, some wiser than others. All nine have never agreed for long on how to go about pursuing this equal justice.

The court building sits on the other side of a stately park from the Capitol building, where the politicians of the Senate stand at the gateway through which all nominees to the court must pass. As he prepared to face the Senate to win its vote of approval, Clarence Thomas was following a path taken by some of the country's greatest judicial thinkers as well as some of its lesser talents.

After winning Senate approval, Thomas would specifically take the place of Thurgood Marshall, the court's first black justice and one of the major legal activists of his time. In his quarter century on the court, Justice Marshall had participated in an era of liberalism that expanded civil rights and civil liberties. Toward the end, he had watched Republican presidents appoint justices who would start to undo much of what he had accomplished in a timespan beginning with the liberal Warren court and continuing through the Burger court, to an increasingly conservative Rehnquist court. The history of which Marshall had been an integral part would be of the utmost importance to Thomas, because it forms a map to the landscape of modern American law. To Marshall, this landscape already looked like a disaster. To Thomas, it looked like an opportunity.

Marshall was an angry and sick old man by the time he announced his retirement, five days before his eighty-third birthday. He had had a heart attack, his eyes were glazed with glaucoma, his two ears worked only with the help of hearing aids. He had fought pneumonia and bronchitis and a life-threatening blood clot in his foot. As his health deteriorated he had refused entreaties from his doctors and friends to take care of himself, to stop eating, drinking, and smoking. His always large, six-foot-two inch frame had ballooned out to two hundred and fifty pounds. He was killing himself, and he knew it.

In a more active time Thurgood Marshall had been in a position to do something about racism; he had combated it more successfully than any other person then living. He had been both the architect and the commanding general of the systematic legal challenge to segregation. By the time he argued *Brown* v. *Board of Education* at the age of forty-five, Marshall had already won thirteen of the fifteen cases he had taken to the Supreme Court, an astounding record. His arguments in *Brown*, coupled with the fortuitous appointment of Earl Warren as chief justice in the middle of the deliberations on the case, helped turn a divided court into a unanimous one against the doctrine of separate but equal school systems.

Marshall's days of arguing in front of the Supreme Court as a lawyer ended in 1967, when President Lyndon Johnson named him a justice. This was in the heyday of the Warren era. He replaced Tom Clark, a conservative justice, and consolidated the power of the liberal wing.

He was no less liberal than many of the great liberals of his time like Warren and William J. Brennan, Jr., although his approach to the cases was more pragmatic than philosophical. In other words, as his critics would later say, he was more interested in the result of a case than in the way he reached it.

Those were heady times for liberals, no less so at the court than on the college campuses. The court, through much of its history, had seen its role primarily as the protector of the property interests of the rich and the power of the states. But the Warren court championed the rights of taxpayers and voters, of the poor, of the press, of children, of religious and racial minorities, and of the criminally accused.

The Warren court also whittled away at the sovereignty of the individual states. First, it gave more power to govern to the more progressive national government in Washington at the expense of state legislatures. Second, it gradually pushed responsibility onto the states to uphold the Bill of Rights. This restricted local police forces and courts to many of the same restraints under which federal authorities had always operated. For example, Marshall in 1969 wrote the opinion, in the case of *Benton* v. *Maryland*, which held that the states had to comply with the Fifth Amendment bar against double jeopardy—against charging someone twice in court with the same crime.

Much of what the Warren court did to expand the rights of minorities and criminal suspects was based on two seemingly simple but vague pairs of words: "due process" and "equal protection." The Fifth Amendment guaranteed that citizens could not be "deprived of life, liberty, or property, without due process of law." However, the Fifth Amendment limits only the federal government, not state governments. The Fourteenth Amendment applied the same language to state governments, extending the basic rights to all citizens, including the freed slaves, and also asserted that everyone was entitled to "equal protection" of the laws.

The Warren court liberals saw in those words, standing alone or in conjunction with other rights enumerated but not elaborated on in the Constitution, the basis for a wholesale extension of civil protections. For them, this meant providing what they saw as fundamental fairness to the underprivileged, the outnumbered, and the accused.

Conservatives argued that such reasoning turned the Constitution into a kind of Rorschach test that allowed judges to read their own values and force them upon the country. Many of them wanted to stick to the original intent of those who wrote the Constitution, using history as a divining rod of those intentions. Liberals countered by arguing that the strength of the Constitution was that it could be interpreted. They thought of it as a living document that allowed adjustments for changing situations. The arguments of both the conservatives and the liberals had truth to them. The deciding factor in this debate was who controlled the court.

The Warren court was activist. It almost delighted in overruling the Supreme Court's earlier precedents, even though such decisions were by tradition treated with great deference for the sake of social and legal stability. But, as the years passed, many of the changes it engineered have become so accepted that they now seem essential to a modern, just society. Many have forgotten how these changes came about at the hands of Warren, Marshall, Brennan, William O. Douglas, and Hugo Black—the most influential and longest lasting of the liberal justices.

In 1962, all American voters achieved the right of equal representation under Brennan's now universally applied one man, one vote doctrine. In 1963, the Warren court decided that the words "due process" in the Fourteenth Amendment meant that the states would have to provide lawyers to poor people charged with serious crimes. In 1965, the court established "the right of privacy" in deciding the case of *Griswold* v. *Connecticut* and invalidating a state law prohibiting married couples from using contraceptives. This right is mentioned nowhere in the Constitution, but because of the *Griswold* decision, most Americans now think it is. In 1967, it was the liberal interpretation of due process and equal protection that allowed the court in 1967 to strike down a Virginia law outlawing interracial marriages.

(Clarence Thomas has often railed against the Warren court's broad interpretation of due process and equal protection. Without that 1967 decision his marriage to a white woman from Virginia twenty years later might still have been illegal.)

Over time, the Warren court overstepped the bounds of what middle America was willing to embrace. The *Brown* decision had received public support in many regions of the country, and some support from progressive elements in the South. But it was the cases after *Brown*, in which the court ordered broad changes in the country's social structure to get rid of segregation and achieve racial equality, that trouble began. And it was not confined to the South.

Many Americans did not really want new freedoms and equalities at the expense of precious religious and social beliefs, or at the cost, for example, of loosing on the streets criminals whose confessions had been obtained without a lawyer present. It was not, after all, the average person who benefited most from these judicial changes, but those who came into conflict with the authorities. Calls went up to impeach the chief justice, in vain. But the Warren court had gone too far, inciting conservatives to battle, and sowing the seeds of its own eventual destruction.

President Johnson inadvertently speeded up the process by trying to manipulate the makeup of the court. In 1965, he persuaded Arthur Goldberg, a prominent labor lawyer who in just three years on the court was already establishing himself as a brilliant justice, to resign in order to become ambassador to the United Nations. President Johnson told Goldberg he had to have him at the UN to replace Adlai Stevenson. But his real reason was that he very much wanted his close friend Abe Fortas on the court instead.

Fortas, the son of an English cabinetmaker, wanted no part of the deal. He had helped found the hugely successful Washington law firm of Arnold, Fortas, and Porter, and was enjoying making money by the bushel. He declined the presidential offer of a seat on the court, more than once. Finally, the always brash president from Texas told Fortas, "I'm announcing your nomination at ten o'clock tomorrow in the White House. You can come if you like." Fortas showed up, and quickly demonstrated he could be Goldberg's equal in judicial brilliance.

But when President Johnson nominated Fortas to succeed Earl Warren as chief justice in 1968, the Republicans stalled, sensing that they had a good chance of winning the presidency with Richard Nixon in November. (This explicitly political Supreme Court battle helped set the stage for the Democrats' opposition to Bork eighteen years later.) Johnson was forced to withdraw Fortas's nomination as chief justice, as well as that of Homer Thornberry, a Texas judge, to replace him. The next year, after Nixon was elected, it was revealed by *Life* magazine that Fortas, accustomed to the high life of his private practice, had taken a $20,000 fee from a foundation set up by an indicted stock manipulator. He resigned from the court in disgrace, shunned even by his closest friends there. The intellectual Goldberg, meanwhile, was a failure as a diplomat and no better when he ran for political office, so he returned to a relatively obscure life in private law practice. By virtue of his maneuverings, Johnson had essentially lost the Democrats two seats on the high court.

This was the end of the Warren era, although its momentum for change would continue for quite a time. The empty seats were filled by the appointments of two Republicans, Warren Earl Burger, as chief justice, and Harry A. Blackmun. When Hugo Black died in 1971, he was replaced by another conservative, Lewis F. Powell, Jr., tipping the liberal-conservative scale. And the conservative John Harlan was replaced by an obscure ultraconservative, William H. Rehnquist, who had only recently been in the public eye as a second-level official in the Justice Department. Even President Nixon, who appointed him, did not seem to have much respect for him, referring to the Supreme Court on one of the Watergate tapes as "a group of clowns . . . Renchburg and that group."

From all outward appearances Thurgood Marshall had a grand time his first three years on the court. He did not write the more important decisions of those years, but he had a unique perspective at the conferences where the justices met in confidence to hash out their positions in upcoming opinions, and during oral arguments, when the justices listened to both sides debate the case. Marshall was the justice who had both experienced discrimination and defended criminals. Under Warren's tenure, these were considered valuable qualities.

Marshall's mood changed, though, as the liberal majority began to slip away so soon after his arrival. He was also taking abuse from the black-power movement coming to the fore in the 1960s. The black radicals of the time criticized him as an Uncle Tom for participating in what they perceived as a white-man's government. He was hung in effigy at demonstrations, and derided for his choice of a Hawaiian woman of Filipino descent, Cecilia Suyat, for his second wife, after the death of his first spouse. As long as the court continued to stand up for the rights of those whom he insisted on calling Negroes, Marshall could dismiss the criticism with impunity. But as the court began to turn its back on minorities in the 1970s, and kept on doing so in the

1980s, his mood began to change. It was almost as if he saw that his radical black critics were right about his participation in the white establishment. He became bitter, lashing out at his colleagues on the court, even his friends, for any slight that he would quickly interpret as racism.

While Marshall soured, his close friend and fellow liberal, Brennan, responded by working harder. Brennan was the son of an Irish immigrant who had become police commissioner of Newark, New Jersey, and brought to his job on the court both political acumen and personal warmth. He was as conservative as any man alive in his approach to family life, but became the nation's leading liberal philosopher. It was largely because of Brennan that the Warren court's decisions survived two decades after the liberal majority had evaporated. Some of the groundbreaking decisions associated in the public's mind with the Warren era were actually issued by the Burger court.

Although he was not liberal, Burger himself wrote the unanimous but widely controversial *Swann* v. *Charlotte-Mecklenburg* decision that first explicitly endorsed the use of forced busing to achieve integration in schools. He also wrote another unanimous decision, *Griggs* v. *Duke Power Co.*, interpreting the 1964 Civil Rights Act as prohibiting employment tests that have a racially disproportionate impact. It was again Burger who wrote the *Lemon* v. *Kurtzman* decision, which made it virtually impossible for government bodies to involve themselves even indirectly in religious activities. The court also held, over the dissents of Burger and Blackmun, that Nixon could not stop *The New York Times* or *The Washington Post* from publishing the secret *Pentagon Papers* on the Vietnam War.

The Burger court put the brakes on the momentum of the Warren era, but did not reverse it. It tuned or snipped many of its decisions, adding exceptions to rules, for example. But it did not throw out most of the decisions wholesale. And sometimes, it added major decisions to the Warren legacy. In 1972, the court handed down *Furman* v. *Georgia* invalidating all the nation's death penalty laws. In 1973, the shocker was *Roe* v. *Wade,* and the establishment of women's constitutional right to abortion.

The nominees by President Nixon to the court were of medium to excellent caliber, with the exception of the ill-fated G. Harrold Carswell. (As Nixon's nomination of Clement Haynsworth, Jr., a respected federal appeals court judge, was being turned down by the Senate in a political payback for the Fortas affair, Nixon's wife, Pat, turned to Justice Hugo Black's wife, Elizabeth, at a White House luncheon and said "Honey, wait till you see what you get next." It was Carswell.) Burger was a less-than-brilliant chief justice, but politically, he bumbled down the middle of the road. Blackmun and Powell became fine judges. With the exception of Rehnquist, the justices President Nixon appointed were not ideologues but experienced lawyers and judges whose vote on any new issue could not always be anticipated. Rehnquist, a conservative version of William O. Douglas, proved to be intelligent but too far out on the right wing to have any influence on his brethren at the time.

The court was comfortably moderate, catering neither to the left nor the right. When Douglas was finally forced to retire, having suffered a stroke in 1975 after thirty-six years on the court, President Ford outraged conservatives by passing over Robert Bork as too controversial. He named instead a moderate Republican judge, John Paul Stevens, from a prominent Chicago family.

There was a tradition in the United States of choosing justices not only by their politics, but by their qualifications and stature. Presidents were often surprised by those they had put on the court. Given complete independence for life, justices had the liberty to think for themselves. For instance, President Franklin D. Roosevelt, who succeeded in turning the court in favor of his New Deal economics with appointments like Black and Douglas, also appointed another seeming liberal who turned out to be one of the court's greatest judicial conservatives, Felix Frankfurter. And it was the Republican President Dwight D. Eisenhower who appointed two of the major liberals of the Warren court, the chief justice himself and Brennan. The only appointment to the court, before Arthur Goldberg, by John F. Kennedy, the most liberal of modern presidents, was Byron White, a moderate conservative.

All this changed when Ronald Reagan was reelected president in 1984. Frustrated by his inability to achieve his conservative social agenda during his first term, Reagan agreed to give the court to the conservative movement that had swept him into power. His appointees were carefully vetted for ideological purity. Sandra Day O'Connor, the granddaughter of an Arizona pioneer rancher and herself a pioneer as the first woman on the court when Reagan appointed her in 1981, was a mainstream conservative with some moderate tendencies. But when Burger retired in 1986, Reagan chose the extreme Rehnquist to replace him as chief justice. President Reagan was starting to build an activist conservative court for which the correct ideology was a prerequisite to membership. This was the court to which Clarence Thomas was eventually nominated.

When Rehnquist became chief justice, he had served fifteen years on the court and become known as the lone dissenter. He had refused to go along with the decisions of the Burger court, even as it grew more conservative. Indeed, Rehnquist was so unwilling or unable to moderate his views to attract a majority that the liberal Brennan confidently told friends that the new chief justice was no threat. Brennan thought he could continue to control or at least moderate the direction of the court.

But almost unnoticed in the attempt to block Rehnquist's elevation to chief justice was the appointment of Antonin Scalia, a fundamentalist Catholic of Italian immigrant parentage who read the law in the same literal way he read the scriptures. Scalia, who was named to replace Rehnquist as an associate justice, has a superb legal mind but one that has been shown to lack judicial compassion. Although Scalia is socially personable, his opinions can demonstrate a streak of viciousness toward those pleading their cases before the court as well as toward those among his fellow justices who disagree with him. He has expressed deep class antagonism toward those who would favor affirmative action for blacks at the expense of white immigrants. Few in the legal world thought that President Reagan could find anyone to the right of Rehnquist, but that was an underestimation of the ability of his administraton to implement its conservative will.

The President's next choice was Robert Bork, another legal fundamentalist, but one with a decidedly more outspoken record than Scalia. When Bork was defeated for the seat vacated by Justice Powell, Reagan eventually named California federal appeals court judge Anthony M. Kennedy. Another Catholic Republican, Kennedy was only a step closer to the mainstream than Scalia and Rehnquist.

By 1988, a conservative majority held sway over the court, although it was a tentative one. Rehnquist, Scalia, and Kennedy constituted a far-right bloc, with O'Connor often joining them. White was a frequent fifth vote for the conservatives, particularly in criminal cases. Blackmun and Stevens were moderates who could go either way, but who were increasingly recoiling from the ideological agenda set by Rehnquist. Brennan and the ever-more-distraught Marshall were the only liberal holdovers from the Warren days.

If the country wanted a conservative court, this was perhaps the perfect situation. The court had strong, articulate voices on the right and the left. It also had a pragmatic center, weighted to the right, but capable of shifting to the left. This was a court in which decisions were debated fiercely from both political sides, which meant that the legal merits of the cases could not be ignored.

At the opposing ends of the court's political spectrum were Marshall and Scalia. This was illustrated concisely during oral arguments the court heard in a Louisiana case in which the state wanted permission to execute an insane prisoner, Michael Perry, with gruesome ingenuity. The state proposed to inject the man with a drug that would bring him back to reality long enough so that he could be legally executed. Marshall had written the decision four years earlier holding that it was cruel and unusual punishment to electrocute the insane.

Scalia, who liked to dominate the questioning of lawyers from the bench, had reacted with scorn to the arguments of Perry's lawyer that he had a right to resist forced medication. Scalia thought such a right was a "luxury" for those on death row.

Marshall interjected a question into the arguments.

He asked the state of Louisiana's lawyer: "Is this medicine given by injection or by the mouth?"

"Both," the lawyer said.

"Well, if all you say is true," Marshall said, with rising sarcasm, "in the interest of Louisiana, while you're giving him the injection, why don't you just give him enough to kill him then? It would be cheaper for the state."

But the court's balance was soon destroyed. In 1990, Brennan at the age of eighty-four suffered a second stroke and retired. In the next term of the court, Marshall, lacking Brennan's vote and persuasive powers, was consistently in the minority. Brennan's replacement was the mild-mannered New Hampshire judge David Souter. Although he did not exhibit any of the chief justice's right wing zeal, Justice Souter voted regularly with Rehnquist.

Under Rehnquist's leadership, the court was now able to start re-shaping the judicial landscape. It put new restrictions on the First Amendment rights of freedom of speech and of the press.

With six generally conservative justices instead of five, Rehnquist could now afford to lose a vote in any one case and still prevail. Thus, even though Justice O'Connor voted against him, Rehnquist led a five-man majority in the decision on the *Rust* v. *Sullivan* case that came as a blow to abortion-rights advocates and many others as well. The court held that the federal government could prohibit doctors or nurses at federally funded family-planning clinics from even mention-ing abortion while counseling pregnant women. The decision, which said that freedom of speech was not involved here, shocked people across the nation. The court was no longer the liberal demon of America, but the opposite. On some issues, its decisions were more conservative than the general public, a majority of which favored abortion rights.

The Rehnquist Court was particularly aggressive in attacking the Warren Court's expansion of the rights of the criminally accused. In *Arizona* v. *Fulminante*, the court even superseded precedents set well before Earl Warren became a justice. That ruling—that the ultracon-servatives won by a narrow five votes to four—had to do with illegally obtained confessions. The court held that if the authorities illegally obtain a confession from a suspect and even if that confession is used against the suspect at trial, the conviction does not necessarily have to be thrown out. The verdict stands as long as a judge determines there was enough other evidence for a jury to have reasonably convicted him. Of course, by that point it would be impossible to ask the jury what it thought.

The court continued to tighten the rules limiting the rights of prisoners to appeal from state courts to federal judges, even where gross abuses of justice occurred. Thus, appeals by condemned peo-ple—even those whose lawyers uncovered last-minute evidence of prosecutorial misconduct or proof of the innocence of their clients—were turned down on the basis of procedural flaws or assertions of lack of jurisdiction.

In cases involving the death penalty, the Rehnquist court acted with particular zeal. The Burger court had reinstated the death penalty in 1976, but the Rehnquist Court went much further. In a decision written by Scalia, the court ruled that it was not cruel and unusual punishment to execute criminals as young as the age of sixteen. The decision was based on the fact that twenty-two states had laws permitting such executions. Whether or not these states had actually been making use of these laws was not the point, according to Scalia.

While there is broad public support for the death penalty, the public is more divided on the subject of executing teenagers or the mentally retarded, which the Rehnquist court also permitted.

Perhaps the most telling case decided by the Rehnquist court was handed down the day Thurgood Marshall resigned. This case involved two particularly awful murders in Tennessee by Pervis Tyrone Payne, who was convicted of stabbing to death an acquaintance and her toddler daughter in a fit induced by anger, drugs, and alcohol. Payne also severely wounded the woman's three-year-old son.

Payne was sentenced to death. But to obtain that death sentence, prosecutors called an unusual witness, the grandmother of the surviving child. She had not seen the crime, but had been living with the consequences.

The grandmother testified in front of a jury that the child "cries for his mom. He doesn't seem to understand why she doesn't come home. And he cries for his sister, Lacie. He comes to me many times during the week and asks me, Grandmama, do you miss my Lacie? And I tell him yes. He says, I'm worried about my Lacie."

The emotional power of such testimony could overwhelm a jury. Indeed, never in two centuries of American jurisprudence had this kind of testimony been allowed. Until that day, evidence could only be introduced when it tended to inform the jury about the character of the crime or the defendant.

Over Rehnquist's dissent, the court had made two earlier rulings that such "victim impact" statements were not permissible. But by 1990, Rehnquist finally had the votes he wanted. From the thousands of petitions seeking reviews of lower-court actions that flood into the court every year, Rehnquist found the Payne case. The briefs in the case had not raised the victim impact issue. The chief justice, backed now by a majority, ordered the parties to rewrite the briefs and speeded up the hearing of the case so that it could be decided before the court adjourned for the summer. The court held that emotional evidence like the grandmother's was permissible.

The nut of Rehnquist's argument was that if the defense could have character witnesses like the accused mother and girlfriend, then it was only fair to bring in witnesses for the victim. Of course, criminal trials are not competitions between victim and accused, but resolutions of allegations about violations of the laws of the land.

Rehnquist also had to justify overruling the decisions in the two earlier cases on this same issue. Adherence to precedent—known in legal terms as *stare decisis*—was the foundation of the court's stability. When it came to precedent, the Rehnquist court in this case was as radical, in the judicial rather than the political sense of the word, as the Warren court had been. The Rehnquist court was an activist court with an agenda.

That agenda was made startlingly clear by Rehnquist himself. "Considerations in favor of *stare decisis* are at their acme in cases involving property and contract rights, where reliance issues are involved; the opposite is true in cases such as the present one involving procedural and evidentiary rules," he wrote.

The chief justice had made a startling statement about his philosophy. As far as Rehnquist was concerned, individual freedoms were not nearly so worthy of the court's protection as property rights.

Marshall and Stevens, joined by Blackmun, were furious. "Today's majority has obviously been moved by an argument that has strong political appeal but no proper place in a judicial opinion. . . ." Stevens wrote. "The great tragedy of the decision, however, is the danger that the 'hydraulic pressure' of public opinion that Justice Holmes once described, has played a role not only in the court's decision to hear the case, but even in the resolution of the constitutional issue involved. Today is a sad day for a great institution." In judicial terms he had accused the majority of bowing to politics rather than striving for justice.

Marshall, in the final words of his career, expressed outrage at the decision. "Power, not reason, is the new currency of this court's decisionmaking. . . . Today's majority ominously suggests that an even more extensive upheaval of this court's precedents may be in store," he wrote, warning that "scores of established constitutional liberties are now ripe for reconsideration. . . . Cast aside today are those condemned to face society's ultimate penalty. Tomorrow's victims may be minorities, women, or the indigent. Inevitably, this . . . will squander the authority and the legitimacy of this Court as a protector of the powerless."

An hour after this decision was handed down, Marshall resigned. The man who had repeatedly vowed that he would have to be carried out of the court feet first quit as much out of disgust as ill health. With his retirement, there seemed little chance that the court would continue the efforts of the 1960s to right the wrongs of a century of discrimination against slaves who were released but not wholly freed.

This had been predictable, since Rehnquist had been elevated to what is perhaps the country's second most powerful job and then given the votes to carry out his intentions. From the days he had been a law clerk, Rehnquist had fought progress in civil rights. While clerking for Justice Robert Jackson in 1952, Rehnquist had written a memorandum that strongly criticized the arguments Thurgood Marshall had just made as a lawyer before the court in the case of *Brown* v. *Board of Education*.

"One hundred and fifty years of attempts on the part of this Court to protect minority rights of any kind—whether those of business, slaveholders, or Jehovah's Witnesses—have all met the same fate," Rehnquist wrote. "One by one the cases establishing such rights have been sloughed off, and crept silently to rest. If the present Court is unable to profit by this example, it must be prepared to see its work fade in time, too, as embodying only the sentiments of a transient minority of nine men.

"I realize that it is an unpopular and unhumanitarian position, for which I have been excoriated by 'liberal' colleagues, but I think *Plessy* v. *Ferguson*[the 1896 case upholding segregation in the South] was right and should be re-affirmed."

Rehnquist became an an assistant attorney general in the Justice Department and was then nominated to the Supreme Court. His memorandum on *Brown* was dug up at the time of his confirmation hearings and created a stir, threatening his nomination. But Rehnquist asserted that he had simply been asked to put in words Jackson's views on the subject, not his own. He said he had been a clerk writing what a justice wanted. The evidence indicates otherwise. Jackson's former secretary, Elsie Douglas, called that assertion "incredible" and said Rehnquist had "smeared the reputation of a great justice." Indeed, Jackson sided with Marshall's arguments in the case and voted to overturn *Plessy*.

Rehnquist may have lied to the Senate to get himself confirmed. He certainly evidenced no support for civil rights once he became a justice. During his twenty years on the Supreme Court, he has voted against nearly every major civil rights decision.

When Clarence Thomas was nominated by President Bush, no Democrat had been appointed to the court in the twenty-four years since Marshall's appointment. By then, there were no true liberals left to challenge Rehnquist's leadership of the court. The only two moderate Republicans left on the court, Blackmun and Stevens, became its liberal wing by default. But two votes would have little influence in a court with seven conservatives.

For the senators preparing for Thomas's confirmation hearings, the fundamental question no longer had anything to do with balancing the Supreme Court. The Republicans had already succeeded in packing it with conservatives. The question was where Thomas would come down in the new power struggle going on within the court's right wing.

The battle for control of the Supreme Court—and the decisions it would be making on issues as important to the country as abortion, crime and the environment—would now take place in a conservative context. But this struggle could have as much importance as the decades-long conflict between liberals and conservatives that preceded it.

If the Senate approved his nomination, Thomas would enter a microcosm. Most of the court's spacious building is closed to the public, so that the nine justices can work, if they wish, in undisturbed intensity. From the parking garage beneath the building, an elevator takes the justices up to the corridor where their chambers are located. The justices have their own dining room, library, and gymnasium. Their days are spent drawing up their opinions with their law clerks and playing the intricately serious game of deciding how to vote. One justice's move on a certain case affects the others. In the conference room, the inner sanctum where their final decisions are made, even the presence of their law clerks is prohibited.

As a newcomer to this world, who would Thomas look to as an example? Who would befriend him? Who, if anybody, would he ask for advice? Who would win his vote when it came down to drafting decisions?

And Thomas's vote would matter. In its lopsided way, the court was closely divided between moderate conservatives and radical conservatives. On the far right were Rehnquist and Scalia, who received frequent support from Kennedy. They vied for authority with the court's more middle-of-the-road conservatives, White and O'Connor. Souter, after his first term on the court, appeared to be more in keeping with the moderate conservatives.

If Rehnquist, Scalia, and Kennedy were to gain control of the court's direction, the remaining decisions of the Warren Court would not just be overturned, they would be obliterated from history. In previous years, when the vote on a decision was close, Rehnquist had to hold his strongest views in check in order to win at all. He was forced to rule on many issues in a far narrower way than he would have wished.

If Thomas helped the radical right take control, the court could experiment with a conservative reengineering of society. Might the court go beyond O'Connor's 1989 ruling in *Penry* v. *Lynaugh* that it was all right to execute the moderately retarded? Might it approve the killing of the profoundly retarded who are convicted of murder?

Would some future Supreme Court, having overruled *Roe* v. *Wade*, carry the idea further? Would it consider ruling for the right to life for the fetus, which would make abortion unconstitutional?

An activist, right-leaning court may well go beyond dismantling what the liberals had built. Rehnquist has hinted of plans to consider the expansion of property rights at the expense of the environment. The idea is to broaden the current interpretation of the Fifth Amendment's prohibition against taking private property for public use without just compensation. If this happens, restrictive zoning or environmental regulations could be considered a taking of property that should be compensated from the public treasury. Rules that increasingly restrict development of the nation's coastlands and wetlands could be affected. Local and state governments enforcing such regulations might be forced to drop them or pay impossible amounts of money to property owners.

Another major conservative move, one supported fervently by O'Connor, would be to return the growing power of the national government to the states. This could portend a divisive restructuring of our system of government at a time of increasing economic complexity. Rehnquist, too, would support this. High on his wish list for reversals is the 1985 decision in *Garcia* v. *San Antonio*, which held that the federal government could order that Texas city's transit authority to pay its employees the federal minimum wage and overtime.

If Thomas were to join the Scalia-Rehnquist-Kennedy bloc, as the conservative movement clearly had good reason to believe, those four need only pick up one other vote from among the remaining five justices in order to have their way. Or the right wing could just wait for George Bush to nominate another hardcore conservative. With Blackmun pushing toward his eighty-third birthday, and Stevens suffering from cancer of the prostate gland, it might not be a long wait if Bush were to win the 1992 election.

Before Thomas would make it to the Supreme Court, though, he was going to be grilled by the Senate Judiciary Committee on his philosophy. The senators would try to find out where Thomas would fit into this newly conservative court.

# Chapter 11

September 10, 1991: The biggest day of Judge Clarence Thomas's life started with an odd bit of public imagery. He walked past the marble pillars into the cavernous splendor of the Senate Caucus Room in the Russell Senate Office Building arm-in-arm with Senator Strom Thurmond, the aging South Carolinian who was once a symbol of Southern racism. Except for their matching conservative ideologies, no two men could have been more different than Senator Thurmond and Judge Thomas. Dozens of photographers crowded forward, snapping every move that Thomas made. They barked orders at the short, muscular Supreme Court nominee to turn this way or that, and he readily complied. As the Senate Judiciary Committee opened its hearings, Clarence Thomas, at age forty-three, was center spotlight in the nation's attention.

These hearings, the start of the final passage to the Supreme Court, were smoothed in advance for Thomas. No fewer than six senators, three of them Democrats, had formally introduced him to their colleagues on the committee. Senator John Danforth, Thomas's protector since their days together in Missouri, had led the way by eloquently framing the debate into a discussion that Thomas could not lose. He urged his fellow senators not to just ask the nominee legal questions, but to ask him about himself.

"What was it like growing up under segregation?" Senator Danforth suggested they ask him. "What was it like to be there when your grandfather was humiliated before your eyes? What was it like to be laughed at by seminarians because you're black? Everyone in the Senate knows something about the legal issues before the Supreme Court. Not a single member of the Senate knows what Clarence Thomas knows about being poor and black in America."

Had the Senate not been composed largely of successful white men from privileged backgrounds, Senator Danforth would not have been able to to get away with this. And the Episcopalian minister would not have been able to do what he did next, had the Senators not felt guilty about the failures of government to alleviate the sufferings of the underclass. Danforth, acting as minister and senator, was able to raise the specter of affirmative action as a kind of cross with which he exorcised the crucial issues related to civil rights from the arsenal of the Democrats. He cited an analysis by William Raspberry, a writer for *The Washington Post*, who analyzed the competing visions of Thomas and the civil rights community. Thomas's vision was made to seem the more logical.

"At issue is whether it is wiser to pursue government policies that target blacks generally—contract set-asides, affirmative action, hiring and promotion, race-based special admissions, and so on, or to fashion approaches based on specific social, educational and economic conditions. Oversimplified, the two opposing propositions can be stated this way. One, race-specific approaches; two, approaches that target the conditions—joblessness, drug abuse, family disintegration, and undereducation."

Further smoothing the way for Thomas were Kenneth Duberstein, the political consultant who had been grooming Thomas all summer, and Fred McClure, the White House liaison with Congress. These two, along with Danforth, would coach Thomas through the hearings.

But when the time came for the main proceedings, Thomas walked forward alone to sit at a table facing the committee's dais. He looked up at the long bench behind which sat the fourteen white male senators who would interrogate him and judge him. The bench and Thomas's table, all heavily wired with microphones, were covered in thick green cloth to muffle sounds extraneous to the testimony.

Thomas's three coaches took seats on the front row behind him and slightly to his right. Flanking him on the left were most of his family. His wife, Virginia, sat nearest him. His son, Jamal, who was now eighteen, took a seat as did his mother, Leola Williams. His sister, Emma Mae Martin, was also there, the same sister who still lived in the rundown house in Pin Point and whom he had defamed by criticizing her dependence on welfare. Thomas's brother, Myers, now an accountant for a major hotel in Birmingham, Alabama, was not present, having already refused to talk to the media.

A small sea of people filled the rest of the grand chamber. Designed to comfortably seat three hundred people beneath a thirty-five foot high ceiling bedecked with magnificent chandeliers, the Caucus Room was jammed. Reporters, their pens poised to scribble, sat at tables behind the first row of chairs; television crews adjoined their cameras; row upon row of spectators filled the seats; and, at the back and sides of the room, more people willing to stand in order to watch squeezed against the walls and massive Corinthian columns of Italianate black-veined marble that had been quarried in New Jersey.

Senator Joseph Biden of Delaware, the Democratic chairman of the Judiciary Committee, gaveled the hearings to order. On his left were seven Democrats and on his right six Republicans, including the senior senator Strom Thurmond. Behind the senators was a row of their staffers, virtually all of them also white, ready to pass their bosses advice or messages. As the senators shuffled through the papers and notes their staffers had prepared for them, Senator Biden asked the nominee to swear the standard oath.

"Judge Thomas, do you solemnly swear to tell the truth, the whole truth, and nothing but the truth, so help you God?" Thomas replied with the required "I do."

Senator Biden had earned a reputation as a conciliatory man, someone who wanted to do what was right and also be liked by everyone. With his thinning hair, which he combed carefully to mask his bald spot, and with his tendency to orate in rambling sentences, Senator Biden was not a prosecutorial figure.

But Thomas was understandably tense. Everything he said would be analyzed. Every gesture he made would be noted. The nominee sat with his shoulders squared and his arms folded on the table in front of him. He was wearing the uniform of Washington—fashionable eyeglasses, a dark suit, white shirt and red tie—a far cry from the overalls he had favored as a student, but not so different from the uniform of his Catholic school days.

Senator Biden began gently in his attractive, informal style, picking up on the idea Senator Danforth had been pushing.

"Well, Judge, Jack Danforth talked about what's at issue. I want to make it clear at the outset of my questioning that there is a great deal more at issue than whether or not your view on how to deal with the civil rights of America deviates from the view of any single group of people."

Thomas had been exhaustively prepared over the ten weeks since the Kennebunkport nomination. He expected five days of cross-examination. All summer, Thomas had labored on his performance, often working in an office at the Justice Department until eight or nine at night with two department lawyers. He studied the legal cases and issues he would be asked about as if he were preparing for the bar exam. In addition, he had spent a number of intense days in Room 180 of the Old Executive Office Building, across from the White House, going through what some in the White House termed "murder boards." The Thomas team from the White House and Justice Department sat at a large horseshoe shaped conference table, with the judge in the middle. Senator Danforth, two private lawyers, and others took turns asking questions, playing the roles of various senators, pummeling the nominee with hostile questions on the sensitive topics like abortion. He had been rehearsed for this drama with the Senate down to the movements of his hands and the tone of his voice.

Thomas was playing not just to the senators, but to a nationwide audience watching live on cable and public television. The public had forgotten about him over the summer. Two-thirds of those Americans questioned in polls just before the hearings said they didn't have an opinion on whether he should be confirmed. This meant that the opposition had failed to get across its message, but it also meant that his initial high level of support was mercurial. The hearings would determine not only how the committee and the full Senate would vote, but also how the all-important general public would feel. And since the Congress is increasingly like a call-in show where the audience gets to

vote for its favorite contestant, the latter might well determine the former.

Thomas needed no reminder that the Senate Caucus Room had been the scene of Robert Bork's demise, as well as that of some of the most dramatic investigations in American history. The Senate had suffered over the sinking of the Titanic in this room, as well as the Teapot Dome scandal, Pearl Harbor, McCarthy, the Vietnam War, and Watergate. A new, more modern and technically up-to-date hearing room had been built nearby for big events just like this, but the Judiciary Committee had wanted to cling to the sense of history and grandeur provided by the Caucus Room.

To prepare himself, Thomas had watched the videos of Bork's committee hearings, a vivid lesson on the dangers of speaking your mind—at least if your views are as extreme as those of Robert Bork. He also watched the supremely successful tapes of David Souter's performance, in another chamber, the year before. Souter, an experienced, conservative, and quiet judge from New Hampshire, had managed to no comment the toughest issues in such an amiable way that everyone liked him for it.

But Clarence Thomas was no David Souter. For one thing, he did not have Souter's mastery of the law to help him dodge the tough questions with legal mumbojumbo. And unlike Souter, he had ten years in public office. Thomas had a public record, most of it from his controversial times at the EEOC, and he had been outspoken more than once.

It was clear at the opening of the hearings that Thomas's record was going to be scrutinized, and severely. The hearings would not be as amiable as the committee chairman's opening remarks. Senator Patrick J. Leahy, the Vermont Democrat who had not previously expressed any opposition but who is a solid liberal, immediately told Thomas, "The last thing I seek in a Supreme Court justice is ideology." He added, Thomas's words "strike me as the views of a combative, hard-line ideologue."

Still, the early betting was that Clarence Thomas, assuming he handled himself as well as he had in his hearings for the EEOC chairmanship and the federal judgeship, would sail through the Judiciary Committee, the major obstacle on the way to confirmation. The

committee was made up of eight Democrats and six Republicans. Thomas needed eight votes. Five of the Republicans' votes were assured, the sixth likely. Some insiders thought that he would pick up three or even four of the Democrats.

Duberstein, the political consultant who had quarterbacked the effort to get Thomas onto the Supreme Court, was optimistic, if guardedly so given the sometimes fickle nature of national politics. As Thomas began testifying, Duberstein watched intently and happily, for the nominee was getting off to a good start with his opening remarks. Making notes and whispering advice to McClure and Danforth, Duberstein was in his element. He was a pro at playing insiders' politics.

Brooklyn born and streetwise, Duberstein has devoted his career to politics. Having begun as a Republican congressional aide, he worked his way into the Reagan White House. Duberstein had handled a number of ticklish assignments, including helping with damage-control during the Irangate scandal, and dealing with Nancy Reagan and her suspicions about members of her husband's staff. He eventually became Reagan's chief of staff. In 1989, he became head of his own political consulting firm. When Duberstein took on Thomas, he was still fresh from his victory in getting Justice Souter onto the high court. If Thomas was the star of this opening day of the hearings drama, it was Duberstein who was the director.

When it came time for his his opening statement, Clarence Thomas powerfully, and shamelessly, deployed the Pin Point strategy. He hit on the poignant parts and glossed over the ambiguities of his biography and, where necessary, embellished his beliefs:

> My earliest memories are those of Pin Point, Georgia, a life far removed in space and time from this room, this day, this moment. As kids, we caught minnows in the creeks, fiddler crabs in the marshes. We played with plovers and skipped shells across the water. It was a world so vastly different from all this.
>
> In 1955, my brother and I went to live with my mother in Savannah. We lived in one room in a tenement. We shared a kitchen with other tenants, and we had a common bathroom in the backyard which was unworkable and unusable. It was hard, but it was all we had and all there was.

Our mother only earned $20 every two weeks as a maid, not enough to take care of us, so she arranged for us to live with our grandparents later in 1955. Imagine, if you will, two little boys with all their belongings in two grocery bags. Our grandparents were two great and wonderful people who loved us dearly. I wish they were sitting here today, sitting here so that they could see that all their efforts, their hard work were not in vain, and so that they could see that hard work and strong values can make for a better life.

By this point some of the people lined up along the walls between the high marble columns were dabbing their eyes with handkerchiefs. Even Hank Brown, the Republican Senator from Colorado, had to take off his glasses to wipe his eyes. The Democrats evidenced no such difficulty.

Thomas paid homage not only to his grandparents, but to the civil rights leaders he credited with paving the way:

But for the efforts of so many others who have gone before me, I would not be here today. It would be unimaginable. Only by standing on their shoulders could I be here. At each turn in my life, each obstacle confronted, each fork in the road, someone came along to help. . . . So many others gave their lives, their blood, their talents. But for them I would not be here.

Thomas went on to praise the man he was named to replace, whose work and opinions he had so often attacked:

Justice Marshall, whose seat I've been nominated to fill, is one of those who had the courage and the intellect. He's one of the great architects of the legal battles to open doors that seemed so hopelessly and permanently sealed and to knock down barriers that seemed so insurmountable to those of us in the Pin Point, Georgia's of the world.

And he had nice words for the civil rights groups he had so often pilloried:

The civil rights movement—Reverend Martin Luther King and the SCLC, Roy Wilkins and the NAACP, Whitney Young and the Urban League, Fannie Lou Hamer, Rosa Parks and Dorothy Height. They changed society and made it reach out and affirmatively help. I have benefited greatly from their efforts. But for them, there would have been no road to travel.

After adding more about his grandparents, Thomas continued:

It is my hope that when these hearings are completed, that this committee
will conclude that I am an honest, decent, fair person. I believe that the
obligations and responsibilities of a judge in essence involve just such basic
values.

A judge must be fair and impartial. A judge must not bring to his job,
to the Court, the baggage of preconceived notions, of ideology, and certainly not an agenda.

Senator Biden, who can be quicker on his feet than his critics give
him credit for, reacted immediately, trying to set the record straight
and get beyond the verbiage.

"Let me begin at the outset by pointing out to you, I for one do not
in any way doubt your honesty, your decency or your fairness. But
. . . I am interested in what you think. . . . The fact that you're honest,
the fact that you're decent, the fact that you're fair, the fact that you
have honed sensibilities, mean a lot to me. But what I want to do in
the next half hour and the next several days is to go beyond that. I will
concede easily because it's true those points, no question. As we
lawyers say, let's stipulate to the facts—you're honest, decent, and
fair."

Although few people knew it, on that same day, Clarence Thomas's
decency and fairness were being dangerously challenged. One of the
Senate staffers, Jim Brudney, was an old Yale law school classmate of
Anita Hill whom she trusted. She telephoned him with details of her
story.

Jim Brudney was an unlikely character to get publicly embroiled in
anything as volatile as the Anita Hill affair. A cautious man, he is one
of the few people on Capitol Hill who avoid the press whenever
possible. He graduated summa cum laude from Amherst College and
got a master's degree at Oxford before going to law school. He distinguished himself by having been selected as a law clerk by Supreme
Court Justice Harry Blackmun.

When the Thomas hearings began, Brudney had nothing to do with
Clarence Thomas or the Senate Judiciary Committee. His only relationship was tangential. Brudney had settled into working for Senator

Howard Metzenbaum, who was a member of the Judiciary Committee. But Brudney's job was that of chief counsel and staff director for the Senate subcommittee on labor, which Senator Metzenbaum chaired.

On the day before the hearings opened, Hill had finally concluded that she was willing to talk. She called back Ricki Seidman of Senator Kennedy's staff. Four days had gone by since Seidman had called Hill, and with the hearings set to begin the next day, the opportunity to do anything with her information was rapidly passing. But Seidman knew that Senator Kennedy did not want anyone on his staff pursuing this case. She came up with an alternative, suggesting to Hill that she talk to her old classmate, Brudney.

It was the next day, when attention was focused on the events in the Senate Caucus Room, that Anita Hill spilled out her ugly-sounding story to Brudney over the telephone line connecting Oklahoma with his Capitol Hill office. Brudney thought the information was highly significant. He told Hill that Thomas might be forced to withdraw his nomination. Once he had hung up the phone, Brudney rushed down from his fourth-floor office in the Dirksen Senate Office Building and over to the the Caucus Room in the nearby Russell building. He pulled Bill Corr and Chris Harvie, Senator Metzenbaum's aides on the Judiciary Committee, out of the hearings to tell them what he knew.

Up until then Corr and Harvie had only known of the rumor about Anita Hill and some vague sexual harassment charge. Now, serious allegations had been handed directly to them by a fellow aide to Metzenbaum. Brudney's story from Hill could not be considered official information since it had not been confirmed in any objective way. Hill might be the source of erroneous charges, they couldn't know. But if the charges were checked out and found to be true, this was very hot material.

Meanwhile, Senator Biden, who as chairman opened the proceedings, had started a dangerous line of interrogation. Thomas's philosophy, as well as his character, was up for scrutiny. The senators wanted to ascertain what kind of legal mind was hidden behind Thomas's carefully prepared façade. Senator Biden had not begun with the intention of sabotaging Thomas. Far from it. The committee chairman wanted to keep the hearings on calm ground. He was not the kind of man who hankered for a fight. While his staff wanted him to vote against

Thomas, Senator Biden was inclined to vote in favor of him. But the senator first wanted to try to square parts of Thomas's convoluted record. His vote as committee chairman would normally carry significant weight with the rest of the Senate.

Senator Biden asked the nominee about a 1987 speech to the Pacific Research Institute, in which Thomas had praised a libertarian legal scholar named Stephen Macedo: "I found attractive the arguments of scholars such as Stephen Macedo who defend an activist Supreme Court that would strike down laws restricting property rights." The statement Thomas endorsed was potential trouble, because of its emphasis on judicial activism—just the thing that the nominee had said he was against—as well as its radical emphasis on property rights.

Thomas seemed thrown by the question. He tried to back away from the words he had declaimed in his speech, which had touched on one of his favorite concepts, that of natural law. He seemed nervous, holding his left hand to his chin, propping his index finger against his cheek and punctuating his answer with pauses. This was not the confident, argumentative, humorous Clarence Thomas whom his friends and family knew.

"Senator, again it has been quite some time since I have read Professor Macedo and others. That was, I believe '87 or '88. My interest in the whole area was in reassessing and demonstrating a sense that we understood what our founding fathers were thinking when they used phrases such as 'all men are created equal' and what that meant for our form of government. I found Macedo interesting and his arguments interesting as I remembered. And it has been quite some time. But I don't believe that in my writings I have indicated that we should have an activist Supreme Court or that we should have any form of activism on the Supreme Court."

Senator Biden pressed him again, asserting that his answer did not square with what he had said in 1987. The nominee responded with an effort to distance the Clarence Thomas of 1991 from the Clarence Thomas of several years earlier. For the Judiciary Committee, he was prepared to play down any part of his philosophical history as controversial as natural law. He claimed matters at the EEOC had preoccupied his mind.

"I don't see a role for natural law in constitutional adjudication," Thomas said. "My interest in exploring natural law and natural rights was purely in the context of political theory. . . . I pursued that on a part-time basis. I was an agency chairman."

Senator Biden had been ready for such a response.

"Well, Judge, in preparing for these hearings, some suggested that that might be your answer. So I went back through some of your writings and speeches to see if I misread them. And quite frankly, I find it hard to square your speeches with what you are telling me today."

The committee chairman read Thomas some of his quotes: "The higher law background of the American government . . . provides the only firm basis for a just and wise constitutional decision."

Senator Biden continued, "And judge, what I'd like to know is I find it hard to understand how you can say that—what you're now saying . . . that you're only talking about the philosophy in a general philosophic sense and not how it informed or impacted upon constitutional interpretation."

"That in fact was my approach," Thomas replied. "I was interested in the political theory standpoint. I was not interested in constitutional adjudication."

The nominee explained that his interest in natural law was in trying to find a constitutional basis to outlaw slavery. The problem with this explanation, though, was that Thomas had repeatedly gone further than the issue of slavery in his discussions of natural law. In particular, he had talked about it in the context of the right to own property or engage in commerce—innocuous enough on the face of it, but underneath suggesting a radical rethinking of the government's right to apply zoning, health, and environmental restraints on the use of property, and to apply health, safety, and quality regulations on American business.

Senator Biden had warmed to the argument, which may have sounded abstruse to anyone not versed in the philosophical underpinnings of constitutional law, but the discussion was crucial to getting a look into Thomas's mind.

Biden went on: "I have pages and pages of quotes where you talk about natural law not in the context of your grandfather, not in the context of race, not in the context of equality, but in the context of commerce."

The senator reached back into Thomas's record and quoted: "Natural law when applied to America means not medieval stultification but the liberation of commerce." and "Economic rights are as protected as any other rights." Senator Biden pointed out that economic rights had in modern times been treated by the Supreme Court as less deserving of protection than personal rights. Becoming exasperated despite himself, Biden finally threw up his hands. "Can you tell me, can you enlighten me on how this was just some sort of philosophical musing?"

"Well, that's exactly what it was," Thomas declared. After further badgering, the nominee asserted that he was not a member of the new conservative school of thought on property rights and that decisions of the Supreme Court earlier in this century allowing government regulation of business were correctly decided.

While Thomas was trying to give reassuring answers, he was simultaneously undermining himself by raising questions about his credibility. Was the nominee waffling about what he believed in order to avoid any controversial answers during the committee's questioning? (Clearly, he had decided that his goal in these hearings was not to make a stand, but to get confirmed. In fact, when William Gates, then in the midst of his own confirmation difficulties for the top job at the CIA, called Thomas up to commiserate with him, the judge told him, "My motto is 'Don't get mad, don't get even, get confirmed.' ")

Senator Biden kept pressing Thomas on his philosophy. Duberstein and Thomas's other coaches were disconcerted. The hearings were getting off to a bumpy start. Thomas's relatives weren't any happier. Leola Williams, sitting on the front row, looked uncomfortable with the way things were going. Senator Biden, with the Washington politeness that doesn't necessarily connote ideological agreement, had graciously escorted Thomas's family beforehand.

"Growing up the way we did, I didn't know people could be cruel like he was," Thomas's mother said. "I couldn't believe what Biden did. He took a picture with us, he was friendly and, then, when he got up in front of everybody, he started cutting Clarence down, just as if he was teaching school, as if Clarence was in kindergarten. That really hurt."

Senator Biden proceeded to spring *the* question on Thomas. It was the single issue Thomas wanted most to avoid, that his coaches had warned him about repeatedly.

"Now, judge, in your view does the liberty clause of the Fourteenth Amendment protect the right of women to decide for themselves, in certain instances, whether or not to terminate pregnancy?"

"My view is that there is a right to privacy in the Fourteenth Amendment," Thomas replied tersely, hoping to dodge the purpose of the question, which was to draw out his legal thoughts on abortion.

Thomas's answer was important, but not fully responsive. The right to an abortion had been founded on the concept of a constitutional right of privacy. By this reasoning, a right to privacy protected a woman's right to do what she wishes with her body. Judge Bork had said there was no such right, ensuring that his nomination would go down in controversy. Each nominee since Judge Bork had said there was a right to privacy, but had refused to say whether this view guaranteed a right to an abortion. Any stand on the issue would divide the Senate and the country.

Senator Biden kept pressing: "Well, judge, does that right to privacy in the liberty clause of the Fourteenth Amendment protect the right of a woman to decide for herself, in certain instances, whether or not to terminate a pregnancy?"

"I do not think that at this time that I could maintain my impartiality as a member of the judiciary and comment on that specific case," Thomas said, referring to *Roe* v. *Wade*, the landmark case legalizing abortion.

Thomas would be asked different versions of this same question at least seventy times in the next few days. He would always answer it in the same way—and rightly so. Supreme Court nominees are not candidates for elective office bound to make promises to the electorate. As Thomas himself had already said, judges are supposed to try and come to each case impartially, without the baggage of preconceived notions. Abortion was certainly current on the Supreme Court's agenda. It would be wrong of any nominee to comment on a specific case or controversy.

But that does not mean that the senators would be wrong in examining what Thomas previously had said on the subject, as women's groups in favor of abortion rights had done back in July in the weeks following Thomas's nomination. The senators also were not wrong in examining how the nominee's philosophical beliefs might lead him to vote on an abortion case brought before the Supreme Court. A majority of the members of the Senate as a whole, like the majority of the American people, were pro-choice, even if they did not always vote that way. Suspicions were high that Thomas was against allowing abortion.

Senator Biden tried to pin down Thomas. The senator asked him about the speech he had made to an audience at the conservative Heritage Foundation on Capitol Hill, only several blocks from the Supreme Court. This was the speech that an abortion-rights group had discovered and employed to rally women's groups around the cause of defeating the nominee. In the speech, Thomas had praised a tract by Lewis Lehrman, a founder of the Heritage Foundation, on the use of natural law to argue for outlawing abortion.

As he faced the Judiciary Committee Thomas attempted to explain that praise away by saying he was playing to his audience.

"I was speaking in the Lewis Lehrman auditorium of the Heritage Foundation. I thought that, if I demonstrated that one of their own accepted at least the concept of natural rights, that they would be more apt to accept that concept as an underlying principle for being more aggressive on civil rights."

The more Thomas tried to wriggle out of what he had said in the past, the more insincere he appeared to the committee.

The coup de grâce came when Senator Biden asked Thomas about his participation in 1986 in the controversial White House Working Group on the Family. Appointed by President Reagan and chaired by Gary Bauer, the group produced a report recommending that unmarried teenage mothers be denied welfare benefits and asserting that the "fabric of family life has been frayed by practices including no-fault divorce, liberal sexual attitudes, and ease in obtaining welfare."

Senator Biden asked Thomas if he had read the report before it was released. Thomas tried to duck the question, saying he only had drafted one section on low-income families. Under questioning, he finally admitted he had never read the full report, before or after it was published, even though he was one of the authors.

That was bad enough. Then Senator Biden asked him about criticism in the report of a Supreme Court decision striking down an overbearing Cleveland city ordinance. In attempting to preserve the traditional family character of a neighborhood, the ordinance made it illegal for unrelated people or even extended families to live together.

A grandmother had been told she could not live with two grandchildren who had been born to different children.

The White House report had said that the Supreme Court's decision to overrule the ordinance "in effect forbade any community in America to define 'family' in a traditional way."

Thomas said had he only known that was in the report, he would have objected, acknowledging that such a law might well have made his own upbringing impossible.

Senator Biden, concluding his first round of questioning, told Thomas that "quite frankly, at this point you leave me with more questions than answers."

The battle for the high ground continued even during the regular twenty-minute bathroom breaks and at lunchtime. The first break after Senator Biden's questioning was pandemonium, as Thomas's well-organized public relations team went into action to try to salvage the day. The Republicans felt that they had lost the Bork battle in part because they were not aggressive in their "spin control"—getting out their interpretation of the event—in the marble hallways outside the Senate Caucus Room. During the Bork hearings, reporters had milled around with the audience, which included lots of representatives of the liberal lobby groups, picking up commentary. For Thomas, the White House and its allies among the right-wing groups were determined not to lose out in this serious game.

Senator Danforth would charge out of the Caucus Room and head for "the stakeout," a wide corridor by the entrance to the room where a bank of television cameras had been set up to record spontaneous interviews. During the hearings Danforth's press aide, Steve Hilton, would hand him a note with the latest tactic, already coordinated with the White House, for the upcoming break. "Your script for the next break is . . ." said one such note that I read over Danforth's shoulder before he folded it up. Senator Danforth would then introduce to the cameras another of Thomas's supporters, thus monopolizing as much of the break time as possible.

Tom Jipping, the coordinator on judicial nominations for Library Court and other right-wing groups, and Ricky Silberman, the EEOC vice chairman and head of a citizens-for-Thomas group, grabbed reporters to give them copies of the first Thomas speech that Senator

Biden had asked him about. It showed clearly that the committee chairman had taken the quotation completely out of context. It was no wonder that Thomas was confused.

"I found attractive the arguments of scholars such as Stephen Macedo who defend an activist Supreme Court that would strike down laws restricting property rights," was what Biden had read to Thomas. The speech had continued, "But the libertarian argument overlooks the place of the Supreme Court in a scheme of separation of powers. One does not strengthen self-government and the rule of law by having the nondemocratic branch of the government make policy."

Thomas's speech had in fact taken issue with Macedo as to the propriety of judicial activism. Of course, there was no easy way to explain away all the other controversial statements Biden had quoted from. But the full text of the Macedo comment was slipped to one of Thomas's principal defenders on the Judiciary Committee, Senator Orrin Hatch of Utah, a Mormon and militant conservative on judicial matters. When the hearings resumed, Senator Hatch embarrassed Senator Biden with this information. The chagrined committee chairman said he had told Thomas the previous Friday he would ask about that particular speech. This small imbroglio raised other questions, about why the Democratic chairman was slipping exam questions, as it were, to a Republican nominee.

Jipping and Silberman were part of a team working out of what they called "the war room," a conference room down the hall from the Caucus Room in the offices of Republican Senator Thad Cochran of Mississippi. Others working there included Judy Smith, the black deputy White House press secretary, who all summer had fielded reporters' questions on Thomas; Constance Newman, the black director of the Office of Personnel Management, who had helped orchestrate the effort to win support for Thomas among African-American groups; and several people from the Republican National Committee.

Other White House officials, including Lee Liberman, were working directly out of Senator Danforth's office one floor below the Caucus Room. The Thomas hearings were bringing together the executive, legislative and judicial officials—representatives of the three branches of government that under the American system are supposed to remain independent of each other. The collusion made those witnessing the hearings uncomfortable.

Back in the hearing room, Thomas continued to retreat from his earlier speeches. This time, Senator Ted Kennedy was doing the questioning. Senator Kennedy, who had led the Democratic charge against Judge Bork, now wanted to avoid public attention in the wake of the recent scandal in Palm Beach.

The Massachusetts senator was in no position to question another man's integrity. He did, nevertheless, play a tepid version of his former role, pushing Thomas on his record regarding the role of the federal goverment and the status of women in the workplace.

"In a 1987 interview with a publication called *Reason*, you question the need for many important federal agencies. You said, and I quote, 'Why do you need a Department of Labor, why do you need a Department of Agriculture, why do you need a Department of Commerce? You can go down the whole list. You don't need any of them, really.' You were quoted correctly, were you not?" he asked.

Thomas responded defensively and a bit repetitiously, "Senator, I again don't know the context of that quote. I don't know what I said before or after. Of course, I think all of us would certainly be in favor of—and I certainly count myself among those Americans who are for safe working environments and who are strongly for protections from abuses and exploitation from individuals who have more clout and more power. And I'm for safe working environments, and I'm for the standards that protect workers. And I'm certainly, as I've made clear during my tenure at EEOC, strongly in favor of laws that prevent employers from discriminating against individuals."

Thomas was more wary now, and rightly so. In fact this was also somewhat out of context. Although not crystal clear in the interview, Thomas seemed to go on to say that while in a perfect world federal regulation would not be necessary, this was not a perfect world. Kennedy eventually read the full quote, but only after he let Thomas squirm.

Also squirming by then were the members of the nominee's family, for whom the name Kennedy had a wonderful aura.

"We loved the Kennedys," Leola Williams, said with an aggrieved tone of voice as she remembered that first day in the Senate Caucus Room. "We prayed for that family."

The hearings had quickly become a game that some of those in-

volved privately called "crazy quotes." These quotes were hunted up
not only by members of the senators' staffs but also by the staffs of the
liberal groups. Some of the questions posed to Thomas by the Democrats were actually solicited by the senators from the groups. In addition, selected senators had been given confidential copies of a lengthy
analysis of Thomas's speeches, and the contradictions within them,
painstakingly drawn up the NAACP Legal Defense Fund. Called the
Clarence Thomas Sourcebook, the ninety-nine page document was the
most thorough examination of Thomas's written record available.

"We look for the outlyers," said a staffer for one of the liberal
groups who had participated in the hunt for wild statements or other
magically incriminating words. "Then we say, 'Oh look, he said this.'
The process isn't serious. The process is inherently political in order
to grasp the attention of the senators both literally and figuratively.
We've got to find something spectacular, because otherwise those guys
won't be interested. Don't I wish I could just write this analysis,
'Clarence Thomas is a serious-minded but unsophisticated guy who in
past years has become increasingly conservative,' instead of looking
for one stupid line out of a speech?"

The mad hunt for wild quotes was due in part to the senators'
unwillingness to deal with the substantive issues behind the nomination, including Thomas's stand on civil rights and his lack of qualifications for the job.

Had Thomas had any great experience as a judge, or as a lawyer, this
might not have been the case. His word bites "became more important
and fell more heavily because of the underlying truth that everybody
knew that Clarence Thomas should not now have been appointed to
the Supreme Court," the staffer continued.

But most of the quotes hurled at Thomas that day were not taken
out of context. They were his own words, if not always his own
thoughts. And Clarence Thomas, coached by Duberstein, was ready to
disavow them if that's what it took for him to get onto the Supreme
Court. He was even willing to disavow his intellectual mentor, Thomas
Sowell, the academic economist whose writings attack the liberal or-
thodoxies on discrimination, including the belief that statistics showing inequalities can be proof of bias.

Senator Kennedy narrowed in on the the economist's views on
women in the workplace, wanting to know if Thomas agreed. The

senator asked the nominee if he still believed the views he expressed in a 1987 interview that the reason women are underrepresented in certain jobs was by their own choice, that they may choose to have babies rather than go to medical school.

"I think it's important to state this unequivocally, and I've said this unequivocally in speech after speech. There is discrimination," Thomas replied, marshaling a strong reply. "There is sex discrimination in our society. My only point in discussing statistics is that I don't think that any of us can say that we have all the answers as to why there are statistical disparities."

Senator Kennedy asked Thomas about his praise for Sowell's analysis that women were voluntarily staying out of certain jobs. Thomas had called the analysis "a much needed antidote to clichés" about women's earnings in professional status. Kennedy continued:

> Mr. Sowell explains that women are paid 59 percent of what men receive for the same work by saying that "Women are typically not educated as often in such highly paid fields as mathematics, science, and engineering, nor attracted to physically taxing and well-paid fields such as construction work, lumberjacking, and coalmining, and the like."
>
> As a matter of fact, there were no women employed in the coalmine industry in 1973. In 1980, after the federal government had begun an effort to enforce antidiscrimination laws, there are 3,300 women working in coalmines. Does that surprise you at all?
>
> If there was discrimination, that doesn't surprise me. . . . But the point that I was making with respect to Professor Sowell again is a statistical one. . . . I thought that it would be more appropriate . . . in looking at how to solve these problems, that you disaggregate the problems and you be more specific, instead of lumping it all into one set of statistics.

When Senator Kennedy pressed Thomas further on Sowell's analysis of women, Thomas all but disavowed the man who had started him down the intellectual path to his present conservatism.

"Senator, I think that someone like a Tom Sowell is certainly one who is good at engaging a debate. And I think it's important that there be individuals who look at statistics in his way. What I did not indicate, that first of all, that I agreed with his conclusions."

For good measure, Thomas also threw in a disavowal of Lehrman's article on natural law and unborn babies when Kennedy asked him about his Heritage Foundation speech.

"I do disagree with the article, and I did not endorse it before," Thomas said.

The questioning of Thomas alternated in half hour segments between Republican and Democrat, in order of seniority. The Republicans for the most part tried to undo any damage done by the Democrat before them. They threw Thomas softball questions like this one by Senator Hatch: "So when you become a justice on the United States Supreme Court—and I believe you will—you intend to uphold the Constitution of the United States? Is that correct?"

"With every fiber of my body," Thomas replied.

When Senator Howard Metzenbaum heard what Jim Brudney had come up with, he did not broadcast it to his colleagues. He did the opposite. Although liberal and unhappy about Thomas's nomination from the start, the senator was not about to stand out front on this issue. He told Brudney to hand the information, as if it were a hot potato that needed cooling, over to Chairman Biden's Judiciary Committee staff. This was what the Senate's procedures called for; nonetheless, Senator Metzenbaum, like Senator Kennedy, was placing Anita Hill's charges in a judiciary-committee limbo.

The Judiciary Committee, like other Senate committees, is not a unified organization but rather a Balkanized collection of political ministates under one umbrella. Each of the seven Democrats serving on the committee under Senator Biden chairs his own subcommittee. The staffers for each of these subcommittees are hired by, work for, and follow the political agenda of its chairman, not Senator Biden. Thus Corr's title was chief counsel of the judiciary subcommittee on antitrust, monopolies, and business rights, which was chaired by Senator Metzenbaum. Corr, though, served also as Metzenbaum's chief adviser on the Judiciary Committee. Further splits were built into all levels of the congressional committee system because separate staffs worked for the majority Democrats and minority Republicans.

By handing the information about Hill over to Chairman Biden's staff on the committee proper, Senators Kennedy and Metzenbaum were giving up control over it. They knew, or should have known, that they were putting Anita Hill in the hands of someone who would not be responsive to what the law professor had to say.

Joseph Biden, the son of a Pennsylvania car dealer, had won election to the Senate from Delaware nineteen years earlier, barely old enough to squeeze past the age requirement. He turned the necessary thirty years of age after his election but before his swearing in. Having appeared on the national political scene as a boy wonder, Senator Biden mused as the hearings began that he never thought he would be weighing the nomination of a Supreme Court Justice five years younger than he was.

Senator Biden is a likable man and an excellent orator who has a reputation for talking too much and not being particularly bright. He had gotten poor grades as an undergraduate at the University of Delaware and not done any better at the law school of Syracuse University—an institution certainly not in the same league as Yale, where Clarence Thomas had matriculated. Nonetheless, Biden emerged during these hearings as one of the few senators on the committee who could think quickly for himself without being pushed along by his staff. He certainly had a grasp of the intricacies of such esoterica as the concept of natural law, although that served mainly to bore the national television audience.

Senator Biden was intent on being recognized as a nice guy as well as a legal brain. He was so cordial to the minority Republican senators on the Judiciary Committee, in his constant effort to be fair, that he got more respect from them than he did from the majority Democrats. With his preoccupation with popularity, which some termed an obsession, Senator Biden was not known as a chairman who exercised leadership.

This preoccupation may have been the results of the way life had bounced him around. Just forty-one days after his first upset election to the Senate, a car carrying his wife and children home with a Christmas tree was smashed by a truck. His wife and infant daughter were killed, his two sons injured. He had to be cajoled into taking the Senate oath of office.

Fifteen years later, in the middle of the Bork hearings that he also chaired, he was forced into a humiliating withdrawal from a race for the Democratic nomination for president. His campaign was derailed by a pair of revelations about his propensity to use other people's words. It was discovered that in a campaign speech he had appro-

priated the words and even the biographical background of Neil Kin-
nock, a British Labour Party leader. In addition, he was accused of
plagiarizing from a text to write a law school paper. He had, in fact,
footnoted a reference to the source of the information, but not sufficiently to indicate that he had used a full five pages of the text. Not
long afterwards he found himself in an ambulance being rushed to a
hospital for neurosurgery. A brain aneurysm had almost killed him.

Biden also struggled to be a man for all seasons politically. He won
his first Senate race on an anti–Vietnam War platform, his second on
an antibusing platform. He was liberal on most issues, including
endorsing the right to abortion, but he searched mightily to find a
compromise position on the death penalty. He settled ambiguously on
endorsing the death penalty while simultaneously limiting it with
antidiscrimination language.

"He is somebody with liberal instincts and a blue collar background
who wants more than anything not to be Ted Kennedy," is the way one
Washington insider put it. "He wants to be a tough-love Democrat,
hard on crime, antibusing but pro-choice."

The senator had never given up on his ultimate political dream, and
still harbored hopes of running for the presidency. There was no way
that Joe Biden wanted to be seen as being tough on Clarence Thomas.
That would alienate blacks, conservatives, and Southerners in one fell
swoop. He had already been unreasonably attacked the year before by
the *Wall Street Journal* for "lynching" Thomas in his earlier confirmation hearings for the seat on the Court of Appeals. At the end of
those hearings, Senator Biden had joined the vote favoring Thomas by
thirteen to one. Senator Metzenbaum had been the lone dissenter.

When the information about Anita Hill was dumped into Senator
Biden's lap, he was already sitting on charges of impropriety against
Thomas. On the eve of the hearings, *The Boston Globe* had reported
that Thomas, when he chaired the EEOC, had abused his privilege of
traveling on the federal tab. Thomas had billed the government for
some twenty personal trips to give speeches or visit friends, covering
himself by paying brief visits to local EEOC offices. The reporting on
this, by the *Globe*'s Walter Robinson, was based in part on research
done of EEOC files by the liberal group People for the American Way.
The reporting had a potential punch because it is a federal crime to

misuse federal funds or make misstatements on federal documents such as travel vouchers.

Thomas Saltonstall, the former director of the EEOC's Boston office, refused to comment publicly to the *Globe* about his boss's travels. He did seem to know enough, though, about a trip Thomas took to Boston that he was willing to testify to the committee about it. Some of those following the hearings, including me, had learned about Saltonstall, and were waiting for the testimony. Saltonstall would have told the committee that on one occasion he had been called to Thomas's hotel room outside Boston to watch him eating dinner with Thomas Sowell. Saltonstall was dismissed a few minutes after making his appearance. This brief encounter apparently was the "EEOC business" reason for the trip. But Saltonstall never told his story to the country. He had insisted on being subpoenaed if he was to testify. But the committee did not issue a subpoena, and he would not come on his own initiative.

In addition, Thomas had made other trips for which the EEOC could not, or would not, find the travel vouchers. This, too, made Thomas's opponents in the lobby groups suspicious *and* hopeful that something significant was to be found there.

But Chairman Biden flatly refused to pursue the matter, despite pressure from his fellow Democrats. For one thing, it was the kind of crime that more than one politician has been found guilty of. Most politicians, however, are not held to the same ethical standards as a nominee to the Supreme Court.

Perhaps in part because of his own nasty experiences with allegations of wrongdoing as well as his strong desire to come across as a nice guy, Biden had never liked to pursue ethical questions, of any sort, against judicial nominees. And he had been made more nervous by the television advertisements of the week before that had attacked him and Senators Kennedy and Cranston.

When I found out about the fight going on behind the scenes in the Judiciary Committee over the travel issue, I asked one of Senator Biden's aides why the chairman was reluctant to pursue it. "He just doesn't like to go after this personal stuff," the aide responded.

———————

Although few people realized it at the time, there was reason by the end of that first day to believe that Thomas was not going to make it through the Senate Judiciary Committee as easily as had been predicted. Anita Hill was not the reason. By then, only two senators even knew about her. The problem was with the performance of Thomas himself.

If Thomas was going to win the committee vote, he had to have the backing of the senators that made up its middle ground—the moderate Republicans and the conservative Democrats. This was touchy stuff. For example, both supporters and opponents of the nominee were hoping for the vote of Senator Howell Heflin, the conservative Democrat from Alabama who was notorious for sitting on the political fence. A former judge himself, Senator Heflin anguished over his decisions, weighing and reweighing the merits of the case. He held an important swing vote, one that potentially could bless one side or the other with victory. This had been illustrated when Senator Heflin played the key role in defeating President Bush's nomination of another black conservative, William Lucas, to the top civil rights post at the Justice Department.

After the first day's proceedings, Senator Heflin said in a televison interview with Cable News Network that he was concerned that Thomas seemed to be disavowing things he had said so ardently in the recent past.

"We are somewhat left in a quandary as to whether there is some confirmation conversion taking place here," Heflin said, meaning that under the pressure of wanting the Senate to confirm him, Thomas was verbally refashioning himself.

Thus the stage was set perfectly the next morning for the contentious old liberal, Senator Howard Metzenbaum, to go after Clarence Thomas as he had before at his confirmation hearings for the appellate judgeship and at grilling sessions before other Senate committees. Thomas braced himself for a spate of barbed questions, trying to look as if he wasn't as leery of the senator as the senator was of him.

Metzenbaum was seventy-four. He had worked his way through college selling Fuller brushes and popular magazines, then hit the jackpot running parking lots at airports. He didn't seem to give a damn what his colleagues thought of him, and was famous for killing the pork-barrel bills that funneled government money into their states. He was one of the few senators left who was unashamed by his own liberalism, often complaining that the Democrats were acting too much like Republicans. He was fond of saying that the country "does not need two Republican parties."

"Yesterday," Senator Metzenbaum began his interrogation, "I thought we would finally get some answers on your views. Instead of explaining your views, though, you actually ran from them and disavowed them."

Sitting only several feet behind Thomas, Emma Mae Martin glared at the senator. She had forgiven her brother for his unkind remarks about her welfare dependency and she wanted to defend him from this stranger.

"If I wasn't a Christian I'd take my Bible and slap that senator in the head," she muttered.

The senator hammered Thomas on abortion, using the rhetoric of the pro-choice movement.

"Frankly, I'm terrified that if we turn the clock back on legal abortion services, women will once again be forced to resort to brutal and illegal abortions. The kinds of abortions where coathangers substitute for surgical instruments. The consequences of *Roe*'s demise are so horrifying to me and the millions of American women and men, I want to ask you once again, appealing to your sense of compassion, whether or not you believe the Constitution protects a woman's right to abortion?"

Senator Metzenbaum tried the same question from thirteen different angles. Of course, he had no luck. He never had much chance of making any progress because most of the time he was reading from a script prepared by his staff and printed out in large letters before him. The scripts not only provide questions but also anticipate the answers, giving the senator different options as to how to continue depending on Thomas's response. This was no way, however, to conduct an effective cross examination.

This dependency on staff aides was not necessarily a function of age. Senator Kennedy, fifteen years Metzenbaum's junior, also read from staff-prepared scripts. So did most of the rest of the senators. Those who didn't stick to a script, like Republican Alan Simpson of Wyoming, ran the risk of making public fools of themselves. The outstanding exceptions on this committee were Senator Leahy on the Democratic side and Senator Arlen Specter of Pennsylvania on the Republican. Both of them had formerly worked as prosecutors. Senators Biden and Hatch were also capable of independent action.

But the reality is that most senators are not both smart enough and well-informed enough in the intricacies of constitutional law to engage in a running dialogue with a Supreme Court nominee without embarrassing themselves. To be fair, judging a judicial nominee requires an enormous amount of study, which is difficult for senators who must keep up with dozens of issues at once. And in the case of Thomas, the senators had to deal with the intricacies of the nominee's fluctuating philosophy. He was no simple read.

Senator Leahy, when it was his turn to speak, was able to push Thomas enough to elicit a most provocative statement on the subject of the landmark abortion case, one that would cause the nominee trouble and weaken his credibility. The senator, a tall, balding man who could gaze down from the dais at the nominee through his glasses, employed the calm and straightforward demeanor of a Vermonter.

"Judge, you were in law school at the time *Roe* versus *Wade* was decided. That was eighteen years—seventeen to eighteen years ago. I would assume—well, back up this way. You would accept, would you not, that in the last generation *Roe* v. *Wade* is certainly one of the more important cases to be decided by the U.S. Supreme Court?"

"I would accept that it's certainly been one of the more important, as well as one that has been one of the more highly publicized and debated cases," Thomas replied.

"So I would assume that it would be safe to assume that, when that came down you're in law school where recent case laws are discussed, *Roe* v. *Wade* would have been discussed in the law school while you were there."

Senator Leahy was leading Thomas into a trap.

"The case that I remember being discussed most during my early part of law school was I believe in a small group with Thomas Emerson [a Yale professor] may have been *Griswold* [the original right-to-privacy case] since he argued that. And we may have touched on *Roe* v. *Wade* at some point and debated that, but let me add one point to that. Because I was a married student and I worked, I did not spend a lot of time around the law school doing what the other students enjoyed so much, and that's debating all the current cases and all of the slip opinions [early, unbound versions of Supreme Court decisions]. My schedule was such that I went to classes and generally went to work and went home."

The former prosecutor was not buying that escape. "Well, Judge Thomas, I was a married law student who also worked, but I also found that at least between classes we did discuss some of the law, and I'm sure you're not suggesting that there wasn't any discussion at any time of *Roe* v. *Wade?*

Nervous and fumbling, Thomas responded, "I cannot—I—Senator, I cannot remember personally engaging in those discussions. The groups that I met with at that time during my years in law school were small study groups."

"Have you ever had discussion of *Roe* v. *Wade* other than in this room?" an increasingly skeptical Leahy asked, provoking laughter from the audience at the absurdity of the question. "In the seventeen or eighteen years it's been there?"

"Only, I guess, senator, in the fact that, in the most general sense, that other individuals express concerns one way or the other and you listen and you try to be thoughtful. If you're asking me whether or not I've ever debated the contents of it, the answer to that is no, Senator."

Senator Leahy persisted, "Have you ever, private gathering or otherwise, stated whether you felt that it was properly decided or not?"

"Senator, in trying to recall and reflect on that, I don't recollect commenting one way or the other. There were, again, debates about it in various places, but I generally did not participate. I don't remember or recall participating, Senator."

"So you don't ever recall stating whether you thought it was properly decided or not?"

"I can't recall saying one way or the other, Senator."

Leahy was understandably incredulous. Thomas was asserting that in law school he had never even discussed *Roe* v. *Wade*, the most controversial case of the era, handed down while he was studying law. According to his law professors, *everyone* at Yale was talking about *Roe* in 1973, the year of the Supreme Court decision on the case. Further, he was claiming that he had never debated the merits of the case and never taken a position on it in private conversation. Very few people to whom I talked that day believed that Thomas was telling the truth.

In trying to make himself sound harmless, even opinionless, Thomas had lost support from more than one quarter. The moderate members of the Judiciary Committee could not but doubt the nominee's sincerity, even his veracity. Also, Thomas was alienating the right-wing groups that had helped organize the nomination for him in the first place.

"By the second day, Clarence Thomas had begun to sound too much like David Souter to be Clarence Thomas," said Tom Jipping. "Conservatives had had high expectations about this hearing. We knew what he believed in, we knew what his character was and we were looking at this as an opportunity for him to come back at the committee and champion what we all believed in. It wasn't that what he said was objectionable. It was what he didn't say that we were hoping he would. After the first day, we just thought he might be off to a shaky start. After the second day, we were more confused by his [performance] and disappointment was increasing."

Behind the scenes, a drama began that few other than the actors themselves knew about. Jipping's boss and one of Thomas's most important backers was more than disappointed. Paul Weyrich, the conservative organizer who was running Library Court as well as the group called Coalitions for America, was shaken. Weyrich felt that Thomas's integrity was in question after the exchange with Leahy. By the end of the week he had ordered Jipping to stay away from the hearings and told him he was seriously considering withdrawing his support. Jipping was afraid he would publicly announce opposition to Thomas. Had he done so, and stated his reasons, it could have killed the nomination right there.

Weyrich believed that Thomas *had* taken a position on abortion when he had visited his pro-choice groups when he was at the EEOC.

Weyrich was too principled to overlook what seemed like, at best, a misstatement of the facts. He remembered that Thomas had been asked about abortion at that meeting. "My recollection of his answer would have seemed to indicate he had a point of view," Weyrich said later in an interview at his office.

Weyrich was upset at the way Thomas was dodging questions about his beliefs, the very beliefs that had earned so much backing from his own and the other allied groups of the conservative movement.

"I thought his lack of candor was disingenuous. . ." Weyrich said.

"Watching it on television it was frankly nauseating."

Jipping worked almost all night going through the transcripts of Thomas's testimony, rehashing the meeting Thomas had had with their coalition, and preparing a memorandum he hoped would at least keep Weyrich from going public.

Having gathered his arguments, Jipping reported to his boss that neither he nor other participants in the meeting with whom he had talked remembered a discussion about abortion. In any case, Jipping had an argument that defended Thomas with a legalistic splitting of hairs. Thomas had not denied discussing abortion, Jipping's argument went, he had testified that he had not discussed *Roe*. Jipping went on to point out that when Thomas had used the word "discuss" in his testimony, he was referring only to his time at law school, not the many subsequent years. Weyrich was persuaded by Jipping's analysis that Thomas had at least preserved his integrity. In print, he said, Thomas statements looked much better—"rather clever," in fact.

Thomas had in reality gone much further than to say he had not discussed *Roe* at Yale. He told Leahy he had never entered into a debate about the merits of *Roe* and never taken a position on it.

Jipping's legalisms were not convincing next to the clear denials Thomas had given under oath. If Thomas was not telling the whole truth about *Roe*, as common sense would seem to indicate, it meant he was willing to dissemble to get onto the Supreme Court.

No matter how tricky or unpleasant the questions posed by the more aggressive Democratic senators on the committee, Clarence Thomas showed no obvious signs of discomfort or nervousness. For five days, beginning on September 10, the Supreme Court nominee was subjected to long hours of interrogation. Each day, with his shoulders squared, he leaned forward slightly at the witness table, alone, with pen and notepad his only visible weapons of defense. Senator Biden's gavel controlled the length of the sessions, during which Thomas had to look up at his questioners on the raised dais as he formulated his answers. But the nominee never looked cowed; he came across as genial if terse.

Thomas's invisible defense was in play, the defense Duberstein had rehearsed with him over and over again. He was not supposed to charge into arguments about the issues waved at him like red flags, though he loved to debate, and he was not to touch the tempting controversies dangled in front of him, particularly abortion. He was supposed to keep his mouth shut as much as he could. Under the unblinking eye of national television, Thomas stuck to the plan.

In Savannah, Lester Johnson watched the performance of his old friend beamed onto his television screen and kept shaking his head.

"That wasn't the real Clarence Thomas talking," the attorney said later in an interview. "Not with those short, drilled sentences. He was not defending his beliefs. He was doing what they had trained him to say."

Virginia Thomas, accustomed to the Senate's hard politics and its straight-backed chairs, sat resolutely behind her husband, evidencing no more emotion than he did under the rain of questions. When Senator Biden called breaks, though, she was quick to her feet, stepping forward to be with her husband. Thomas's mother and sister, Leola Williams and Emma Mae Martin, also stepped close to the nominee to show support.

Clarence Thomas's verbal grilling was followed by three days of testimony by an array of witnesses who came to the Senate Caucus Room to offer praise, or blast criticism. The senators listened to friends of Thomas, enemies of his politics, critics of his legal qualifications, and backers of his beliefs.

The hearing process of the judiciary committee appeared to be working well. Senators and people of all convictions publicly debated who Thomas was, and what he stood for. Clarence Thomas might have been somewhat recalcitrant when he did not want to fully answer a senatorial query, but, all in all, it seemed he was being thoroughly tested. The hundreds of spectators listening in the mammoth Caucus Room and the millions more paying attention on radios or television sets were learning all there was to know. They could not have guessed that the committee was not telling them the whole truth, that charges of sexual harassment had not been investigated.

One of the early witnesses against Thomas was Erwin N. Griswold, a Republican but one who didn't want to see Thomas on the high court.

Griswold had been a professor of law at Harvard University for thirty-two years, much of that time as dean. He also had served as solicitor general in the Johnson and Nixon administrations from 1967 to 1973, to be followed in that post by Robert Bork. Upon leaving government service, Griswold opened a private practice in Washington. With his experience, his reputation and his eighty-seven years behind him, he could say what he thought.

No one questions that Judge Thomas is a fine man and deserves much credit for his achievements over the past forty-three years. But that does not support the conclusion that he has, as yet, demonstrated the distinction, the depth of experience, the broad legal ability which the American people have the right to expect from persons chosen for our highest court. Compare his experience and demonstrated abilities with those of Charles Evans Hughes or Harlan Fiske Stone, with Robert H. Jackson or the second John M. Harlan [his grandfather, the first John M. Harlan, also was a high court justice], with Thurgood Marshall or Lewis F. Powell, for example.

To say that Judge Thomas now has such qualifications is obviously unwarranted. If he should continue to serve on the Court of Appeals for eight or ten years he may well show such qualities and I hope he does. But he clearly has not done so yet.

I have no doubt that there are a number of persons, white, African American, or Hispanic, male or female, who have demonstrated such distinction. I do not question that the President has the right to take ideological factors into consideration and it seems equally clear to me that this committee and the Senate have a similar right and power. But that is no reason for this committee or the Senate approving a presidential nominee who has not yet demonstrated any clear intellectual or professional distinctions.

And the down side, and this worries me profoundly, is frightening. The nominee, if confirmed, may well serve for forty years. That would be until the year 2030. There does not seem to me to be any justification for taking such an awesome risk.

Senator Hank Brown of Colorado, a relative newcomer to the Senate and one of the quieter members of the Judiciary Committee, moved to try to parry Griswold's damaging comments. Senator Brown is a lawyer as well as a tax accountant and a meat-packing executive. He asked Griswold to compare Thomas with Justice William O. Douglas, who was appointed to the court at age forty with a similar background in federal regulatory agencies.

"In the case of Douglas," Griswold replied, "you are starting out with a really great mind. I don't see any signs of corresponding intellectual ability in the present nominee."

The best reason for opposing Clarence Thomas was not his extreme views. That would be reason enough, but it was something the senators were finding impossible to sort out. The point was that the nominee did not yet have the experience, or the knowledge, or the intellect to do the job. The stakes at the Supreme Court are too high to offer on-the-job training, particularly when the recipient gets to keep the job even if he never masters the trade.

During the course of the hearings, Thomas's lack of understanding of constitutional law was becoming abundantly apparent to those knowledgeable in this highly specialized field.

(It was only recently that Thomas had become serious about following developments in constitutional law. In his earlier years in government, his attitude had been cavalier at times. In 1984, for instance, Thomas had admitted to ignoring a Supreme Court ruling on a case in which he had been at least somewhat involved, that of *Grove City College* v. *Bell*, in which the high court made an important ruling that narrowed the interpretation of the laws against sex discrimination in university programs receiving federal aid. While under oath in a legal deposition involving another case, Thomas said he had not read the Grove ruling. "Someone may have given it to me, but I probably trashed it," he declared. He acknowledged that he had participated in shaping the Republican administration's brief in the case a couple of years earlier while at the civil rights office of the Education Department, but as for reading the result, he said, "I have a lot of other things to do.")

In front of the crowd in the Senate Caucus Room, Thomas's most embarrassing moments with constitutional law came while trying to respond to a question from Senator Patrick Leahy of Vermont about the most important cases decided by the Supreme Court since his Yale law school days.

Thomas stumbled about, struggling to come up with some examples. He mentioned *Roe* and *Griggs* v. *Duke Power Company*, the 1971 case in which the high court first held that Congress has the right to outlaw employment discrimination. He said he couldn't think of any others "off the top of my head. As you mention them, perhaps I could accord some weight to them, but just not off the top of my head."

Part of Thomas's problem was that he had misunderstood Senator Leahy's question, thinking that the senator had asked about the major decisions *while* he was in law school. Even so, Thomas's law school years, beginning in 1971 and ending in 1974, were bountiful ones for the Supreme Court. Cases that might roll off the tongue of a constitutional scholar, in addition to *Roe* and *Griggs*, would include *Swann* v. *Charlotte-Mecklenburg*, the 1971 case that permitted school busing; *Lemon* v. *Kurtzman*, the controversial First Amendment case that established the modern standard for separation of church and state; *Furman* v. *Georgia*, which threw out all death penalty laws; *Branzburg* v. *Hayes*, in which the court held that a reporter could be charged with contempt for refusing to testify to a grand jury concerning a crime; *Keyes* v. *Denver*, the first school desegregation case in a district where segregation had not been a matter of law; *Miller* v. *California*, which made a major change in the obscenity standards; and *The New York Times* v. *United States*, the famous decision refusing to stop the *New York Times* from publishing the *Pentagon Papers*.

Thomas's performance made constitutional law professors of all stripes cringe. Why, then, was Thomas's competence not made an issue, except by Griswold? The answer may be racially tinged. On the one side, the Republicans relished the idea of a black Supreme Court justice who had a distaste for sweeping social programs for the underprivileged and disadvantaged. They would do what they could to help Thomas. On the other, the Democrats felt checkmated. They couldn't ridicule a black nominee for his lack of learning; they might look elitist at best, and racist at worst; they were trapped by their own ideology.

Two other major issues were also ignored by the Democrats. Thomas's abysmal record in handling age discrimination cases, which had been the central controversy in the hearings for his appellate court nomination, was hardly mentioned. This was an issue with great middle-class appeal, but the Democrats hadn't been given any political backing by the American Association of Retired Persons, which had failed to take a stand. The powerful vote of the elderly was not being held out as a reward. An additional difficulty with this issue was that it was too technical to play well on television—and making a good impression on the national television audience was a part of what these hearings were about.

The other ghost issue, of course, was affirmative action. But the

Democrats had no stomach for this fight in 1991, especially since they were arguing the issue against a black man who had experienced the cruel lashes of racial bigotry since childhood. Once again it took a Republican, Senator Arlen Specter, to press the issue.

The Pennsylvania senator was good at making his point, particularly when it came to judicial nominations. He had been both a prosecutor and a professor of law. Nowhere did he feel more comfortable than when seated at a Judiciary Committee hearing deftly corraling a nominee with questions. Unlike most of his colleagues on the committee, Senator Specter understood the intricacies of constitutional law and he loved to debate them. Politically, the senator was a loner, not to be trusted by the other Republican senators and their staffs. He had often sided with the Democrats on social policy, voting for abortion rights and busing.

Among the Republicans on the Judiciary Committee, he was the most frequent ally of the Democrats. He was often the toughest questioner of Republican nomineees, even if he ended up voting for them for the sake of partisan politics. Senator Specter had sparred brilliantly with Judge Bork before reluctantly voting against his nomination. By 1991, though, the senator faced an election challenge from the right wing of his own party, and he was likely to vote for Thomas. But that didn't mean he would be silent.

Laying his groundwork, Senator Specter went over some of the strong statements the nominee had made in the past about racism. He read Thomas one of his comments in the piece by Juan Williams that had appeared in *The Atlantic*. "There is nothing you can do to get past black skin," Thomas had said. "I don't care how educated you are, how good you are at what you do, you'll never know the same contacts or opportunities, you'll never be seen as being equal to the whites."

Removing his reading glasses and using them to gesture down at Thomas, Specter asked the nominee to reconcile that and similar comments with his opposition to affirmative action. "Why is it that you come down so strongly against any group action to try to put minorities or African Americans in the position that they would have been in as a group but for the discrimination?" Specter asked.

"Senator, I think that over my years in public life, as well as my adult life, I've made it clear what I think of racism and discrimination . . ." Thomas said. "I think that we all have to do as much as possible to include members of my race, minorities, women, anyone who's excluded, into our society. I believe that. I've always believed that. And I've worked to achieve that."

"What's the best way to do it?" Specter continued. Thomas replied:

I think that is the question: how best to do it? I think that you have a tension. You want to do that, and at the same time, you don't want to discriminate against others. You want to be fair. At the same time you want to affirmatively include. And there's a real tension there. I wrestled with that tension. I think others wrestled with that tension. The line that I drew was a line that said that we shouldn't have preferences, or goals, or time-tables or quotas. I drew that line personally as a policy matter, argued that, advocated that, for reasons that I thought were important.

One, I thought it was true to the underlying value in the statute that we be fair to everyone. And I also drew it because I felt, and I've argued over the past twenty years, and I've felt that [it was] important that whatever we do, we do not undermine the dignity, self-esteem and self-respect of any-body or any group that we're helping. That has been important to me and it's been central to me.

I think that all of us who were well intentioned on either side of the debate, at any given time, wanted to achieve the exact same goal. I would have hoped, if I could revisit the '80s, that we could have sat down and constructively tried to hammer out a consensus way to solve what I con-sider a horrible problem.

Thomas was handling the questions well. But Specter kept pressing. He wanted to know how Thomas's answer that he was seeking fairness squared with his sharp criticism of the 1986 Supreme Court decision that required a union to accept a quota for black workers. The high court's ruling required a New York sheet-metal workers' local, which had for decades fought legal action to force it to admit blacks, to increase its minority membership to more than 29 percent. When Thomas had chaired the EEOC, his agency had argued against such a ruling. Thomas's stand had been that those workers who could actu-ally prove they were discriminated against by the union should benefit from the case, not the future applicants who would be admitted under the percentage goal.

The senator asked how Thomas could have come to this conclusion given the history of the case. Since it was clear from the union's intransigence that it would have continued to discriminate if given free rein, why wasn't it reasonable to set a hiring goal?

"I felt, as a policymaker, that the best way to enforce the law, to enforce antidiscrimination laws, is to increase the remedy, the direct remedy, for discrimination," Thomas replied, failing to parry the senator's thrust.

Having made his point, Senator Specter began another aggressive line of questioning. Casting his eye onto Thomas's past, he asked the nominee how he could be so much against affirmative action when this was exactly the kind of social engineering that had gotten him into law school at Yale University.

Thomas surprised Arlen Specter—and many others listening to his testimony—by saying that he was not against affirmative action in the college context as long as it was targeted at disadvantaged kids of any race, not just at blacks. Thomas indicated he would not, however, extend the same argument to job hiring.

"Well, Judge Thomas, that's fine for those of us who have gone to Yale," said Specter, who also was a Yale law school alumnus. "But what about the African-American youngster who doesn't have an educational background and is fighting for a job?"

In this verbal bout, Thomas succeeded in explaining the principles behind his stand against affirmative action. But Senator Specter succeeded in exposing some of the weaknesses in Thomas's position. The other senators didn't rush into the fray, though. The Republicans wanted to smooth over Thomas's record rather than look for fractures in his philosophy. The Democrats were not interested in taking advantage of Specter's skillful questioning; they wanted to avoid the all-too-sensitive racial issue.

As Thomas's testimony neared an end, it looked as though the nominee was going to make it through without any major tribulations. His weaknesses were not being closely examined. Behind the façade of formality in the Senate Caucus Room, the Republicans and their aides were starting to feel confident that the Supreme Court was going to gain another conservative justice.

The Democrats and their aides were feeling helpless. They had been unable to get a solid grip on any of the things that disturbed them about the nominee; Thomas had slipped out of the abortion question, and the committee members had been unwilling to wrestle with him on the other issues. Desperately some of the aides put in overtime hours. They kept the lights burning into the night in their Senate offices as they searched for a way to unsettle the nominee who had been so well coached by the Republicans in the executive branch, and so cleverly backed by the groups of the radical right.

These behind-the-scenes political realities were invisible to most Americans. It looked as though Thomas was on the road to winning confirmation because of his race and his image as a man who pulled himself up by the bootstraps from utter poverty to a productive life. Thomas had done his best during the hearings to throw in illustrations of how his character might enhance his role on the Supreme Court; he told the committee that he could bring to the high court an understanding of how its decisions affected the underprivileged.

As an example, Thomas recounted that every day when he looked out of his current office window at the appellate court, he noticed the busloads of miserable prisoners being driven away. "I say to myself almost every day, 'There but for the grace of God go I,'" he testified. His implied promise was that he would take prisoners' rights to heart. Whether or not he meant this would only become clear if he had a chance to issue opinions from the Supreme Court bench.

It was character that was selling the nominee, just as George Bush and Kenneth Duberstein had planned from the start. Keeping his penchant for arguing under tight control, Thomas finished his testimony with his image largely intact.

Politically powerful African-Americans were distracted over the crucial weekend of Thomas's testimony by the lavish annual dinner of the Congressional Black Caucus. Thousands of guests poured into the Washington Hilton for the gala dinner sponsored by the caucus, which is made up of the nation's black representatives to Congress. The caucus had come out in opposition to the Thomas nomination early on. But Clarence Thomas wasn't mentioned in any of the speeches made that evening. While serious dramas about the future of the Supreme Court were being played out elsewhere in the capital, the party went on, complete with a fashion show featuring gorgeous women.

In the following days, dozens of witnesses came forward to have their say about Clarence Thomas. With a mechanical fairness, Chairman Biden alternated anti-Thomas with pro-Thomas witnesses.

Balancing the testimony of the eminent legal scholar, Erwin Griswold, was the testimony of the equally eminent Guido Calabresi, the current dean of the law school at Yale University. He, too, had a fine legal background, having been a Rhodes scholar, a Supreme Court law clerk to Justice Hugo Black, and a Yale law professor.

Calabresi said that he had not had Thomas as a law student, but that he had gotten to know him well during the years the student from Pin Point spent in Yale's halls. Calabresi, although he disagreed with Thomas politically, wanted to convince committee members that this was a nominee who had the capacity to grow intellectually.

The young Thomas had shown "a capacity for independent thought that is always unusual, but is especially so among students, who pretend all too frequently to conform to the current mood," the dean testified.

> His approach to law when he was a student was not especially linked with the left or with the right. What characterized him was he could not be predicted—that he was always seeking more information in order to decide what made sense to him, and that whatever position he took was his own and was powerfully and eloquently held.

Calabresi told the senators that he had recommended Thomas to Danforth, then the Missouri attorney general.

> I was glad I did so then, and I'm glad I did so now. Many of his views have changed several times since those days. That does not surprise me. It is almost inevitable with people who are truly struggling with ideas and wrestling with the great issues of the day. I would expect that at least some of his views may change again. I would be less than candid if I did not tell you that I sincerely hope so, for I disagree with many, perhaps most, of the public positions which Judge Thomas has taken in the past few years.

Calabresi interpreted Thomas's philosophical wanderings as positive.

[Thomas's] history of struggle and his past openness to argument, together with his capacity to make up his own mind, make him a much more likely candidate for growth than others who have recently been appointed to the Supreme Court and who, whatever they may have said at their confirmation hearings, had, in fact, been set in their ways and immovable back to their law school days.

Such a capacity for growth as a justice develops his or her own constitutional philosophy is essential if a person is to become a truly great justice. None of the great justices of the past, not Justice Black, nor Justices Harlan or Stewart, not Justice Holmes nor Justices Brandeis or Cardozo, not even Justice Frankfurter, for all his years of teaching constitutional law, came to the court fully formed. The court itself and the individual cases that came before them shaped them, even as they shaped the court. In the end, it was a combination of character, ability, a willingness to work really hard and openness to new views that made them great justices. These qualities, if there truly is openness, matter far more than past positions. Many a justice has changed his mind dramatically since going on the court.

To conclude his argument, Calabresi relayed an anecdote about Thomas as a student reacting to a bad mark.

Early on [in his law studies, Thomas] did get a poor grade . . . from one of the toughest teachers in the school. When that happens, most students stay as far away from such a professor as they possibly can. Not Judge Thomas. He not only went back to the same teacher for another course, but chose to do his senior essay, his dissertation, for that teacher, and this time he received an honors, the highest grade given in the school. The quality this demonstrates has stood Judge Thomas well in the past. It will stand him well in the future.

Most of the other witnesses for Thomas lacked Dean Calabresi's stature. And most testified for the obvious reason that some portion of Thomas's political philosophy appealed to them. Law enforcement officials, for instance, could guess that the nominee would not be prone to expanding the constitutional rights of criminals.

A typical pro-Thomas panel of witnesses, who would all testify at the same sitting, included Captain Johnny Hughes of the Maryland State Police, who was speaking for the National Troopers Coalition; Bob Suthard, a former superintendent of the Virginia State Police;

James Doyle, a former assistant attorney general in the state of Maryland, who became a lobbyist for special interests at the state legislature; Donald Baldwin, who was speaking for the National Law Enforcement Council, and Sheriff Carl Peed of Virginia's Fairfax County.

Chairman Biden, trying as always not to offend anyone, struggled with the sheriff's name.

"Sheriff, is it pronounced 'ped'?" Biden asked anxiously, hoping that the name rhymed with red.

"Peed," the sheriff replied, pronouncing his surname to rhyme with seed and refusing further comment.

"Peed," Biden repeated, abashed. "I am sorry. I'm not very good at this, you see."

Peed had come to speak for the National Sheriffs Association. He told the senators that sheriffs across the country believed Thomas to be "a person of the highest caliber, an anticrime person, a judge who recognizes the tough job facing law enforcement professionals today."

Like Peed's, most of the testimony was predictable. A panel of black law professors testified against Thomas. One of the Franciscan nuns who had taught Thomas spoke on his behalf, as did the president of Holy Cross College. Representatives of abortion-rights groups repeated their criticisms.

Molly Yard, representing the National Organization of Women (NOW), appeared despite the fact that she was still recovering from a stroke. She was determined to give the senators a piece of NOW's feminist mind.

"In fact Judge Thomas is not the enigma he would like to be," she said. "Both his words and his actions show him to be cold and callous. This man insulted women who have suffered discrimination in employment by calling their legitimate complaints clichés. He said that women avoid professions like the practice of medicine because it interferes with our roles as wives and mothers. This type of medieval claptrap would doom any politician running for electoral office. How then can it be considered acceptable for a Supreme Court nominee?"

John Hope Franklin, the highly respected historian of the civil rights movement, canceled his testimony at the last minute. He was said to be disgusted with the senators' failure to question Thomas thoroughly on his civil rights record. The executive director of the NAACP, Ben Hooks, did appear to speak for his organization, criticizing Thomas for rising to the top and forgetting his brethren. Hooks spoke for his organization and kept absolutely silent about his own secret contribution to Thomas's success.

In attendance in the audience was one of the true symbols of the civil rights movement, a fragile, elderly Rosa Parks, whose refusal to sit in the back of a bus touched off the Montgomery bus boycott and the civil rights marches that led to desegregation. She was so weak that she was practically carried into the hearing room. A member of the audience sent a note to Biden, asking him to recognize this woman who made American history. The chairman ignored Rosa Parks, though, fearing, perhaps, that a mention of her name would appear partisan.

Many on the panels of witnesses who came to speak for Thomas were relative unknowns in national politics. One of these was John E. Palmer, president of EDP Enterprises, a food service company that feeds troops at Fort Leonard Wood, Missouri, as well as Fort Riley, Kansas. He came to speak for the Heartland Coalition for the Confirmation of Judge Clarence Thomas. Others were Robert Woodson, president of National Center for Neighborhood Enterprise, and Alphonso Jackson, executive director of the Dallas Housing Authority.

The witnesses on the other side were generally better known. Joseph L. Rauh, a longtime mainstay of the civil rights movement, spoke against the nominee. Also speaking against Thomas were representatives of the Congressional Black Caucus, who had cooled down from their weekend, and the Coalition of Black Trade Unionists, which was represented by William Lucy, a veteran labor leader.

It was evident that Clarence Thomas was not a man from either of the establishments, left or right. He had not developed a wide circle of acquaintances in the capital, and the far-right groups that so fervently supported his nomination did not wish their cause to be publicly identified. Their representatives attended the hearing, but kept out of public view as much as possible.

A quick-eyed reporter caught sight of Elizabeth Law, one of the radical-right lobbyists, during an intermission, but was unable to identify her. John Mackey, a Justice Department official, sidled over to Law and advised her to "go for a walk" to escape detection. The political teams working for Thomas out of Senator Danforth's and Senator Cochran's nearby offices didn't want the press to get the full story of who was supporting Thomas. Better to avoid the political complications, and stick with the message of Thomas as a man of character. They had no intimation of how severely Thomas's character was going to be critiqued in the coming weeks.

As the first days of the hearings passed, Anita Hill was in Oklahoma agonizing. She had already talked to members of the staffs of Senators Kennedy and Metzenbaum. She believed that the Judiciary Committee should investigate her charges, and speedily. But she couldn't force the committee and, in particular, its chairman, to do so; she had to wait and wonder. She was reluctant to step forward more boldly. It had been difficult enough telling her story to Jim Brudney, her old classmate on Senator Metzenbaum's staff. She had made it clear that she was not ready to have her name spread around in public. All her life she had been a private person, not one to broadcast the details of her private life to the world. If something was bothering her, her habit was to confide in a few close friends. Hill also knew that if what she had to say was not treated carefully and secretly, this episode from her past could blow up into an uncontrollable scandal. This at a time when she had finally found a comfortable professional home at the University of Oklahoma's law school at Norman.

Hill's allegations against the Supreme Court nominee were now going to be in the hands of Senator Biden, who was not exactly eager to get involved. Biden's staff had told Metzenbaum's staff that they would not call Hill. She would have to initiate the conversation.

This was difficult for Anita Hill to do. As she told Metzenbaum's staff and Kennedy's, she was reluctant to come forward. Her reluctance had also become clear to me, but I knew I was not in a good position to press the issue. Since I was working for a daily newspaper with a circulation of about 800,000, I was not the person Hill wanted to talk to just then about some of the most intimate and painful details of her life. She didn't want her name even mentioned in public as yet, and certainly not in connection with Clarence Thomas.

Hill was not the person who had started the controversy rolling; it had been initiated by telephone calls from Senate staffers in Washington, who had learned her story from the Alliance for Justice, which had come into the know by way of a woman classmate in whom Hill had confided. Hesitant, Hill had not spoken up until the first day of the hearings. But if Ricki Seidman of Senator Kennedy's staff had not prompted Hill, the law professor would never have said a word.

"Absolutely not!" Hill answered later when asked a question about whether she would have come forward independently. "It was a troubling decision for me to make, even after they came forward to me. It's not something that I wanted to grandstand about. And I realized that it has been a long time since these incidents occurred. And therefore, weighing that factor I had made a personal choice, to not become involved. However, I'm not sure in retrospect that even that would have been the good choice, but having been approached by the Senate, I felt that I had an obligation to come forward."(Hill also said she had not come forward earlier, particularly in 1990 when Thomas had been nominated to the federal appeals court, simply because "they never approached me.")

By September 12, the third day of the hearings, as Thomas continued to spar with the senators about the record of his political and judicial life, Anita Hill had decided she couldn't continue to stand with one foot in the door, waiting to see if someone on Senator Biden's staff would open it and invite her in to tell her story. Now that the issue had been raised, Hill had decided she would not be able to regain her peace of mind unless it was dealt with. That morning she telephoned Harriet Grant, the committee's nominations counsel and the person with whom she would discuss the next step. Harriet Grant did things by the book, Joe Biden's book. Her job was to brief Senator Biden on the information she had collected on judicial nominees—not just for the Supreme Court, but the whole federal judiciary. This included information from the extensive questionnaire sent each nominee by the committee. The committee, however, had no heavy-duty investigative capability. For that it relied on the FBI, which did background checks on every nominee. But the FBI was an executive-branch agency, reporting first of all to the White House, which made the judicial nominations to start with; the conflict-of-interest was built in.

Grant's reputation among the liberal groups opposing Thomas was that she was straitlaced—no doubt exactly what she wanted it to be. She did not seem eager to share information with them, or to look into potential problems that they might raise with her.

When Hill telephoned on Thursday, September 12, Grant was willing to listen. Hill had to break off the conversation, though, because she had go to teach a law school class that morning. Grant called Hill back that evening. Over a long-distance line between the capital and Oklahoma, Hill once again told the story of what had happened to her when she worked for Thomas. As a lawyer who understood the need to corroborate any story like hers, Hill provided Grant with the means to do that. She gave Grant the name of a friend, Susan Hoerchner, a judge in California, in whom she had confided her troubles with Thomas at the time.

After her conversations with Grant, Hill understood that her name and her charges against Thomas would not be made public, but that the information would be given to the members of the committee. That was exactly the way Hill wanted it—both ways. She wanted to avoid publicity, but she had decided that her story was too important to keep to herself. She felt that she was doing the right thing. Hill seemed to have no idea that the door she had opened was leading her into a morass; she evidently didn't understand Washington politics.

Senator Biden wasn't eager to come to Hill's aid. As far as Biden was concerned, someone close to him said later, "It was political nitroglycerine. We didn't know at this stage what was going to happen. What if we passed this thing around and it leaked and she said, 'I've been abused by the judiciary committee.' Or we could get killed the opposite way, by doing nothing. There is a perception that with the public you are putting a stick in the hornets' nest by digging up dirt, that that would also backfire. The public's feelings on this are very ambiguous. They want to see us thoroughly investigate nominees. But if we ask them should we dig up dirt on nominees they would say we should investigate them but not dig up dirt. That's the line that we have to walk all the time. I think from the start or shortly thereafter it was clear this was going to be a political disaster for us; it was just a question of which political disaster."

To this day, it remains unclear as to whether Biden even tried to understand Hill's position on the sensitive issue. Later, when Biden reconstructed the confusion of events that eventually dumped Hill in the eye of a public storm, the senator had a version of what happened that did not jibe with Hill's. Senator Biden said that Hill had been told that the committee members would not be informed about her charges unless a full investigation took place. In the interests of fairness, such an investigation would require that Thomas be given a chance to respond. According to Biden, Hill had not agreed that Thomas be told about her charges, thereby miring the Judiciary Committee in a state of inaction. Hill had told Grant, according to Biden's office, that at least "it was cathartic to tell someone about it."

Biden, according to his staff, felt strongly that he was not going to circulate "some anonymous charge." They said that Biden thought he had made sure that Hill understood this. Biden, who had spent much of the previous year drafting a law that would protect women who were victims of violence, also believed that women should not be coached or pushed into coming forward.

Days passed and the committee did nothing. Neither Grant nor anyone else on Biden's staff followed up on the allegations that the chairman of the EEOC had sexually harassed a member of his staff before being nominated to the Supreme Court of the United States. No one called Hill back to press her to come forward publicly. No one called other EEOC staffers to ask if they had experienced anything like what Hill said happened to her. No one even called Judge Hoerchner, who was willing to provide crucial corroboration. Senator Biden, who had had his own problems with attacks on his character, was content not to press for more information on the sexual harassment charges, which might be inconclusive or messy to deal with, or both. In the meantime, Thomas finished testifying, and the assortment of witnesses followed with their various opinions.

Finally, on September 18, after six days had passed with no action on the part of the committee, Judge Hoerchner called Washington. Judge Hoerchner made it clear to the committee that she could back up Anita Hill's charges. She thought Hill's case should be heard, at least unofficially, by the judiciary committee. Even this didn't force the committee into action.

The next day as the hearings were nearing their close, Hill picked up her telephone again and dialed the committee staff. It was another Thursday, September 19; a full week had gone by since Hill had spoken with Grant, the chief nominations counsel. Anita Hill wanted to know what had happened with her information. Nothing, she learned. Hill then asked what options she had to get the information before the senators on the committee, saying she did not want to abandon her concerns.

On Friday, September 20, the last day intended for the hearings, the committee staff made a move. It was proposed to Hill that the FBI be brought in to investigate her charges specifically. Her name would have to be provided to the FBI. The federal investigators would then interview both Thomas and Hill, who would no longer be able to remain in the background. Hill, still unsure of herself, hesitated. She asked to be telephoned again the next day. Hill continued to equivocate, in the view of Senator Biden and his staff, who had no real idea of the woman with whom they were dealing. At the time, the committee chairman had not made the effort to call the Oklahoma professor and talk to her directly. No staff member had been dispatched out to Oklahoma to meet with Hill in order to assess her character, to get her detailed account of what had gone on with Thomas, and to give her a live rundown of what was happening in the capital.

Most of the other senators on the committee had no idea about the drama that was going on behind the scenes with Anita Hill. By the weekend, with the hearings seemingly over, the best guess was that the majority of senators would vote in favor of Thomas. With a nod from the Judiciary Committee, a favorable vote from the full Senate was all but guaranteed. The next to the last hurdle on Thomas's path to the Supreme Court seemed to be dropping away. Nine of the fourteen senators on the committee seemed ready to approve President Bush's nominee when it came time to vote at the end of the week. It looked as though the six Republicans would hold solid with the president's choice, and three of the eight Democrats would lean far enough right to also vote for Thomas.

Senator Specter, the maverick among the Republicans, who had tangled with Thomas over his civil rights philosophy, announced that he would vote in favor of the nominee. Specter said that Thomas was qualified, if barely so, and that the Supreme Court needed diversity. The senator also was impressed by the strong stand Thomas had taken during the hearings against overruling the high court's precedents. That suited the senator's respect for the sanctity of constitutional law.

Senator Dennis DeConcini, the conservative Arizona Democrat, also planned to cast a favorable vote. DeConcini was one of those who believed deeply in the presidential prerogative in nominations. A former prosecutor and a multimillionaire whose family had large real estate holdings, DeConcini was the only Democrat to have been elected to the Senate from Arizona in three decades. To stay in office he thought he had to maintain his conservative image. Still, DeConcini had voted against Bork, with little in the way of ramifications in his 1988 reelection campaign, even though the angered judge had traveled to Arizona to campaign against him.

But at the time of the Thomas nomination, DeConcini, like Kennedy, was in no position to go out on a limb. He had become the most notorious of the Keating Five, the group of five Democrats who had pushed the Federal Home Loan Bank Board to lay off a troubled savings and loan owned by Charles H. Keating, Jr., the savings and loan magnate from Arizona. Having received $80,000 in campaign contributions from Keating, DeConcini was a prime target of the Senate Ethics Committee investigation into the scandal. He was in no position to alienate the White House by voting against Thomas.

In any case, there was no indication then that DeConcini's vote would matter. Senator Howell Heflin, after sounding the alarm about Thomas's "confirmation conversion," had apparently backed off. The venerable Alabama Democrat had asked Thomas a series of softball personal questions when he had his chance for a second crack at the nominee. Most onlookers took that as a sign that Heflin had decided to vote in favor.

There was a further indication that the "Southern strategy" to get Thomas confirmed was paying off. J. Bennett Johnston, an influential Southern politician from Louisiana who had been instrumental in the defeat of Bork, had announced that he would support Thomas if his nomination got to the Senate floor. In addition, there was every sign that Biden would vote for Thomas.

The weekend after the hearings was a long one for Anita Hill. The committee's proposal for an FBI investigation meant that investigators whom she neither knew nor trusted would suddenly be asking questions about what she felt had been an extraordinarily difficult time in her life, so difficult that she had retreated from it, coming home from Washington to the friendlier land of Oklahoma. She could expect no tact. Worse, she would have to hand over the use of her name to investigators who would also be questioning Clarence Thomas. Although the FBI investigation was not supposed to be public, it meant taking a risk. She still wanted her name kept out of the public arena.

The only experienced advisers to whom Hill turned were staff aides on the Judiciary Committee. She kept getting the message that unless she submitted to FBI involvement in the case, the committee would not handle her charges. Calls went back and forth between Oklahoma and Washington. Although Hill had worked in the capital, she did not have a clear concept of the power politics of a controversial Supreme Court nomination, according to Shirley Wiegand, another professor at the Oklahoma law school, who had become a close friend of Hill.

Wiegand and Leisha Self, another woman member of the law school faculty, were Hill's personal confidants over the weekend. The two women helped Hill talk out her concerns, but neither had any national political experience by which to advise her.

"The only advice she took was from those she talked to on the committee. She didn't know how the procedure worked, and I didn't know either," Wiegand said later in an interview. Hill's colleague was convinced that outside interest groups—feminists or liberals with an interest in derailing the Thomas nomination—were not talking into Hill's ear.

Explaining how Hill made her decision, Wiegand said, "I know it was not taken with the advice of any of the interest groups. I know of a couple of calls to the [law] school [by outsiders], but for the few of us involved, we felt it was very dangerous to accept help from them. That was not what she had in mind. Later, when the folks [from various interest groups] started trying to get involved, she made it very clear that she didn't want them involved. She knew that would be misinterpreted. She doesn't align herself with political factions. She still doesn't call herself a feminist."

Hill "made the decision herself," Wiegand said. "I had told her that if I were her, I wouldn't know what to do. I couldn't give her the answer."

Although Hill did hold quiet convictions about women's rights, it was not political considerations that embroiled Hill's decision, according to Wiegand. "She is a private person and she didn't want to disrupt Clarence Thomas's life or her life," Wiegand said, but finally Hill proceeded, thinking this was her "civic duty." She also had expected the FBI documents to remain confidential, that even with this next step, she and Thomas would not come under the scrutiny of the general public.

Finally, Hill decided to proceed. On Monday, September 23, she called the committee. She said she wanted to send her own statement of what had taken place between her and Thomas; she was willing to have the FBI make its investigation, using her name. Later in the day, Hill faxed her four-page, unsworn statement to the committee. Those who read it were shocked.

The allegations in the law professor's statement were almost too bizarre to be believable. When Thomas was her boss, according to Hill, he had repeatedly called her into his office, ostensibly on work-related matters, only to start talking about sex. He talked in vivid terms about the pornographic movies he had seen. Scenes he found particularly fascinating showed women copulating with animals, group sex, and rape, all of which he described to Hill in great detail. He kept asking her to go out with him, with obvious implications.

Biden, who had all but shunted aside the grotesque details under-pinning the sexual harassment charge, realized something had to be done fast. He could no longer afford to ignore Hill's accusations, even though it was already past the eleventh hour in terms of the committee vote. Senator Biden had planned to have the vote on the Thomas nomination before the week was out, by Thursday or Friday. Obvi-ously, the vote could not take place on schedule if an FBI investigation was underway. Biden immediately got in touch with officials over at the White House and arranged for the FBI to proceed with speed.

When Hill got home that evening to her house in Norman, on a quiet, suburban street, only a few miles from the law school, she found a message on her answering machine from the Oklahoma City office of the FBI. She called the office and was told the FBI wanted to interview her as soon as possible. The city is a half hour drive from Norman. When two agents, a man and a woman, arrived at about 6:30, she answered their questions about her allegations meticulously. When they asked if she would be willing to take a polygraph test, she agreed to do so.

Two days later, Wednesday, September 25—five days after the hearings had supposedly ended—Thomas received a telephone call at home from the White House. The call shattered his hopes that his nomination was smoothly on its way. This was the first he knew, officially anyway, that anything was wrong. Thomas was told that some unspecified allegations needed to be investigated. He had already passed the standard FBI background check. What could this be about? Without further explanation, he was asked to call the FBI to make an appointment.

Two hours later, two agents came to his home in suburban Virginia. When he heard who was making the charges he said: "Anita? You've got to be kidding. This can't be true." He denied the charges. It was never disclosed whether Thomas, like Hill, was asked the standard FBI question about willingness to take a polygraph, and if so, what his response was.

That same day Hill had again called the Judiciary Committee, where she usually talked with Grant, who relayed information to the chairman. Hill was told that the statement she had faxed two days earlier had not been distributed to the other committee members. It was hard for her to believe that there was still nothing happening. But Hill was assured that her statement would be used, or at least that the information in it would be brought to the attention of senators preparing to cast their votes on Thomas.

For anyone keeping a close eye on the Judiciary Committee, it began to appear that all was not well. Senator Biden's office would not provide the seemingly simple information about when the senators on the committee would actually cast their votes. Biden had expected to have the vote by the week's end. Even staffers for other senators on the Judiciary Committee couldn't get any information from Senator Biden's staff.

Late in the day, I learned from sources in the Senate that the FBI had reopened its investigation of the nomination. But I couldn't immediately discover the reason. There was some intimation that whatever the FBI was doing was not serious—which certainly was the prevailing attitude in the Judiciary Committee. That night, I learned that the FBI investigation involved sexual harassment. Putting two and two together, I figured out that the reopening of the investigation must have something to do with Anita Hill. Still I needed to get more solid information before writing a news story about this potentially major development.

In the meantime, Senator Biden was busy. That evening and the next day, he briefed the Democrats on the Judiciary Committee about the new investigation. The top senators of both parties—George J. Mitchell of Maine, the Senate majority leader, and Robert J. Dole, the Senate minority leader—were informed, as well. The senators were told that Hill's statement and the report that the FBI had almost produced from its interview were available. They were not given copies. Some looked at the documents, others did not bother.

Senator Biden had let Senator Thurmond decide how to handle the Republicans. Thurmond, the committee's ranking Republican, approached the matter like a Southern gentleman. (He once had said to a group of women testifying before him: "These are the prettiest witnesses we have had in a long time. I imagine you are all married. If not, you could be if you wanted to be.") Senator Thurmond ignored the matter. He decided this fuss over a sexual harassment charge was not significant enough to discuss with colleagues. It was to be a cause of great embarrassment for those senators left in the dark.

Those Democrats who had more interest in Hill's charges decided it was too late to do anything more. Any one of them could have employed Senate rules to put the vote off for a week, but none did. In some cases they did not think the matter was important enough. Others thought that without her willingness to come forward publicly—her statement and the FBI report were supposed to be held in confidence by the Senate—little could be done. Around this time, only one senator, Democrat Paul Simon of Illinois, is known to have actually made the effort to talk to Anita Hill. There is no indication from Senator Biden that he ever talked to Hill before the Judiciary Committee voted on Thomas.

Regardless of what Hill had to say, Chairman Biden proceeded to schedule the committee vote for Friday. This, in the opinion of one Senate staffer, "sealed the fate of Anita Hill." It left no time to deal seriously with her allegations.

On Thursday, September 26, the committee was startled by a development that had nothing to do with Anita Hill; Senator Howell Heflin announced on the Senate floor that he would vote the next day against Thomas. One of the most conservative of the Southern Democrats, Senator Heflin voted with the Republicans more often than not.

The aging Alabaman had been a great local trial attorney and then run successfully for the post of chief justice of the Alabama Supreme Court, where he reformed the entire state court system. Although he had been a senator for well over a decade, Heflin was more of a judge than a politician, more of a deliberator than an orator. He was famous for his tortured indecision.

Indeed, according to one Senate staffer, he had carried to the Senate floor two speeches on Thomas—one in favor of the nomination, one against. At the last minute, Senator Heflin decided to go with the speech lambasting the nominee. He said he was going to vote against Thomas for not being honest in his testimony and for having swung too far to the right. Coming from a conservative like Heflin, this was saying something.

"First let me say," the senator began, "I support a conservative court; my votes for Chief Justice Rehnquist and Justices O'Connor, Scalia, Kennedy, and Souter support my basic philosophy in this regard. However, I am not for an extremist right wing court that would turn back progress made against racial discrimination as well as the progress that has been made for human rights and freedoms in recent years."

While Thomas had an admirable background, the senator continued "my review of his writings and speeches raised questions in my mind that he might be part of the right-wing extremist movement." Thomas appeared to the senator to be a libertarian who would hold property rights above the rights of society to regulate commerce in order to protect the public safety, health, and welfare. This would mean "no minimum wage laws, no occupational safety and health laws, no environmental protection laws, nor laws providing for federal inspection of aircraft or food and meat products."

"During the course of the hearing," Heflin added, "Judge Thomas's answers and explanations about previous speeches, articles, and positions raised thoughts of inconsistencies, ambiguities, contradictions, lack of scholarship, lack of conviction, and instability. During the hearing I expressed that such created an appearance of confirmation conversion and that he was an enigma because of his puzzling answers and explanations."

Heflin cited Thomas's shifting his opinion on the concept of natural law and how it applied to consitutional law. The senator wondered aloud whether the nominee had changed his position for "expediency's sake."

The senator seemed particularly offended by Thomas's lack of conviction about Justice Oliver Wendell Holmes. In a 1988 speech to a conservative audience, Thomas had cavalierly dismissed the venerated justice. ("No man who ever sat on the Supreme Court was less inclined and so poorly equipped to be a statesman," Thomas had said.) In front of the Judiciary Committee, Thomas had described Holmes as a "great judge."

"His remarks about Holmes indicate a lack of scholarship and objectivity when he used dogmatic words in harshly attacking Holmes before a receptive audience," the senator said.

Heflin went on to note that Thomas had attacked Holmes for the very view on natural law that Thomas now claimed to share—that it should not be used in constitutional interpretation.

"Adding to his previous inconsistencies on the doctrine of natural law, Judge Thomas's responses suggest to me deceptiveness, at worst, or muddleheadedness, at best."

Heflin's announcement put Senator Biden on the spot. If he proceeded to vote for Thomas, he would be the only Democrat on the committee other than Senator DeConcini to do so. He would appear out of step with his party. A vote either way now presented difficulty.

If the chairman voted against Thomas it could well cause a tie of seven senators opposing the nomination and seven supporting it. This technically would mean that the nomination would fail. But the committee had long since surrendered the power to kill Supreme Court nominations. In the event of a tie, the nomination would still be sent without a recommendation to the floor for a full Senate vote. Nevertheless, a tie would breathe new life into Thomas's opposition. Senator Biden anguished. He was overheard screaming at Ron Klain, his chief counsel on the committee, who was pushing him to vote against Thomas.

Thomas, the White House, and most conservatives in Washington were waiting apprehensively for Biden to make up his mind. It was early Friday, September 27, the morning before the committee vote, that Biden announced his decision on the Senate floor. His speech began with what would prove to be one of the most embarrassing statements in Senate history, since he began by assuming that the questions Hill had raised about Thomas's character should be ignored.

"For this senator, there is no question with respect to the nominee's character, competence, credentials or credibility," Biden said after dispatching Anita Hill's sworn statement to the FBI to what he must have thought would be oblivion. "For me, the question that concerns me the most is Judge Thomas's judicial philosophy. The approach he would bring to deciding how to interpret the ennobling phrases of the

Constitution in matters of contention, on ambiguous questions con-
fronting the Supreme Court."

Biden went on, however, to render a dissertation on why Thomas
should not be confirmed. It often sounded like a speech written to
support Thomas, which it may originally have been. Indeed, Biden
conceded that "every instinct in me wanted to support Clarence
Thomas." But while his heart told him to vote for the man from Pin
Point, his head cautioned him to do otherwise.

Biden's first complaint was that Thomas had not been receptive to
the committee's questions, particularly about the right of privacy.
That, he said, is every nominee's right.

"But if this choice is the nominee's to make, the decision about
what we do in response to the nominee's action is for us, for the
Senate, to make. I cannot force a nominee to be complete and engaging in his answers; but I am not obligated to vote for the confirmation
of a nominee who fails to do so, either. Throughout his testimony,
Judge Thomas gave us many responses—but too few real answers.

"Perhaps some have advised him that this would be the best route
to confirmation—and perhaps they are right about the politics—but
it is a political strategy that I do not intend to endorse by voting for
Judge Thomas's confirmation."

This was a statement of some historical importance, putting the
White House on notice that the "stealth" approach to a Supreme
Court nomination, which had worked so well with Justice Souter, was
not an automatic pass through the Senate to the court.

Biden's second complaint was that Thomas's ideas were beyond the
pale.

"Judge Thomas has praised some extreme ideas about 'economic
rights,' ideas which, if applied as their authors intended, would invalidate virtually every single modern legislative scheme to regulate the
economy, the environment and the workplace. . . . The ideas that
Judge Thomas embraced are part of an ultraconservative agenda to use
the courts to fundamentally alter the legal framework within which the
government operates."

Indeed, Biden was trying to build on a foundation he had started
with the rejection of Robert Bork to establish a fairer standard for
Supreme Court confirmations, one in which the Senate would require
some signs of moderation on the part of the President. Biden felt that

Thomas's defeat on sexual harassment allegations would not help that cause.

He ended by appealing, no doubt in vain, "for a course of moderation in judicial selections." He said that there was "a fervent minority within the President's party engaging in an open campaign—open and notorious, I might add—to shift the Court dramatically to the right."

Before the fourteen senators on the Judiciary Committee reconvened in the Senate Caucus Room to make their votes final and official, the staff of Senator Biden made a belated move. Copies of Hill's statement were distributed to the Democrats on the committee. It was only then, one hour before the vote, that the Democratic side of the committee was all fully informed. On the Republican side, some of the senators still didn't know the name Anita Hill.

Meanwhile, the Caucus Room, where hundreds were gathering to witness the vote, was abuzz with talk of another alleged scandal. This had to do with the possibility of a serious breach of ethics by Thomas in his role as a judge on the federal appeals court.

The *Legal Times,* a Washington weekly serving the legal community, was reporting that Thomas had drafted—but not issued—an opinion that, if known, could have mired his nomination in serious trouble.

The opinion, circulated within the court by Thomas in June several weeks before he was nominated, would have overturned the Federal Communications Commission's (FCC) granting a woman an FM radio station license in Maryland. A woman was granted the license rather than a man because of a conscious effort, mandated by Congress, to promote diversity on the airwaves.

This opinion by Thomas, which seemed to have disappeared, flew in the face of a Supreme Court decision of the previous year that had upheld a similar preference based on race. If Thomas had authored such an opinion, it might confirm fears that the nominee would disregard precedents laid down by both Congress and the Supreme Court in order to promote his own conservative agenda. It also seemed to conflict with Thomas's answer to a question from Specter during the hearings, in which he had said he had no reason to disagree with the Supreme Court decision.

By September the opinion had still not been issued, and the paper said that court staff had speculated that it had been held back by Thomas to prevent controversy, a terrible breach of ethics if true. But there was no proof.

The story also renewed discussion of allegations by the liberal group Supreme Court Watch that Thomas should have excused himself from a case on the appellate court involving the Ralston-Purina pet food company founded by Jack Danforth's grandfather. Senator Danforth owned at least $7.5 million in Ralston-Purina stock, and stood to benefit greatly from Thomas's decision setting aside a damage award against the company. Legal ethicists were divided over whether Thomas should have bowed out of the case.

As the Judiciary Committee session got underway, Senator Specter debunked the *Legal Times* story, saying he had talked with Thomas that morning and had been assured that the delay had nothing to do with the nomination. What he did not say then was that he had also talked to Thomas about Anita Hill and received similar assurances. Specter congratulated Biden for moving ahead on the vote "with dispatch."

Unswayed by the controversies still swirling around the nominee, Senator DeConcini voted with the Republicans for Thomas. But the remaining seven Democrats voted against him. The committee found itself completely divided. The tie vote was a stunning message of no confidence from a committee that had been expected to hand Thomas an easy victory. Never had a Supreme Court nominee failed to get a favorable committee vote and still been confirmed by the Senate.

After all the drama of the voting and attendant rhetoric, Chairman Biden said he wanted to make "one last point." Only a handful of the committee's senators, several staffers, and perhaps a few people in the audience knew that he was talking about Anita Hill. He continued:

As I've indicated to you, I think this is a close call. I also indicated in my discussion with Judge Thomas that I believe there are certain things that are not at issue at all. And that is his character, or characterization of his character. And I have not heard anyone saying anything to the contrary to what I'm about to say. But if this does occur, I have assured Judge Thomas and assure my colleagues, I will be an advocate for Thomas's position. And that is that this is about what he believes, not about who he is. And I know my colleagues will refrain and I urge everyone else to refrain from personalizing this battle, to the extent that it is one on the floor of the Senate. And I don't expect that to happen on the floor of the Senate. I don't expect it to happen off the floor, but I hope it won't happen on the floor in the Senate.

Among all the verbiage, Biden was saying that he considered the matter of the sexual harassment charges closed.

An unwritten but ubiquitous rule of American journalism is that reporters are supposed to keep their own travails out of the news. Most of the time this is utterly appropriate. In the case of Anita Hill versus Clarence Thomas, though, the standard rule falls away because so many people have been trying to guess at what happened when.

Although I was the first reporter to break the news of Anita Hill's charges, I also was the reporter who had sat on the story of the year for two months. Good reasons held me to my caution. This was not the first time I had been so close and yet so far. As the Middle East correspondent for *Newsday*, I worked on the Iran-Contra story for six months only to see the news break in a Lebanese newspaper.

In the case of Anita Hill, I was slowed by several things. I knew that she was unwilling to come forward and publicly discuss what had happened to her, and that my newspaper was unlikely to run the story without her name and cooperation. I had also made a promise to a person whom I agreed to protect with anonymity. The promise to the source who had first given me Hill's name was that I would not attempt to telephone her and get her to talk about sexual harassment. I could certainly call, since she was one of many past and present EEOC employees who were being interviewed by the media about their former boss, but I had to talk about other issues. In the meantime, I kept informed about the progress others were having with Hill. My source feared that a call from a reporter, particularly a male reporter, asking questions about this sensitive matter, might drive the hesitant Hill underground.

When I heard Biden bringing up the issue, albeit obliquely, I resolved to get the story by means other than my original source. At this point, I had learned from others that the FBI was investigating Hill's charges of sexual harassment. The problem was that I did not know what the specific allegations were; I didn't have enough information for a full story. My story on the committee vote did mention that the FBI's investigation into Thomas had been reopened to delve into a "personal matter."

The tie vote provoked a flurry of activity on the part of Thomas's opponents. They had been braced for the committee to vote in favor of Thomas; the impasse meant that Thomas's performance in the hearings had been so unimpressive as to raise doubts among the senators. Filled with new hope that the full Senate might vote down the President's nominee, the liberal coalition went into last-minute action.

The Alliance for Justice sent out an alert to all its members around the country, urging them to lobby some thirty-five senators whose votes could decide the nomination. People for the American Way put out a press release declaring that "the conventional wisdom on this nomination just went out the window." A group of Thomas's opponents, including Ralph Nader, and Joseph Rauh from the Leadership Conference on Civil Rights, paid for an advertisement in the *Legal Times* asking for anyone who had ever discussed the issue of abortion or the case of *Roe* v. *Wade* with Thomas to please come forward.

The Judiciary Committee's tie vote slowed what would have been a flood of endorsements for the nominee in the Senate. As a new week of politicking began, Thomas seemed to be losing some votes his backers had counted upon, but gaining new ones. Nothing was settled. By midweek, I had ensconced myself in the Senate press gallery to keep a check on the upcoming vote and to get a fix on the Hill case. From the press gallery—several rooms jammed with journalists, desks, computers, typewriters, and coaches that adjoined a gallery overlooking the Senate floor—it was possible to keep in touch with several developments at once.

At that point, Thomas seemed to have the backing of eleven Democrats, enough to put him over the top even if three of the Senate's forty-three Republicans defected from the President's plan for the high court. Thomas's opponents, however, had succeeded in gaining precious time. The final vote on the nominee had been put off until the following week. This might be long enough for someone to come up with something with which to defeat Thomas. And Anita Hill was still very much in the minds of some people in the capital.

One morning while working up in the press gallery I received a message that a senator then on the floor wanted to talk with me. About what, I didn't know. I was a newcomer to Washington politics, and despite twenty years in newspapering that had taken me to dozens of countries, I was still impressed that a member of the United States Senate would have something to discuss with me. It was with some self-importance that I rushed down to meet the senator in the President's Room. I found him waiting in the chamber, which was decorated with gilt-edged mirrors and leather coaches, and situated just off the Senate floor. It was where presidents used to sign last-minute bills into law.

The senator, an opponent of Thomas, had a tip for me regarding a news article I had written earlier about the nominee. It proved to be of little use; but when asked if he had any hopes of stopping the nomination, he gave me a straightforward answer.

"Not unless someone with important information who is insisting on keeping it confidential comes forward publicly," the senator said.

For me, this was a lightning bolt, a chance to confirm that at least some of the senators knew about Hill's allegations of sexual harassment and thought them serious enough to potentially derail the Thomas nomination. "You mean the law professor from Oklahoma?" I asked.

His eyes opened in amazement. "How did you know about that?"

I couldn't answer his question directly. I had promised to keep my sources of information confidential.

"What exactly is she saying he did?" I asked, trying to nail down some information about what the FBI had been investigating. It didn't work. The senator backed away from me, shaking his head to indicate he could not talk about Hill.

That was it. He hadn't told me anything factual, but when I added what I already knew, the conversation was illuminating. It was clear he thought the Hill story had a lot of potential even at this late hour of the nomination process. Why else would the senator be thinking about it? Were other senators considering it as a possible means of defeating Thomas? The political sticking point seemed to be that Hill still wanted to keep her private life out of the public eye.

The conversation also superseded my obligation not to call Anita Hill and ask her about sexual harassment. The subject had been broached with me, albeit unintentionally and indirectly, by a senator. As I was heading down a corridor away from the President's Room I happened upon a legislative aide to another senator who was opposed to the Thomas nomination. He stopped to chat with me cordially, but I shocked him by asking immediately about Hill. He, too, looked at me wide-eyed, before walking off without saying another word. Just the mention of Hill's name was hitting raw nerves.

I rushed back to the *Newsday* bureau halfway down Pennsylvania Avenue toward the White House. From there, I could look straight out at the windows of the FBI headquarters. I telephoned Hill and caught her in her office at the law school between classes she was teaching. As best I could over the telephone, I tried to establish a rapport, though I had no real idea who she was, or how she thought. All I knew were the basics—she was a law professor in her mid-thirties. All I could hear in her voice was formality; she spoke precisely, with neither warmth nor hostility.

Reminding the professor that we had talked several weeks before about Thomas's politics, I prepared to ask about how the EEOC chairman had treated her. When I finally mentioned sexual harassment, she sighed. But she didn't elaborate. I suggested that I get on a plane that evening and talk to her the next day in person. When she asked for two hours to consider the plan, I was ecstatic to to have a chance to speak to her directly; but when I called back, Hill sounded distant. She wanted to think about it overnight.

For several days we went through this high-pressure back-and-forth: Professor Hill was torn. She indicated that she wanted the world to know her story, but she was afraid of the consequences. She said she did not want publicity.

At one point, she asked me whether I thought it would make a difference if she told her story to the world. Would it be taken seriously? For the purposes of getting the information, I should have said yes. But I could not bring myself to press her hard. I did not use the usual reporter's bag of tricks—the appeal to the conscience, the mention of history in the making, the line about how the information would become public inevitably. I did not reassure her about how quickly her story would all blow over. I did not even employ the classic ruse of pretending to know more than I knew. I had a sense, for once, that what I was dealing with was very sensitive. Unlike the officials in the White House, unlike the senators on Capitol Hill, unlike the men and women who accepted nominations for high posts, Hill did not want attention.

Anita Hill was one of the more reluctant people I had ever tried to interview. She had not gotten involved in Thomas's nomination on her own initiative. Only when staff aides to senators in Washington contacted her did Hill begin to take an interest in the matter of Clarence Thomas. Led to believe that senators on the Judiciary Committee wanted to hear what she had to say, Hill made an effort to tell them. But when her story fell on deaf ears in the committee, she did not contact the press. The press contacted her. And even then she would not cooperate. She threw up a final obstacle for me on Friday evening, October 4, by now a week after the committee had voted itself into a tie and thrown the Thomas nomination into uncertainty. After I had made reservations once again to fly out to Oklahoma, Hill said she would talk to me only if I could get the statement she had sent the Senate. She would confirm what was in her statement, but she refused to be the one to open the floodgates of the national media.

Hill had exhausted me. I was ready to leave the office, go home for the weekend and give up on getting anything out of this Oklahoma law professor. The vote of the full Senate on the nomination was only a few days away. Time had all but run out. But before I left, the chief of the Washington bureau, Gaylord Shaw, stopped by my desk to see what had happened. He had been an investigative reporter for the Associated Press and *The Los Angeles Times* before moving to *Newsday*.

"Don't give up yet," he said to my great annoyance. "Keep after her."

The White House, Thomas, and various of his closest supporters had been on pins and needles all week. They knew about Hill's charges and were praying they wouldn't have to deal with them. By that Friday

evening, some in the Thomas camp risked a small celebration. The
Senate and the media would not be doing much over the weekend;
there was reason to hope that Anita Hill's name would never have to
be mentioned publicly. The final vote on Thomas had been scheduled
for the coming Tuesday.

On Saturday, I trudged back into the office, wishing that I had gone
sailing on Chesapeake Bay. Instead I decided to make an all-out
assault on the story. I called Hill. I called the liberal groups. I called
a dozen Senate staffers at home. I called every senator on the Judiciary
Committee for whom I could hunt up a home telephone number.

I called the senator with whom I'd had the go-round in the President's Room. He was sympathetic with my desire to get the information, but he insisted that it was confidential. Hill had not wanted her
name released to the public. He did make an offer. He would give me
the information about the charges against Thomas *if* Hill told him it
was all right. She could call him and give her permission. This, I
thought, just might be a formula that would work: Hill could say
truthfully that she had not given me the information, and the senator
could say quite properly that he had not violated anyone's confidentiality. But when I telephoned Oklahoma, Anita Hill frustrated me
again. She couldn't go so far as to give her permission. She didn't want
even a secret part in making the charges public.

"What a straight arrow," I thought to myself as I hung up. I called
the senator back. He once again refused to help me without her
permission.

I kept trying. It was getting late and the deadline for the Sunday
paper had passed when one of my telephone calls made it through to
someone who knew what was going on, and was willing to talk. As is
standard in journalism when a story deals with sensitive material, I
agreed to keep the name of this person confidential. I knew already
that this source was trustworthy, that the information was good.

(While I cannot reveal the identity of the person who provided me
this information, I can say it was not given to me as a passive beneficiary of any last-minute plot to ambush Thomas. To get the story, I
had badgered and coaxed more than one person. And I would not have
been able to do that if I had not been following the case of Anita Hill
for months.)

Over the telephone, my source described what Anita Hill had told the Judiciary Committee—Thomas had repeatedly discussed sexual matters with her in a suggestive and humiliating manner while he was her boss at the EEOC. At the time, Hill was twenty-five years old.

"He made suggestions to her about what kind of sex she engaged in, asking her in great detail about different forms of sex," my source explained.

Thomas had not touched Hill, had not explicitly threatened to fire her if she did not have sex with him. But Hill had been so upset by the harassment that she had confided in her friend who had verified the story for the Judiciary Committee.

The Supreme Court nominee had been accused of sexual harassment and senators had known about it but done nothing. The story was now in my hands, and the chain reaction began that would carry this news across the country before the night was out. I called Shaw, the bureau chief, at his home in suburban Virginia. He wasted no time in calling New York to alert the paper's top editors, who instantly recognized that we had big news. He ordered a modern-day version of "Stop the presses," which entailed ripping up the front page to accommodate the newsbreak from Washington.

Shaw rushed from home to the bureau and helped get the details to fill out the story. He telephoned the White House press office, talking to the spokesman pulling weekend duty. Shaw explained what we were going to run in the paper. The first reaction from the White House was: "Oh shit!"

The White House, of course, also had the report by the FBI. By mandate, the agency reported to the White House first and then the Senate.

I telephoned Hill. She confirmed the information that my source had given me. At this point, I had the essential elements of a rock-solid story. I had a named person, a responsible person—a *law* professor—confirming that she had made serious charges against Thomas in a sworn statement to the FBI. I had a source who had seen the FBI report. Someone else, one of Hill's friends, had talked to the Judiciary Committee and corroborated her charges. Furthermore, from what Shaw was learning, it was becoming clear that not only senators but also officials in the White House had known about Hill. Soon, the public was going to know, too.

I wrote a quick, short version of the story for the first edition on

Sunday, October 6. *(Newsday* prints close to a million copies of the paper for Sunday, so its presses must begin running early on Saturday evening.) Then I started calling senators at home.

The first member of the Judiciary Committee I reached was Orrin Hatch, the Republican from Utah. His first words were angry and instantly accusatory. "I am going to kill Metzenbaum and Neas," he said, leaping to the conclusion that the senator from Ohio and the head of the Leadership Conference on Civil Rights were to blame.

"I am incensed. I am ready to go on the [Senate] floor and kick some tail. It makes me so mad that they would try to smear somebody with something like this," he said. "Whoever did this ought to be shot. This is a fine young man that they're smearing in the most reprehensible, dirty way possible and that's because they're losing.

"Frankly, it's false and it's typical of the way they're trying to smear various nominees," Senator Hatch also declared, having dismissed Hill's charges as if there had already been a trial and a verdict on the matter.

Then I got Senator Alan Simpson of Wyoming on the telephone. Like his colleague, he was angry.

"They've culled this guy's record better than grain drills in a pasture," the Wyoming Republican complained, using a ranching metaphor to describe how meticulously the Thomas opposition had searched for something to use against the nominee.

"Why didn't the woman pursue it? What is the reason for bringing it up if the person never pursued it?" he continued, defending the decision to ignore Hill's charges.

The next senator I reached was a Democrat, Paul Simon, who was out of town at a class reunion at Dana College in Blair, Nebraska. On hearing the news of my story, Senator Paul Simon reacted as suddenly as the Republicans. But, rather than debunking Hill's charges, he called for a postponement of the Senate vote on Thomas, which was now three days away.

"I think it is a serious enough charge that the committee ought to look at it and if necessary the vote ought to be postponed," he said.

"I would say it adds to the credibility concern," he went on. Simon and others opposed to Thomas had criticized him for tailoring his testimony for the hearings, rather than frankly stating his views. Now that the charges against Thomas were public, the Democrats might decide to make something of them.

The White House called back with a full statement confirming the story:

> On September 23, the allegation was brought to the attention of the Judiciary Committee. The Judiciary Committee immediately informed the White House. In consultation with the committee, the White House promptly directed the FBI to conduct a full, thorough and expeditious investigation. Upon completion of the FBI investigation on September 26, the report was submitted to the White House and the committee. The White House reviewed the report and determined that the allegation was unfounded. The President continues to believe that Judge Thomas is eminently qualified to serve on the Supreme Court and expects him to be confirmed promptly.

Although the White House's statement sounded forthright, it was not wholly accurate. The allegation had been brought to the attention of the Judiciary Committee weeks earlier. The FBI had not had time to conduct a complete investigation. The agency had hurriedly interviewed Hill and Thomas, whose stories conflicted, and questioned Hill's friend as well as others with relevant information. The officials in the White House knew no more than the FBI or the senators who had read the FBI report. The basis on which the White House had determined the allegation to be unfounded was apparently a political one.

Finally, I called Hill again for a more extensive interview. She said that Thomas had begun sexually harassing her in 1981 when she first worked for him at the Department of Education. She said the harassment stopped for a while and she thought it was over, but it began when she moved with Thomas to the EEOC. All of this came over the telephone line in careful, calm sentences. Hill sounded relieved that the indecision was over. Her story was out and she had not been the one to provide the first, vital information.

"One of the things I am most concerned about is that I really had no intention of going public to the press with this statement," Hill said, referring to the details of her charges that she had faxed to the Judiciary Committee. "I had really only wanted and only intended to speak to the committee. My efforts to do that were not followed through as promised by the committee, as far as I could tell."

Hill told me her reasons for keeping quiet over the years. For a long time, she said, she had been afraid to speak against Thomas because of his power.

"For a certain period of time, in the past ten years, I really thought there might be some retaliation," she said. "It was really fear of retaliation from someone in an administration that was fairly powerful, and I did not want this to happen. Because of the sensitive nature of the information, I did not think it would serve any purpose to have it common knowledge. But I thought that having the information in front of the [Judiciary] Committee was relevant and helpful [in evaluating] how Thomas viewed the issue of sexual harassment on a personal level and how he used his office and peers in his position."

She also explained that she was talking, after all her refusals, because it was clear now that the story would be in print by morning. "To be honest with you, I believed that the story was going to be told anyway, and I wanted to be able to give my impression and not have it be the subject of other people's interpretation."

Her sharpest comment was in response to my asking her why she had never filed a complaint about Thomas's behavior.

"Who would I file it with? He was the chairman of the EEOC."

By nine Saturday night, October 5, the story of Hill's allegations against Thomas was going out from *Newsday* over the wires, electrical thoroughfares connected to three hundred newspapers nationwide. The story was being carried by The Los Angeles Times–Washington Post news service. (*Newsday*, which is owned by the same corporation as *The Los Angeles Times*, is a part of this service.) A few hours later the Sunday edition of *Newsday*, with the story on the cover, started rolling off the presses.

In order to follow up on the story, I decided to fly to Oklahoma the next morning. I needed to find out all I could about this woman and her background. Before quitting for the night, I called her again to ask for an interview over lunch. But that sort of leisurely interview was not destined to be. The quiet of Hill's life was coming to an end for a while.

She went out to dinner Saturday night with Shirley Wiegand, another professor at the University of Oklahoma law school, who was her best friend, and Mark Gilette, also a law professor and a friend. She calmly told her friends what had happened; none knew what to expect. But by the time Hill got home, she began to get an idea. Her telephone was ringing off the hook. It never stopped all night long. She didn't answer, but it kept her from sleeping.

The next morning, I was on a flight to Oklahoma City, which had the nearest airport to the University of Oklahoma at Norman. I didn't know what to expect either. On previous occasions, I had written what I thought were big stories, only to find the general public uninterested. On the other hand, there might well be pandemonium in Norman and in Washington.

When Hill awoke that morning, she saw someone, presumably a reporter, already waiting near her doorstep. At six forty-five, she called Wiegand. Hill had not expected her story to create a major sensation, but now she was wondering. Wiegand decided that Hill should clear out in case she was deluged by the media. Hill drove to Wiegand's nearby house and while the two women drank coffee and read the Sunday newspapers, the media began converging on suburban Norman. Television vans were parking in front of Hill's house. At nine, National Public Radio (NPR) broadcast an interview by Nina Totenberg with Hill as part of its morning news program, which aired across the country.

Sure enough, when I arrived in Norman before noon, I found reporters and cameras everywhere. Television vans—from local stations, network affiliates, and the networks themselves—were lining suburban Berry Road in the staid, middle-class, and racially mixed neighborhood where Hill lived. Reporters stood in groups in the street. No one had any idea where Hill was. The blinds were drawn in the windows of her demure house of pinkish brick. Neighbors of Hill's who ventured out to talk to the reporters had only nice things to say about her. They included Dewey Selmon, a former pro football player, who said that Hill had been chosen to represent the immediate community in a dispute over the use of undeveloped land behind their houses.

The press had besieged the law school, even though it was Sunday. The school, in a modern building set off from the university's main campus, was normally a low-key place. Several law professors who had come in to do some work were giving interviews instead. They, too, had praise for Hill and her credibility, including a few who said they had favored the Thomas nomination. Hill herself was staying out of sight.

It was impossible to find anyone with anything bad to say about Anita Hill. Typical of the comments were those of Professor Osborne M. Reynolds, Jr. "I would believe anything she says, anything."

In the five years she had been at Oklahoma she had already become a respected faculty leader. She was a member of the executive committee of the faculty senate and had been named scholar in residence in the university provost's office.

Hill herself wasn't around to have lunch in public with me or anybody else. I checked into a nearby Marriott Hotel, having had plenty of interviews with colleagues of Hill but, frustratingly, none with the elusive professor. In my search to locate Hill, I telephoned law professors at home, including Wiegand, who had taken charge of keeping her friend out of sight. There weren't too many places to hide in the small, flat town of Norman, so Wiegand had checked Hill into the same Marriott hotel. She, of course, didn't tell me that Hill, as I later learned, was ensconced in the hotel only two rooms away from mine.

Under the noses of the local and national media, Hill did manage to sneak out of the hotel to take her usual Sunday walk with Wiegand. She also had a law student distribute a statement to the reporters gathered outside her house. It said: "My interest has been in fulfilling my responsibilities to the political process as I see them: That is to provide the Senate with information about a nominee. Allegations that my efforts are an attempt to disparage the character of Clarence Thomas are completely unfounded."

Otherwise, Hill was staying behind her locked door, getting updates from Wiegand about the press's progress in Norman. She was going to talk to the reporters, but she first had to prepare for a press conference that would be more uproarious than anything she had faced in her life.

Meanwhile, people elsewhere in the country were being asked about her credibility. Almost everyone who knew Anita Hill seemed to respect her. One was Professor Stephen L. Carter, of the Yale Law School, a figure of prominence in the black legal community. Professor Carter had just written a well-received book that challenged affirmative action with ideas similar to those of Thomas. Carter had no political reasons for praising Hill, with whom he had gone to law school.

"I've known Anita Hill for fourteen years and she is a person of enormous integrity and spirituality. She is a person of great compassion and thoughtfulness and if she said something like that occurred it would have to be considered very seriously," Carter told *The New York Times*. Editors at the *Times*, which was scooped by *Newsday* on the story, deleted from some of its Monday editions all mention that the story had been broken by their competitor in New York.

In Washington, the reaction to the story built up steam slowly. Many of the senators and congressmen were in their home states over the weekend and didn't realize that sexual harassment was an issue with explosive potential. It was members of the women's movement, like Judy Lichtman of the Women's Legal Defense Fund, who reacted first. Lichtman started calling friends with connections to political leaders.

One of the women called Tom Donilon, a Washington lawyer and adviser to Senator Biden, to try to impress upon him how important the story was. This would soon cause an avalanche, Donilon was told, because of the way that sexual harassment cuts to the quick of power relationships between men and women. Only two of the one hundred senators who would be voting on the Thomas nomination were women, a fact that would delay senatorial reaction. Donilon seemed concerned, although not convinced that his caller's urgency was necessary. He promised to call Biden.

Thomas's longtime backer, Senator Danforth, talked to the press outside his Washington house. He said Hill's charges were a desperate "eleventh-hour attack more typical of a political campaign than of a Supreme Court confirmation." He attacked the credibility of Hill's charges by explaining that the professor had not broken off all contact with Thomas after leaving Washington. She had, he pointed out, invited Thomas on behalf of her Oklahoma law school to come out to talk to students. How did that mesh with the portrait of a woman who had fled her boss in Washington? While Thomas remained curiously silent, Danforth said that the nominee "forcefully denied" the allegations.

When the week began in Washington, the Senate was outraged by the news of Hill's charges against Thomas; but the reason behind the outrage was that the charges had been made public, not that Thomas might have sexually harassed an employee, or that the Judiciary Committee had all but ignored the charges.

The Senate floor became a forum for senatorial indignation. But the senators were more interested in finding out how their secret had been let out of the bag than they were in finding out what the sexual harassment charges were all about. There were more calls Monday for an investigation of the so-called leak—a label that sounded erroneously as if someone had handed me the full, ready-to-print Hill story—than there were calls to look into the charges.

"There should be an investigation of how this got out," said Senator Danforth, once again springing to Thomas's defense. "I think this is a very serious problem. I don't think we're doing the country any good by subjecting people to mortification."

Senator Simpson took out his frustrations on me from the Senate floor, recounting in a somewhat garbled way how the story had gone from me to the radio, then from the inside of *The Washington Post* to its front page. "I got a call in my house, Saturday night, seven o'clock. *Newsday*, you know, guy breathing so hard he could hardly contain himself. 'Oh, Senator, what about this?' I said, 'What about it?' Apparently, then from *Newsday* the ping-pong ball went to National Public Radio and then from there in not too long a period we have it all floating in America. Something well known to everyone for—at least those who are most intimately connected in the decision—and then, of course, taking on a life of its own, coming from page A6 in one of our major newspapers to the front page, right there."

The charges themselves were not taken seriously.

"Is this the whole thing, the rantings of a disgruntled employee who has reduced herself to lying?"asked Senator Strom Thurmond.

Senator Orrin Hatch accused opponents of Thomas of "sprouting trumped-up charges like mushrooms after a spring rain. How low will they go?"

Senator Arlen Specter divulged that he had talked to Thomas about Anita Hill just before the committee vote and that he was satisfied with Thomas's denial. He said that given "the lateness of the allegation, the absence of any touching or intimidation, and the fact that she moved with him from one agency to another, I felt I had done my duty and was satisfied with his responses." Specter, the ace lawyer on the Judiciary Committee, seemed to have ignored the fact that the law did not require physical contact to establish sexual harassment, and that words could be severe weapons of intimidation.

Some Democrats, notably Paul Simon and Edward Kennedy of the Judiciary Committee, urged a delay so the charges could be further investigated. Senator Simon pointed out that it was no longer just a matter of sexual harassment, but whether Thomas had lied under oath to the FBI when he denied the charges.

But many of the Democrats were not taking the matter seriously. They, too, had suffered from leaks of information at times in the past. Senator DeConcini, who had been humiliated because of a leak by Republicans about his involvement in the Keating savings-and-loan scandal, argued that Hill's charges were not worth getting upset about. "In my judgment the allegations cannot be substantiated. And to put this vote off would be a travesty of justice and of this process."

Biden said that the fact that the public now knew about the charges changed nothing.

"None [of the Judiciary Committee members] believed that the information which we then posessed necessitated a delay in voting. I see no reasons why the addition of public disclosure of the allegations—but no new information about the charges themselves—should change this decision."

Even George Mitchell, the liberal Senate Majority Leader from Maine, was adamant that there could be no delay in the vote. His reason was technical—he and the other senators had made an agreement the week before to vote on Tuesday and he wanted to keep it.

The fact that Mitchell thought that senatorial accord was more important than a lone black woman's charges of harassment exemplified the old-boys'-club atmosphere in which the Senate worked. The

two women members of the Senate, Nancy Kassebaum and Barbara
Mikulski, had not changed the atmosphere in the marble hallways.
The senators still gave most of their top-rank legislative jobs to men
and their bottom-rank clerical jobs to women. They enjoyed an exclu-
sive gymnasium, swimming pool, sauna, and steam room. And they
didn't seem to have broken a long tradition of closing ranks to protect
their unwritten rules of male decorum.

Once Hill's charges were out in the open, most of the senators didn't
immediately grasp the concept of how verbal sexual assault could
traumatize a woman, particularly coming from a boss. It was asking
the powerful to understand the feelings of the powerless.

There was more than a gender gulf in the way, though; there was
also quite possibly a racial divide, as well. It was easier to support a
black man backed by the white establishment than to believe a black
woman challenging the establishment. This was the sort of senatorial
thinking that initially gave Clarence Thomas, the judge, the edge over
Anita Hill, the professor of law. The senators also had to deal with the
raw emotion inherent in Hill's charges, and the responses that were
elicited.

Danforth, the minister and politician, was visibly distraught at what
he perceived as a vicious last-minute attack on the character of a man
who he knew from long experience could not possibly have done what
was alleged. Thomas was his friend. In addition, the senator had put
his own very considerable prestige on the line with Judge Thomas. If
this development ruined Clarence Thomas's bid for the high court, his
rejection would be Danforth's rejection as well. It would also mean
that he would not have the satisfaction and prestige of having his own
protégé on the Supreme Court. On the Senate floor that Monday,
October 7, Senator Danforth said,

Judge Clarence Thomas is my personal friend. When I was called by the
White House on July the first and told that he would be nominated to the
United States Supreme Court, that was one of the happiest days of my life.
I have known Clarence Thomas for seventeen years. I hired him when he
was a law student at Yale and asked him to come to work at my office in
Jefferson City [Missouri] when I was state attorney general. He worked for

me again in my Senate office. I have kept very close touch with him ever since. I know him very well.

It was one of the happy days of my life because, first, I believed that the Supreme Court was getting a person who is very well qualified for that job. I know that the President said that he was the best-qualified person for the job, and of course, the detractors of Clarence Thomas have rushed to attack that particular proposition. But I honestly believed and do believe that he is the best person for the job. I think he is the best person for the job not only because of his ability, but because of his humanity, because of his background, because of the experience which he brings to the Supreme Court, and because of his character.

To the senator, the attack on Thomas seemed exactly like the sort of last-minute chicanery with which all politicians are familiar.

Those of us who are politicians, elective politicians, know that on the weekend before an election we expect something dreadful to happen. We know to have our campaign workers tune in the television sets to find out what is being carried on the news, or what new commercial is being run in the last days of the campaign when it's too late for us to respond. We politicians expect that. Sleazy as it is, that apparently is the nature of American politics today. Now, this phenomenon of American politics has been imported into the process of confirming nominees for the Supreme Court.

Danforth said he had not even bothered to read the FBI's report. He didn't believe it necessary. He trusted Thomas and he doubted Hill because she had not charged Thomas at the time of the alleged harassment.

I don't know anything about these charges, except that Clarence Thomas is my friend and I've asked him about them, and he says they're not true. I do know that the events complained of allegedly took place between eight and ten years ago. I understand that no formal complaint was made.

Over at the White House, the charge was not taken very seriously. President Bush told reporters he was "not the least" concerned about

Hill's charges. Administration officials said they did not think the Thomas nomination was in trouble. They would be more worried before the day was out.

Hill made her first public appearance in Oklahoma on Monday, October 7. It was a press conference in a law school classroom jammed not only with reporters but also with her students and fellow teachers.

When Hill walked to the lectern, she was greeted with a standing ovation. It was a message to people across the country, who could watch live on Cable News Network (CNN), that as far as those who knew Hill best were concerned, this was someone to be taken seriously. Lest that message be too subtle, the dean of the law school and representatives of student associations read statements lauding their professor.

But the most effective witness for Anita Hill was Hill herself. She was petite, poised, and stylishly dressed, looking nothing like the stereotype of a feminist troublemaker. As she began to speak, she came across as modest, temperate, and reasonable.

> The first point that I want to address with you is the idea that this is somehow a political ploy that I am involved in. Nothing could be further from the truth. There is no basis for that allegation that I am somehow involved in some political plan to undermine the nominee. And I cannot even understand how someone could attempt to support such a claim.
>
> But I would ask that what you do is to look at the facts that this has taken a great toll on me personally and professionally and there is no way that I would do something like this for political purposes.

Hill pointed out that it was not she who had gone to the Senate, but Senate staffers who had come to her.

> I responded to the committee's approach and I only responded after they approached me. I felt that as a citizen, as an individual who had information, that it was my obligation when approached to come forward and I did that.
>
> We have been discussing this for some time now and that's another point that I want to make. The control of the timing of this information and the release of this information has never been with me. I have never had any

control about when this information would be released. I spoke with the
Judiciary Committee about it in early September and through a number of
discussions it was not until the twentieth of September that an FBI investigation was suggested to me . . . some people have said that I waited until
the eleventh hour to bring this to the press. I never came to the press. The
press came to me.

[This was true; speaking for the press, I knew I had badgered her.]

I would like to say that I want an official resolution to this. My integrity
has been called into question, and by people who have never spoken to me,
that have not considered the facts carefully, as far as I know. And I want
an official resolution of this, because at this point the issue is being de-
flected and people are talking about this as a political ploy. And all that is
an attempt not to deal with the issue itself. It is an unpleasant issue. It's
an ugly issue. And people don't want to deal with it generally and particularly in this case. . . . I resent the idea that people would blame the
messenger for the message rather than looking at the content of the message itself and taking a careful look at it and fully investigating it.

Hill was ushered out of the room and upstairs to the office of Dean
David Swank for a breather from the mob of reporters. I was allowed
in to talk to her for a few minutes and saw a different person than the
confident woman who had appeared on national television. Leaning
back into a chair, she looked completely drained. This was only a taste
of what awaited her.

She had refused to discuss the details of her allegations, but had
come across as a very credible, reasonable human being. Back in the
capital, the response to Hill's words was immediate among Thomas
supporters in the Senate.

"Boy, this is trouble," said Senator Simpson, who had been working on a speech lauding Thomas when he received a phone call telling
him to tune in his television to Oklahoma. The senator was already
furious about the allegations, but he was a politician who knew the
importance of television impact.

"She didn't seem like a flake or an idiot and she presented herself
with extreme sincerity and honesty," said Carl Hampe, an aide to
Senator Simpson. "I think he saw a formidable political opponent."

Chapter

14

By allowing herself to be pushed onto the national stage, unwilling though she was, Hill had catalyzed a controversy that was soon to spin out of her—or anyone's—control. She quickly discovered that the public spotlight was not a comfortable place. Her privacy was a thing of the past. The country wanted to inbibe every available fact, description, and rumor about her. Who was this woman who had quietly waited the better part of a decade before letting her wild-sounding charges fall like a bomb on a federal judge seeking comfirmation to the Supreme Court?

The media as well as supporters of Thomas on the political right hurried to investigate Hill. The friends she had made from the time of her girlhood school days to her professorial teaching days were questioned. Colleagues and acquaintances were interrogated, as were her aging parents and many of her siblings. One hardened reporter after another kept coming up with the same result—a chorus of praise for Hill, her character, and her integrity. She seemed too good to be true.

Only over time did it become clear that Hill was a defender of civil rights and women's rights. She registered as a Democrat and had political differences with Thomas, but she was also known for being reasonable and keeping ideology out of her decisions. Her only immediate critics—other than the insiders of the Thomas camp who were outraged from the start—were a very few students at the ultra-conservative and now defunct Oral Roberts University law school, who did not like her politics or teaching style.

Until she sent the nation into an uproar, Anita Faye Hill was never a troublemaker. Her parents hadn't raised her that way. She was the youngest of the thirteen children of Albert and Erma Hill to grow up on their farm, an austere piece of the eastern Oklahoma prairie.

The farm lies several miles outside of the inconspicuous town of Morris, whose population had shrunk to barely a thousand as Oklahoma oil lost its premier place on the national market and Oklahoma agriculture dwindled. This is a region of dry, rolling grassland, whose monotony is stamped by square grids of unbending roads. The Hill farm is part of a community named Lone Tree because its most significant landmark was once a windswept hill crowned by a single stout tree. The gate to the Hill farm is a primitive weaving of barbed wire and wooden planks that doesn't encourage visitors. The house itself sits on a lonely knoll among some scrub oak trees and a jumble of farm machinery, reminders of work long done and work yet to do.

The house is small, of weathered board, and without frills. The steps to the door are cinderblocks that over the years have been pressed into the earth. The furnishings are aging. A picture of Jesus Christ hangs on one wall, and on another is a display of photographs of the Hill children.

Their mother, at the end of her eighth decade, still sits with her back as straight as a ruler. Erma Hill was dressed in a gray suit that dared not wrinkle and her silver hair was pulled back in a bun from which not a single hair escaped. With a long, hard stare, Mrs. Hill rivets visitors, making them wonder where they found the audacity to come to her house on her farm and ask prying questions. She did answer a few, though, about her daughter's character.

"I raised her to be an honest, truthful, godfearing child," Mrs. Hill said, pausing before adding a summation. "And to go work for what she got." Albert Hill used to grow crops on his two hundred and forty acres of hardscrabble farmland, and the children all helped with the labor. They also were expected to excel in school and go to church without even thinking of complaining.

"All of them went every Sunday to the Lone Tree Baptist Church," Mrs. Hill said. "There wasn't any question." The church stands in a bit of pasture up the road and fits into the landscape. It is a modest edifice and the white paint is flaking off its planks. But once it was the social center for the community, the place where people gathered for church dinners and events.

Anita Hill might have had a slightly easier time of it than her siblings because farm machinery had improved when she was born in 1956. And she was the baby of the family, whose members call her by her middle name.

"The youngest always gets the attention of all the older ones," Mrs. Hill remarked before ending the conversation by saying, "I have to get back to work now. I've some ironing and I have yet to start fixing dinner."

Albert Hill was equally terse in response to inquiries about his daughter. Having come in from hammering something behind the house, he said, "She's a good daughter. She does what's right." He stood in the doorway with muddy boots, offered a callused hand to shake and then returned to his work on the farm where he now was running a herd of cattle.

From the knoll where the Hill house sits, you can see in a full circle, and the prairie sky is so huge it makes the earth seem humble, almost two-dimensional.

Anita Hill has avoided giving many interviews since leveling her charges against Thomas, but her siblings are willing to talk about how life was on the farm.

"We worked an awful lot," remembered Winston Hill, one of Anita Hill's older brothers, who has become the minister at the Lone Tree church. "By five or five-thirty, by the time the sun came up, we were up. Six was getting late. In the day, we'd go to school, then we'd come home and then do the farmwork and then we'd do our homework.

"When Anita was coming up, she worked cotton and peanuts. Cotton is horrible. Your fingers get torn up pulling cotton and your back hurts. You work all day and you don't get a lot fast. It's a slow process. The harvest is in August, too, so it's hot. You're sweating. Your main thought is one day I'll be out of this, one day I'll be through with this. Peanuts weren't any fun, either. The biggest problem with peanuts is that you were coated with the dirt and the dust.

"This all had a long-term effect on your mind. We had a sense of responsibility because we knew no one else was going to do this work for us. If we didn't pick the cotton, it would still be right there in the field. It wasn't going anywhere."

If the Hill children misbehaved, occasionally they were switched with a stick. But Winston Hill remembers moral punishment as being much more effective.

"Dad was one for sitting you down and talking. He could talk to me and make me feel about this big," he said, holding up his hand with the thumb and forefinger about a quarter of an inch apart and narrowing his eyes to squint at the miniaturized image of himself. "He could instill in you a feeling of guilt for whatever you had done. The feeling from him was I trusted you and you betrayed me, your father."

Mrs. Hill added another dimension to the discipline. "The main thing she taught us was to live so we could respect ourselves. Faye and the rest of us got a lot from her. She made us assume our abilities, particularly when it came to school. If you brought home anything less than a B that was terrible. If you brought home a C you had to have a very good excuse." One school year, when Mrs. Hill was pregnant, an older girl brought home a poor grade. It was a crisis, Winston recalled, and Mrs. Hill immediately walked the several miles to the school and back in order to confer with the teacher about what had gone wrong.

"And if you were capable of making A's, then you brought home A's. She would look over the report cards. If I had a grade lesser than an A, I'd be terrified. I didn't want to hear what she would have to say. She never did whip me about anything, but she'd give you a verbal beating. She'd make you realize you let her down and, even worse, you let your own self down." At high school graduations, the Hill children were often the stars. Among them, five were valedictorians—including Anita and Winston—and one was a salutatorian.

Winston, after years in Los Angeles performing as a blues singer in the tradition of boyhood idols like Count Basie and Ella Fitzgerald, returned to Oklahoma and has become the minister at the Lone Tree church. "I think the reason I've done this is the way I was brought up. I'm in love with music but the whole nightclub scene didn't appeal to me."

"All those Hill kids had one thing in common. They were all smart," said Eddie Hill, a cousin who grew up on a neighboring farm.

"Faye Hill was always outstanding," added Eddie's wife, Dolores, who also grew up in Lone Tree. "She was quiet and she always read a lot. She had a determined mind. Her goal was to finish school, make A's, be a lawyer and work in the White House. She used to talk about these kinds of things, when everyone else was talking about daily life and whether they were going to get married. Not Faye. You would always see her with a hard-back, thick book." Some of those books were inherited by the children of Dolores Hill, who brought out one as proof. It was a worn copy from a set of the Junior Encyclopaedia Britannica.

Anita Hill's early years passed in a segregated world. Although the farms worked by whites were mixed in with those of the blacks, the races stayed apart. So did the Cherokee Indians, scattered throughout eastern Oklahoma, descendants of the tribes who were forced from their native lands in the American southeast in 1838. Many of the Indians brought with them black slaves, who would be freed after the Civil War.

Until she was fourteen, Hill attended a school for black children in a tiny crossroads town straight up the road from the farm. The central school for white students was in Morris, but gradually it was being integrated. As the farm population decreased, the outlying schools were made increasingly marginal. One by one, they were merged into the Morris system. Unlike other places, the Morris schools experienced minimal trouble with integration.

"Most of the blacks and whites grew up near each other. Although they didn't socialize, they didn't carry these racial grudges you find elsewhere. Maybe it's because there's enough space for everyone out here," said Roy C. King, a retired superintendent of the Morris schools.

When Hill entered the primarily white Morris Junior High School, she flourished. Susan Clark, a white classmate who would become a good friend, said that Hill's presence changed the academic atmosphere.

"Suddenly I had competition," Clark remembered. "Up to that point, I had not had a lot of competition in terms of being the smartest in the class. But we had a very friendly competition and it probably benefited both of us." Clark graduated as the class salutatorian, in second place behind Hill.

"Anita Hill was intelligent and she also worked real hard. With that combination, it was nobody's surprise when she came out at the top of the class," King, the retired superintendent, said.

Susan Clark remembered her academic rival as "very strong-willed. I knew back then that she was going to do something with her life. She was a quiet type of person but if somebody asked her for her opinion, she would speak out. She wasn't just a bookish type. She had a sense of humor and she had opinions."

Although Morris was something of a backwater, its culture dominated by pickup trucks, cowboy hats, and hefty male egos, Hill had grown up with more sophisticated convictions. Both she and Clark were keenly aware of the political and social issues gripping the country. In the larger town of Okmulgee seven miles away, school integration brought unrest and nastiness.

"Anita discussed black rights. We didn't have anything going on in Morris, but we knew about the trouble in Okmulgee. Anita cared. She was looking out into the world beyond," Clark recalled. The classmates had a common interest in women's rights. "We didn't have a wide range of experience or knowledge," Clark said, "but we knew that women generally had a second-class place. We didn't want to accept that. Women's rights were important to us."

In the graduating class of Morris High School, fewer than a fifth of the fifty-eight students were black. But Hill fit in easily. In the school yearbook, she appears several times, as secretary of the student council and a member of the National Honor Society, as a member of the Future Homemakers of America and the Pep Club. In her senior class picture, she is wearing a white dress and a gold cross decorates her chest. She is slim and wears dark-framed glasses. Others in her class went for more risqué poses, with plunging, feathered necklines.

"She always had a calming effect on me," said Clark, who went on

with Hill in 1973 to Oklahoma State University in Stillwater, a compla-
cent city in central Oklahoma. Nothing radical, or even very exciting,
was going on there. Most Oklahomans were conservative Democrats,
old-fashioned populists who stayed well behind the cutting edge of
politics.

True to character, Hill spent a lot of her time with her books, having
chosen psychology as a major. Socially, she experimented with nothing more wild than alcohol, to which she didn't take much of a liking.

"It was work first, then socializing," Clark said.

Hill sometimes went to the Strip, a series of bars near the campus,
a focal point for extracurricular activities. But she did not become a
regular.

"She didn't like the taste of beer. I remember one time she tried to
make it more drinkable by mixing it with Pepsi. I think that was the
worst idea she ever had," Clark said.

Hill went to parties but was not interested in immediately hitching
herself to a man.

"For both of us, marriage wasn't the big thing," Clark said. "Romance, husbands and all that was the furthest from both our minds.
Maybe it was our belief in women's rights, in the idea that women
could make careers for themselves."

In their junior year, the two women from Morris rented an off-
campus apartment together. Clark's grades soared that year because of
Hill's example.

"Anita always gave me that feeling: Don't goof up here, Susie. I'd
sometimes feel uncomfortable with myself, thinking, 'Gosh, I wish I
could be so perfect.' She had poise. When we had finals she could bear
up under anything. I was fretting. She was studying, of course, but she
never got in a tizzy. And I don't remember her being a slouch. Even
in her bathrobe, she looked poised. She had a way of carrying her head
up. You knew she was a moral person."

During her college years, Hill served as a counselor for freshman
students and was on the advisory board of the university's Women's
Council.

Hill graduated from Oklahoma State in 1977 with honors. She was
a National Merit Scholar and a university Regents Scholar. She was on
the university president's honor roll and the dean's honor roll.

She had been accepted at several prestigious law schools and she chose Yale. She had been awarded an NAACP Legal Defense Fund Scholarship to attend the school. During the three years at Yale, Hill lived by herself in an apartment off-campus and diligently worked her way through the law school regimen. She didn't stick with any social or political clique, making friends among black and white students, conservatives and liberals.

"Some of her good friends were not just white, but they were some of the most conservative students at Yale Law," remembered Mark Del Bianco, a classmate from those days who now practices law in Washington.

As for Hill's character, Del Bianco repeated what others had also observed. "She's just smart, hardworking and decent," he said.

Another classmate, Jerry Miranowski, said that Hill did not wear her politics on her sleeve. "She was not a very political person. It was more issue to issue on things that would mean a lot to her. She was not ideological."

Miranowski had perhaps the most telling comment to offer on Hill. "She was great," she said. "You're probably tired of hearing that, but if there was one person I would absolutely believe of the one hundred and seventy-five of my law school classmates, that person would be Anita Hill."

In class, Hill was quiet, but not too shy to bring up questions, according to Del Bianco. She was neither a "turkey" nor a "gunner," neither a poor student nor an aggressive, hand-waving one. One of her professors, Geoffrey Hazard, remembered Hill as "a competent student, not outstanding, competent."

After earning her law degree in 1980, Hill went directly to Washington to take a job with the law firm of Wald, Harkrader & Ross. She had worked for the firm during one of her law school summers. Some of her colleagues there remember her as capable and hard-working. But she stayed only a year with the firm, before taking a job that approached her childhood dream of working in the White House.

She was hired for a position in the Office of Civil Rights at the Department of Education, as the assistant to Clarence Thomas, a rising star in the Republican administration. Although Hill had come from the Democratic tradition of Oklahoma and found herself working with Republicans, she had a position of the sort that had always interested her. Among other things, she was dealing with the rights of blacks and women in the upper echelon of national policymaking. She was quiet about her convictions.

But from the start, some of the strict right-wingers at the agency looked at her askance, complaining that she did not fit politically with the new Reagan administration. Some of her more liberal friends wondered, too, how she was faring among strict Republican colleagues.

"I was surprised that she was working under him [Thomas], because he was more conservative on civil rights than she was. He was pretty conservative even back then," her former classmate Del Bianco said. But the job was a good opportunity for a young lawyer.

After following Thomas to the EEOC, Hill left Washington with a suddenness that she didn't explain to most of her colleagues. She told only a few friends that one of the reasons she had departed was Clarence Thomas's behavior.

Del Bianco noticed that something strange had occurred in Hill's attitude toward Thomas. Years after she had left Washington, he mentioned to her that Thomas had been named to the federal appellate court. Hill's reaction was negative.

"I said something to her like, 'I see Judge Thomas, your old boss, was appointed.' And if there's anything good to say about a person, she'll say it. But there was a look of pain on her face, and her comment was very noncommittal. It left the impresssion that, if she couldn't say good things about him, then there must be something wrong."

In 1983, Hill retreated to her home state, taking a job as an assistant law professor at the tiny O.W. Colburn School of Law at the ultrareligious Oral Roberts University in Tulsa. Having escaped the pressures of Washington, Hill seemed content within the shelter of academia. She acquiesced to the evangelistic rituals at the school, which included taking the school's Code of Honor Pledge. She declared her faith in God and vowed "to keep my total being under subjection from immoral and illegal acts and habits, whether on or off the campus." She also pledged, "I will not lie, I will not steal, I will not curse, I will not be a talebearer."

She regularly made the hour and a half drive from Tulsa to Lone Tree to visit her parents. Nothing had changed much on the farm.

Erma and Albert Hill still rose at dawn to go about the chores, and every Sunday morning they went to the little weathered Baptist church.

Anita Hill had come to deeply appreciate the old homestead on the austere knoll under a vast sky. From up there, the prairie wind sounded as if it had been blowing that same way forever. The farm was, in her words, "a part of America that is getting lost in the rush of modern times and quick development."

In 1986, Hill moved on to Norman, the state's principal college town, taking a position at the University of Oklahoma's law school. There she felt at home. The law school is a modern, orderly place with earnest students and a close-knit academic community of three dozen law professors. Hill flourished at the university, gaining tenure after four years and making fast friends with several other members of the generally liberal faculty.

Her colleagues have grown to trust her enough to elect her to the law school's Committee A. This is the executive committee comprised of three professors and the dean that decides the dicey issues of the faculty's salaries, promotions, and tenure.

Hill registered to vote as a Democrat upon her return to Oklahoma, and she is the only black woman professor at the law school, but she has avoided creating controversy. Within the law school, she has taken on the role as adviser to minority students, Indians as well as blacks. She endorses women's rights and pushes for minority hiring but expresses her views quietly. She has served on the board of a women's advocacy center and donated time to help the handicapped.

Once in Oklahoma, Hill maintained a cool and cordial relationship with Clarence Thomas, which colleagues of hers explained as part of her usual pragmatism.

With no inkling of what Hill would eventually say about Thomas, a committee at the law school decided to invite him there to speak. This was during the time that Thomas was chairman of the EEOC. The law professors gave Hill the job of inviting him. "Hill was reluctant to extend the invitation, but rather than make an issue of it, she did what the committee wanted," a colleague said.

Another law professor at the university, Shirley Wiegand, would become Hill's best friend. The two women made a strict habit of taking three five-mile walks each week, for exercise and conversation.

"Perhaps we get along so well because we both came from farms out in the country," Wiegand said. Wiegand, though, comes from Wisconsin, is married, and has a grandchild. She also describes herself as a feminist and the law school's stalwart left-winger.

"I'm left-wing in Oklahoma terms, which means I'm pretty tame by most standards," Wiegand explained.

Hill, on the other hand, is far more reticent about her political views. She doesn't talk about her political party affiliation and she doesn't make judgments through an ideological prism, Wiegand says of her friend.

For instance, when Judge Bork was being grilled by the Senate Judiciary Committee in 1987, Hill did not condemn him for his philosophy, which differed in many ways from hers.

"She did not like the process of his rejection," Wiegand said. "She would judge him as a total person. She would want a judge who would be intellectually honest, rather than being prejudiced because of his stand on a certain issue. She might have disagreed with his judicial conclusions, but she appreciated that he had thought them through."

At that time, of course, Hill had no idea that she would be entangled in a senatorial brawl that would make the Bork hearings look genteel. When Hill went to Washington to present her sexual harassment charges against Clarence Thomas, Wiegand accompanied her friend.

Upon her return to Norman, Wiegand found herself facing rumors, which she took with amusement, that she and Hill were lesbians.

"I think that's the last weapon men have against women, saying that they are lesbians," Wiegand said.

She recounted how she laughed when a reporter from the scandal-mongering supermarket tabloid, *The National Enquirer*, telephoned to ask her if she was a homosexual.

"I laughed. I should have said, 'Unfortunately I'm not,' " Weigand said, laughing again. "I had my husband write a letter to the paper—I guess you can't really call it a paper—telling them their piece was ridiculous.

"Truly, it says a lot about the people making the accusations. They insist on labeling her because she hasn't fallen into line and attached herself to a man." According to Wiegand and Leisha Self, another professor, Hill has a low-key social life.

"Anita is very independent," Self said. "I don't think she's looking for the right man. I don't think she has it as a goal in her life. A calm life is important to her."

Self also remarked on Hill's strength. "She is strong in a way that I didn't expect anybody could be. Others and I have talked about it and agreed that we couldn't have held up under the same scrutiny. And when I thought about it, I realized I've never seen Anita cry. I've seen other women on the faculty cry and, certainly, I have cried."

Hill sometimes goes out to a movie or a jazz club and drinks a beer—without Pepsi—or a glass of wine. And weekly, she goes out with a group of professors from the law school that calls itself The Bar Review.

"Every Thursday we go to a different restaurant. We eat, talk, drink a little," said Mark Gilette, another professor. "We talk about issues at the law school, athletics, basketball. She's a sports fan and fairly learned in pro basketball. She likes the Chicago Bulls. She's more of a listener than a talker. The number of political conversations I've had with Anita can be counted on one hand. Most people in academics are more vocal. There is no doubt on women's rights and civil rights as to which side she stands on, but she just doesn't bring it up."

"Although Anita Hill is not a feminist in a strident way," said Professor Self, she is "strong in her beliefs that women should have equal rights in our society." Hill has credentials as a mild-mannered feminist. For two years, she served on the board of directors of the Women's Resource Center in Norman, an organization that helps victims of domestic violence and sexual assault. The center runs a shelter for battered women and staffs a rape-crisis hotline.

Hill's task was to provide legal advice to the center and attend board meetings.

"There are sixteen members on the board," explained Jo Ann Smith, the center's executive director. "At these meetings, while everybody else was giving war stories and opinions about one issue or another, Anita Hill would be sitting and paying attention. Then when she would speak she would bring everything together and she would be so succinct that the decision would often be made. As a person, she is both intelligent and analytical."

Smith describes the center as one of the most controversial organizations in Norman. For out in the middle of Oklahoma, where male chauvinism has never died, being a feminist is tantamount to being a radical. "In the 1980's, people came to consider me an extremist when basically all I do is help women."

The center has a carefully worded credo: "We believe that women have the right to live in safety, to be treated with dignity, to make choices and to hope."

"Here in Oklahoma, that statement is considered militant," Smith said.

Hill also served on the board of Handitrans of Norman, a charitable organization providing transportation for the feeble, the old and handicapped.

At the university, Hill has served as an adviser to the Black Law Student Association and is a member of the President's Advisory Committee on Minority Affairs. And minority students often come to her office, seeking counsel.

Johnna Oberly, a second year law student and a Native American who has both Comanche and Osage blood, said that Hill had been instrumental in uniting minority students. Hill helped write the charter for the coalition that brought together black, Native American, Asian, and Hispanic law students.

"She is very level-headed," said Oberly of Hill. "She always thinks everything out. A lot of times, she's ten steps ahead of students and ready to bring us back to earth. As minorities we tend to feel defensive, but she looks for the practical solution without losing sight of the principle. She has a strong personality but she's very reasonable."

The subjects that Hill principally teaches are contract law and commercial law, dry and detailed subjects. She also conducts a civil rights seminar. Her scholarly work sounds as if it is both arcane and harmless. Her list of legal publications includes titles like "The Relative Nature of Property in the Context of Bankruptcy" and "A Comparative Study of the Convention on the Limitation Period in International Sales of Goods and Articles 2-725 of the Uniform Commercial Code."

As if to show her human side, Hill has taped snippets of humor and wisdom to the door of her office. One is a fanciful depiction of three black women sitting behind a court bench in judicial robes that is

captioned THE SUPREMES COURT. Another is a picture of Eleanor
Roosevelt accompanied by a quotation: "You gain strength, courage
and confidence by every experience in which you really stop to look
fear in the face. . . . You must do the thing that you cannot do."

# Chapter 15

Senator Jim Exon was getting ready to leave his home in Lincoln, Nebraska, to fly back to Washington when his wife Patricia stopped him. "Jim, you ought to listen to this," she told him, calling his attention to the television showing Anita Hill's press conference. As they watched it, the conservative Democrat had to admit to his wife that he was impressed by Hill, even though he had announced three days before in the Senate that he would vote for Thomas. For Exon, who was seventy, this whole issue of sexual harassment in connection with a Supreme Court nominee was both startling and new.

Other pro-Thomas Democrats in the Senate, such as liberal Joe Lieberman of Connecticut, were getting an earful from their wives as well as they headed back to the capital. In the government, in the press, in the public at large, it was mostly women, who responded to Anita Hill; they reacted intuitively, knowing little about Hill but realizing, from their own experiences or those of their sisters or daughters, that sexual harassment happens all the time.

Daniel Patrick Moynihan, the former Harvard professor and ambassador, now a senator from New York, was another Democrat who was prepared to vote for Thomas before the story broke. Many of

Thomas's ideas about the disintegration of the black family and welfare dependency were similar to theories that Moynihan had raised in
the 1960s, when liberal orthodoxy was at its zenith. His concepts had
created a furor and were dismissed by many as racist, just as Thomas's
ideas were dismissed by the civil rights community. Thomas's
unorthodox views had appealed to Senator Moynihan.

But Hill's press conference unleashed the fury of women on the
New York intellectual politician and the rest of Thomas's senatorial
supporters. Three thousand outraged callers dialed Moynihan's offices
in both New York and Washington on the Monday that Hill addressed
the nation, and again on Tuesday, the day the Senate vote on Thomas
had been scheduled. The vast majority of the callers were demanding
a delay of the vote or an outright rejection of Thomas, and Moynihan
listened. Moynihan had not been singled out among his colleagues:
every senator's office was under telephonic bombardment. Even senators who had never realized the importance of sexual harassment as an
issue understood what it meant when thousands of constituents
shouted against it over the telephone.

The onslaught overloaded the Senate telephone system. The cir-
cuitry had not been designed to handle this astounding number of
calls; some offices lost their telephone service altogether. Much, but
not all of the outcry, was spontaneous. Lobbyists for women's-rights
groups were roaming the Senate: if they learned that a certain senator
was not being sufficiently bombarded, they hustled messages out to
their people in his state to get busy.

By the time Senator Exon arrived in the capital, his office, too, had
received a flood of calls. A former governor, Exon was no novice when
it came to the rough-and-tumble of moral issues in politics. Two years
earlier he had led the charge against former Senator John Tower as the
Texan tried to be confirmed as Secretary of Defense. Senator Exon had
based his attack on charges of Tower's drinking and womanizing. This
had provoked a counterattack from the failed nominee, who raised
unsubstantiated charges that Exon was "one of the two or three biggest boozers in the Senate." When Senator Exon hurried to the Senate
floor Monday evening, October 7, to demand a delay on the Thomas
vote, it was a sign that the support for Thomas was beginning to crack.

Even Arlen Specter, who had been so adamant that Thomas's denial
had sufficiently disposed of Hill's late-breaking charges, had changed

his tune overnight. By early Tuesday, he was on morning television endorsing a postponement of the vote by a day or two in order to "put any doubts to rest."

By then, the atmosphere on Capitol Hill was electric. In Senate office buildings, the telephones were ringing madly; in the Capitol itself, indecision reigned. The anteroom and the corridors near the entrance to the Senate floor were filling with Hill supporters, journalists, and television crews. Over in the House of Representatives, in the other wing of the Capitol, trouble was brewing as well.

Senator Moynihan was one senator who got the message loud and clear. He wanted the Thomas vote delayed but he faced a major procedural problem. Senate rules required that a postponement of the vote would require the unanimous consent of all one hundred senators. The Senate majority leader, George Mitchell, was insisting that this obstacle could not be overcome; the vote would have to be held that day if anyone objected to the delay. Mitchell was trying to work out a deal, but preferred to follow established procedure. But Moynihan could be ingenious.

On Tuesday morning he created a furor on the Senate floor with an unusual parliamentary maneuver. Moynihan made a motion that the Senate simply adjourn for a week, which would have the same effect as postponing the vote. Moynihan's motion infuriated Republicans as well as the Democratic leadership. Senator Mitchell came running from his office into the decorous Senate chamber, waving his arms to call a halt to the proceedings. The majority leader pulled Moynihan aside and told him in no uncertain terms that he, and he alone, decided when to adjourn. Senator Moynihan backed down, but he had made his point. There were ways to delay the vote.

By noon, the vote was still on. The lavishly painted reception room at the entrance to the Senate floor had filled with members of women's-rights groups waiting to pounce on any senator coming off the floor. The Senate guards were having trouble maintaining their usual politeness while protecting senators trying to get onto elevators and back to their offices. Some were quick to capitulate; others, including Senator Biden, were not. Biden remained adamant that his committee had handled Hill properly.

"The Judiciary Committee did not screw up on anything," the chairman barked as he brushed by reporters.

Normally an even-keeled institution, the Senate was being slapped about like a ship without a mast by the waves of gender warfare. Nothing had disrupted the institution so raucously since the days of the civil rights bills, when archsegregationist Strom Thurmond had wrestled a Texas Democrat to the floor outside a committee room to prevent him from providing a quorum for a vote.

At lunchtime, seven congresswomen marched from the House side of Capitol Hill, their elbows pumping and their heels clacking as they climbed the steep steps to the Senate. They were rudely rebuffed by the senators. The Senate Democrats, fifty-six men and one woman, were having their weekly luncheon and could not be disturbed. Twice the women of the House knocked on the closed door of the luncheon room, and twice they were shooed away. Finally, Senator Mitchell made a grudging compromise. After dessert, he would meet with the congresswomen in his office.

Undaunted, the congresswomen—led by Louise Slaughter of New York, and Patricia Schroeder of Colorado—marched over to the office buildings in search of senators to lobby. Women staffers came out into the hallways and shouted encouragement to the representatives on their mission into the bastion of male power. "Right on! Right on!," they yelled.

Prodded by the outpouring of sentiment loosed by Hill's allegations, the traditional liberals tried to rally their followers to the cause. Senator Ted Kennedy, who had stayed out of the limelight due to his own tarnished personal history, tried to inject some reason into the proceedings. "There is no justification for an unseemly rush to judgment in a few hours when a delay of a few days can make such an important difference," he said, arguing for just a little more time to evaluate what Hill had to say about Thomas.

The rhetoric grew heated when Senator Alan Cranston of California took the Senate floor. At the age of seventy-seven, Cranston had been known for years as the liberal organizer of the Senate. He had played a major role in defeating Bork. He was also one of only nine senators who had been willing to vote the year before against confirming David Souter for the Supreme Court.

"I have been appalled at the prospect that the Senate would proceed to vote on the nomination of Clarence Thomas without reconvening the Judiciary Committee to hear the very serious allegations which have been made by Professor Hill," Cranston began. "I am appalled at statements being made that these are not serious charges because they involve verbal, not physical, abuse, " he continued. "I am appalled at the stunning admissions of a lack of sensitivity to the problem of sexual harassment. I am appalled by the vicious attacks upon Professor Hill, which have been made on and off the Senate floor. What has a majority of this body been saying to all the women who are subjected to sexual harassment? Who have been, are now, or will be subjected to sexual harassment?"

But in 1991, Cranston's influence was not what it had been in the past. He had lost power not so much because of his battle with cancer but due to his losing battle with the Senate Ethics Committee.

In 1986 in the middle of a tough reelection contest with Ed Zschau, a moderate California businessman, Cranston had turned for help to Charles Keating, the owner of Lincoln Savings and Loan. That year and in ensuing years, Keating provided more than a million dollars to Cranston or to projects directed by him and his son. As with DeConcini, Cranston, and the three other senators who became known as the infamous Keating Five, the savings-and-loan owner would later call on Cranston for help. Among the five, however, Senator Cranston was singled out for criticism by the Ethics Committee. The scandal destroyed his otherwise distinguished career of twenty-two years in the Senate, forcing him to abandon his cherished post in the Senate leadership and announce that he would not seek reelection in 1992. Cranston was no more the person to lead the charge than Kennedy.

It seemed that wherever you looked in the Senate, the moral authority to challenge the nominee's behavior had been dissipated.

It took a Southern moderate, Democrat Jim Sasser from Memphis, to make the liberals' best case. Senator Sasser was a lawyer and not known for speaking out on issues beyond those of the Budget Committee, of which he was chairman. Sasser got to the heart of the matter right away, arguing that the Senate, rather than Clarence Thomas or Anita Hill, was on trial in that day's debate:

> Make no mistake about it. We're engaged here today in a test of the integrity of the United States Senate. A substantial number of Americans now suspect that we are rushing to judgment on perhaps the most profound responsibility we have as United States senators. Millions of Ameri-

cans are just like myself. We learned of this allegation by way of the news media and by watching the press conference of Professor Hill on the television networks just yesterday, and we should take seriously our responsibility to advise and consent on nominations to the highest courts in this land, and I believe my colleagues do take that very seriously.

I would say to my colleagues that, if we do anything else, the American people are going to believe that Judge Thomas was railroaded through confirmation, that he passed through this Senate with a wink and a nod, and that he goes to the highest court in this land for the rest of his natural life, if he chooses to serve there, with the taint that neither we, nor he, nor the passage of time can wipe away. And I submit . . . that, if we do that, we will have called into question in one stroke the judgment of the executive branch in proposing Judge Thomas to the Supreme Court, the fairness of the legislative branch in our examination and in fulfilling our responsibility to advise and consent, and lastly we will have cast in doubt the character of the judicial branch. . . . I would submit that, at this juncture, the country simply cannot afford that.

It took the only woman Democrat, Senator Barbara Mikulski of Maryland, to educate her colleagues about sexual harassment. Senator Mikulski is the product of a Polish neighorhood in East Baltimore— streetwise and politically tough despite her diminutive four-foot-eleven-inch stature. She is an ardent feminist who, in her 1986 campaign for the Senate, demolished Linda Chavez, her Republican opponent. Chavez tried to tarnish Mikulski by making innuendos about her status as a single woman and describing her as a "San Francisco-style liberal." The tactic failed to impress the Maryland voters. In the Senate, she took a strong feminist position:

What disturbs me as much as the allegations themselves is that the United States Senate appears not to take the charge of sexual harassment seriously. We have indicated that it was not serious enough to be raised as a question in the Judiciary Committee. We did not think it serious enough to apprise the Senators themselves that this was an allegation. I'm a member of the United States Senate and I think I work hard and do my homework, and so do many of my other colleagues. And as I have called around the Senate, I find that my own colleagues knew nothing of this until it broke as a media story over the weekend.

And then over here we have Professor Anita Hill, whose background up from the roots of very severe rural poverty, not too unlike Judge Thomas himself—one out of Oklahoma, one out of the clay hills of Georgia—who has made these allegations. She has said she has come forth with pain because reliving this situation has indeed been extremely painful for her. If we do not give full airing to this, she will always be the woman who made these allegations. And now, we face the fact that even yesterday, Professor Hill was attacked on the Senate floor with unprecedented venom. A woman was attacked on the Senate floor with unprecedented venom when she was herself talking about being a victim. We owe it to Professor Hill not to attack her on the Senate floor, but to submit her to a line of questioning about the events that she alleges to see if, in fact, they are true.

If you talk to victims of abuse the way I have, they will tell you they are often doubly victimized, by both the event in which they are abused and then subsequently by the way the system treats them. And what now has occurred is that they say that this could not be taken seriously enough to be brought to our attention.

To anybody out there who wants to be a whistle-blower, the message is: Don't blow that whistle because you'll be left out there by yourself. To any victim of sexual harassment or sexual abuse or sexual violence either in the street or even in her own home, the message is nobody's going to take you seriously, not even the United States Senate.

To the private sector, who now has to enforce these laws on sexual harassment, whether we call it sexual humiliation or whether there's overt physical aggression, sexual terrorism, the message to the private sector is: Cool it, guys. Even the Senate takes a walk on this one.

The Republicans were fighting back with everything they could find. They knew that a delay, as reasonable as it seemed, would provide an opportunity for Thomas opponents to make high drama of the sexual harassment charges and perhaps come up with other potential slurs against the nominee's character. A postponement of the vote might be fatal to the nomination. Thomas supporters feared, as one of them put it, a "death by a thousand cuts." Ricky Silberman, Thomas's longtime loyalist over at the EEOC, said, "It was war." And in war, anything goes.

Late Monday night, Senator Alan Simpson went on national television to launch a counterattack. He appeared on ABC's *Nightline* program with documents that the Thomas camp hoped would sink Hill's case. The senator had telephone logs from Thomas's office that seemed to show that Hill had continued to call the nominee, and therefore had stayed on a friendly basis with him long after she had left Washington.

It was Senator Danforth who had uncovered the logs after repeated conversations earlier in the day with Thomas and his secretary. The telephone records had shown eleven messages from Hill for Thomas, which the secretary had taken down in clear handwriting. One message read, "Just called to say hello. Sorry she didn't get to see you this week." Hill had left this on January 31, 1984, just seven months after allegedly departing from the EEOC in fear of Thomas. Most of the messages simply read "Pls call." One, that the secretary recorded at 3:40 P.M. on January 3, 1985, said "Pls call tonight," and included the name of Hill's hotel and room number in Washington. The most recent message was less than a year old, recording that Hill had called to invite Thomas to speak at the Oklahoma law school. (At Hill's press conference, her colleagues at the law school had reiterated that she had been unenthusiatic but cooperative about their request that she invite Thomas.)

Senator Danforth called a press conference of his own on Tuesday and handed out copies of the telephone logs. He was convinced the phone records would turn the tide in favor of Thomas. How could this woman claim to have been treated so badly and then have remained friendly with her tormentor? The senator also passed out copies of a signed affidavit from Thomas, who had not appeared in public since Anita Hill's allegations had been published. The affidavit read:

I, Clarence Thomas, having been duly sworn, do hereby swear and affirm the following:

1. As I told the Federal Bureau of Investigation on September 28, 1991, I totally and unequivocally deny Anita Hill's allegation of misconduct of any kind toward her, sexual or otherwise. These allegations are untrue.

2. At all times during the period she worked with me, our relationship was strictly professional. During that time and subsequently, the relationship has been wholly cordial.

3. I am terribly saddened and deeply offended by these allegations.

However, there was one strange inconsistency in Thomas's statement that has never been explained. He was supposedly interviewed by the FBI on September 25, yet he said in the affidavit he was interviewed on September 28. That was three days after the FBI report was completed, and one day after the committee vote.

Other information that could help to discredit Hill's charges had come in as well. Charles A. Kothe, the founding dean of the law school at Oral Roberts University, sent the Senate a statement in which he described how he had come to hire Hill with Thomas's recommendation. Kothe said that Thomas had visited the school and his own home on several occasions and that Hill had been friendly to the nominee at the time. Kothe went on to speculate about the origin of Hill's charges in a way that he would later retract, but only after Danforth and his allies had used the speculation and built upon it.

"I find the references to the alleged sexual harassment not only unbelievable but preposterous. I am convinced that such are the product of fantasy," Kothe said.

Meanwhile, on the Senate floor, Orrin Hatch made another move to bolster the Thomas cause. The Republican member of the Judiciary Committee read a letter from a former aide to Thomas at the EEOC, Armstrong Williams, who now was a Washington public relations man. Williams's view of Hill was contrary to that of almost everyone who had ever met her. He said he had worked with Hill at the EEOC and found her to be "untrustworthy, selfish and extremely bitter" after being passed over for the job as the agency's chief legal counsel. He described Hill as a "very selfish person who wanted everything to go her way." Williams's statements about Hill sounded preposterous but so, too, did Hill's statements about Thomas, to many of those who knew him.

The backers of Thomas had managed to turn around and take a few cuts at Hill, particularly with the telephone logs. These message records seemed to bolster Thomas's case, at least without some explanation from Hill. But by the time Senator Danforth distributed the copies—with many messages carefully blacked out as if to hide something else—the momentum initiated by Hill's charges was barreling out of control.

As Tuesday wore on, more and more votes fell away from Thomas, who had been fairly confident of an easy victory the week before. On Friday, Clarence Thomas had had a solid sixty senators ready to vote for his confirmation, with a chance of getting more to follow the herd once it was clear he would win. By midafternoon Tuesday, one hundred days after Clarence Thomas had been nominated by President Bush, Thomas could count on only forty-one senators to definitely vote for him. An equal number were ready to vote against his confirmation, and as many as nineteen senators were undecided or calling for a postponement. The victory that had seemed so close just a few days before had evaporated.

The Republicans senators backed off. They decided to let the nominee decide himself whether to have them go ahead with the vote, according to a source in the White House. They knew Thomas would lose if the vote proceeded as scheduled, but the quandary was that he might also lose if it was delayed. The senators wanted him to make the call.

Senator Danforth took upon himself the mission of dealing with the quandary. He had an agonizing conversation with Thomas. When he came to the floor to announce the decision late in the afternoon, pain was written all over his face. His speech was rambling and bitter. His performance was a far cry from the Tuesday morning sermons the senator-priest delivered at St. Alban's Church, a bastion of the city's Episcopal elite. It was not like his usual methodical and principled floor speeches, sermons themselves really, on behalf of the civil rights bill or in opposition to the death penalty.

Danforth was a fine example of noblesse oblige. His grandfather had founded the Ralston-Purina company and made millions, but at the same time had preached nobility and humility to his progeny. Jack Danforth had gone to Princeton University, then earned degrees in both divinity and law from Yale. In college, he had fallen under the sway of an aunt, Dorothy Compton, a liberal Democrat and activist who taught him about racial justice.

Armed with his two seemingly contradictory graduate degrees, Danforth went to Wall Street to practice law in a big firm. In his spare time, he served as chaplain to dying cancer patients. He eventually returned to his birthplace in the privileged suburbs of St. Louis. In 1968, he won a campaign for Missouri's attorney general and hired as his aides the best people he could find inside and outside the state, including Clarence Thomas. Eight years later, he was elected senator and became known in Washington as Saint Jack for his injection of morality into political arguments.

But Danforth's saintly moniker cut both ways. He had been known to wrap himself in morality when some thought he was not on the side of the angels. For instance, he salvaged his seat from a challenge in 1982 by Harriett Woods, a liberal leader and women's-rights activist, by shifting into a negative campaign that attacked her support for abortion and busing.

When the confirmation of his protégé for the Supreme Court went suddenly wrong because of what he thought was an underhanded attack, Senator Danforth seemed to have lost control of himself.

"The cheese slipped off the cracker," said one observer. "He just lost it. He personalized it. He just went nuts. Many people on [Capitol] Hill had the impression that his behavior was very uncharacteristic. He is a very righteous individual, that's what makes him so appealing. But when the righteousness turns into something else, it turns ugly."

Danforth lashed out at what seemed to him a plausible target; he attacked one of the liberal groups that had been lobbying against Thomas. He charged People for the American Way with calling up members of the EEOC staff and asking for "dirt" on Clarence Thomas. Lacking evidence, Danforth's speech implied, wrongly, that People for the American Way had orchestrated the Hill charges.

The organization vehemently denied the allegations. It had, in fact, been trying desperately to patch up relations with Danforth ever since the last bitter struggle over a Supreme Court nomination, that of Judge Robert Bork. Although many other moderate Republicans had voted against Bork, Senator Danforth had fought for the Yale professor and taken his defeat hard. Because the Democrats' majority in the Senate was thin and reliant on conservatives, a liberal lobbying group like People for the American Way was in trouble without the support of a moderate Republican leader like Danforth. Any chance of repairing that relationship in the near future went out the window with Danforth's speech.

Saint Jack also accused an unnamed colleague of leaking the FBI report on Hill, which would be a federal crime. But neither *Newsday* nor the rest of the media that pounced on the Hill story ever reported possessing the FBI document. The information that had caused the brouhaha could as easily have come from other sources including Hill's four-page statement to the Judiciary Committee, the release of which would be no more than a breach of Senate rules. Indeed, it is such leaks, which happen every week of the year, that grease the workings of the Senate.

In his rambling anger, Senator Danforth railed sarcastically against the idea of a delay:

Let's keep this ball in play. We need delay. We need more time for the People for the American Way to make their phone calls, digging up the dirt. We need the interest groups to have more time to gin up their opposition. There's blood in the water. We need more time for the sharks to gather around the body of Clarence Thomas. Oh, we need a delay. The Judiciary Committee, when they said it doesn't warrant further action, they blew it, it is said. I don't think so at all.

One hundred days ago today, Clarence Thomas was nominated for the Supreme Court of the United States. For one hundred days, the interest groups and their lawyers and various staff members of the Senate have combed over the record of Clarence Thomas. For one hundred days, they've examined footnotes and law review articles, to question him about sentences and articles taken out of context, speeches from—made in a political context, which are then analyzed and criticized before the Judiciary Committee. One hundred days, this has gone on, and people say: "Oh, no, wait. We need more. We need more time." That's a tactic. . . . I have been asked by the press today, why not delay? Why not delay? One hundred days isn't enough. The Judiciary Committee's word for it isn't enough. Why not delay? Why not keep this circus—and I use that word in the Roman context—why not keep this circus going? The lions aren't satisfied yet. Why not just have a delay? And my answer throughout the day has been: "I don't think there should be a delay because all of the relevant evidence is before us now."

The senator also predicted, correctly, that a delayed vote and a senatorial inquiry would not necessarily resolve the matter of one person's word against another.

The charge of Ms. Hill, the response to the charge by Clarence Thomas denying the allegation of Ms. Hill, it is not as though at some future time after some appropriate hearing, the skies will miraculously open, the clouds will dissipate and we will know the answer to these charges. I am quite sure that if we have a delay, no matter how long that delay would be, people would say: "Well, we need another delay or we still have doubts or she proved her point or he proved his point." The questions will still exist.

People say clear the clouds away, there's a cloud of doubt. Well, we can't do anything while the cloud of doubt exists. . . . [T]he cloud of doubt was created by a violation of the rules of the United States Senate. Think about voting down the nomination of Clarence Thomas solely on the basis of a violation of Senate rules. Think about voting down the nomination of Clarence Thomas solely because an FBI report was distributed to the media illegally. Talk about scandal—that is scandal.

So . . . I have said to the press and I have said to some of my dear friends in the Senate today, I don't think there should be a delay. This poor guy has been tortured enough, and at the end of the delay, they're going to continue at it, and at the end of the delay, they're going to say: "Wait, there's somebody else. There's something else. Let's have another delay." I have said in my opinion, a delay would serve no purpose whatever, and that's how I feel about it.

Then, Senator Danforth dropped the biggest news of this amazing day.

But . . . it's not my call. At least in my mind, it's not my call. Because a person who I respect so greatly and a person I love dearly said to me on the phone: "They have taken from me what I have worked forty-three years to create. They have taken from me what I have taken forty-three years to build, my reputation." And he said: "I want to clear my name."

Thomas had not made this decision to fight to cleanse his reputation until the last minute. By Tuesday afternoon, it was obvious to Thomas and his advisers that if he had pressed for a vote that day, he would have been defeated then and there.

Clarence Thomas said to me on the phone: "I have to clear my name. I have to restore what they have taken from me. I have to appear before the appropriate forum and clear my name."

That is the proposition . . . that I am asked to put to the United States

Senate: forty-eight hours and a proper forum for Clarence Thomas to try
to clear his name.

Clarence and Virginia Thomas had spent the night of Monday and
all day Tuesday at the four-story Georgetown house of their friends the
Silbermans. Larry Silberman was a judge with Thomas on the Court
of Appeals, while Ricky had been his deputy and one of his teachers
of conservative ideology at the EEOC. The refrigerator had been
stocked with champagne for the celebration they had expected to have
that night with all of Republican Washington.

As the day progressed, Thomas grew more heartsick and despon-
dent. It was clear that he had shed some tears. "Why, Ricky? You
know how I am. Why would anyone do this to me?" Thomas asked.

Every time Thomas agreed to eat something and the Silbermans
moved to order some takeout fried chicken or Chinese food, the
telephone would ring with more bad news from Danforth. Thomas
would lose his appetite again.

When asking for a delay became Thomas's only hope, the senators
had no further reason to hang on to their vote as scheduled. But it took
another four hours for them to negotiate the terms. Senator Danforth
must have known that it would be impossible to hold a hearing in
forty-eight hours. But by fighting for two days he was able to hold the
delay down to a week.

Once he realized the import of what was happening, Senator Biden
had wanted a two-week postponement in order to have time for fair
hearings on the controversy. But even that would have been too short
a time to get to the bottom of allegations about sensitive events that
may have occurred so long ago. When Senator Danforth and his fellow
Republicans backed Senator Mitchell and the Democrats into a postponement of a week, the fate of Anita Hill was essentially sealed once
again. A serious investigation of her charges could not be accomplished in so short a time. There was always the remote possibility of
an additional delay—as Senator Robert Dole, the minority leader,
suggested. But the majority leader, Senator Mitchell, and the committee chairman, Senator Biden, were gentlemen who liked to stick to
their word. A week's delay would mean a week and, in the meantime,
hearings would be held.

Hurried as they would be, the hearings would not be able to come to some sort of truthful decision on Hill's charges; this much was obvious to many of those doing the negotiating. The new hearings might amount to nothing more than a mandatory symbolic exercise. The women's groups were on the senators' backs, and the committee members had to deal with the public perception that Hill's charges had not been taken seriously. The Senate was embarrassed. Let's go back and do it right, those caught in the middle suggested to Dole and Mitchell, and then, assuming nothing more comes out, we'll go ahead and approve him. The outcome of the Hill hearings, barring a miracle, was preordained.

It was clear, too, from that Tuesday night that the Republicans and the Democrats would be playing by two different sets of rules. Biden held a meeting that very evening with Thurmond, who had to be consulted as the ranking minority member of the Judiciary Committee, to discuss the new hearings. Biden stressed that he would approach the hearings as a neutral and fair fact-finder. Thurmond had a different, vindicating attitude, according to some of those involved. "We know the facts," he kept saying. "He's innocent. We're going to prove he's innocent." Given those contrasting approaches, the chances of a miraculous clarity emerging from the hearings were nil.

But it took Wyoming's Senator Alan Simpson to say out loud that the Republicans had none of the Democrats' hang-ups about being gentlemen. Not in this case. Simpson, who for fourteen years had held the Senate seat that was once his father's, was known for his trenchant humor and unusual candor. The six-foot-six cowboy was the Senate's minority whip and President Bush's closest friend on Capitol Hill. A fixture in both Wyoming and Washington politics, Simpson was not afraid of losing his constituency with what he often referred to as his big mouth.

Earlier in 1991, during the Gulf war, Simpson's nasty and less logical side had gotten the better of him when he lashed out against Peter Arnett, the CNN reporter who stayed in Baghdad to broadcast firsthand accounts of the bombing. Simpson was not fond of the press to start with and the sight of an American newsman telling Iraq's side of the story incensed him. He first labeled Arnett as an Iraqi sympathizer for doing the job of a newsman. The senator then went overboard by alleging that the Vietnamese man to whom Arnett's sister was married had been active in the Vietcong. Arnett was then covering the Vietnam war for the Associated Press; the implication was that Arnett, who won a Pulitzer Prize for his Vietnam reporting, was an enemy sympathizer. The senator never produced evidence to support these remarks.

But Senator Simpson also could verbally hack a path through the political jungle in the direction of veracity. At times during the Thomas nomination, Senator Simpson acted as the Senate's fool, in the Shakespearean sense of the supposedly crazy man who dares to speak the unbridled truth. Senator Simpson criticized Hill and the media, but then went on to warn, and perhaps threaten, about what was about to happen to Hill, and to Thomas, now that the capitol games were getting not only serious, but also rough.

I think it's a cruel thing we're witnessing. It's a harsh thing, a very sad and harsh thing, and Anita Hill will be sucked right into the—the very thing she wanted to avoid most. She will be injured and destroyed and belittled and hounded and harassed, real harassment, different than the sexual kind. Just plain old Washington variety harassment which is pretty unique in itself.

So maybe we can really put them on the grill. I've heard the old phrase, "The gridiron singes but does not burn." And I've never believed that one.

And maybe we can—maybe we can ruin them both. Leave them both wounded and their families wounded. Maybe in cynical array they can bring the curtain down on them both and maybe we can get them both to cry. That'll be something that people will be trying to do.

It's a tragic situation and it's very sad to observe.

# Chapter 16

Americans everywhere were taking sides in the burgeoning controversy over the Supreme Court nomination. They were noisily debating each other though they had few actual details of the story. But there was one woman editor at a newspaper in North Carolina who said she knew instantly what to think.

"Yeah, she's telling the truth! She's gutsy," Angela Wright said to herself, when she first saw Anita Hill on television. In an interview, Wright said she had reason to believe this Oklahoma law professor whom she had never met. Wright had also worked for Thomas at the EEOC. She arrived eight months after Hill had departed for Oklahoma and she said her own experiences with the chairman were not dissimilar.

Wright did little more than muse about it all until she began reading news accounts of how cavalierly the Senate was treating Hill's charges. She was incensed, particularly, by the way she thought Hill had been vilified by Senator Arlen Specter.

At the age of thirty-seven, Wright was then settling into journalism, after a turbulent career in Washington as a political public-relations adviser. Having left the capital and studied journalism at the University of North Carolina at Chapel Hill, she took a job at the Winston-Salem *Chronicle,* a small black weekly newspaper, She was managing editor of the weekly when she was hired away by *The Charlotte Observer,* a prestigious daily paper. The *Observer* made her an assistant metropolitan editor, which was a low-level but high-pressure management position. It was a good job, but what Wright really wanted to do was write. She hoped to become a columnist, and she had been encouraged by her bosses to turn out some sample writing pieces to show her stuff.

So, motivated by what was going on in Washington, Wright sat down and wrote. She had few good words for Thomas, in part because he had fired her as head of public relations at the EEOC by crudely taping a note to her office chair. She also had words that supported Hill's charges.

"I know Thomas is capable of doing these things, so women should be furious at the way Anita Hill is being treated," she wrote in the sample column.

Wright showed her writing effort to a few colleagues, but as far as she was concerned that was the end of it. The column was never intended for publication. Wright said she had no intention of getting publicly involved in any Washington brouhaha.

But somehow, out of the blue, Wright received a telephone call from Washington on Wednesday evening, the day after the Senate had postponed its vote on Thomas's nomination. The call would snatch her up out of the relative obscurity of her native North Carolina and, briefly, make this newswoman the biggest story in the nation. The call was from Mark Schwartz, one of Senator Biden's staff lawyers on the Judiciary Committee. He knew about her column; one of her colleagues apparently had tipped off the Senate. Would she be willing to share the contents of her column with the committee? She refused. Would she come to Washington? She said no.

"This environment was brewing," she said later. "It was not the way this should have been handled. It was not fair to Anita Hill, it was not fair to Clarence Thomas, and it was not fair to his wife. . . . This should not have been played out on prime time. The charges were serious enough to be treated in a serious manner. . . . After eleven years in Washington, I had figured out what they were after. It was a circus atmosphere, shameful, full of political posturing."

But later Schwartz called back, this time with Cynthia Hogan, another committee lawyer, on the line. Wright began to waver. Finally, she agreed to give a statement to a bipartisan group of committee staffers the next day.

"I wanted them to know I believed Anita Hill, that I knew about this behavior," Wright said, not thinking of her role as that of "the second woman," the witness who might add crucial proof to Hill's story. Wright said she only had wanted to help corroborate Hill's story without drawing too much attention to herself.

Like Anita Hill, Angela Wright was a young, very attractive, single black career woman who had worked for Clarence Thomas at a time when his life was in turbulence, both personally and professionally. Otherwise, the two women were very different. By her own account, Wright was hot-tempered and quick with her tongue; she also had what she described as "the guts of a bull." This combination got her into plenty of trouble in Washington, where it is the low-key person who more often survives in the government bureaucracy.

In the late 1970s, Wright had come to Washington to work for Congressman Charlie Rose, a Democrat from North Carolina. By the time Clarence Thomas was nominated to the Supreme Court, Rose had become well known in the capital for his aggressive defense of the tobacco and peanut interests that were so powerful in his state. Rose had fired Wright after she stalked out of the congressman's office yelling about some act of unfairness. She did not return for the rest of the day. Wright said later of this incident that she had deserved to be fired. "I'm the kind of person who learns from my mistakes. I don't do those kinds of things again."

But she did equally intemperate things when she quit another job, this one at the Agency for International Development (AID), the large bureaucracy that manages the country's foreign aid program. Wright was director of media relations. But she had not gotten along with her boss at AID, Kate Semerad. Wright acknowledged that her letter of resignation was "nasty," describing Semerad as "silly" and "insensitive," and accusing her of using "racist tactics." To make matters worse, she sent copies of the letter to "everyone in the world," she said. "I carbon-copied the White House, I carbon-copied personnel, I carbon-copied everybody I could think of," admitting she now regretted her actions. Angry, Wright wanted vindication. She responded as helpfully as she could to inquiries from aides to Senator Jesse Helms who were trying to find information that would prevent Semerad from getting a promotion.

She could leave AID because Clarence Thomas had offered her a job in 1984 as the EEOC's director of public affairs. It was a serious position that necessitated managing a staff of twenty-seven, handling frequent contacts with the press, organizing seminars, and putting out agency publications. Her departure from the EEOC a year later was also abrupt. The reasons the chairman fired her were disputed, and would eventually play a part in the larger Hill-Thomas controversy.

But by the time the controversy exploded, Wright seemed to have gained more control over her life. Her bosses at the Charlotte newspaper respected her and supported her. "In nearly two years at the *Observer*, Angela has been a strong editor and shown solid judgment under pressure," Jane Shoemaker, the paper's managing editor said after the Judiciary Committee's interest in Wright became public. "She's independent. She tells people what she thinks. We support her."

On Thursday morning October 10, one day before the start of the scheduled hearings into Anita Hill's allegations against Clarence Thomas, a group of people gathered around a speaker-phone in a Judiciary Committee office. Ready to listen to Wright's statement were eight committee staffers and a court reporter acting as a stenographer. Wright spoke from home, where she was accompanied only by her dog. She had not even retained a lawyer.

At the Senate end of the line were two members of Biden's staff, Cynthia Hogan and Harriet Grant, the chief nominations counsel; two aides representing Strom Thurmond, Terry Wooten, chief counsel of the committee's minority Republican staff, and Melissa Riley; and aides to other key committee senators, Howell Heflin and Patrick Leahy from the Democratic side of the committee, and Arlen Specter and Orrin Hatch from the Republican side. Everything was at stake in this conversation. Clearly, Thomas's nomination could not survive a second set of harassment charges from another credible witness. The staffers needed to know what Wright was claiming had happened to her, and whether she was believable.

The group had agreed that the actual questioning would be limited to Hogan and Wooten. Hogan led. She asked Wright if Thomas had ever said anything inappropriate to her.

"At one point, Clarence Thomas made comments about my anatomy," Wright said for the committee's record. "Clarence Thomas made comments about women's anatomy quite often. At one point, Clarence Thomas came by my apartment at night, unannounced and uninvited, and talked in general terms, but also in conversation he would try to move the conversation over to the prospect of my dating him."

Wright was able to recall some specifics, but totally unable to provide any dates or other circumstances of the incidents. The EEOC chairman had frequently suggested he wanted to date her, she said. He made some kind of improper comment perhaps one out of every four or five times she saw her.

"We are talking about a thing that, you know, pretty much pops out of Clarence Thomas's mouth when he feels like saying this. We are not talking about, you know, traumatic single events here."

There was one incident that she said she remembered well. It happened at a retirement party she had been asked by Thomas to organize for her predecessor, Al Sweeney. Thomas had not always been polite with his opinion about Sweeney, according to Wright. She said that Thomas once had told her, "Al Sweeney is old, he's no good. He has one foot in the grave, and the other one on a banana peel."

Wright described the retirement party. "We were sitting at the banquet table while the speakers and things were going through their speeches, and Clarence Thomas was sitting right next to me and he at one point turned around and said, 'This is really a great job,' blah, blah, blah. And he said, 'And you look good and you are going to be dating me, too.' That was not like the only time he said something of that nature."

Wright said this sort of talk was a Thomas theme.

"In general, given the opportunity, Clarence Thomas would say to me, you know, 'You need to be dating me, I think I'm going to date you, you're one of the finest women I have on my staff,' [or] 'you know, we're going to be going out eventually.' " By "given the opportunity," Wright explained that she meant when no one else was present.

The second of three specific incidents that Wright said she remembered was the occasion when Thomas showed up uninvited at her apartment on Capitol Hill one night.

"He came to my apartment, I opened the door, I offered him a beer. We talked. He sat at what was actually a counter separating the kitchen from the living room area. We sat on bar stools and talked in general about general things and, you know, the conversation would turn to his desire to date me, and I would adeptly turn it to some other topic." Thomas left after midnight, after ignoring a series of hints that it was time for him to leave, she said.

Wright said the third incident occurred at an out-of-town seminar she had arranged for him. There, she said, her boss complimented her on her dress and asked her what size her breasts were.

Asked if she told anyone about that incident, she said she had talked about it to Phyllis Berry Myers, Thomas's former director of congressional affairs at the EEOC. Myers had already been quoted in *Newsday* and other papers as saying that Thomas had never acted improperly toward her or anyone else to her knowledge. At that point, Myers was being recruited by the White House to testify on behalf of Thomas.

Wright quoted Myers as saying something very different at the time when they both worked at the EEOC. According to Wright, Myers responded to her by saying, "Well, he's a man, you know, he's always hitting on everybody." Myers later denied to reporters ever making that comment.

In 1985, barely a year after she had begun working at the EEOC, Angela Wright learned she was being fired when she read the message the chairman had stuck to her chair. As a political appointee—Wright described herself as a moderate Republican—Thomas had the right to fire her anytime, she said. She immediately went to Thomas's office to ask him the reason for her dismissal. Thomas told her that generally he had been unhappy with her job performance and complained that she had failed to fire some of her staff.

Thomas told her, "Well, Angela, I've never been satisfied with your work," Wright recounted to the group of committee staffers huddled around the speaker-phone.

"I said, 'Why have you not been satisfied with my work, and why have you not told me this up to this point?'

"He said, 'Well, I told you to fire those folks down there, and you haven't fired a soul down there.' And I said, 'Well, Clarence, these people are career employees, not like I can just go in there and say you are fired. It takes almost an act of Congress to get them removed.'

"He said, 'Well, I just in general am not satisfied with your work.' "

Cynthia Hogan then asked Wright the sensitive question.

"Do you think that your failure to respond to any of Judge Thomas's comments to you had anything to do with his firing you?"

"You are not the first person who has asked me that question," Wright responded. "Several people at EEOC asked me that question. . . . About the only thing I can tell you is that he did tell me at one point during that conversation when I asked him about why he was firing me that he was real bothered by the fact that I did not wait for him outside his office after work. It was a statement that I dismissed as one of his statements."

"Well, did that comment make you think that perhaps the firing had to do with your failure to respond to his comments?" Hogan asked.

"It did not make me think that at that moment. What I was thinking at that moment was he was grasping for all kinds of reasons. In retrospect I guess that is a possibility but that is not the first thought that came to my mind when he said it."

Hogan then asked her if she knew Anita Hill, to which Wright responded that she had neither known nor heard of her before that week. Asked whether Hill's allegations were "in or out of character for Clarence Thomas, as you know him?" Wright said, "I feel that the Clarence Thomas that I know is quite capable of doing just what Anita Hill alleges."

Wright said she had confided in other women at the agency about Thomas's behavior toward her, and that they had similar stories to tell her about the chairman's conduct. Wright refused, however, to name any of them except Myers, saying it was not fair to drag anyone else into the controversy. She did agree to ask other women if she could give the committee their names.

Hogan's questioning had been solicitous and sympathetic. But next came Terry Wooten's turn at the speaker-phone. Wooten was a middle-aged lawyer from South Carolina who had worked five years for

Senator Thurmond. It was to Thurmond, the committee's ranking Republican, that Wooten owed his allegiance. And Thurmond wanted desperately to discredit Angela Wright.

Wooten, understandably, pressed for details, specifics that Wright said she had trouble recalling. But she did volunteer something else.

"You know, Clarence Thomas I think felt very comfortable around me, and I want you to understand that I am not sitting here saying to you that I was sexually harassed by Clarence Thomas. I am a very strong-willed person and at no point did I feel intimidated by him. Some other woman might have, but these were not situations that I ran home and ruminated on and wrote down in my diary."

What Thomas had done was "annoying and obnoxious," Wright told Wooten, but she did not feel threatened and therefore did not consider the chairman's behavior harassment.

At that point, Cynthia Hogan jumped back in for the Democrats, not wanting Wright to exculpate Thomas. She asked if Wright had meant sexual harassment in the legal sense. Wright answered that she thought what Thomas had done could be classified under the law as sexual harassment.

In general, Wright was forthright in describing her feelings about Thomas and his suitability for the high court. "I never wavered in my feelings about that. I don't think, I don't think that Clarence Thomas is a good man and I did not think that he should be on the Supreme Court."

The Clarence Thomas she described was very different from the man who had been portrayed to the American people. He was, she said, "not a very nice person." His attitude towards agency employees was cynical and callous, she said. It was his wont to make comments, other than sexual ones, that she felt were untoward.

Wright recounted how Thomas had acted at one EEOC meeting, during which some of her colleagues had been complaining about the racial atmosphere in Mississippi, where the chairman and some of his staff had taken a trip. She said, "I remember Clarence sitting there and rearing back in his chair with a cigar in his mouth and saying, 'I have no problem with Mississippi. You know why I like Mississippi, because they still sell those little Pickaninnies dolls down there. And I bought me a few of them, too.' "

Wright's questioning by the committee staffers went on for nearly two hours. When Angela Wright hung up the phone in the early afternoon, she thought that was the end of it. She was wrong. Hogan called her back in the late afternoon to tell her she had been subpoenaed to come to Washington to testify. Federal marshals would be coming by her house to serve the subpoena. Senator Biden had been acutely embarrassed by charges that, as the committee chairman, he had not pursued Hill's charges. He was not going to be lax or confused again—at least not yet.

Wright was shocked. "When they told me about the subpoena, I figured it was the price I was going to pay for daring to say something against a Supreme Court nominee. . . . I felt like I had been transported to a foreign country."

Hardly had she put down the telephone when she saw herself on television being named as "the other woman"—a label she did not think was appropriate. Then her phone started to ring incessantly; reporters were calling her number nonstop, just as they had four days earlier with Anita Hill's. She ignored the calls. People were knocking on her door. She ignored them, too. When her sister arrrived to help, she asked Wright why she had not let in the federal marshals, who had been standing on her doorstep for nearly half an hour.

There were only two days to prepare for perhaps the most unusual hearings in the Senate's history. Both sides were frantic.

Lawyers and political experts who believed in the importance of what Hill had to say were springing into action spontaneously. Whether Hill wanted it or not, she was going to have supporters when she arrived to testify in Washington. Hill herself had not, at the outset, seemed to realize how deadly serious were the political games that went on beneath the elegant dome of the Capitol. Others did.

On Tuesday night, after the Senate agreed to postpone the confirmation vote and hold a second round of hearings, Emma Jordan received a telephone call at her home in Washington from another law professor, Judith Resnick of the University of Southern California. Both women were well-known experts in the mundane and exacting legal field of the commercial code. Jordan, a professor at the Georgetown University Law Center, was prominent, being president-elect of the Association of American Law Schools. Resnick, Jordan recalled, had heard that Jordan, who is black, might know Anita Hill, who also specialized in the commercial code.

"I understand you can reach Anita Hill. There are a bunch of law professors who want to help," Resnick told her. They began to talk about "what a dream legal team would be" for Hill. They put together a list of some of the best lawyers in the country who might want to help in key fields: someone with experience in Supreme Court nominations, someone with trial experience, someone with expertise in the issue of sexual harassment, and so on. The legal profession is not yet as specialized as medicine, but there are vast differences in knowledge within the different areas of the law. A single lawyer couldn't handle all the issues of the coming hearings, but a variety of attorneys and experts would take some organizing.

Jordan hung up and tried to get through to Hill at her home in Norman, but the line was busy. Early Wednesday morning, she gave it another try. When Hill answered, Jordan asked her if she had arranged a legal team. Hill had only heard eleven hours earlier that there were to be hearings. She had been put in touch by friends with Charles Ogletree, a well-known black criminal defense lawyer then teaching at Harvard Law School, but she had not established her representation. Jordan was stunned.

There was almost no time. Most major legal events are arranged months ahead of time, and proceed only after careful examination of the relevant law books. Even Clarence Thomas had been given nearly two and a half months to prepare for his first appearance before the Judiciary Committee. Anita Hill and her lawyers would have to get ready in two days.

With a network of conference calls, Ogletree, Jordan, and Resnick put together the rest of Hill's team. Susan Deller Ross, another Georgetown lawyer and a prominent expert in the law of sex discrimination, was signed up. Ogletree recruited Michele Roberts, a Washington lawyer with whom he had worked in the capital's public defender's officer, to help prepare Hill's testimony. John P. Frank, a venerable constitutional lawyer from Phoenix who had written twelve books on the Supreme Court, agreed to fly immediately to Washington to participate. Frank brought in his associate, Janet Napolitano, and recruited an old Washington hand, Warner W. Gardner. Even Lloyd

Cutler, the former counsel to President Jimmy Carter who had fought for the confirmation of his friend Robert Bork, was enlisted. Hill, who on Tuesday had no lawyer, by Wednesday had an all-star ad hoc legal crew behind her. If anything, too many lawyers were now involved, a situation that, not unsurprisingly, would lead to conflicts.

Anita Hill would also need guidance with the now heated politics, and with the press. Janet Napolitano called Diane Thompson, a Washington consultant who had worked for Senator Barbara Mikulski. Thompson called another former Mikulski aide, Wendy Sherman, who had become a high-powered political consultant working with a Washington-area firm called Doak, Shrum, Harris, Sherman, Donilon. The consulting firm was closely tied to liberal Democrats, including Teddy Kennedy and Howard Metzenbaum, as well as Mikulski. Sherman had previously worked at Emily's List, which raises funds for women political candidates, and had run the Washington office of the Dukakis presidential campaign. She in turn brought in Louise Hilson, of Devillier Communications in Washington, to handle the press. Over Wednesday and Thursday, the Hill entourage kept growing.

Each of these people worked for free, paying their own expenses. Most of them did not even know Anita Hill. "Why should we presume we should do for her without knowing whether it was so or not?" asked one of Hill's volunteers. "The answer to that question was clear. Why would someone come forward if she didn't have a story to tell? She deserved representation and a fair shake in a town that we all know can eat you alive, not even intentionally."

After the decision to delay the vote on Thomas, the atmosphere at the White House was nervous and gloomy. There were fears of a snowball effect, with new charges layering the old ones. There were rumors of the "second woman" fueling the pessimism. The Bush administration was splitting internally, along familiar lines. Pragmatists, like Marlin Fitzwater, the presidential press secretary, counseled Bush to keep a low profile. Some in the White House were hoping that Thomas would give up on the nomination, and Fitzwater wanted Bush to give him a push. The ideologues, like Boyden Gray, were ready for a fight. But even Gray was so depressed that he couldn't help but wonder aloud whether Thomas was a "dead duck."

On Wednesday Bush did the absolute minimum for Thomas, inviting him into the Oval Office for what is known in politics as a photo opportunity—a chance for a pack of news cameramen to take quick pictures and for the President to make a few careful remarks at the most. Bush said he was reaffirming his total confidence in the nominee, but this was little more than going through the motions.

For Clarence Thomas, this was his first public appearance in the four days since the Hill story had broken. But he made no real effort to defend himself against the charges. Asked by shouting reporters as he left the White House if he was going to "stick it out," Thomas said only "Yup."

The Republican camp on Capitol Hill was also in disarray. Many of the Republican staffers on the Judiciary Committee had watched Hill's press conference and found her convincing. "It was absolute chaos," one of them said. "People were just freaking out about what to do, assembling strategies, trying to marshal evidence. Who knows Anita Hill, what can we find out about her, is there truth to this story?"

Senator Hank Brown, the new Republican on the committee, took the initiative to call Hill on the telephone. They talked for twenty minutes. After the senator had hung up, he stared off into space for a while. "She tells a very credible story," he said, causing his staff to worry that he might turn against Thomas and change his vote.

As Friday's hearings neared, and Thomas had not withdrawn, the debate in the White House focused on strategy. The pro-Thomas hawks—including Gray, Lee Liberman, and Bill Kristol in the vice president's office, and led by Thomas himself—"wanted to take everything head on," said a high-level White House official. The other camp—Kenneth Duberstein and the staff of the large White House public relations apparatus—believed that a softer approach to the charges might work better. The idea, the White House source said, was that Thomas should not necessarily deny everything and that he could not get away with stonewalling and saying, "Look, this is my privacy. I'm not going to say anything about that."

That this second approach was contemplated raises the question as to whether the White House believed Thomas's blanket denial of the charges.

The White House remained divided. The first round of hearings had created a wariness of Duberstein's original, soft-shoe approach toward getting Thomas confirmed. It had not worked well; Thomas actually had lost votes by being evasive and seeming not to be himself. Of course, it is quite possible he would have lost more votes if senators knew just how conservative he truly was. In the end, Thomas himself made the strategy decision about how to go into the second round. He refused to work with Duberstein and the other White House proponents of the go-easy school.

Back in Savannah, Thomas's mother was taking the events hard, too. After learning about Hill's charges, she went into a state of emotional shock. Stubbornly, she had tried to continue with her nursing assistant's job at the hospital. But every time she entered a patient's room, she saw the ugly news on television.

"I ended up stayin' home in bed. I was just crying, because I couldn't stand to see them dirtying Clarence's name the way they were," she said.

Thomas continued to stay out of the public eye but privately he was devastated by what was being said about him. It was a low point for him, according to his friend Lester Johnson, the Savannah attorney. Johnson telephoned Thomas after the Hill charges broke.

Johnson recalled the conversation. "He said, 'I've never felt this bad in my whole life. I've been through days when they called me nigger, told me I was thick-lipped and had nappy hair, but this affects my whole family. This is the worst thing anybody could ever do. If they're going to attack my philosophy, fine. If they're going to attack me for being an Uncle Tom, that's okay. But if they're going to attack me for sexual harassment that's the bottom. The only thing that's been keeping me up is God.' "

Meanwhile, the forces of the presidency were engaged in trying to discredit Anita Hill. Lawyers loyal to the White House were calling around everywhere, trying to dig up anything. On Thursday they hit paydirt. A former partner at Wald, Harkrader & Ross, the Washington law firm where Hill had worked for a year before she went to work for Thomas, had something negative to say. He told the Republicans that Hill had been asked to leave the firm because of a poor evaluation that may have involved ethical misconduct. This information would aid in rallying nervous and vacillating Republicans.

Danforth organized a powerful demonstration of support for Thomas from women who had worked with the nominee. Some eighteen women came to stand up for Thomas at a press conference the senator organized. Nine spoke, saying they had neither seen nor heard any impropriety involving Thomas. "I never, never saw Clarence Thomas treat me or any other woman in other than the most professional and courteous fashion," said Pam Talkin, the EEOC's former chief of staff. "He was almost puritanical."

But in the precious few days before the hearings were to begin, tension increased. The White House and the Republican senators were furious at Chairman Biden's decision to bring in Angela Wright, without conducting an FBI investigation first and without, they claimed, keeping them fully informed. From the moment Wright's name had come up, Republicans put pressure on Biden to keep her out of the hearings.

On Thursday night, all six of the Republican senators on the Judiciary Committee gathered for a final strategy session in Senator Thurmond's office in the Russell building, one floor down from where the Hill hearings would begin the next morning. They were joined by Danforth and Duberstein, while Fred McClure participated by phone from the White House. The senators' aides came as well, so that some twenty people packed the room.

It was decided that the Republican side of the committee would employ a different format from that of the first set of hearings. The senators who were the two sharpest questioners in the group, Hatch and Specter, were to take the lead. The Republicans were particularly anxious to keep Senator Alan Simpson out of it as much as possible, fearing that he would not control his words and would be so nasty to Hill that he would create sympathy for her.

Senator Hatch was too pro-Thomas to credibly question Hill. He would instead question Thomas, trying to lead him through his denial and also prompt his views on Hill. Senator Specter was the perfect choice to take on Hill directly. From his days as a prosecutor in Philadelphia, he had verbal and legal skills that no one else on the committee, Republican or Democrat, could match. Specter, having been consulted about this assignment ahead of time, had already asked the FBI to conduct a further investigation into some of the allegations against Thomas.

Specter's other advantage was that he was a liberal Republican; his interrogation of Hill would not have an ideological tarnish that Hill supporters could point out. Specter, in fact, was in favor of abortion rights, a stand that lent him favor in the eyes of liberal women's groups. He also was not closely tied to the White House's policy on judicial nominations. He was the only one among the Republican senators to have asked tough questions of Thomas. Previously, he had voted against Bork.

At the last-minute meeting, one of the Republicans had offered advice to Specter, saying, "We should be very, very easy on Hill and just nail her with the witnesses we bring in."

"Well, we've got to ask her some questions," Specter replied.

"People felt, 'Well, Specter, you're doing it. We'll respect your judgment. You haven't said you're going to do something crazy so the ball's in your court,'" a participant recounted.

The decision about how tough to be on Hill was left up to Specter. His politics were suspect within right-wing ranks, but no one questioned his abilities or his tactical judgment. For the Republican strategists, there were additional reasons for giving Specter the assignment that they did not mention to him then.

Senator Danforth spoke up at the session to warn that Thomas was near the end of his rope. He left the group with worries that Thomas was likely to say the hell with everything and withdraw. Danforth reported a bit of conversation he had had with the nominee.

"What do I say to my son," Thomas had said to his senatorial friend, "when he hears this stuff about me bragging about how big my penis is? Why do I have to go through this? What am I even doing here?"

The Republicans were careful while developing their plans to keep their ultimate goal in mind—to win or hold the votes of the more than a dozen Democrats who were favoring Thomas, at least before the Hill charges were known.

"The strategy was that we had to provide cover for the Democrats that would vote with us, that would be the purpose of the hearings," said Carl Hampe, Senator Simpson's aide on the committee. "Everything we did kept that in mind. We just wanted to poke enough holes in Anita Hill's story, but in doing so we had to make sure that we didn't come off as so nasty that we forced sympathetic Democrats to vote against him."

The Democrats, by comparison with the Republicans, were disorganized. There was some disagreement about how to proceed. At first

they considered bringing in outside counsel to conduct the questioning for their side, but the hotshot Washington criminal defense lawyers they asked wouldn't do it. There was no great appetite in Washington for taking on Clarence Thomas, not on this issue. In the end,
it was decided at a meeting in Biden's office on Wednesday to do as
the Republicans were doing, to appoint two senators to lead the questioning. Some of the Democrats, like Senator Kennedy, were relieved
they would not be in the spotlight.

The Democrats decided that Senator Howell Heflin, who had a
reputation as a savvy interrogator, would question Thomas. Heflin
seemed a perfect choice, in that the senator was a conservative from
Alabama, and the Southern Democrats would be looking towards him
for guidance. Also, Senator Patrick Leahy, an aggressive questioner,
was designated to question Hill. Biden, as chairman, would have
preferred not to be involved in questioning. But he decided that after
the criticism of his initial handling of Hill's charges, the last thing he
wanted to do was to appear to be ducking the job. Biden, therefore,
decided to question both Hill and Thomas. But after Leahy thought
over the arrangements, he decided he didn't want to question Hill
only; he had begun to worry about the political consequences with the
women's vote if he was not delicate enough with Hill and her extraordinarily sensitive issue. Leahy decided to balance his act by questioning Thomas, also. To make the whole procedure symmetrical, it was
decided that Heflin would also question both Thomas and Hill. In the
end, the Democrats had an overlapping panel of questioners that was
not fated for great success.

But the Democrats' overarching problem was that, unlike the
Republicans, they had no clear strategy or even goal. And unlike the
Republicans, they were concerned about being fair. Fairness seemed
higher on their list of priorities than effectiveness or, in a larger sense,
justice. They agreed at that Wednesday meeting to approach the
hearing as an attempt to ascertain facts, not as an opportunity to dig
into the character of the nominee. They were not ready to play hard-
ball with Thomas, even if most of them thought he did not belong on
the high court.

"This is endemic for the Democrats," said one Democratic aide on
the Judiciary Committee. "Any one of us could have said, 'We have

to get serious about this. The Republicans are out to win. They are treating this like a war. We have to get our shit together.' " But no one did.

As a party the Democrats had not decided they were against Thomas. The Democratic leadership in the Senate, headed by Senator George Mitchell of Maine, was ambivalent. On the one hand, they didn't want to look like they were smearing a black man. On the other hand, they now wanted to get across a message about how concerned they were about this issue of sexual harassment. They were chagrined by the way they had bungled Hill's case and by the consequent appearance of insensitivity to an issue of importance to many of their women constituents.

The Democrats felt compromised also by the Republicans' charge that they had leaked at the critical last moment a secret FBI report to scuttle the Thomas nomination. Ted Kennedy, Howard Metzenbaum, and Paul Simon, the most liberal of the Democrats on the committee, were under suspicion of leaking, and so they all were inclined to stay out of the fray in the second round of hearings. The Democrats were going to be nice guys, while the Republicans were aiming for the jugular.

"My argument has been, and I know this is Biden's and everybody else's, that we're not going in to advocate for or against Judge Thomas or for or against Professor Hill or anything else," Leahy told a reporter on the eve of the hearings.

During her last few days in Norman before leaving for Washington, Anita Hill was finding it almost impossible to continue her regular schedule, but she was trying. The law school's single building, which was surrounded by the normally serene lawns of the Oklahoma campus, was mobbed with television cameras and reporters. Hill had to fight just to get from one class to another. Some of her male students of football-team proportions would form a phalanx to get her through the corridors. Not unlike Thomas and his supporters, many of Hill's friends were disgusted with the performance of the press.

The Judiciary Committee had arranged for Hill to fly to the capital on Wednesday afternoon, leaving her the next day to prepare her testimony. Since she was under subpoena, the committee would pay for her travel and accommodations. But just to get her through the media throng, out of the law school, and through the airport in Oklahoma City would require some strategy.

The security people from the university devised a plan. With all the cameramen waiting expectantly for Hill's departure, one of the security force drove a car up to the south side of the law school and opened the door. The television crews all ran outside. Meanwhile, the security staff took Hill out the north door and escorted her through the airport before the journalists figured out the hoax.

On Thursday, the rest of the Hill team converged on Washington. Ogletree flew in from New York and happened to find himself on the same plane as William Bradford Reynolds, the former Reagan Justice Department official who had been on the losing end in Bork's confirmation hearings. The two men had known each other for some time and they sat together, talking about the upcoming hearings. Reynolds said he knew Thomas well and was quite certain he was telling the truth. Ogletree expressed with confidence the idea that Hill's veracity would be established in the hearings. He never once mentioned that he was to be Hill's lawyer and coach.

That may be because he had no intention of taking charge of Hill's team. Ogletree had been a famous public defender in Washington. It was said that he just could not lose. But now he was on a research leave from Harvard, trying to establish the serious academic credentials he needed for tenure, a decision that was pending in a year. He had been warned by friends to keep a low profile during this period. For a law professor, there is no life without tenure. But he also felt uncomfortable with being too visible on Hill's behalf for other reasons. He had participated in the drafting of the NAACP's report against Thomas. Now he sensed correctly that the organization had no stomach for a controversy on such a personal level, one pitting a black woman against a black man.

As Ogletree was arriving, the rest of the makeshift legal team was hastily trying to put together a plan with Hill at the offices of a large Washington law firm, Pepper, Hamilton & Scheetz. For Hill, the scene was a bit like old times; her former firm, Wald, Harkrader & Ross, had merged with the Pepper firm four years earlier. Donald H. Green, a trial lawyer who had come over to Pepper from the Wald firm, had agreed to make a conference room available to his former associate, a decision that some Republicans in the firm were very unhappy about. Green at that point knew nothing of the charges circulating among the Republicans about the circumstances under which Hill had left the company.

When Ogletree got there, the person in charge seemed to be John Frank. It would have been hard to imagine someone more qualified. Frank had just published a book about another Supreme Court nomination, of Clement Haynsworth, that was rejected by the Senate in 1969. *The National Law Journal*, a weekly newspaper for lawyers, had listed him among the country's one hundred most powerful lawyers and described him as a "legendary" appellate and trial lawyer. He was the lawyer who argued the famous *Miranda* v. *Arizona* case before the Supreme Court in 1966 that required police to read suspects their rights before questioning them.

But Ogletree had not been in the room ten minutes, according to a profile of him published in *The American Lawyer* magazine, when he started firing questions at Hill. The Judiciary Committee, he told her, had an affidavit challenging specific sections of her statement to the committee. What was her response?

"I don't care what their affidavit says, it's not true. That's not what happened," Hill replied. "Good, that's just how you should respond," Ogletree told her. The other lawyers in the room breathed a sigh of relief. Not realizing that Ogletree was checking Hill's response to the most outrageous questions imaginable, they had mistakenly thought for a moment that the hypothetical affidavit existed.

Ogletree also warned Hill that she would be on her own when she was testifying the next day. "Don't expect any help from the committee," he said.

While the lawyers prepared Hill and lined up corroborating witnesses behind locked doors on one floor of the law firm, the more politically oriented members of the team met upstairs to coordinate their press strategy. The situation was chaotic; hundreds of phone calls poured in from reporters.

Among those attending that meeting were Wendy Sherman; Janet Napolitano, Frank's associate; Louise Hilson, the media consultant who had been a longtime Capitol Hill aide and whose husband was political director of the Democratic Senatorial Campaign Committee; Nikki Heidepriem, a consultant who worked with the National Abortion Rights Action League; Lisa Letterer, who did public relations for several women's groups; and Sonia Jarvis, an old friend and Washington roommate of Hill's who was a lawyer for the National Coalition on Black Voter Participation in Washington. They were not unlike Hill's team of lawyers—mostly liberal Democrats with feminist leanings. Heidepriem and Letterer, in fact, stayed in the background so as not to draw attention to the involvement of feminists in Hill's support group.

The preparations went on late into the evening, before Hill and the others broke for a dinner at the Washington home of her nephew, who worked for *The Washington Post*. Hill, who had been cool through this whole process, finally had gotten upset when she discovered typographical errors in the meticulously worded statement that she was to read to the committee the next morning. She insisted that it be done properly. Sonia Jarvis had to retype it.

There was little coordination, at least at first, between the legal team and the political team. The lawyers were doing what they knew best—readying Hill to give her testimony and to undergo cross-examination. They did their work as well as possible under extraordinary circumstances. But what some of them seemed not to understand was the political nature of what they would face the next day.

A major portion of Anita Hill's family team also converged on the capital to support "Faye" during the hearings. The whole family had been planning to spend the coming weekend back at the old homestead on the hilltop in Oklahoma celebrating the eightieth birthday of Erma Hill. All thirteen of her children had made arrangements to be there in Oklahoma. The birthday reunion plans were shattered as half the family ended up flying into Washington instead. One of Hill's brothers, all five of her sisters, and her parents came to Capitol Hill. For Hill's father, Albert, the hasty trip to Washington was his first experience flying on an airplane.

Although the whole brouhaha was upsetting to the members of the family, they stayed loyal to their youngest. "We're close enough that we can feel each other's hurts over the miles," said Winston Hill.

The Republicans did understand the nature of what was ahead. "It was just war and we were all enlisted in the war," said Ricky Silberman, the EEOC's vice chairman, who was a Thomas loyalist. And they knew that the first battle that had to be won involved the case of Angela Wright.

There was an immediate decision in the Republican camp to make a direct attack on Wright, based on her personnel records. A reporter for Knight-Ridder Newspapers reported that Senator Hatch, a pious Mormon not known to swear, had said that Wright "is going to have her ass handed to her." Hatch vehemently denied making the comment.

What he did say, while appearing on national television, was that "from what I heard I think she's going to be in trouble if she goes in there and starts to say these things about Clarence Thomas." A bald threat to Wright and the Democrats.

At least three different versions of Wright's employment problems were promulgated by Thomas's supporters and given to the media. Senator Alan Simpson said that she had twice been fired from other jobs after making sexual harassment claims, an allegation that Wright denied and Simpson never substantiated. Clint Bolick, the conservative Washington lawyer who had worked under Thomas at the EEOC, said Wright was fired because she had made derogatory remarks about homosexuals. Ricky Silberman, however, said that Wright had been fired because of incompetence. She told *The Washington Post* that Thomas used to tell her Wright "fell in the worthless category."

Thomas himself, though, had given Wright an excellent reference to *The Charlotte Observer* less than two years before. Thomas had said Wright was "an excellent employee" who worked "very well under stress" and that he owed her an apology for letting her leave, the newpaper reported.

In all the tension and the fast-breaking news that week following Hill's revelations, the media failed to pay enough attention to its own public opinion polls. The outpouring of outrage from politically minded women, who had started off the week buttonholing senators, masked the fact that the public at large did not believe Anita Hill from the start.

A poll conducted for *The Washington Post* indicated that Americans still supported Thomas's confirmation two to one, a drop from the nominee's standing in September but still a comfortable margin. A *New York Times* survey had similar results on the confirmation question, with 47 percent of those polled saying that Hill's charges were probably not true, while only 21 percent believed her. At the same time, there were signs of a backlash from black men against the personal attack on "a brother." Anita Hill would have a lot of convincing to do the next day.

# Chapter 17

Clarence Thomas was visibly impatient Friday morning. He was sitting at the same table, in the same splendid Senate Caucus Room where he had already undergone five days of excruciating questioning about his judicial philosophy the month before. As Chairman Biden rambled on about the importance of sexual harassment and of fairness, Thomas sat up straight, the heel of his left foot incessantly thumping the floor. He looked like a man about to explode.

Late the night before, Thomas and his advisers had decided that he should testify about the charges of sexual harassment first. The idea was to steal Anita Hill's thunder by putting Thomas's denial in place beforehand. He had a neat set of typed pages on the table in front of him. Thomas had allowed no one, he said, other than his wife, Virginia, and Senator Danforth to read this statement. "No handlers, no advisers," in Thomas's words. Duberstein had been banished to the background. Sitting behind Thomas now were his wife, her face set in grim determination, and the Missouri senator, his face haggard with worry and fatigue. When it came time for Thomas to speak, after five days of silence, he started out slowly, reading easily. The hundreds of people jamming the room were silent, their expressions concentrated, rapt, concerned, stern.

I have been racking my brains and eating my insides out trying to think of what I could have said or done to Anita Hill to lead her to allege that I was interested in her in more than a professional way and that I talked with her about pornographic or X-rated films.

At no time in the two years they had worked together had Hill indicated to him or anyone close to him that a problem existed, Thomas said. He knew nothing about Hill's contentions until the FBI suddenly had visited his house to interview him about the subject on September 25.

But with that said, if there is anything that I have said that has been misconstrued by Anita Hill or anyone else to be sexual harassment, then I can say that I am so very sorry and I wish I had known. If I did know, I would have stopped immediately and I would not, as I've done over the past two weeks, have to tear away at myself, trying to think of what I could possibly have done. But I have not said or done the things that Anita Hill has alleged. God has gotten me through the days since September 25, and he is my judge.

As he spoke much of the nation was watching. All three commercial networks were broadcasting live from the hearing room on Capitol Hill. In living rooms and offices, in beauty parlors and bars, Americans stopped what they were doing to listen to the embattled nominee.

When I stood next to the president in Kennebunkport being nominated to the Supreme Court of the United States, that was a high honor; but as I sit here before you one hundred and three days later, that honor has been crushed. From the very beginning, charges were leveled against me from the shadows, charges of drug abuse, anti-Semitism, wife beating, drug use by family members, that I was a quota appointment, confirmation conversion, and much, much more. And now, this.

I have complied with the rules. I responded to a document request that produced over thirty thousand pages of documents, and I have testified for five full days under oath. I have endured this ordeal for one hundred and three days. Reporters sneaking into my garage to examine books I read. Reporters and interest groups swarming over divorce papers looking for dirt. Unnamed people starting preposterous and damaging rumors. Calls all over the country specifically requesting dirt.

As Thomas proceeded the sound of his voice and the level of his anger increased. He began to shed the humility in which he had cloaked himself during the first set of hearings. What had been billed as an opening statement was sounding more and more like an angry withdrawal.

This is not American; this is Kafkaesque. It has got to stop. It must stop for the benefit of future nominees and our country. Enough is enough. I'm not going to allow myself to be further humiliated in order to be confirmed. I am here specifically to respond to allegations of sex harassment in the workplace. I am not here to be further humiliated by this committee or anyone else, or to put my private life on display for prurient interests or other reasons. I will not allow this committee or anyone else to probe into my private life. This is not what America is all about. To ask me to do that would be to ask me to go beyond fundamental fairness.

Yesterday I called my mother. She was confined to her bed, unable to work and unable to stop crying. Enough is enough.

I am proud of my life, proud of what I have done and what I have accomplished, proud of my family, and this process, this process is trying to destroy it all. No job is worth what I have been through, no job. No horror in my life has been so debilitating. Confirm me if you want. Don't confirm me if you are so led, but let this process end. Let me and my family regain our lives. I never asked to be nominated. It was an honor. Little did I know the price, but it is too high.

I enjoy and appreciate my current position and I am comfortable with the prospect of returning to my work as a judge on the U.S. Court of Appeals for the D.C. Circuit and to my friends there. Each of these positions is public service and I have given at the office. I want my life and my family's life back, and I want them returned expeditiously.

Instead of understanding and appreciating the great honor bestowed upon me, I find myself here today defending my name, my integrity, because somehow select portions of confidential documents dealing with this matter were leaked to the public.

I am a victim of this process. My name has been harmed. My integrity has been harmed. My character has been harmed. My family has been harmed. My friends have been harmed. There is nothing this committee, this body, or this country can do to give me my good name back. Nothing.

At this point, people in the Senate Caucus Room looked at one another knowingly. Senator Hank Brown turned around and glanced at one of his aides. So did Senator Herb Kohl, on the Democratic side of the committee. Reporters instantly began to forumulate the day's news story in their heads, for it seemed that Thomas was about to withdraw.

I will not provide the rope for my own lynching or for further humiliation. I am not going to engage in discussions nor will I submit to roving questions of what goes on in the most intimate parts of my private life or the sanctity of my bedroom. These are the most intimate parts of my privacy, and they will remain just that, private.

Then, he stopped, his powerful expression of anguish finished.

Then the Judiciary Committee started to bumble; in the frenetic days since the vote delay, the committee had not worked out the procedures for the hearings on Hill's charges. Chairman Joseph Biden, with deep circles of sleeplessness defining his eyes, opened his remarks with a directive that was nothing but confusing.

"Professor Hill," he said, "as recently as late last night, continues to ask us to maintain the confidentiality of her statement to the committee." This seemed to mean that the senators would be stymied in their questioning; if they would not be permitted to use Hill's statement, how in the world would they proceed?

This unreasonable limitation sent murmurs of puzzlement through the audience. Was Hill, even at this point, refusing to cooperate? Senator Danforth, in his seat behind Thomas, was shaking his head back and forth in disbelief. The chairman's statement infuriated Senator Orrin Hatch, the Republican from Utah who, like Thomas, seemed ready to explode. He shouted at Biden, shaking his fist at him as he spoke, his voice rising in shrill outrage.

"It would be the greatest travesty I have ever seen in any court of law, let alone an open forum, in the nomination process of a man for justice of the United States Supreme Court to allow her attorneys or her or anybody on this committee or anybody else for that matter to tell us what can or cannot be used now that this man's reputation has been very badly hurt."

Then Biden and Hatch went at it in front of the whole nation like a couple of brawling schoolboys. Just minutes into the hearings, the process went out of control.

"Will the senator yield?" Biden asked.

"No, I'm not finished," the righteously indignant Hatch shouted. "I intend to use that statement because it is fair to use it. I don't want to hurt—"

Glaring at Hatch, Biden interrupted, "Senator, let me—"

Hatch interjected, "Let me finish."

"No, I will not. Let me make a point," Biden insisted.

"Yes, you will. Yes, you will," Hatch snapped back.

Finally, Biden managed to explain what was going on.

"Professor Hill says that she wants to tell her story. She did not release the statement, she says. And she wants her story told by her. Because we have given the opportunity to the judge to speak first, if he so chose, and he has, that she wants to be able to use her statement in her own words that she has thus far not released and has not spoken to publicly—she has not spoken to publicly—when she comes and addresses the committee. Now, why don't we get on with this process?"

Further objections flew from Senator Strom Thurmond and Senator Alan Simpson, before Senator Ted Kennedy stepped in and sensibly suggested a recess to work out the dispute. But Hatch wanted to keep fighting. He attacked the Democrats.

"I object to a recess . . . if somebody on this committee or their staff had had the honesty and the integrity before the vote to raise this issue and to ask for an executive session and say this has to be brought out. Nobody did, and then somebody on this committee or their staff—and I'm outraged by it—leaked that report, an FBI report that we all know should never be disclosed to the public because of the materials that generally are in them. They take it down as it's given, it's got raw stuff in it—and it's been leaked. Half—the media knows everything in it. And I think the American people are entitled to know if they want to."

The argument degenerated to the point that Hatch threatened to resign from the committee. The Utah senator did, finally, agree to a recess.

It would be wrong to assume that the outrage expressed by Hatch or the other Republicans was pure political posturing. Hatch, Simpson, Thurmond, and their staffs had known both Clarence Thomas and his wife for years. Thomas was one of them. Virginia Thomas had been a lobbyist for the Chamber of Commerce and the Department of Labor, and had worked closely with these same people. They had gotten to know Thomas socially, not only through his public role at the EEOC but also through his wife. Virginia Thomas was a political cousin to the Republican senatorial family.

There also was something about Clarence Thomas that inspired a passionate faith in him among many of those who met him.

"The people who know him swear by him," said Mark Disler, a lawyer who worked for Senator Hatch on the committee and who, like the senator, had been friends with Thomas for years. "It is difficult to describe the depth of people's feelings about him. I got calls at two A.M., five A.M. at home from people who wanted to help during the hearings. People are very, very loyal to him, which is a reflection of the quality of his character. I have never heard him make a risqué comment. There's an outgoingness about him. He wants to treat people right, with respect and dignity. He always called his driver 'Mister,' for example. While he is a proud person, there is no touch of arrogance or self-importance about him."

At the same time, there may have been some method to Hatch's madness. Hatch, for one thing, knew very well that the FBI report itself had not been leaked. With their cries of outrage at the way Thomas had been treated, the Republicans were making Thomas into the victim rather than Anita Hill. As the senators recessed, both Republicans and Democrats had worked themselves into a state.

As the first light struck the Capitol dome that morning, Hill was in her nearby hotel on the telephone to Ogletree, asking him to take charge. She had gotten the sense that for Tree, as the lawyer was known to his friends, her personal welfare was the most important issue. Hovering around her were feminists who wanted to make sexual harassment the issue, or diehard Thomas opponents who wanted to make him the issue. Hill's concern was simply that she have the opportunity to say what she wanted to say and survive to teach another day.

But Ogletree hesitated. It was becoming clear that President Bush and his administration would stop at nothing to get Thomas confirmed, including attempting to destroy anyone who got in the way. Ogletree was at a vulnerable stage in his life, with all the security of lifelong tenure at stake.

And he may have sensed, correctly, that there was another reason for wanting to put him out front. The black community was being ripped apart, sister against brother, by Hill's accusations. Many black men, and some women, felt that whatever Thomas may have done or not done a decade earlier was irrelevant. The behavior Hill described, even if true, was not serious enough to justify turning against one of their own when he was finally about to make it in the white world. In their eyes, Hill was being disloyal. As a well-known black figure with a fierce reputation for fighting for poor black people, Ogletree was the right symbol as well as the right person. While Thomas had befriended lobbyists for South Africa, Ogletree had challenged apartheid. On a 1989 trip to that country, for instance, Ogletree caused a stir while visiting a prison; he had upset white authorities by shouting encouraging political slogans to the black inmates, according to Clinton Bamberger, a Maryland law professor who had accompanied him.

It was Emma Jordan, the black law professor, who particularly wanted Ogletree behind Anita Hill when the cameras started rolling. Ogletree was not sure he wanted to be used in that way and, according to some of those on Hill's team, a tension developed between the black lawyers in the group along the gender fault line.

Hill was staying in almost complete secrecy at the small Capitol Hill Hotel, four blocks from where she would be testifying. She was accompanied there by her best friend from Oklahoma, Shirley Wiegand. Hill intentionally "was sequestered," in the words of Wiegand. She did not want to deal with anybody other than her lawyers, Wiegand said, because of her distaste for publicity and also her fear that anything she did in Washington could be misunderstood. Hill didn't want to be directly involved with any of the liberal groups, according to Wiegand, "because she feared it would be misinterpreted by those who disliked what she said and who wanted to make it look like she was in the grip of wild, radical feminists."

Most members of Hill's team did not know her whereabouts. The rest of the group was staying downtown at the Washington Marriott. When Hill did not get the assuring answer she wanted from Ogletree, word was passed along to Jordan and Ross. The two women lawyers hurried to Ogletree's room in the hotel and argued him into relenting; he would do his best to take charge of her case.

When Hill's handlers gathered for breakfast downstairs at the hotel, the tension within this thrown-together group of heavy-hitters was evident. It could hardly have been otherwise, given the speed with which everything was being done. Added to the male versus female tension was black versus white. John Frank, the legal giant, who was white, seventy-three years old, one of the nation's most respected lawyers and an expert in Supreme Court nominations, had been supplanted as leader by Ogletree, a black untenured assistant professor who was barely more than half his age. There was also an underlying tension between the black women lawyers and the white women consultants. Luckily for Hill herself, she was on the periphery of these simmering animosities.

That morning the lack of fundamental organization in the Hill camp was also evident. The group had no solid strategy as to how to deal with the media and the imminent political circus. Ogletree did not want to be out front talking with reporters. The group of people who were supposed to handle Hill did not even know exactly how they were going to get to Capitol Hill or where they would gather there. No suitable office had yet been arranged at the Senate for them to use as a temporary headquarters. Senator Kennedy had offered them a room, but it was not close to the critical Caucus Room in the Russell office building. What Hill really needed was a political advance team, but there had been neither the time nor the inclination to assemble one.

When they arrived at the Capitol in a combination of taxis and private cars, Wendy Sherman, the Senate veteran, started walking the corridors and found an empty hearing room and offices belonging to the Rules Committee just down the hall from the Caucus Room. They were just settling in when the hearings opened with Clarence Thomas in the spotlight.

In order to stay out of the fray, at least at first, the Hill team watched on television from the privacy of the Rules Committee's rooms as Thomas spoke and then Biden began. The chairman's statement about

Hill's statement caused a small uproar—everything seemed to be
going awry for the Hill handlers. Until late the night before, they had
thought that Hill would testify first. But when Thomas and the White
House decided at the last minute they wanted to preempt Hill and her
charges with an opening by Thomas, Chairman Biden agreed without
anticipating the confusing consequences. Biden and his staff had been
informed by Hill's lawyers that they did not want the Judiciary Committee to go over Hill's statement with Thomas until she had a chance
to speak for herself. They hadn't realized their stance had been misunderstood. So when Biden asserted that Hill was still objecting to the
committee going public with her statement, making Hill look foolish
at best, her people "went ballistic" as one of them put it.

"We clearly were concerned this was powerful testimony being
made without the context of her story," said one member of the team.
"It was terrible. Normally she would testify first, but this was not a
court of law."

Everyone started yelling at Ogletree, saying that Hill had to testify
immediately before any senators jumped into the public act. Jeff Peck,
an aide to Biden, caught an earful from the Hill people. "She must
come up," they were demanding, "and she must come up now."

While the senators, safely closeted from the public eye in a back
room with no staff present, were fighting over what to do, Thomas and
his wife were left sitting in the Caucus Room with the audience and
dozens of reporters. Because of the arrangements in the room, I was
seated immediately behind Virginia Thomas, as were some other journalists. She stood up and stared me down, recognizing me as the one
who had written the first newspaper article about Hill's charges. After
hearing Thomas's statement, I was thinking about the pain my story
had caused him and his family. I too stood up, to try to say something
helpful to her, but she stopped me. "D-O-N'-T T-A-L-K T-O M-E," she
said, elongating each sound, her voice full of hatred. "D-O-N'-T T-A-L-K
T-O M-E," she repeated. I sat down, not blaming her for the enmity.

Finally, after a ferocious meeting, the committee agreed that Hill
would testify next, before Thomas had a chance to say anything more.
Hill had been down the street at the hotel, watching the proceedings
on television. She was hurried first to the Rules Committee rooms,
where someone handed her a Bible. She sat down in a leather chair in
an outside office, next to a fireplace, apart from her frantic advisers.

She was composed and, not saying anything to anyone, she appeared to be bracing herself for what was coming. She drank a glass of water as the Capitol police cleared the corridor so she could make her entrance to the Caucus Room.

Dressed in a prim, light-turquoise suit, Hill gave a brief description of her background and explanation of her decision to go to work for Thomas. Then, she related for the first time in public her detailed account of what had happened when she worked for Clarence Thomas. Her words, spoken in a flat tone almost as calmly as if she were reading a college paper, would quickly turn the Thomas nomination into the most lurid in the Supreme Court's history. She began by saying that only three months after she had begun the job at the civil rights office in the Department of Education, Thomas asked her to go out with him.

> What happened next and telling the world about it are the two most difficult things—experiences of my life. It is only after a great deal of agonizing consideration and sleepless number—a great number of sleepless nights that I am able to talk of these unpleasant matters to anyone but my close friends.
>
> I declined the invitation to go out socially with him and explained to him that I thought it would jeopardize what at the time I considered to be a very good working relationship. I had a normal social life with other men outside of the office. I believed then, as now, that having a social relationship with a person who was supervising my work would be ill-advised. I was very uncomfortable with the idea and told him so. I thought that by saying no and explaining my reasons my employer would abandon his social suggestions. However, to my regret, in the following few weeks, he continued to ask me out on several occasions. He pressed me to justify my reasons for saying no to him. These incidents took place in his office or mine. They were in the form of private conversations which would not have been overheard by anyone else.

Anita Hill said that Thomas did not stop at asking her out. As time went on he started talking about sexual matters with her at work as well.

Because I was extremely uncomfortable talking about sex with him at all
and particularly in such a graphic way, I told him that I did not want to
talk about these subjects. I would also try to change the subject to education matters or to nonsexual personal matters such as his background or
his beliefs. My efforts to change the subject were rarely successful.

Hill then attempted to explain one of the great mysteries behind her
own actions. Why, if he was behaving in such an awful way, had she
followed him from the Department of Education to the Equal Employment Opportunity Commission?

During the latter part of my time at the Department of Education, the
social pressures and any conversation of his offensive behavior ended. I
began both to believe and hope that our working relationship could be a
proper, cordial, and professional one.

When Judge Thomas was made chair of the EEOC, I needed to face the
question of whether to go with him. I was asked to do so, and I did. The
work itself was interesting, and at that time it appeared that the sexual
overtures which had so troubled me had ended. I also faced the realistic
fact that I had no alternative job. While I might have gone back to private
practice, perhaps in my old firm or at another, I was dedicated to civil
rights work, and my first choice was to be in that field. Moreover, the
Department of Education itself was a dubious venture. President Reagan
was seeking to abolish the entire department.

For my first months at the EEOC, where I continued to be an assistant
to Judge Thomas, there were no sexual conversations or overtures. However, during the fall and winter of 1982, these began again. The comments
were random and ranged from pressing me about why I didn't go out with
him to remarks about my personal appearance. I remember his saying that
some day I would have to tell him the real reason that I wouldn't go out
with him.

He began to show displeasure in his tone and voice and his demeanor
and his continued pressure for an explanation. He commented on what I
was wearing in terms of whether it made me more or less sexually attractive. The incidents occurred in his inner office at the EEOC.

Hill went on to describe an incident that seemed utterly bizarre.

One of the oddest episodes I remember was an occasion in which Thomas
was drinking a Coke in his office. He got up from the table at which we were

working, went over to his desk to get the Coke, looked at the can and asked, "Who has put pubic hair on my Coke?" On other occasions, he referred to the size of his own penis as being larger than normal, and he also spoke on some occasions of the pleasures he had given to women with oral sex.

Hill paused and sighed before finishing the last sentence. Members of the audience, including normally blasé reporters, could not believe what they were hearing. A month before we had all been in this same room listening to talk about legal concepts such as natural law and the right of privacy. Now, we were listening to a discussion of the size of a Supreme Court nominee's penis.

Hill said she began to fear Thomas would fire her, so she started to look secretly for another job, dreading that he might make it difficult for her if he found out. In February 1983, she was hospitalized for five days with severe stomach pains that she attributed to stress from the situation at work.

In the spring of 1983, an opportunity to teach at Oral Roberts University opened up. I participated in a seminar—taught an afternoon session and seminar at Oral Roberts University. The dean of the university saw me teaching and inquired as to whether I would be interested in furthering— pursuing a career in teaching, beginning at Oral Roberts University. I agreed to take the job in large part because of my desire to escape the pressures I felt at the EEOC due to Judge Thomas.

When I informed him that I was leaving in July, I recall that his response was that now I would no longer have an excuse for not going out with him. I told him that I still preferred not to do so. At some time after that meeting, he asked if he could take me to dinner at the end of the term. When I declined, he assured me that the dinner was a professional courtesy only and not a social invitation. I reluctantly agreed to accept that invitation, but only if it was at the very end of a working day.

On, as I recall, the last day of my employment at the EEOC in the summer of 1983, I did have dinner with Clarence Thomas. We went directly from work to a restaurant near the office. We talked about the work I had done, both at Education and at the EEOC. He told me that he was pleased with all of it except for an article and speech that I had done for him while we were at the Office for Civil Rights. Finally, he made a comment that I will vividly remember. He said that if I ever told anyone of his behavior that it would ruin his career. This was not an apology, nor was it an explanation. That was his last remark about the possibility of our going out or reference to his behavior.

Now Hill began to address the other great question about her handling of the situation. Why had she kept calling him, as evidenced by the telephone logs kept by Thomas's secretary and brought forward by the Republicans?

From 1983 until today, I have seen Judge Thomas only twice. On one occasion, I needed to get a reference from him, and on another he made a public appearance in Tulsa. On one occasion he called me at home and we had an inconsequential conversation. On one occasion he called me without reaching me, and I returned the call without reaching him, and nothing came of it. I have on at least three occasions, been asked to act as a conduit to him for others.

I knew his secretary, Diane Holt. We had worked together at both EEOC and Education. There were occasions on which I spoke to her, and on some of these occasions undoubtedly I passed on some casual comment to then Chairman Thomas. There were a series of calls in the first three months of 1985, occasioned by a group in Tulsa, which wished to have a civil rights conference. They wanted Judge Thomas to be the speaker and enlisted my assistance for this purpose. I did call in January and February to no effect, and finally suggested to the person directly involved . . . that she put the matter into her own hands and call directly. She did so in March of 1985.

Hill said she telephoned Thomas again, by request, to obtain research information for that meeting.

There was another call about another possible conference in July of 1985. In August of 1987, I was in Washington, D.C., and I did call Diane Holt. In the course of this conversation, she asked me how long I was going to be in town and I told her. It is recorded in the message as August 15. It was, in fact, August 20. She told me about Judge Thomas's marriage and I did say congratulate him.

Hill talked about her feelings.

It is only after a great deal of agonizing consideration that I am able to talk of these unpleasant matters to anyone except my closest friends. As I've said before these last few days have been very trying and very hard for me and it hasn't just been the last few days or this week. It has actually been over a month now that I have been under the strain of this issue. Telling the world is the most difficult experience of my life, but it is very close to having to live through the experiences that occasion this meeting. I may have used poor judgment early on in my relationship with this issue. I was aware, however, that telling at any point in my career could adversely affect my future career. And I did not want early on to burn all the bridges to the EEOC.

   As I said, I may have used poor judgment. Perhaps I should have taken angry or even militant steps, both when I was in the agency, or after I left it. But I must confess to the world that the course that I took seemed the better as well as the easier approach.


Unbelievably, the country was now gripped in one of the most bizarre dilemmas in congressional history—whom to believe? The grotesquely explicit accusations of the professor of law, or the impassioned denials of the nominee to the Supreme Court?

Angela Wright, meanwhile, was wending her way toward Washington. She was scheduled to appear as the second witness willing to accuse Thomas of behavior that seemed to amount to sexual harassment.

   When she got to the airport in Charlotte the morning that the hearings reopened, she found herself pursued by reporters and cameramen. A stewardess flagged her down and took her into the pilots' lounge until it was time to board the plane. But as she attempted to board, the media throng surged forward, and one television camera smashed into her chin, knocking her back against the wall. At the boarding gate, a crowd had gathered, including a cluster of women who were yelling Yehs and a cluster of men who were dishing out Boos.

   Once on the plane, seated in the coach section, Wright still was not out of reach of the controversy that had engulfed her. A male passenger stopped next to her seat and stared hostilely. The crew decided to move her to first class. Even there she did not feel completely safe, going so far as to wonder whether someone might have put a bomb on board to stop her from getting to Washington.

   She faced another mob of reporters at the airport in Washington.

But her colleagues at the newspaper had arranged for her to be met by a lawyer who whisked her away from the runway in a limousine. One television crew chased the limousine, finally losing it on the George Washington Parkway.

This whole experience was quite a reversal for a professional journalist.

"I told a lot of folks, I think every journalist should wake up one morning and have their face splattered all over the news and all over the television in not too flattering a manner, and to have people start picking at their private life, picking at, you know, who is this person. No human being can withstand the type of scrutiny that we inflict on certain people and often without any real relevancy to the issue at hand. We just dig for new angles and I think we manage to invade other people's privacy with no real regard to what's going to happen," Wright said later in an interview.

Clarence Thomas undoubtedly felt the same way.

Sitting behind Anita Hill as she gave her opening statement was her coterie of lawyers. This was not quite the right image—Hill did not look like the Oklahoma farm girl who had come to Washington just to tell the truth. This was not what had been planned. But, with the mixup in who would testify when, Hill's large family did not make it to the Caucus Room before Chairman Biden ordered the doors closed.

When the doors were opened again after her statement, twelve members of her family and two other supporters filed in. The group included her parents, whose serious and calm demeanors disguised internal turmoil, various brothers, sisters, and other close relatives. The dramatic entrance of all of them, though, demonstrated exactly what was intended—this was a very close, down-to-earth family. Hill's countenance suddenly lighted with big smiles as her mother, Erma, and then her father, Albert, hugged her. Her father had never been in Washington before and would have much preferred to be home on the Oklahoma prairie. Her mother was missing the reunion her family had planned for her eightieth birthday.

The family's entrance threw Chairman Biden into embarrassment. He was responsible for the protocol of the hearings and here, suddenly, was the Hill family milling about without anywhere to sit. The lawyers had monopolized the seats behind Hill. The hearing was disrupted as Biden and his staff furiously orchestrated a search for suffi-cient chairs.

After the family contingent was finally settled in behind Hill, Biden began questioning her. He asked for more information about her background. He wanted particularly to know the circumstances under which she had departed Wald, Harkrader & Ross ten years earlier, and whether she had been asked to leave. It was apparent that Biden had seen some of the material being gathered by the Republicans that alleged that Hill had left the law firm because her work had been considered inadequate.

But Hill denied that the law firm had been unhappy with her performance. "I was interested in seeking other employment," she said. "It was never suggested to me at the firm that I should leave the law firm in any way."

Then Biden began asking about the sexual incidents, his demeanor somber. He asked about the Coke can incident.

"The incident involved his going to his desk—getting up from a work table, going to his desk, looking at this can and saying, 'Who put pubic hair on my Coke?' " Hill replied, as somber as her questioner and pausing slightly before uttering some of the more explicit details of her story.

Were there other such incidents that occurred in Thomas's office, Biden asked. Hill said there was one in particular.

"This was a reference to an individual who had a very large penis and he used the name that he had been referred to in the pornographic material."

"Do you recall what it was?" Biden asked.

"Yes, I do. The name that was referred to was Long Dong Silver." The name of this pornography star would now become part of daily American parlance, and of the history of Supreme Court nominations.

Biden asked Hill, with a straight face, whether this sort of discus-sion about pornography had been related to her work.

"Very often I went in to report on memos that I had written. I'm sure that that's why I was in the office," Hill replied.

The chairman asked her whether these conversations embarrassed her.

"The pressure to go out with him I felt embarrassed about because I didn't—I had given him an explanation that I thought it was not good for me as an employee working directly for him to go out. I thought he didn't take seriously my decision to say no and that he did not respect my having said no to him.

"I—the conversations about sex I was much more embarrassed and humiliated by. The two combined really made me feel sort of helpless in a job situation because I really wanted to do the work that I was doing. I enjoyed that work, but I felt that that was being put in jeopardy by the other things that were going on in the office and so I was really, really very troubled by it and distressed over it."

Then, Biden wanted to know whether Hill would tell the committee "what was the most embarrassing of all the incidences that you have alleged." The more Biden asked, the more outrageous were the details that Hill described.

"I think the one that was the most embarrassing was his discussion of pornography involving these women with large breasts and engaged in a variety of sex with different people or animals. That was the thing that embarrassed me the most and made me feel the most humiliated."

Biden pressed her for details of Thomas's own words.

"I really cannot quote him verbatim. I can remember something like 'You really ought to see these films that I've seen or this material I've seen. This woman has this kind of breasts that measure this size and they've got her in there with all kinds of things. She's doing all kinds of different sex acts,' and you know, that kind of—those were the kinds of words, where he expressed his enjoyment of it and seemed to try to encourage me to enjoy that kind of material as well."

"Why did you think he was saying these things to you?" Biden asked.

"Well, coupled with the pressure about going out with him, I felt that implicit in this discussion about sex was the offer to have sex with him, not just to go out with him. There was never any explicit thing about going out to dinner or going to a particular concert or movie. It was, 'We ought to go out,' and given these other conversations, I took that to mean 'We ought to have sex, or we ought to look at these pornographic movies together.' "

Hill, whose primness was evident to anyone watching her, said that for her these conversations "were very ugly. They were very dirty and they were disgusting."

Then Biden went to the limit. He pressed her—"for the record"—for details of what Hill said was Thomas's repeated boasting about the size of his manhood.

"Did he just say 'I have great physical capability and attributes,' or was he more graphic?"

"He was much more graphic," Hill replied as demurely as seemed possible.

Biden pushed some more. "Can you tell us what he said?" he asked.

"Well, I can tell you that he compared his penis size, he measured his penis in terms of length, those kinds of comments."

As Biden ended this round of questions, the great Caucus Room was strangely quiet. Hill's wrenching testimony, added to Thomas's equally wrenching and completely conflicting testimony, had left the crowd feeling overwhelmed. The confirmation process had careened beyond imaginable bounds; it had become a surreal spectacle. Sworn testimony was being taken about errant pubic hair, the penis of the nominee, and women fornicating with animals.

Next it was the Republicans' turn to question Anita Hill; the senator appointed was Arlen Specter.

"Professor Hill, I have been asked to question you by Senator Thurmond, the ranking Republican, but I do not regard this as an adversary proceeding," he began.

"Thank you," Hill replied.

"My duties run to the people of Pennsylvania, who have elected me, and in the broader sense as a United States senator, to constitutional government and the Constitution. And my purpose, as the purpose of the hearing generally, is to find out what happened."

After giving Hill those assurances, Specter then went on to question her as if the proceedings were a criminal trial and she was the suspect. Even so, there would be no rules of evidence, no rights for the accused and no defense attorney to raise objections or cite points of law.

Specter's role as Hill's inquisitor was, in part, the result of a masterful White House strategy to coopt the least trusted Republican on the committee and take advantage of his precarious political position at that moment.

"The brilliant, strategic reason underneath this was that Arlen

Specter was feared to be a loose cannon," said an aide to one of the other Republicans on the committee.

> He dealt Bork a death blow and everyone knew that he had a very tough primary with people running to the right of him. He needed to curry the favor of the conservatives. What better way of doing that than giving him a shot at destroying Hill? It also fed his tremendous desire to demonstrate to his old law partners and former colleagues in the Philadelphia bar that he hadn't lost his stuff—that he was still a great trial lawyer. They [the Republicans] wanted to make this Arlen's day in the sun. Arlen may not shine on too many things in the Senate, but what he does shine on is these nominations. So this was giving him the golden egg. Everyone knew that his personal desires and his political concerns would combine to produce a very good show.

Specter hit Hill with a staccato burst of what he thought were inconsistencies in her statements, or with her past statements to friends or acquaintances.

In one series of questions Specter asked repeatedly whether Hill had told lawyer Carlton Stewart at an American Bar Association convention in Atlanta "how great Clarence's nomination was and how much he deserved it."

"I only said that it was a great opportunity for Clarence Thomas. I did not say that it was a good thing, that this nomination was a good thing," Hill replied.

What about a statement by another former Thomas aide, Phyllis Berry Myers, that Hill's allegations "were a result of Ms. Hill's disappointment and frustration that Mr. Thomas did not show any sexual interest in her"? Concentrating on his prosecutorial agenda, Specter alternately wrinkled his brow and frowned as he methodically aimed precise question after precise question at the witness.

"We [Myers and Hill] were not close friends," Hill answered. "We did not socialize together, and she has no basis for making a comment about my social interest, with regard to Clarence Thomas or anyone else. . . . I might add that at the time that I had an active social life, and that I was involved with other people." Hill leaned forward as if to impress the earnestness of her words on the senator.

The senator pressed Hill hard as to why she had not given the FBI as much detail of her alleged experiences, such as the pubic hair on the Coke can, as she had given the public in her testimony. She answered that the FBI agents had not quizzed her about specifics and that she was more "comfortable" speaking in generalities.

Specter also wanted to know how she could have decided not to report the harassment many years earlier if it had occurred as she said.

My question is, understanding of the fact that you're twenty-five and . . . shortly out of law school and the pressures that exist in this world, and I know about it to a fair extent. I used to be a district attorney and I know about sexual harassment and discrimination against women, and I think I have some sensitivity on it. But even considering all of that, given your own expert standing and the fact that here you have the chief law enforcement officer of the country on this subject and the whole purpose of the civil rights law is being perverted right in the office of the chairman with one of his own female subordinates—what went through your mind, if any-thing, on whether you ought to come forward at that stage, because if you had, you'd stop this man from being head of EEOC perhaps for another decade. What went on through your mind? I know you decided not to make a complaint, but did you give that any consideration, and if so how could you allow this kind of reprehensible conduct to go on right in the headquar-ters without doing something about it?

"Well," Hill replied, "it was a very trying and difficult decision for me not to say anything further. I can only say that when I made the decision to just withdraw from the situation and not press a claim or charge against him, that I may have shirked a duty, a responsibility that I had. And to that extent I confess that I am very sorry that I did not do something or say something, but at the time that was my best judgment. Maybe it was a poor judgment but it wasn't dishonest, and it wasn't a completely unreasonable choice that I made given the circumstances."

With this Specter's allotted time was up—for the moment—and Senator Patrick Leahy's turn came. In trial parlance the Vermont senator would try to "rehabilitate" the witness—patch her where she had been damaged by Specter. Under Leahy's questioning, Hill gave another reason for being reticent with her story about Thomas. She said she had feared being fired from her teaching position at Oral

Roberts if she had filed a complaint against Thomas after she left the EEOC. She also testified that when she was working for Thomas, he asked her for dates five to ten times.

But when Leahy asked her whether she had talked to anyone about the harassment at the time it occurred, Hill dropped a bombshell. There were three such people, Hill said, naming them all. If she could produce testimony from those three, it would go a long way toward corroborating her story and giving Thomas trouble.

The Republicans would have to do something to save Thomas. But they were prepared. They had known that she would have at least one such witness, so to counterbalance that testimony they had a theory of how to explain it away. Hill, according to two witnesses, was prone to fantasy.

"Professor Hill, do you know a man by the name of John Doggett?" Senator Specter asked her on his next turn.

The question seemed to throw her. Finally she said, "Yes, I have met him."

"I ask you this, Professor Hill, in the context of whether you have any motivation as to Judge Thomas. What was your relationship with Mr. Doggett?"

Again, Hill seemed confused. "I don't recall. I do not recall. We were friends, but I don't—it wasn't anything—I just don't know," she said.

Specter, having blindsided Hill, now acted the gentleman, saying he would provide her with a copy of Doggett's statement before questioning her further. At this, many in the committee room broke their stunned silence to whisper about this counter-bombshell: "Who is Doggett?" Meanwhile, copies of the statement—which Hill, her lawyers and Chairman Biden had *not* seen—was being handed out to reporters in the hallway by Steve Hilton, an aide to none other than the Senate's moral leader, John Danforth.

The statement itself was a piece of work. John Doggett averred that Hill, at a party on the occasion of her departure from Washington, had taken him aside. According to the statement, Doggett and Hill had known each other casually in Washington, but had never dated. Hill, the statement said, had told Doggett at the party, "I am very disappointed in you. You really shouldn't lead on women and then let them down."

Doggett, a black Texas lawyer who had gone to Yale with Thomas, proceeded in his statement to give a psychological analysis of Hill's behavior. "I came away from her going-away party feeling that she was somewhat unstable and that in my case, she had fantasized about my being interested in her romantically . . . it was my opinion at the time and is my opinion now that Ms. Hill's fantasies about my sexual interest in her were an indication of the fact that she was having a problem with 'being rejected' by men she was attracted to."

Doggett was entitled to his opinions, but the decision to present his rather creative analysis as testimony was an indication of just how desperate the Republicans were. According to one Judiciary Committee aide, some dispute had gone on among the Republicans about whether to use Doggett's testimony. But Senator Specter, the aide said, had insisted. He was not alone in his interest in the Texas lawyer. One administration official remembered seeing President Bush himself carrying Doggett's statement that day.

Senator Specter picked up on the matter of Doggett again in a later round of questioning that afternoon. Hill's response was that she did not have any romantic interest in him, and that indeed she could hardly remember this man, whom the committee had yet to question in public.

"As I recall," Hill said, "I told you that I had very limited memory of Mr. Doggett. The event that he is talking about was a party where there were thirty or forty people. I was talking to a lot of people. They were people who I had known while I was here in Washington. And we might have had some conversation, but this was not the content of that conversation. I do not—I have very limited memory of him. I did not at any time have any fantasy about a romance with him. As I said, my memory of him is limited. I do remember at some point seeing him jogging near my home, but beyond that, I have a very limited memory of any interaction that I had with him or how I might have met him, anything like that."

Senator Specter had a second witness lined up to testify about the fantasy theory. The senator asked Hill about another written statement she had not seen, this one made by Charles Kothe, the former dean of the Oral Roberts University law school. In an unusual academic deal the school had been sold to evangelist Pat Robertson, and moved from Oklahoma to Virginia.

Kothe had stated, "I find the references to the alleged sexual harassment not only unbelievable but preposterous. I am convinced that such are the product of fantasy," Specter quoted the former dean.

Hill did not hesitate with her response. "Well," she said, "I would only say that I am not given to fantasy. This [the sexual harassment account] is not something that I would have come forward with if I were not absolutely sure about what it is I am saying. I weighed this very carefully, I considered it carefully and I made a determination to come forward. I think it's unfortunate that that comment was made by a man who purports to be someone who says he knows me. And I think it's just inaccurate."

By the time the hearings ended, the fantasy theory would be almost totally discredited. But that mattered little. What mattered was its immediate impact on the senators and millions of other Americans listening to the testimony. And, as farfetched as it was, the fantasy theory was the best the Republicans could come up with to explain how Hill could have told three people about the alleged harasssment at the time it occurred.

While attention focused on the Hill versus Thomas plot unfolding in the Caucus Room, subplots were being acted out in other places in the capital. Donald H. Green, a Washington trial lawyer with Pepper, Hamilton & Scheetz, started getting a flurry of telephone calls about his old associate, Anita Hill.

Green had been a partner at Wald, Harkrader & Ross, the firm where Hill worked for a year before starting work for Thomas. Green had been the chairman of the firm's committee that evaluated the performance of its young lawyers, or associates.

The first call, on the opening day of the hearings, was from Terry L. Wooten, chief counsel of the minority staff of the Judiciary Committee, who worked for Senator Thurmond. Wooten was in charge of lining up witnesses to testify for Thomas. The Republicans wanted not only information that would bolster Thomas's image but also any that could tarnish Hill's.

"He said, 'Why was she fired?' " Green recounted later. "That was his first question to me."

Dispatching with the idea that Hill had been dismissed from the firm, Green told Wooten, "Whoever said that was a liar." Wooten next inquired as to what ethical problems Hill had at the firm. Green, a former Marine and Justice Department lawyer, said he knew of no ethical problems.

Wooten warned Green, "You can anticipate the possibility of a subpoena."

Green talked to another former partner who shared his memory that Hill had not been asked to leave the firm. But he kept getting more phone calls from the Republican side of the Judiciary Committee, pressing him for more information. That night he received a call at home from a former partner with close ties to the Republicans.

"Don, I'm calling because I don't want you to be another Alan Fiers," the partner said, referring to the former CIA official who had pleaded guilty to lying to Congress. "This has to do with the Anita Hill thing. Don, I know she was fired, you better tell the truth."

Hill's record at the law firm would remain a strange controversy for some days, but eventually an explanation for the differing opinions about it would come to light.

Back in the Caucus Room, it came time for Senator Heflin to try his hand. The senator's slow drawl transported his listeners to Alabama, or some other sleepy Southern state where lawyers slowly build their points in layers of soft, folksy questions. Of course, Senator Heflin, the former judge with the wisdom of seventy years, was every bit as cagey as Senator Specter, even if their styles were as different as South and North. Whether or not he was as effective in terms of creating sheer drama was a different matter. The jowly Heflin, his shirtfront rumpled over a sizable belly, began by trying to extract from Hill crucial testimony about what had *not* propelled her to come forward with her charges.

"Professor Hill, we heard Judge Thomas deny that he'd ever asked you to go out with him socially, date him, and deny all allegations relative to statements that allegedly he had made to you that involved sex, sex organs, pornographic films and material, those type of things. And you have testified that that occurred, that he asked you to date, go out socially. And you've testified here today relative to the statements that he had made to you about pornographic films and materials and other things," Heflin began, working his way to the core question now in front of the committee, and the nation.

"I, and I suppose every member of this committee, have to come down to the ultimate question of who's telling the truth. My experience as a lawyer, judge, is that you listen to all the testimony and then you try to determine the motivation for the one that is not telling the truth. Now in trying to determine whether you are telling falsehoods or not, I've got to determine what your motivation might be. Are you a scorned woman?"

"No," Hill said.

"Are you a zealot civil rights believer that progress will be turned back if Clarence Thomas goes on the Court?"

"I—no, I don't. I think that—I have my opinions but I don't think that progress will be turned back. I think that civil rights will prevail no matter what happens with the Court."

"Do you have a militant attitude relative to the area of civil rights?"

"No, I don't have a militant attitude."

"Do you have a martyr complex?"

Breaking the grave expression she had maintained, Hill couldn't help but laugh at this, seemingly at the absurdity of the idea that she might have wanted to suffer this public grilling.

"No, I don't."

"Well, do you see that coming out of this you can be a hero in the civil rights movement?"

"I do not have that kind of complex. I don't like all of the attention that I am getting, I don't—I would not—even if I liked the attention I would not lie to get attention."

This was absolutely key to deciding whom to believe, Hill or Thomas. Did Hill have a motivation to lie? Thomas did, in order to get on the Supreme Court, but only if he would stoop to the extraordinary depth of perjuring himself in sworn, public testimony.

"Well, the issue of fantasy has arisen. You are—have a degree in psychology from the University of—Oklahoma State University." As Heflin went along, his questions were punctuated with short pauses and long pauses, that came sometimes after single phrases and sometimes after single words so that his listeners were left hanging in suspense or, over time, distracted by the monotony.

"Yes."

"And you studied in your psychology studies when you were in school and what you may have followed up with, the question of fantasies. Have you ever studied that from a pyschology basis?"

"To some extent, yes."

"What do you—what are the traits of fantasy that you studied, as you remember?"

"As I remember, it would have—it would require some other indication of loss of touch with reality other than one instance. There is no indication that I'm an individual who is not in touch with reality on a regular basis that would be subject to fantasy."

Having drawn Hill out on the issues of motive and fantasy, Heflin moved on, trying to discover Thomas's motivation if what Hill had recounted about her experiences with him were true. Now that Hill had made her case in person, Heflin was free to quote from the original statement that had been the subject of such furious dispute at the hearings' outset. Hill had faxed the statement to Washington the previous month and the committee had had it in hand when it voted on Thomas the previous month.

Heflin read Hill's words, " 'I sensed that my discomfort with his discussions only urged him on as though my reaction of feeling ill at ease and vulnerable was what he wanted.' " And then he said, "In other words, you're basically stating that that appeared to be his goal rather than trying to obtain an intimate or a sexual relation with you. It may be that you also felt that. But that raises quite an issue. What do you mean by that? How do you conclude that?"

"Well," Hill answered, "it was almost as though he wanted me at a disadvantage—to put me at a disadvantage so that I would have to concede to whatever his wishes were."

"You think that he got some pleasure out of seeing you ill at ease and vulnerable?"

"I think so, yes."

"Was this feeling more so than the feeling that he might be seeking some type of dating or social relationship with you?"

"I think it was a combination of factors. I think that he wanted to see me vulnerable, and that if I were vulnerable, then he could extract from me whatever he wanted, whether it was sexual or otherwise—that I would be at his—under his control."

"Now, as a psychology major, what elements of human nature seem to go into that type of a situation?"

"Well, I can't say, exactly. I can say that I felt that he was using his power and authority over me, was exerting a level of power and attempting to make sure that that power was exerted. I think it was the fact that I had said no to him that caused him to want to do this."

Hill was talking about the power games that are often a classic ingredient of sexual harassment.

Heflin also asked Hill about the Coke can incident and she said she felt Thomas had been acting inappropriately but she couldn't interpret exactly what he had intended by the remark. Hill apparently did not know that in hard-core pornography Coke cans are employed to penetrate women.

As the day in the Caucus Room progressed, the wound-to-the-breaking-point tension decreased. But the committee and the audience remained riveted by the testimony. The only people departing the room were journalists dashing to telephones and offices to file stories.

By afternoon, Senator Specter was again doing the questioning. He wanted to know about the two things that seemed most puzzling to many Americans about Hill's behavior: her decision to follow Thomas from the Department of Education to the EEOC, and her repeated contacts with him after she left Washington.

She had said, Specter reminded her, that one reason she had gone to the EEOC with Thomas was that she was not sure if she would have a job at the civil rights office of the Department of Education under his successor. But, he asked, wasn't she a Schedule A [civil service] employee with job protection? And hadn't Harry Singleton, Thomas's replacement and old friend from law school, told her she could stay on?

Hill responded that she had not been guaranteed the job. She also said that if she had stayed, she probably would not have been doing the civil rights work that had attracted her in the first place. Anyway, President Reagan was trying to abolish the whole department at the time, she said.

In fact, Thomas himself had told her he could not guarantee that she would have a job at the department once he had gone, Hill testified. At that time, she said, he had stopped harassing her.

"I moved on because I assumed that the issue of the behavior of Clarence Thomas had been laid to rest, that it was over, and that I could look forward to a similar position at the EEOC."

As for the telephone logs showing that Hill had called Thomas at least eleven times after she left his employ, she insisted, "The issue is garbage. Those telephone messages do not indicate that which they are being used to indicate: that is, that somehow I was pursuing something more than a cordial relationship, professional relationship. Each of those calls were made in a professional context. Some of those calls revolved around one incident. Several of those calls, in fact, three, involved one incident where I was trying to act on behalf of another group."

Senator Specter, the tough prosecutor, refused to be dissuaded.

"Now my question to you is, since those calls were in fact made, as you now say, doesn't that have some relevance as to whether the committee should accept your statements about Judge Thomas's sexual harassment in the context of your efforts to call him this many times over that period of time?"

"No. . . . My point is that I have stated to you that I continued—I hoped to continue to maintain a professional relationship for a variety of reasons. One was a sense that I could not afford to antagonize a person in such a high position. Those calls that were made, I have attempted to explain none of them were personal in nature. They involved instances where I passed along casual messages, or instances where I called to either find out whether or not the chairman was available for a speech acting on behalf of someone else, and that no, they have very little, if any, relevance at all to the incidents that happened before those phone calls were made," Hill replied.

Specter was not satisfied.

"You say that they were all professional, and you have accounted for a number of them in your statement. But a number of them have not been accounted for. For example, the log on January 30, 1984, quote, 'Just called to say hello.' 'Sorry she didn't see you last week.' May 9, 1984, 'Please call.' October 8, 1986, 'Please call.' Taking the one, 'Just called to say hello.' 'Sorry she didn't see you last week.'

"First of all, is that accurate?" Specter asked.

"As I indicated earlier, I do not deny the accuracy of these messages."

Hill did not have a satisfactory rationale that would explain all of the telephone messages. Senator Leahy, who questioned Hill next, tried to put the calls in some perspective, pointing out that Hill had averaged only 1.5 calls to Thomas a year.

"Assuming those phone logs are accurate, you weren't exactly—you weren't exactly beating down the doors with phone calls there, were you," he asked rhetorically.

Then Senator Leahy pursued the very important point that Heflin had tried to make. What possible ulterior motive did Hill have for coming forward?

"Do you have anything to gain by coming here? Has anybody promised you anything by coming forth with this story now?"

"I have nothing to gain," Hill responded. "No one has promised me anything. I have nothing to gain here. This has been disruptive of my life and I've taken a number of personal risks. I've been threatened. And I have not gained anything except knowing that I came forward and did what I felt that I had an obligation to do, and that was to tell the truth."

"And my last question," Leahy said. "Would your life be simpler, quieter and far more private had you never come forth at all?"

"Yes. Norman, Oklahoma, is a much simpler, quieter place than this room today."

Finally Senator Specter took his last turn for the day; he had his own point to try to prove about motivation and Hill's truthfulness. Specter went back to a question he had hit her with in the morning regarding what she was told by Jim Brudney, Metzenbaum's aide, about what might happen if she came forward with her charges.

That morning Hill had stumbled on the question, saying she did not recall having had a conversation with Brudney about the consequences of her charges.

In the afternoon, her memory refreshed, Hill acknowledged that she had discussed with the aide "the process for going forward, what might happen if I did bring information to the committee. That included that an investigation might take place, that some—I might be questioned by the committee in closed session. It even included something to the effect that the information might be presented to the candidate or to the White House. There was some indication that the candidate—or excuse me, the nominee might not wish to continue the process."

This is what Senator Specter wanted to hear. He asked with excitement, "Mr. Brudney said to you that the nominee, Judge Thomas, might not wish to continue the process if you came forward with a statement on the factors which you've testified about?"

"Well, I'm not sure that that's exactly what he said," Hill replied. "I think what he said was, depending on an investigation, a Senate— whether the Senate went into closed session and so forth, it might be that he would not wish to continue the process.

"So Mr. Brudney did tell you that Judge Thomas might not wish to continue to go forward with his nomination if you came forward."

"Yes," Hill answered.

"Isn't that somewhat different from your testimony this morning?" The Pennsylvania prosecutor thought he had driven home his point.

Hill disagreed, saying her early testimony had been in response to an indirect and confusing question based on a misleading newspaper report. She also disagreed with Specter's interpretation of the conversation. "We talked about a number of different options, but it was never suggested that just by alleging incidents, that that would cause a candidate—or the nominee to withdraw," she recalled.

Ultimately, this intricate line of questioning would become an embarrassment to the senator.

Hill remained calm, as she had throughout the day. Although her previous public appearances had been limited largely to the safety of classrooms, she performed as if she were expert at enduring questioning from the U.S. Senate, in front of the entire nation, about the most intimate of matters. Not once, even under the persistent prosecutorial badgering of Senator Specter, did she lose her poise, become angry, or break into tears. Specter had been able to raise some doubts about her behavior, but he had not shaken her story. Staffers on both the Democratic and Republican sides of the committee thought she had done well and there were those on both sides who believed her. At the White House, the mood was glum. President Bush, who earlier in the day had expressed confidence that Thomas would be exonerated, left for Camp David without saying a word to reporters.

After her testimony, Hill was drained. She went back to the rooms of the Rules Committee, joining her lawyers, the other members of her team and the members of her family. There, in a room with a vaulted ceiling and handsome bookcases, where senators usually debate parliamentary tactics, the disparate group joined hands, while a minister close to the family said a prayer, giving thanks for Hill's strength.

The day in the Caucus Room had been the opening of a real battle between two witnesses with opposite stories. It also had served as a metaphor for a larger struggle constant in American society of the latter decades of the century, the conflict between a system dominated by traditional male values and a challenge based upon female values. Beneath the question of who was telling the truth was the divide of party politics, and beneath that the morass of sexual politics.

At nine o'clock Friday evening, October 11, the first day of the reopened hearings, Thomas reappeared, breathing fire and new life into his chances of confirmation.

I would like to start by saying unequivocally, uncategorically, that I deny each and every single allegation against me today that suggested in any way that I had conversations of a sexual nature or about pornographic material with Anita Hill, that I ever attempted to date her, that I ever had any personal sexual interest in her, or that I in any way ever harassed her.

A second, and I think more important point, I think that this today is a travesty. I think that it is disgusting. I think that this hearing should never occur in America. This is a case in which this sleaze, this dirt, was searched for by staffers of members of this committee, was then leaked to the media, and this committee and this body validated it and displayed it at prime time over our entire nation. How would any member on this committee, any person in this room, or any person in this country, like sleaze said about him or her in this fashion? Or this dirt dredged up and this gossip and these lies displayed in this manner? How would any person like it?

The Supreme Court is not worth it. No job is worth it. I'm not here for that. I'm here for my name, my family, my life and my integrity. I think something is dreadfully wrong with this country when any person, any person in this free country would be subjected to this.

This is not a closed room. There was an FBI investigation. This is not an opportunity to talk about difficult matters privately or in a closed environment. This is a circus. It's a national disgrace. And from my standpoint as a black American, as far as I'm concerned, it is a high-tech lynching for uppity blacks who in any way deign to think for themselves, to do for themselves, to have different ideas, and it is a message that unless you kowtow to an old order, this is what will happen to you. You will be lynched, destroyed, caricatured, by a committee of the U.S. Senate rather than hung from a tree.

No Supreme Court nominee had ever dared tell the senators holding the power of confirmation that *their* performance was a travesty, a disgrace, a circus, a lynching. Thomas had thrown off Kenneth Duberstein's coaching in the politic arts of compromise, conciliation, and gentlemanly blandness. His ire was so fiery, so close to the line between shouting and raving, that some Republican committee aides feared his tirade might backfire. Many of his friends in the conservative movement, though, cheered at seeing what they considered to be the real Clarence Thomas for the first time in the hearings. And it quickly became apparent from the halting questioning of Senator Howell Heflin that Thomas's comeback had doused the Democrats.

Heflin began by cautiously ducking Thomas's salvo of words. This would prove to be a major tactical mistake for the Democrats, since it allowed the nominee's words to stand unchallenged. Heflin turned to Hill's testimony.

"Now, you, I suppose, have heard Ms.—Professor Hill's—Ms. Hill—Anita F. Hill testify today," the Alabama senator said, letting his pauses hang in the air.

"No, I haven't," Thomas said, pointblank.

"You didn't listen?" the senator asked him incredulously.

"No, I didn't. I've heard enough lies."

Heflin was taken aback. "You didn't listen to her testimony at all?"

"No, I didn't."

"On television?" Heflin asked hopefully.

"No, I didn't. I've heard enough lies. Today is not a day that in my opinion is high among the days in our country. This is a travesty. You spent the entire day destroying what it has taken me forty-three years to build, and providing a forum for that."

"Well, Judge Thomas, you know, we have a responsibility, too. And as far as I'm involved, I had nothing to do with Anita Hill coming here and testifying," the senator said, backing off. "We're trying to get to the bottom of this, and if she is lying, then I think you can help us prove that she was lying."

"Senator, I am incapable of proving the negative," Clarence Thomas said angrily. "It did not occur." Thomas pointed his finger accusingly at the senators, as he complained that Hill's charges had been leaked to the media when they should have been resolved in confidence.

"Well, I certainly appreciate your attitude toward leaks," Heflin sympathized, irrelevantly. "I happen to serve on the Senate Ethics Committee, and it's been a sieve."

"Well, but it didn't leak on me," Thomas said, still defiant. "This leaked on me and it is drowning my life, my career, and my integrity and you can't give it back to me and this committee can't give it back to me and this Senate can't give it back to me. You have robbed me of something that can never be restored."

"I know exactly how you feel," chimed in Senator Dennis DeConcini, who was himself the subject of a character-damaging leak about his involvement in the savings-and-loan scandal. This, too, was irrelevant to Thomas's plight. He didn't want the mushy-sounding good will of the Democrats, who seemed to have been thrown into a state of intimidation.

Senator Heflin tried again to persuade Thomas to be amenable. He tried to appeal to the nominee's sense of reason.

"Judge Thomas, one of the aspects of this is that she could be living in a fantasy world. I don't know. We're just trying to get to the bottom of all of these facts. But if you didn't listen and didn't see her testify, I think you put yourself in an unusual position. You in effect are defending yourself and basically some of us want to be fair to you, fair to her, but if you didn't listen to what she said today, then that puts it somewhat in a more difficult task to find out what the actual facts are relative to this matter."

That may have been what Thomas intended. But for someone who claimed not to have watched the day's proceedings, he seemed awfully familiar with them. (Later, Thomas said his wife had briefed him throughout the day.)

"The facts keep changing, Senator. When the FBI visited me, the statements to this committee and the questions were one thing. The FBI's subsequent questions were another thing, and the statements today as I received summaries of them were another thing. It is not my fault that the facts changed. What I have said to you is categorical: that any allegations that I engaged in any conduct involving sexual activity, pornographic movies, attempted to date her, any allegations, I deny. It is not true. So, the facts can change, but my denial does not. Ms. Hill was treated in a way that all my special assistants were treated: cordial, professional, respectful."

"Judge," Heflin tried, "if you are on the bench and you approach a case where you appear to have a closed mind and that you are only right, doesn't it raise issues of judicial temperament?"

"Senator, senator, there is a big difference between approaching a case objectively and watching yourself being lynched. There is no comparison whatsoever."

"All right, sir," Heflin said, struggling for what to say next. "Judge, I don't want to go over this stuff, but of course, there are many instances which she has stated, and in effect, since you didn't see her testify, I think it's somewhat unfair to ask you specifically about it. I would reserve my time and go ahead and let Senator Hatch ask you, and then come back."

Heflin had been flummoxed by the man whom he was supposed to cross-examine. His skills at lawyering seemed to have evaporated. So Thomas, unlike Hill, who had immediately undergone a meticulous and able challenge to her testimony from Senator Specter, got a free pass. (Heflin, at one break in the weekend testimony, passed an aide to another senator in a corridor who asked, "How're you hanging in there, Judge?" "By my neck," he replied.)

The job of questioning Thomas about the details of Hill's charges was handed to his fiercest supporter, Utah Senator Orrin Hatch. Hatch had good reasons, beyond his friendship with Clarence and Ginny Thomas, to defend the nominee.

Hatch was a tall man whose complexion was so pale and dress so dapper that in his rare moments of repose he could pass for a department store mannequin. Now a lay minister in the conservative Mormon church, he had been born in poverty in Pittsburgh to a father from Utah who worked as a metal lather. He had been an uncompromising ultraconservative when he first arrived in the Senate in 1977, a leader of the New Right's war against the liberal social agenda. But as he increased in maturity and seniority, Hatch had become a conservative with a social conscience, backing AIDS education and a government child-care bill vehemently opposed by conservatives as government intrusion into the family.

Though he remained conservative on most issues, particularly judicial nominations, New Right figures like Paul Weyrich had condemned Hatch as a traitor to the cause. The charge against Hatch was that he was trying to turn himself into a moderate because he wanted to be on the Supreme Court himself and wanted to curry some favor with his liberal colleagues. But if the Supreme Court was his goal, Hatch would need solidly conservative credentials to get nominated in the first place. And he certainly boosted them with his attacks on Hill in the guise of a friendly cross-examination of Thomas.

Hatch began his questioning by leading Thomas through each specific charge by Hill in order to give the nominee the chance to offer specific denials. He asked Thomas if he had talked to Hill about oral sex, or pornographic films, or about people having sex with animals. Thomas quickly grew cooperative.

"Senator, I would not want to—except being required to here—to dignify those allegations with a response. As I have said before, I categorically deny them. To me, I have been pilloried with scurrilous allegations of this nature, I have denied them earlier, and I deny them tonight."

Hatch continued to ask Thomas the string of exceedingly uncomfortable questions he had prepared ahead of time. Hatch's expression was determined and fixed, similar to that of someone who might be cleaning a dirty toilet.

"Now, did you ever say to Professor Hill in words or substance—and this is embarrassing for me to say in public—but it has to be done, and I'm sure it's not pleasing to you—did you ever say in words or substance something like 'there is a pubic hair in my Coke'?"

"No, Senator," Thomas replied with an air of disgust and impatience.

"Did you ever refer to your private parts in conversations with Professor Hill?"

"Absolutely not, Senator."

"Did you ever brag to Professor Hill about your sexual prowess?"

"No, Senator."

"Did you ever use the term Long Dong Silver in conversation with Professor Hill?"

"No, Senator."

The questioning had been too much for Virginia Thomas, who broke down and sobbed while sitting helplessly behind the man she had married four year earlier.

Thomas, in response to Hatch's questions, went on to draw a contradictory picture of Hill. She was, he said, someone with whom he had a solid professional relationship, someone whose work was good, but also someone who may have been a disgruntled employee.

When Thomas had moved to the Equal Employment Opportunity Commission with Hill, the working relationship between the two of them changed, he said. At the EEOC, Thomas had to cope with many more responsibilities than previously. Because of this, he said that even though she worked as his special assistant, their professional relationship became more distant.

"As a result," Thomas said of Hill, "she did not enjoy that close a relationship with me, nor did she have her choice of the better assignments. And I think that as a result of that there was some concern on her part that she was not being treated as well as she had been treated prior to that."

Moreover, Hill was not well liked by everyone on his staff, Thomas testified.

"I believe that she was considered to be somewhat distant and perhaps aloof, and from time to time there would be problems that usually involved—and I attributed this to just being young—but usually involved her taking a firm position and not—and being unyielding to the other members of the staff, and then storming off or throwing a temper tantrum of some sort, that either myself or the chief of staff would have to iron out."

Anita Hill's work was good, he said, but "the problem was that—and it wasn't a problem—it was not as good as some of the other members of the staff."

Hill had testified that she had not asked for any other job at the EEOC other than the one she had as assistant to the chairman. Thomas, however, said that "she may have sought a promotion" to be his chief of staff and "I think that—and again, I'm relying on my memory, she aspired to that position, and, of course, was not successful, and I think was concerned about that."

Thomas did not mention that in 1982, after they had both moved to the EEOC, he gave Hill a promotion in civil service grade from GS-13 to GM-14, making her a high level manager. With the promotion came a raise of almost $5,000, from a salary of $34,706 to $39,609.

He did say that they maintained a cordial relationship that included occasional visits to her apartment.

"As I remember it, I lived in Southwest Washington and would—as I remember—and, again, I'm relying on my recollection, she lived some place on Capitol Hill, and I would drive her home and sometimes stop in and have a Coke or a beer or something and continue arguing about politics for maybe forty-five minutes to an hour. But I never thought anything of it."

Senator Hatch then summed up his reaction to the charges.

"I have to say cumulatively these charges, even though they were made on all kinds of occasions—I mean, they're unbelievable that anybody could be that perverted. I am sure there are people like that but they are generally in insane asylums."

Of course, from the point of view of this Mormon from Utah, this may have been true. But the EEOC's own files indicate that such behavior is not all that uncommon and that it can be perpetrated by persons who otherwise function normally in society.

Thomas's opponents pointed out later that one of the difficulties with assessing the charges against him was that he had changed so much in the eight to ten years since the alleged behavior took place. The Clarence Thomas who had come to the Senate for confirmation to the Supreme Court was for the most part a confident, dignified, and happily married man experienced in the ways of Washington. The Clarence Thomas who had been Anita Hill's boss was an awkward, newly separated man in his early thirties with little savvy and with huge responsibilities and vexing political problems.

Thomas spoke late into the evening Friday, until the committee adjourned. The entirety of the testimony given in the Caucus Room had amounted to a daylong soap opera of historic importance. It had been an unprecedented opportunity for the voyeuristic public to tune into the private lives of real people and to judge the judge for themselves. It also had been a rare chance to see the nation's top elected officials in action, but shorn of their usual, image-conscious wool. They were performing naked in essence, without the practiced scripts that could have helped them avoid seeming so bumbling or so brutal. If the reputations of the two witnesses and the future of the country's judiciary had not been at stake, the drama could have been highly amusing. Instead, it was nothing but tragic. And it was to be continued.

Given the skittishness of the Democrats about questioning Clarence Thomas, he could have finished his testimony the next day in a few hours. But the Republicans had decided to keep Thomas in front of the nation all Saturday, October 18, taking advantage of the weekend audience watching on television. They had also decided, based on fear that Hill's credible appearance the day before had severely damaged Thomas, to go on the attack. This decision was ratified by President Bush, backed by all the legal resources of the White House, the Justice Department, and other federal agencies. It was implemented, with no holds barred, by Orrin Hatch and Arlen Specter.

Senator Hatch's questioning of Thomas was more a series of small speeches punctuated with symbolic queries such as "Don't you think, Judge?" Senator Hatch managed to make attacks on the credibility of Hill while simultaneously repeating disingenuous compliments about her.

"Judge, there are a lot of things that just don't make sense to me in Anita Hill's testimony," the senator said. "I liked her personally. I thought she presented herself well. There's no question she's a very intelligent law professor. She has graduated from one of the finest schools in the land, law schools, that is, and her undergraduate work was exemplary. She clearly is a very intelligent woman and I think everybody who listened to her wants to like her and many do. But, Judge, it bothers me because it just doesn't square with what I think is—some of it doesn't square with what I think is common experience and just basic sense, common sense."

Hatch critiqued what he said were Hill's successively expansive charges. He accused her of adding details as she went. Her initial discussion with the FBI agents, according to the senator, had been augmented with additional descriptions provided in her written statement to the committee and with the graphic accounts given in her testimony. Hatch was trying to show that Hill had embroidered her story.

In fact, Hatch had a major part of the sequence wrong. Her initial statement was the one faxed to the Judiciary Committee. It was followed the same day by the less detailed interview with the FBI agents. Hatch had to reverse the chronology to build his proof, an erroneous fabrication that no one called him on.

Thomas, in response to another of Hatch's solicitous queries, made a trenchant observation. The allegations against him, he said, played into the age-old racist stereotype of the hypersexual black male. This was exactly what he said he had been guarding against by adopting a rigorous personal code against any kind of sexual banter in the office. (Hill, of course, had testified to the contrary the previous day about Thomas's extremely loose tongue.) Thomas continued:

> Throughout the history of this country and certainly throughout my life, language about the sexual prowess of black men, language about the sex organs of black men and the sizes, et cetera, that kind of language has been used about black men as long as I've been on the face of this earth, and these are charges that play into racist, bigoted, stereotypes, and these are the kind of charges that are impossible to wash off, and these are the kind of stereotypes that I have in my tenure in government and conduct of my affairs . . . attempted to move away from and to convince people that we should conduct ourselves in a way that defies these stereotypes. But when you play into a stereotype, it says though you're skiing downhill, there's no way to stop it, and this plays into the most bigoted, racist stereotypes that any black man will face.

Thomas pointed out that historically this sexual stereotyping was associated with the lynchings of black men that occurred for so many decades in the South. This was a subject that had preoccupied Thomas since his teenage years.

That is the point that I'm trying to make, and that is the point that I was making last night, that this is high-tech lynching. I cannot shake off these accusations because they play to the worst stereotypes we have about black men in this country.

There followed a hilarious dialogue in which Hatch, attempting to jump on Thomas's point, made it appear he had no idea what the nominee was talking about. As clever as he sometimes could be, the prudish senator from Utah seemed ignorant of the black culture in America and one of its central grievances.

HATCH: This bothers me. It bothers me.

THOMAS: It bothers me.

HATCH: I can see why. Let—let me—I hate to do this, but let me—let me ask you some tough questions. You've talked about stereotypes used against black males in this society. In this first statement, "He told her about his experiences and preferences, would ask her what she had liked or if she had ever done the same thing." Is that a black stereotype?

THOMAS: No.

HATCH: Okay. Hill said that he discussed oral sex between men and women. Is that a black stereotype?

THOMAS: No.

HATCH: Okay. "Thomas also discussed viewing films of people having sex with each other and with animals." What about that?

THOMAS: That's not a stereotype about blacks.

Hatch tried again.

HATCH: Okay. "He told her that he enjoyed watching the films and told her that she should see them." Watching X-rated films or pornographic films, is that a stereotype?

THOMAS: No.

Hatch was disproving the very theory he was trying to bolster. But he kept going.

HATCH: "He never asked her to watch the films with him. Thomas liked to discuss specific sex acts and frequency of sex."      .

THOMAS: No, I don't think so. I think that that could—the last frequency could have to do with black men supposedly being very promiscuous or something like that.
HATCH: So it could be partially stereotypical then?
THOMAS: Yeah.
HATCH: In the next statement, she said, "His conversations were very vivid. He spoke about acts that he had seen in pornographic films involving such things as women having sex with animals and films involving group sex or rape scenes. He talked about pornographic materials depicting individuals with large penises or breasts involved in various sex acts." What about those things?

A bingo, at last, for Hatch.

THOMAS: I think the—certainly the size of sexual organs would be something.
HATCH: Well, I'm concerned.

Hatch said this with great emphasis. Thus encouraged he went on.

HATCH: "Thomas told me graphically of his own sexual prowess."
THOMAS: That's clearly stereotypical.
HATCH: Clearly a black stereotype.
THOMAS: Clearly.

Having received a bit of an education, Hatch moved on to an area where he was on more solid ground. He sprang the first of two surprises that Hill's opponents had devised.

Various lawyers from the White House, the Justice Department, and the EEOC had set out hastily to find ways to discredit Hill's testimony. Among those heading up the Justice Department's efforts was Michael Luttig, who had already been confirmed but had not yet been sworn in as a federal circuit court judge. One possibly fruitful line of inquiry, the lawyers figured, was to look for an alternative explanation as to how such a seemingly demure woman as Anita Hill could have heard of Long Dong Silver or of pubic hairs in odd places.

It was a lawyer in the general counsel's office of the EEOC who found a reference to Long Dong Silver in the legal record. But Hatch took public credit for the find.

HATCH: People hearing yesterday's testimony are probably wondering how could this quiet, you know, retired [sic] woman know about something like Long Dong Silver. Did you tell her that?

THOMAS: No. I don't know how she knows.

HATCH: Is that a black stereotype, something like Long Dong Silver?

THOMAS: To the extent, Senator, that it is a reference to one's sexual organs and the size of one's sexual organs, I think it is.

HATCH: Well, there's an interesting case I found called *Carter* versus *Sedgwick County, Kansas*, a 1988 case, dated September 30. It's a Tenth Circuit Court of Appeals case. It's a district court case. It's a district court case within the Tenth Circuit. Do you know where—which circuit Oklahoma is in?

THOMAS: My guess would be the Tenth Circuit. I remember serving on a moot court panel with a judge from the Tenth Circuit, and I believe she was from Tulsa.

HATCH: Well, I have to tell you something. I believe Oklahoma is in the Tenth Circuit. Utah is, also. It's an interesting case. I'm just going to read one paragraph, if anybody wants to read it. And I apologize in advance for some of the language. I really do. It's a civil rights case—interesting civil rights case. And again, I apologize in advance for the language.

He proceeded to read from this three-year-old case in which a black woman had sued a county government in Kansas. She claimed she had been harassed and fired by a man named Brand due to her race and sex.

" 'Plaintiff further testified that on one occasion, defendant Brand presented her with a picture of Long Dong Silver, a photo of a black male with an elongated penis.' "

The implication, and a farfetched one, was that Hill had been somehow familiar with this particular case and had employed its material to slam Thomas. Hill had not participated in the case in any way and it had nothing to do with her specialty in commercial law. But Hatch suggested that liberal groups had fed Hill this information, colluding with her to make up the charges and using this case for embellishing details.

The senator launched into a diatribe. "All these interest groups have scratched through everything on earth to try and get something on you, all over the country, all over this town, all over your agency, all over everybody, and there's a lot of slick lawyers in those groups— slick lawyers, the worst kind. There are some great ones, too, and it may have been a great one that found the reference to Long Dong Silver, which I find totally offensive, and I find it highly ironic—and I find it highly ironic that you've testified here today, that used against you by one who taught civil rights, who came from one of the five best law schools in the country, who is an intelligent and apparently decent African-American, used against you a bunch of black stereotype accusations. What do you think about that?"

"Senator," Thomas replied, "as I've indicated before, and I will continue to say this and believe this—I have been harmed. I have been harmed, my family has been harmed, I've been harmed worse than I've ever been harmed in my life. I wasn't harmed by the Klan. I wasn't harmed by the Knights of Camellia. I wasn't harmed by the Aryan Race. I wasn't harmed by a racist group. I was harmed by this process."

Hatch was ready with another half-baked explanation for Anita Hill's testimony. He asked Thomas whether he had ever said to her, as Hill alleged," 'Who has put pubic hair on my Coke?' Unquote. That's what she said. Did you ever say that?"

"No," Thomas replied. "Absolutely not."

"Didn't you ever think of saying something like that?" Hatch asked.

"No."

Hatch had been a trial lawyer himself, and knew how to drag something out for dramatic effect on the jury.

"That's a gross thing to say, isn't it? Whether it's said by you or by somebody else, it's a gross thing to say, isn't it?"

"As far as I'm concerned it is, Senator. And it's something I did not, nor would I say."

"Ever read this book?" Hatch asked, holding up a copy of a popular horror story published while Thomas was in law school. A Justice Department lawyer had pointed out an interesting passage in the book.

"No," Thomas replied.

"*The Exorcist*," Hatch pronounced triumphantly.

"No, Senator."

"Ever see the movie?"

"I've seen only the scene with the bed flapping," Thomas said.

"And let me tell you," the senator continued with his attack on the lawyers with the liberal groups, "these aren't itty-bitty tort attorney investigators. These are the smartest attorneys from the best law schools in the land. All paid for at the public interest expense. It's what's ruining our country in large measure. Because some of these groups—not all of them—many public interest groups are great. I don't mean to malign them all. But a number of them are vicious."

Hatch did not want to attack Anita Hill head-on. She had been too credible a witness, and it was hard to accuse a black woman of racial stereotyping. So instead the senator went after the only other target, the "interest groups," as he called the citizens' organizations that opposed Thomas.

"We saw it in the Bork matter. And we're seeing it here," Hatch said. "Let me just read to you from *The Exorcist*. You said you never did say this, 'Who has put pubic hair on my Coke?' You never did talk to her about Long Dong Silver. I submit those things were found. On page seventy of this particular version of *The Exorcist:* ' "Oh, Burke," sighed Sharon, in a guarded tone she described an encounter between the senator and the director. Dennings had remarked to him in passing, said Sharon, that there appeared to be, [quote] "an alien pubic hair floating around in my gin." ' Unquote. Do you think that was spoken by happenstance? And she would have us believe that you were saying these things because you wanted to date her? What do you think about that, Judge?"

"Senator, I think this whole affair is sick."

"I think it's sick, too."

Hatch had not proved a thing. He had accused the liberal groups and by implication Hill of falsifying testimony, on absolutely no evidence. But he had succeeded, using techniques no better than those of the infamous Senator Joseph McCarthy, in fogging the image of Hill in the eyes of the public and of those who wanted any possible rationale to believe Thomas. And Biden had done absolutely nothing to stop him.

Arlen Specter, when it came his turn to question Thomas, was not to be outdone by his Republican colleague. Specter, too, accused Hill of perjury, but he didn't hint around about it.

Senator Specter referred Thomas to the issue of the conversation Hill had had with Jim Brudney, the Metzenbaum aide. Under Specter's detailed questioning the day before, Hill had testified about the conversation, changing her story but never admitting to the charge that Brudney had led her to believe that Thomas would quietly withdraw. It was a muddled situation. But Specter declared in the guise of a question to Thomas that it was perjury.

"Judge Thomas, I went through that in some detail, because it is my legal judgment, having had some experience in perjury prosecutions, that the testimony of Professor Hill in the morning was flat out perjury and that she specifically changed it in the afternoon when confronted with the possibility of being contradicted. And if you recant during the course of a proceeding, it's not perjury." The rather foggy implication was that Hill must have realized she perjured herself in the morning and wriggled cunningly out of the difficulty in the afternoon.

Senator Specter was trying too hard, stretching an implication to try, unsuccessfully, to nail Hill with the charge of lying under oath.

Trial lawyers across the country immediately howled in protest at Specter's wild allegation. "Had Specter made that gratuitous declaration anywhere but in the protective cocoon of a Senate chamber, many a lawyer would have offered to take up the cudgel for Hill and fry his rump in a jury skillet," wrote prominent criminal defense lawyer F. Lee Bailey.

Specter himself was well pleased with his own performance that had attached, albeit very shakily, the word "perjury" to the name Anita Hill. When an aide to another senator told him that a television commentator had just credited him with having "drawn first blood" with the perjury charge, Specter looked up with a pleased expression on his face and said "Really?" Specter's staff told other aides that the "first blood" comment really set him off. "He's really on a roll," one of the staffers said.

In his attempt to pander to the conservatives whose support he needed so badly in the upcoming primary, Specter had gone too far. He said later he had not realized how offensive he was looking to many women, whose issues he had a record of supporting and whose votes he wanted. In fact, to try to look good to women, the senator had ordered a female staffer to sit behind him at one point in the heat of the hearings. The idea was that the television eye would show the importance he accorded this woman adviser, even as he tore into Hill. But the ruse didn't help. Thousands of telephone calls protesting his rough treatment of Hill came ringing into both his Washington and Pennsylvania offices. Forty people were put to work in the senator's offices simply answering irate women's calls, which overloaded the telephone system and temporarily put it out of commission.

Not one of the Democratic senators leaped to defend Anita Hill from Specter's and Hatch's relentless counterattacks—although Metzenbaum valiantly defended Brudney, his aide. Nor did one have the courage to properly cross-examine Thomas. It was hard to say which side was the more irresponsible: the Republicans or the Democrats.

Senator Leahy, the steady Vermont senator and former prosecutor, attempted to bring up with Thomas the crucial question of pornography.

"Now, back on the charges that Professor Hill made yesterday, one was of discussion of pornographic films with her. She stated this happened on a number of occasions and that she had found it uncomfortable and asked you not to. Let me ask you, I mean, she's been asked whether this happened, let me ask you, Did you ever have a discussion of pornographic films with Professor Hill?"

"Absolutely not," Thomas said.

"Ever had with any other women?" Leahy asked.

"Senator," Thomas replied adamantly, "I will not get into any discussions that I might have about my personal life or my sex life with any person outside of the workplace—"

"I'm not—I'm not asking—" Leahy tried to say.

"I will categorically say," Thomas interjected, "I have not had any such discussion with Professor Hill."

Leahy, despite his legal skills, had little choice but to retreat to a circumspect distance. Unbeknownst to the public, Chairman Biden had made a controversial ruling at a caucus of the committee that there would be no questions about the personal lives of either Thomas or Hill. Specifically, there would be no questions to Thomas about whether he had viewed pornography at home. This certainly protected Hill from irrelevant questions about her sex life. But it also protected

Thomas from relevant questions about whether he was the avid fan of pornography that friends from his college years had described. Any such evidence would greatly bolster Hill's case, particularly if Thomas or someone else testified that this habit had continued after he came to Washington.

"Please don't misunderstand my question, Judge," Leahy said, addressing Thomas politely. "I am confining it to the workplace. I have no interest in what may be your personal life in this. That's yours. What I'm asking is within—she alleges within the workplace. Make sure I fully understand—I'm asking you this question so that you can—you can give the answer. Am I correct in understanding your answer that within the workplace with Professor Hill, you never had such a discussion?"

"That's right."

"You never had such discussions within the workplace with any other women?"

"That's right."

"Or anyone for that matter?"

"That's right."

The Democrats had little they dared or wanted to talk to the nominee about. When Senator Biden was supposed to be cross-examining Thomas, many of his questions seemed designed simply to eat up time. He droned on with questions about how Thomas operated his office, about whether his staff had direct access to him, about whether he felt a special obligation to watch out for staff members like Hill. Perhaps Biden's bite was diminished by his emergency trip to the dentist at two that morning to have an emergency root canal procedure. The committee chairman was both exhausted and hurting. Whenever there was a break in the hearings, he walked around holding an ice pack to his jaw. His toothache could have been a metaphor for the pain the whole country was suffering during the hearings he was chairing.

The one point that the Democrats were successful in making, the only one, was that Hill seemed to have no plausible motive for fabricating her story. Leahy, Biden, and Heflin all questioned Thomas as to what her motive might be, but the nominee refused to speculate.

Senator Leahy laid out the conundrum for Thomas.

You have Anita Hill, a woman who has gone to Yale Law School, certainly
one of the finest law schools in this country, and I'm sure as its graduate,
you accept that. She's obviously quite bright. You have certainly stated in
past a high regard for her. You've hired her in two positions of significant
trust and responsibility, gone through all the things—going through the
bar exam and all that, not easy tasks for anyone. She held those two
positions of high trust and responsibility, both in the Department of
Education and at the EEOC. She then went to a university where she is a
law professor and has done well enough to become tenured.

Holding that—not only the law degree, but the license to practice law—
something that she has worked extremely hard for for years, protected and
nurtured all this way through, added to her experience and all, why would
she come here and perjure herself, throw away all of that, for what? I mean,
what would she possibly get out of throwing all that away?

"Senator, I don't know," Thomas replied. "I know the Anita Hill
who worked for me, and the relationship that I've had with her from
time to time on the intermittent calls or the few visits over the years.
I don't know what's happened since 1983. All I know is that the
allegations are false and that I don't have a clue as to why she would
do this."

Later Hatch, the sharp-eyed senator from Utah, hinted at a possible
explanation—a difference in ideology. He asked Thomas whether they
had disagreed over Thomas's opposition to the use of quotas. Thomas
said that she was "adamant" in her espousal of quotas and would at
times get "a bit irate" about the issue. In fact, Anita Hill's political
beliefs were vastly different from Thomas's, but no one seemed then
to have a clear concept about her quietly held convictions favoring
rights for minorities and women. Other than the point made by Hatch
about quotas the Republicans failed to exploit Hill's politics as an
issue. They had been busy quarrying for information with which to
bash Hill, but they kept coming up with misleading material such as
tawdry verbiage from *The Exorcist* rather than the facts.

Leahy also attempted to apply some basic logic to the the seeming
paradox befuddling the senators, which was that each witness categorically claimed to be telling the truth. Had Thomas tortured Hill with
running commentaries about the obscene or not?

Leahy constructed a hypothetical incident:

A robbery takes place, armed robbery, sir, and two people standing there, two witnesses see it. And one says, "That robber was tall." The other one says, "No, that robber was short." Well, the fact is the robbery took place. Everybody, including the victim, agrees the robbery took place. But you have two people, honest people standing there and saying, one says, "By God, that was a tall robber." And the other one says, "No, it was a short robber." But the robbery takes place. And we can understand that. And we can understand the difference of view in how somebody might observe an event.

But here it's like two ships in the night. I mean, you seem to be diametrically opposed, certainly in your testimony and Anita Hill's. I think we would both agree that on the basic substance of what we're talking about here, you're diametrically opposed. . . .

Then we have one of two possibilities, obviously. One of you is not telling the truth or is there any possibility that the both of you were seeing the same thing, both of you were seeing the robbery but seeing it entirely differently. Which is it? Is it that one of you absolutely is not telling the truth or one of you—or both of you rather—are viewing the same events differently?

"Senator, I'm not going to get into analyzing that. I will just simply say that these allegations are false. They were false when the FBI informed me of them. When they were subsequently changed to additional allegations, they were false. And they continue to be false," Thomas replied, refusing to be drawn in by Leahy.

Other tactics were employed by Senator Heflin, who had faltered so badly in his earlier questioning of the nominee. He evidently thought he might be more successful by responding to Hatch's invocation of the Long Dong Silver court case and the pubic hairs of *The Exorcist*. He was going to point out that if this information had been available to Hill, it also had been available to Thomas.

"Now, let me ask you," Heflin said in his Alabama drawl, "did you read this case of the Tenth Circuit that involved this Long John Silver?"

The senator seemed not to understand, or to want to understand, that the central character in the discussion of pornography these past two days was not a pirate with a seafood restaurant chain but an actor of sorts with a penis so long that it hung to his knees.

"Senator, this is the first I've heard of it—and I have not read it," Thomas said, referring to the court case and not correcting the senator's misnomer for the pornography star.

"The term 'Long John Silver,' or whatever else might be given to it, I've been told that there is a movie, a pornographic movie, in regards to it. Have you ever heard of the name of that—"

"No, Senator."

Heflin could hardly frame his questions. The paradox, the pornography, and the politics of this second round of hearings seemed to have overwhelmed him.

"Now, this issue of pubic hair in Coke, did you read the book, *The Exorcist?*" he asked.

"No, Senator," Thomas continued with his curt replies.

"Quite a few people have read it, haven't they—from what I understand? I haven't read it, but—"

Howell Heflin was said to have been quite a trial lawyer in his day. He had used his six-foot-three-inch frame and two hundred and fifty pounds to great effect in the courtroom, winning acquittals with elaborate theatrics. But the Senate Caucus Room was not the same kind of forum as an Alabama courtroom, where he had all the time in the world to build his case. He had done a good job with Thomas in the first set of hearings. But this time his questioning had grown inept and clumsy, much like his questioning of Oliver North in that same room four years earlier. (He was remembered in that case for his much-reported comment about North's buxom secretary Fawn Hall that suggested she may have smuggled documents in her brassiere.) Of course, like the other Democrats, he felt hamstrung by the politics, fearful that he would offend those of his constituents who supported Clarence Thomas if he was too harsh with him.

Heflin, a cigar smoker who left his lighted stogies on the windowsill on his way into the hearing room, asked Thomas if he still refused to answer personal questions.

"Oh, absolutely, Senator," Thomas replied. "I will not be further humiliated by this process. I think that I have suffered enough. My family has suffered enough. I think that I have attempted to address all of the questions with respect to my relationship with Ms. Hill in the workforce. And I think enough is enough."

The senator's response was classic Heflin.

"I had an old trial lawyer tell me one time, Judge, that if you've got the facts on your side, argue the facts to the jury. If you've got the law on your side, argue the law to the judge. If you've got neither, confuse the issue with other parties."

Biden, the third in the trio of Democrats designated to question Thomas, had a final matter he wanted to discuss with the nominee. He wanted to address Senator Hatch's diatribe about the liberal groups plaguing the nomination.

"Judge, let me make sure I understand one thing. Do you believe that interest groups went out and got Professor Hill to make up a story, or do you believe Professor Hill had a story, untrue from your perspective, that, as referred to here, groups went out and found? Which do you believe?"

Thomas adopted Hatch's conspiracy theory.

"Senator, I believe that someone, some interest group, I don't care who it is, in combination, came up with this story and used this process to destroy me."

"Got Professor Hill to say—to make up a story?" Biden asked.

"I believe that, in combination, this story was developed or concocted to destroy me," Thomas repeated. He did not speculate as to who comprised the combination.

Now, at the end of a day of outrageous tactics on the part of the Republicans, the committee's two renowned liberals, Kennedy and Metzenbaum, had a chance to speak. Would they attempt to redeem the Democrats' performance, to inject some balance into the proceedings?

"Let me go down the line here," Biden said to his Democratic colleagues. "Anyone—Senator Kennedy, any questions?"

"No, Judge," Kennedy said to Thomas, "we just thank you for coming under extraordinarily difficult circumstances."

"Senator Metzenbaum?" Biden asked.

"I have no comment," was all that Metzenbaum could think to say.

But Alan Simpson still had some thoughts to get off his chest. As if the Republicans had not already gone far enough, Simpson was about to undertake an imitation of Wisconsin's infamous Senator Joseph McCarthy, whose tactics had included waving in the air bogus documents that he claimed proved various, vaguely specified allegations.

"What do we know about Professor Hill?" the Wyoming senator said, slipping again into his role as the committee's Shakespearean fool, sometimes uttering nonsense and sometimes hitting on the truth in a rambling soliloquy. "Not very much."

> I'm waiting for one hundred and five days [the amount of time Thomas had been under scrutiny as the nominee] of surveillance of Ms. Hill, and then we'll see, you know, who ate the cabbage, as we say out in the Wild West. This is an impossible thing.
>
> And now I really am getting stuff over the transom about Professor Hill. I've got letters hanging out of my pocket [Simpson said, flapping his jacket]. I've got faxes, I've got statements from her former law professors, statements from people that know her, statements from Tulsa, Oklahoma, saying, "Watch out for this woman." But nobody's got the guts to say that, because it gets all tangled up in this sexual harassment crap. I believe sexual harassment is a terrible thing. I had a [legislative] bill in a year ago doubling the penalties on sexual harassment. I don't need any test, don't need anybody to give me the saliva test on whether one believes more or less about sexual harassment. It's repugnant, it's disgusting in any form.
>
> So if we had one hundred and four days to go into Ms. Hill and find out about her character, her background, her proclivities, and all the rest, I'd feel a lot better about this system.
>
> And I'm talking about the stuff I'm getting from women in America who are sending me things, and especially women in Oklahoma. Oh, that will all become public. I said at the time [of the Senate debate on the second round of hearings] it would be destructive of her. And some said, "Well, isn't that terrible of Simpson, a menacing threat." It wasn't menacing, it was true, that she would come forward and she would be destroyed. She will [the senator said, addressing Thomas at the witness table], just as you have been destroyed. I hope you can both be rehabilitated.

The "stuff coming in over the transom" about Anita Hill was too bizarre and unbelievable even for the Republicans to use, although the staff of the Republican senators spent much of the weekend pursuing it. Faxes and telephone calls were coming in from former students of Hill at the ultraconservative Oral Roberts law school, an institution so unsuccessful that it had been sold. One student at the University of Oklahoma sent in a letter saying he had heard from other students there that Hill was a "feminist, a racist and an incompetent," in the words of one Republican aide. Reporters had found nothing but praise for Hill from her Oklahoma students. Hot to find anything derogatory, the Republicans tracked down this young man, who apparently was not a student of Hill, at a football stadium where he was watching the Texas-Oklahoma game. But he wasn't much help to the Republicans after all. He said that the students to whom he referred had refused to come forward.

A major part of the effort by Republican staffers on the committee to find dirt about Hill was aimed at trying to verify what came to be known as the pube affidavit. A former Oral Roberts student actually signed an affidavit saying that he and two other students had received graded papers from Hill with little pubic hairs between the pages. How they knew the hairs were pubic in origin is not clear. But this charge caused great excitement in the Republican camp, where it was regarded as political dynamite. Officials at the White House and the Justice Department were advised, and these high-level public servants urged on the Republican staffers. The one student who signed the affidavit had been tracked down while hunting in the Rocky Mountains. But the other two refused to cooperate, even though Senator Alan Simpson agreed personally to call the father of one of them. Without corroboration, the pube affidavit had to go unused.

Other Oral Roberts students described Hill as an ardent feminist. This description of Hill, who did endorse women's rights in a soft, nonideological fashion, was accurate from these students' extremely conservative perspective.

The Republicans kept busy chasing down other nebulous rumors as well. A woman lawyer in Tulsa faxed in a letter saying that she had a friend who claimed to have prepared Hill for her testimony all through the month of August. Another person had overheard a comment in a bar by someone who had supposedly said: "Gee, isn't Anita doing much better now than she did three weeks ago at her mock hearing?" Another claimed to have received a phone call from Kate Michelman before the Hill story broke saying that her organization, the National Abortion Rights Action League, had been working on Hill since July. None of this could be substantiated.

Senator Simpson, having attempted to destroy Anita Hill with innuendo, proceeded to go to work on Angela Wright.

Wright had been waiting all day in the Washington office of her lawyer, expecting to testify. Judiciary Committee staffers called frequently, warning her she could be called at any moment. In the morning two FBI agents, both women, had come by to question her. Wright recalled later that they asked a lot of perfunctory and general questions, until finally her lawyer got frustrated and asked them, "Don't you want to find out why we're here? Don't you want to ask about these proceedings?" The lawyer finally took over the questioning, while the agents took notes.

Meanwhile, a debate was raging among the Democrats about whether to call Wright at all. They were concerned about her poor employment record and even more concerned about intimations from the Republicans that they had something on Wright that would embarrass the Democrats if they called her. In addition, Hill's lawyers were also arguing hotly against calling Wright. Hill's camp thought that Wright, who had a history of being mercurial, would be associated with Hill, who had a history of being reliable. Although there were no connections between the two women other than their willingness to testify against Thomas, Hill's advisers made the judgment call that it would be better not to have any possibly questionable testimony from Wright. They also seemed to be concerned that Wright, because of her statements that Thomas's behavior had never really seriously affected her, might make Hill look overly sensitive. The Hill camp was putting heavy pressure on sympathetic Democrats on the committee to keep off the stand the one person, however flawed, who could add backing to her story.

Simpson seemed to have caught wind of the Democrats' hesitation.

He told Thomas as he continued his soliloquy that "Angela Wright will soon be with us—we think. But now we're told that Angela Wright has what we used to call in the legal trade 'cold feet.' Now, if Angela Wright doesn't show up to tell her tale of your horrors, what are we to determine about Angela Wright? Did you fire her? And if you did, what for? You said that."

"I indicated, Senator," Thomas replied, "I summarily dismissed her. And this is my recollection. She was hired to reinvigorate the public affairs operation at EEOC. I felt her performance was ineffective and the office was ineffective. And the straw that broke the camel's back was a report to me from one of the members of my staff that she referred to another male member of my staff as a faggot."

"As a faggot," Simpson repeated.

"And that's inappropriate conduct and that's a slur and I was not going to have it," Thomas said.

That was enough for Simpson.

"And so that was the end of Ms. Wright who's now going to come and tell us perhaps about more parts of the anatomy, I'm sure of that—and a totally discredited—and we just [may as] well get to the nub of things here—totally discredited witness who does have cold feet."

Then Simpson added to his senatorial parody of the Shakespearean fool by quoting the bard himself—and got it wrong.

"Well . . . you know all of us have been through this stuff in life, but never to this degree. I've done my old stuff about my past and shared that. I won't get into those old saws, but I tell you I do [think] Shakespeare would love this. This is all Shakespeare. This is about love and hate and cheating and distrust and kindness and disgust and avarice and jealousy and envy—all those things that make that remarkable bard read today. But, boy, I tell you one came to my head and I just went and got it out of the back of the book, *Othello*. Read *Othello* and don't ever forget this line. 'Good name in man and woman dear, my Lord'—remember this scene—'is the immediate jewel of their souls. Who steals my purse steals trash, T'is something, nothing. T'was mine, t'is his and has been slave to thousands. But he that filches from me my good name robs me of that which not enriches him and makes me poor indeed.' What a tragedy! What a disgusting tragedy!"

Thomas seemed to wince as Simpson spoke. The parallels to Thomas were perfect, and completely misunderstood by Simpson. The lines that the senator quoted were not those of Othello, the black tragic hero of the play, but of Iago, the scheming villain, who was falsely trying to convince Othello that he was telling the truth.

The second day of hearings had been a good one for Thomas and, thanks to Hatch, Specter and Simpson, a bad one for Hill. Thomas seemed to be recovering nicely after Hill's shattering testimony of the day before. The third and final day of the hearings would be one that included dramatic support for Hill's story and the most memorably audacious testimony of the hearings. The Judiciary Committee, although it had chances, did not extricate itself from the fiasco of its own making.

The hearings resumed Sunday, October 13, with corroboration of what Hill had said from no fewer than four impressive witnesses, all of them respected citizens. Three of these witnesses—Susan Hoerchner, a workmen's compensation judge in Norwalk, California, who had gone to Yale with Hill; John W. Carr, a partner in a well-known New York law firm who had dated Hill when she was at the EEOC; and Ellen M. Wells, a project manager for the American Public Welfare Association in Washington—testified that Hill had told them while she was working for Thomas in Washington that she was being harassed by her boss. The fourth, Joel Paul, a law professor at American University in Washington, testified that Hill had told him in 1987 that she had been sexually harassed by her supervisor at the EEOC.

The Republicans, who for once seemed nervous about questioning the witnesses too closely, failed to press Hoerchner about her initial statement made to committee investigators several days earlier. She had stated that Hill had told her she was being harassed in the spring of 1981, when Hill was still in private practice and before she worked for Thomas. In her public testimony Sunday, Hoerchner said she did not remember the date, but that it was after Hill went to work for Thomas because she mentioned his first name. Democratic committee staffers chalked up the discrepancy to the likelihood that Hoerchner had confused her dates about this decade-old conversation with Hill.

These four witnesses also tried to explain to the row of fourteen male senators on the committee why a woman would not report behavior such as that described by Hill and how she could have remained on friendly terms with her tormentor after severing the professional relationship.

"Well," said Wells, "when you're confronted with something like that, you feel powerless and vulnerable, and unless you have a private income, you have no recourse. And since this is generally done in privacy, there are no witnesses, and so it's your word, an underling, against that of a superior, someone who is obviously thought well of or they would not have risen to the position that they hold. And so if you hope to go forward and, by going forward, move out from under their power and control, you sometimes have to put up with things that no one should be expected to put up with."

Wells also recounted some of her own experience as a black professional woman. She told the senators about what she did to survive and,
by extension, what many others like her had to do.

"It is something that I know my mother told me, and I'm sure
Anita's mother told her: When you leave, make sure you leave friends
behind, because you don't know who you may need later on. And so
you at least want to be cordial. I know I get Christmas cards from
people that I don't see from one end of the year to the other, and quite
frankly, do not wish to," Wells said, eliciting laughter from the audience in the Caucus Room, which still was jammed with spectators,
reporters, and television crews. "And I also return their cards and will
return their calls. And these are people who have insulted me and done
things which have perhaps degraded me at times, but there are things
that you have to put up with. And being a black woman, you know you
have to put up with a lot, and so you grit your teeth and you do it."

Wells testified that she, too, had been the victim of sexual harassment, and had done nothing.

"You do ask yourself, what did I do? And so you try to change your
behavior because it must be me, I must be the wrong party here. And
then I think you perhaps start to get angry and frustrated. But there's
always that sense of being powerless. And you're also ashamed. I
mean, what can you tell your friends and family because they ask you,
well, what did you do? And so you keep it in; you don't say anything.
Or if someone says, 'Well, then you should go forward,' you have to
think again, well, how am I going to pay the phone bill if I do that?
And yes, perhaps this job is secure, but maybe they'll post me in an
office in a corner with a telephone and *The Washington Post* to read
from nine to five, and that won't get me anywhere. So you're quiet and
you're ashamed and you sit there and you take it."

Joel Paul bolstered Hill's credibility by saying that she had supported Robert Bork's nomination to the court in 1987. (In fact, Hill
said later in an interview that she had not endorsed Bork, who had
taught her at Yale law school, but had been critical of the Democrats'
attacks on him during the confirmation process.)

None of the four witnesses had actually seen the harassment described by Hill. But their testimony demolished the theory developed
by Hatch and adopted by Thomas that Hill had "concocted" her
testimony in a conspiracy with the anti-Thomas "interest groups" in

order to keep Thomas off the Supreme Court.

"If there was a plot afoot, it must have originated ten years ago," Senator Herb Kohl of Wisconsin, the junior Democrat on the committee, commented wryly.

To make the conspiracy theory pan out, one of two unbelievable scenarios must have occurred: Hill would have had to be spreading lies to her friends back in the early 1980s. Or all four witnesses must have agreed secretly with leaders of liberal groups to lie under oath before the Judiciary Committee.

The Republicans' case against Hill's credibility was in trouble. They had only one remaining theory to try to develop in their efforts to discredit Hill. This was the theory that she had fantasized her sexual life, including whatever happened between Thomas and her. The foundation of this theory had been built on the prospective testimony of two witnesses for Thomas scheduled to appear later in the day.

In the afternoon, a few hours into the Sunday hearings, Ted Kennedy decided that he was fed up with himself. He called one of his most trusted advisers and said he would not stay quiet anymore. The Democrats on the committee had been bombarded with complaints that they had done nothing to challenge Thomas or defend Hill from the Republican onslaught. Finally, the liberal from Massachusetts had decided to open his mouth.

"Some people just don't want to believe you," Kennedy said to the four Hill witnesses.

They have to understand that. They just don't want to believe you and they don't want to believe Professor Hill. That's the fact of the matter, and you may be detecting some of that in the course of the hearing and the questions this afternoon.

But I hope . . . that after this panel we're not going to hear any more comments, unworthy, unsubstantiated comments, unjustified comments about Professor Hill and perjury, as we heard in this room yesterday.

I hope we're not going to hear any more comments about Professor Hill being a tool of the various advocacy groups after we've heard from Ellen Wells and John Carr and Joel Paul, all who have volunteered to come forward after they heard about this in the newspapers, comments about individual groups and staffers trying to pursuade her.

I hope we're not going to hear a lot more comments about fantasy stories picked out of books and law cases after we've heard from this distinguished panel or how there have been attempts in the eleventh hour to derail this nomination. I hope we can clear this room of the dirt and innuendo that's been suggested [about] Professor Hill, as well, about over the transom information, about faxes, about proclivities.

We heard a good deal about character assassination yesterday. And I hope we're going to be sensitive to the attempts at character assassination on Professor Hill. They're unworthy. They're unworthy.

And, quite frankly, I hope we're not going to hear a lot more about racism as we consider this nominee. The fact is that these points of sexual harassment are made by an Afro-American against an Afro-American. The issue isn't discrimination and racism, it's about sexual harassment. And I hope we can keep our eye on that particular issue.

It was an articulate, hard-hitting speech, but it was too late. All it accomplished was to demonstrate just how effective Kennedy could have been if he had taken part in the hearings the previous two days.

Most informed people in 1991, whether or not they agreed with Kennedy's politics or his personal life, would have had to concede that he had been an outstanding senator for many of his nearly thirty years in office. He continued to rack up legislative accomplishments even through the Reagan years, never shying away from championing the causes of the oppressed. He had helped galvanize public opinion against the apartheid regime in South Africa. He had pushed into law civil rights and fair housing bills. He had led the successful attack against the Bork nomination. He also was the only member of the Judiciary Committee who had been willing to stand up and vote against David Souter, a decision that seemed vindicated in liberal eyes by the justice's initially conservative voting record.

The now silver-haired Kennedy had the most experienced staff in the Senate, whose salaries he supplemented out of his own pocket. Had he allowed those aides to pursue Anita Hill back in August when she first came to their attention, her charges against Thomas might have been made earlier and handled with a good deal more grace. Had he given his staff the green light to start an investigation, Anita Hill might well have burst upon the scene not only earlier but buttressed with supporting testimony that could have forced Thomas's withdrawal.

But this time Kennedy's already well-documented personal problems, exacerbated by the Palm Beach drinking and sex escapade on Easter weekend, had gotten in the way of his political responsibilities. The overindulgence in alcohol and lack of discipline in the senator's life showed in both his swollen facial features and his decrepit performance at the hearings. Sitting throughout at Chairman Biden's left hand, Kennedy had proved to be a tongue-tied embarrassment to himself rather than a moral beacon to others.

At the time that Anita Hill's friends were testifying under oath, she was sitting in the office of Charles Ruff, a Washington lawyer and former U.S. attorney. She was hooked up to a machine measuring her blood pressure, breathing and pulse rate, taking a polygraph test administered by Paul K. Minor, who had headed the FBI's polygraph division and trained FBI agents in the use of the device.

"Have you deliberately lied to me about Clarence Thomas?" Minor asked Hill.

"No," Hill replied.

"Are you fabricating the allegation that Clarence Thomas discussed pornographic material with you?"

"No."

"Are you lying to me about the various topics that Clarence Thomas mentioned to you regarding specific sexual acts?"

"No," Hill replied again.

Minor made a report on the polygraph test and his conclusion exculpated Hill. "There was no indication of deception to any relevant question," he wrote.

Minor and Charles Ogletree, Hill's lead lawyer, wasted no time in releasing the results of the lie-detector test. The Hill camp, now more coordinated, called a surprise press conference that became a tumultuous affair. The polygraphy, Ogletree told the media, was a response to the attacks on Hill's credibility by the Republicans. "Professor Hill had in my opinion to fish or cut bait," he said. In Ogletree's opinion, however, Thomas should not be required to take a similar test because it was not appropriate for a Supreme Court nominee to be subjected to that kind of treatment.

The Republicans heaped scorn on the polygraph tactic. Senator Hatch said it was "exactly what a two-bit slick lawyer would do," a comment that cut Ogletree to the core.

As a practical matter the lie-detector test, while not foolproof, went a long way toward establishing that Hill was not lying. That in combination with her supporting witnesses left the fantasy theory as the only viable explanation, other than the truth, for Hill's statements.

"I have never accused Anita Hill of lying," Senator John Danforth told reporters, carefully choosing his words. "A lie is an intentional statement."

In fact Danforth, the White House, and two lawyers working directly for Thomas had over the weekend been researching an obscure psychological disorder known as erotomania. Certain people with this disorder, and they are usually women, fantasize a romantic relationship with someone, often someone of power.

One of those who brought this possibility to the attention of the White House was Jamie Bush, a nephew of the President. During the hearings, Bush had dined with Jeffrey Satinover, a prominent Stamford, Connecticut, psychiatrist, who had made some riveting remarks. The psychiatrist had told the President's nephew that he had treated a couple of patients who had suffered from erotic delusions. Dr. Satinover said that he had been struck by the impression that neither Hill nor Thomas appeared to be lying; this disorder could be the explanation. He also had heard about the affidavit John Doggett had made stating that Hill had fantasized about him.

Bush was intrigued enough to immediately get on the telephone with the White House, and shortly thereafter Dr. Satinover found himself on an airplane to Washington. There he was directed to Danforth's offices, where another psychiatrist, Dr. Park Deitz from California, was also being consulted. Danforth's office, situated one floor below the Senate Caucus Room, had been serving as the base of operations during the hearings for the Thomas camp.

Satinover was interviewed by the two private lawyers who were advising Thomas. "They asked me about what the condition was, is it possible to assert that Anita Hill suffered from this," Dr. Satinover recalled later. The Stamford psychiatrist said it was impossible to diagnose Hill from a distance. While other psychiatrists have said that erotic delusions would be accompanied by other delusional disorders, Dr. Satinover did not. He maintained that a person could suffer from "erotomania" without showing other symptoms. He agreed, however, that the fantasies usually were romantic in nature, rather than being as sexually explicit as Hill's testimony. "This is one of the points that argues against it, it doesn't necessarily exclude it," he said.

The Hill camp was also consulting psychiatrists and was considering calling one or more as experts who would testify that it was not unusual for victims of sexual harassment to keep their difficulties secret; many never came forward with their accusations.

In the meantime, a bipartisan group of committee staffers was privately interviewing Rose Jourdain, Angela Wright's best friend. Jourdain, an older woman, was seriously ill and lying in a hospital bed at the Washington Hospital Center. She was the woman in whom Wright had confided about Thomas's untoward behavior. Her testimony would immeasurably improve Wright's credibility. But Wright had refused to give the committee staffers Jourdain's name, because she was sick. They had tracked her down anyway without Wright's help.

Jourdain had done a variety of things in her life. She was a writer who had authored a novel and a textbook. She had written and produced a television play. She had worked as a schoolteacher and, for two years, served as a speechwriter for Clarence Thomas. She had become a confidant of Wright's when they worked together at the EEOC, and curiously had been fired the same day. It was Jourdain's opinion that they were both fired because they were ideologically out of sync with the chairman.

The interview was another of those lopsided, last-minute scenes as no fewer than six committee lawyers and a court reporter huddled around a Senate speakerphone interviewing Jourdain, who was lying in her hospital bed with only her daughter at her side. In a telling exchange at the beginning of the interview, Jourdain was asked her name, address and telephone number. After she responded, with each word recorded in the transcript, the sick woman had a request of the staffers. "The only thing," Jourdain said, "I want to ask you is that my address and phone number will not be made public, will they?" "None of this will be made public," she was assured. Every news organization in the capital had the woman's particulars that night.

Jourdain described Wright as initially happy and enthusiastic about her job handling public relations at the agency. As time passed, however, Jourdain said that "she confided to me increasingly that she was a little uneasy and grew more uneasy with the chairman, because of comments she told me that he was making concerning her figure, her body, her breasts, her legs, how she looked in certain suits and dresses."

According to Jourdain, Thomas had often asked to meet with Wright in his office near the end of the day. Wright, nervous about what would occur, would ask Jourdain to wait for her until she came out of the chairman's office. Jourdain also confirmed that Wright had told her about Thomas's uninvited visit to her apartment.

She described one scene in particular that she remembered. Wright had walked into Jourdain's EEOC office, slammed the door shut and said, according to her friend," 'Do you know what he said to me?' And I said, 'No, what did he say to you?' You know, because it had gone on before." Jourdain recounted the gist of what Wright had said to her. "I think it had something to do with, ooh, you have very sexy legs, or something like you have hair on your legs and it turns me on, or something like that. I thought it was nutty, you know what I mean? It was that, but it was very unnerving to a young woman who is sitting there hearing this, you know."

Jourdain was asked by Barry Caldwell, who was on Senator Specter's staff, what she thought Wright's motivation was for coming forward.

"Based on what I know about her, I would tend to believe—no, I don't tend to believe, I absolutely believe that she heard this young black woman [Hill] on the television being raked over the coals, as though this experience that she was having was completely impossible, and you know, that a person in Clarence Thomas' position, black or white, would not have done this, and this woman was somehow coming from left field with some malicious agenda.

"And having had a similar experience, I believe that Angela would have felt it her bounden duty to go on record saying that, and she is a very religious, very morally strong person. You know, she is a person who believes very much in right and wrong."

Caldwell asked Jourdain, hopefully, if there were any negative qualities about Wright that "stick out in your mind. For instance, is she vindictive? Is she vengeful? What about flirtatious?"

"No," Jourdain said to all of these. But she did think of one criticism.

"She tends to spend an awful lot of time with her dog and treat it more as a human being. That is the only thing that I can think of. I have said to her, you know, like this dog gets as much care as a lot of human beings, but that is the only thing I could ever think of that I would say negative."

When Wright found out, while sitting in her lawyer's office in the Virginia suburbs of Washington expecting to be called to testify before the committee, that staffers had pursued Jourdain to her hospital bed, she became upset.

"Actually," she said later, "it reduced me to tears, because all I could think of is 'My God, how many people am I going to get involved in this because I dared to say something.' And it started to hit me that a lot of people want to stay out of this, and I may end up getting them involved in a big mess. Especially Rose is my best friend, my mom, my second mom and everybody, and being sick. I guess part of it, the tears, was because of the fury I felt that they would invade her privacy in her hospital room. I mean, is nothing sacred?"

There was one more woman who came forward to give the Judiciary Committee a view of Clarence Thomas that was different from that of his supporters. Sukari Hardnett, who had worked at the EEOC in 1985 and 1986 and served briefly on the chairman's personal staff, sent a letter to the committee that weekend saying that Thomas had given special attention to attractive female employees.

"If you were young, black, female and reasonably attractive . . . you were always at his beck and call, being summoned constantly, tracked down wherever you were in the agency and given special deference by others because of his interest," wrote Hardnett, who by 1991 was employed as a social worker in Washington.

In an interview, Hardnett recounted a strange incident that occurred in the EEOC chairman's office. Thomas, Hardnett said, had told her that he was looking for a wife and ordered her to summon another woman employee to the office. Then, Hardnett said, Thomas discussed male-female relations with the woman and also asked her if she wanted to have children. Hardnett said she witnessed this scene between Thomas and his employee, whom she did not identify.

Later Thomas told Hardnett, she said, that he was attracted to the woman but that he did not want to father any more chidren.

---

Over the weekend as the public melodrama played in the Senate Caucus Room, the Republicans were also busy behind-the-scenes, collecting their own affidavits. John Burke, a partner from the law firm of Wald, Harkrader & Ross, where Hill had worked, sent in a sworn statement that was critical of Hill. Burke stated that at the time of Hill's employment he was in charge of coordinating assignments of the young lawyers in the tax, general business, and real estate sections of the firm. He said that Hill had performed several assignments for him. Burke said that he had given Hill a negative performance evaluation and that he had told her it would be in her best interests to look for work elsewhere because her prospects at the Wald firm were limited.

Burke's statement contradicted what Donald Green, the Washington lawyer who had been a partner in Wald, Harkrader & Ross, already had told the Republicans about Hill's departure from the firm. Green's discussion of the matter had been made informally over the telephone, whereas Burke's recollection of Hill's performance had just been made formally in writing.

Burke's statement cast a shadow not only on Hill's past, but also on her testimony. Hill had stated that she had left the firm voluntarily. If she had lied about that, she possibly could have lied about the rest.

It also became the basis for a theory that the White House was trying to spread among the members of the press. Bill Kristol, Vice President Quayle's chief of staff, told reporters that the pro-Thomas theory of the case was that Hill had made up the story of her sexual harassment and told it to her friends in order to cover up for her own job failures. Then, the theory held, she had unwittingly been swept into making her complaints about Thomas public after Judge Susan Hoerchner told others what Hill had told her.

The Republicans were also consulting with a polygraph expert, one who had the additional specialty of evaluating non-verbal behavior. In other words, he studied people's gestures and mannerisms to determine if they were telling the truth. This gentleman told the Republican senators that he could determine when Hill was lying outright because she would lift the right side of her mouth. When she was merely dissembling, her eyes would roll upward, he claimed. Using these movements as clues, he said Hill was lying about departing voluntarily from her old law firm.

------------

After Hill's witnesses had finished testifying and Sunday afternoon was drawing to a close, the Judiciary Committee recessed in order to meet behind closed doors and decide how to proceed. Even at that hour, with the vote on Thomas only forty-eight hours away, the senators had not decided on which witnesses or what evidence they would consider before ceasing with the debacle they had created.

The senators, both Republican and Democrat, were tired and tense, and the meeting got a bit raucous. The Republicans were threatening to bring out their heavy ammunition, the pube affidavit and whatever marginal but nasty testimony they could muster about Hill or her supporters. They also wanted to subpoena Hill's personnel records from her old law firm. The Democrats countered by saying they wanted to bring in witnesses who could testify that Thomas liked to watch pornography. The result was a standoff, a bipartisan decision to ratify the ruling Biden had made on his own earlier in the hearings that the committee would not delve into the private lives of either Thomas or Hill.

The Hill team had to make some critical decisions as well. The next panel of witnesses scheduled to testify was a pro-Thomas group of four of his former employees. After that several character witnesses for Hill had been scheduled, to be followed by more witnesses for Thomas. But the Hill camp decided at the last minute against putting any more of their witnesses in the hot seat.

Hill's lawyers hesitated for several reasons as the inner politics of the hearings became increasingly intricate. They feared that this panel of Hill's friends would be interrogated by the Republicans as to why Hill had not told them about her experiences with Thomas. Another reason for the lawyers' decision was that they did not want some members of the panel to have to answer questions about whether or not they had any role in releasing information about Hill to the press.

Hill's lawyers also feared that questions would be asked and intimations made about the marital status and supposed sexual preferences of some on this panel of Hill's friends. The Republicans might possibly try to raise unfair implications about the sexuality of the unmarried women among them, and also of Hill herself. The basis for this fear was Senator Simpson's viciously ambiguous comment the day before about Hill's "proclivities." A man who would make that kind of comment in a public hearing was capable of of using more innuendo. Any woman, no matter how exemplary her life, could be vulnerable.

One member of the Hill team put it this way: "If you are a single woman in a political environment your sexual behavior will be subject to review. You will either be promiscuous or you'll be a lesbian. Those are the choices, you know. Women who run for office, whatever they are, in subtle or unsubtle ways get attacked. If they are married it is how strong is their marriage, or if they are divorced, who created the divorce?"

In the end, the Hill team decided that it was unnecesary to take any of these risks. The highly skilled lawyers thought they had won, that they had successfully presented the case of the Oklahoma law professor. They thought they had proven Hill's veracity for all the Senate to see. They had, after all, managed to make two seemingly convincing points that day—one with the panel of four people confirming that Hill had told them about the allegations and the other with the results of the lie detector test. When a committee staffer warned one of the lawyers that the public did not necessarily agree that Hill had won the day, he was told that his perception of the case was biased because he was a man. Hill's lawyers didn't seem to understand that the Judiciary Committee forum was not a court of law; it was a place where raw emotion and baseless innuendo and sexist prejudice could be as important as evidence.

The result was to cede the entirety of Sunday evening and night to the Thomas partisans. This was prime time for television, so that the millions of Americans watching in their homes would be getting another strong dose of the pro-Thomas case. The only possible exception was the testimony of Angela Wright.

Wright was still in her lawyer's office waiting to be called. But the Republicans were intimating to the committee Democrats that they would attempt to discredit Wright. "They kept on walking around saying we've got a stack of stuff on her a mile high," one staffer said. Most of the Democrats bought what appeared to have been essentially a bluff. Certainly, Wright's poor employment record did not help her credibility, but it did not destroy it, either. The Republicans never established that they had more definite evidence with which to damage Wright. Wright also had going for her the official statement made to

the committee by Rose Jourdain. The decision about Wright's testifying was probably the most important of the whole hearings. The
question of whether more than one alleged victim of Thomas sexual
harassment existed was absolutely critical in many senators' minds.

According to an aide close to Senator Biden and familiar with his
thinking, the committee chairman was the one Democrat who fought
to bring Wright to testify. Biden understood how important the words
of the "second woman" could be, but he could do little with the
thirteen other committee senators united against him. Biden also knew
about the doubts expressed by the Hill camp.

Wright herself, having been ordered to Washington against her will,
felt that she had to clear her name and straighten out the speculations
being made about her testimony. In a later interview, she said that she
wanted to testify even though it might have been difficult. Thomas was
lying when he said she had called anyone a faggot, she insisted. But
she had watched on television the grilling that the Republicans had
given Hill and was well aware of what could be in store for her. In the
end, Wright agreed to a compromise put to her by the committee. She
would not have to testify, but the statement she had made to the
committee Thursday, and Jourdain's statement as well, would be
incorporated into the hearings' official record and eventually released
to the media. In essence, however, the result would be that Wright was
no longer a factor in the outcome of the hearings. Written testimony
was far less dramatic, or convincing, than live testimony. The Democrats had allowed themselves to be intimidated, sidelined at a crucial
point in the game.

As it worked out, the four witnesses for Anita Hill were followed
Sunday evening by four passionate witnesses for Thomas. They all
were black women who had worked for him at the EEOC and said they
never had observed any untoward conduct by the chairman toward
Hill or anyone else for that matter.

The women's testimony, which the Republican senators dragged on
for hours, was not remotely comparable in evidentiary value to the
four witnesses for Hill, even though the two panels were balanced off
against each other. These supporters of Thomas were essentially character witnesses, strong ones, but none had any independent knowledge
of what had or had not occurred. Three of those who testified for Hill,

while not able to prove what happened, could corroborate that she had made her charges about Thomas contemporaneously with the alleged events.

Nevertheless, the Thomas panel was effective. While the Hill witnesses were mostly reserved types, the Thomas witnesses were down-to-earth folks who may have seemed more convincing to the television audience. The Clarence Thomas they described was an entirely different person from the man about whom Hill and Wright had talked.

Diane Holt, Thomas's personal secretary for six years and someone who worked, as she put it, "cheek to cheek, shoulder to shoulder" with him at both the Department of Education and the EEOC, said, "The Chairman Thomas that I have known for ten years is absolutely incapable of the abuses described by Professor Hill." Adding to the weight of Holt's testimony was the fact, which was attested to by both Holt and Hill, that the two women had been good friends.

J.C. Alvarez, a Chicago businesswoman who had worked for four years as a special assistant to Thomas, chose to attack Hill personally. The Anita Hill who had testified Friday was not the same person she had known in Washington, Alvarez said.

"On Friday, she played the role of a meek, innocent, shy Baptist girl from the South who was the victim of this big bad man. . . . The Anita Hill that I knew and worked with was nothing like that. She was a very hard, tough woman. She was opinionated, she was arrogant, she was a relentless debater. And she was the kind of woman who always made you feel like she was not going to be messed with. . . . She was aloof, she always acted as if she was a little bit superior to everyone, a little holier than thou."

Thomas always was proper in the office, Alvarez said.

"Because we were friends outside of the office, or perhaps in private, I might have called him Clarence. But in the office, he was Mr. Chairman. You didn't joke around with him. You didn't become too familiar with him, because he would definitely let you know that you had crossed the line."

Because there was no time for a dinner break given the flood of testimony, Chairman Biden had ordered fifteen pizzas delivered to the committee's anteroom for the senators and staffers. The fast food apparently was difficult to digest, because loud, undisguised burps erupted with some regularity over the committee's loudspeaker system from the microphone in front of Senator Thurmond. The witnesses ignored these extraneous sound effects.

Nancy Fitch, a Temple University professor and also a former Thomas assistant, testified that Hill's allegations were an insult to Thomas's considerable intelligence as well as his great moral character.

"If these allegations, which I believe to be completely unfounded and vigorously believe unfounded, were true, we would be dealing not only with venality, but with abject stupidity, with a person shooting himself in the foot having given someone else the gun to use at any time. There is no way Clarence Thomas, C.T., would callously, venally hurt someone."

Phyllis Berry Myers, another former assistant, was glowing in her praise. "Clarence Thomas's behavior toward Anita Hill was no more, no less than his behavior toward the rest of his staff. He was respectful, demanding of excellence in our work, cordial, professional, interested in our lives, in our career ambitions.

"I have known Clarence Thomas in times of his darkest moments and in his shining triumphs. I've had a role in most of his confirmation battles, none of which have ever been easy. In that capacity, I have been privy to the most intimate details of his life. In all that time, never, never has anyone raised allegations such as Anita has."

Myers also said she believed that Hill had a "more than professional interest" in Thomas and that when her desire for romance was not reciprocated, her feelings were hurt.

The hour was late—past eleven o'clock at night, when John M. Doggett III, the lawyer from Texas, and Charles Kothe, the former Oral Roberts law school dean, finally took the stand along with two other witnesses for Thomas. Kothe and Doggett were the basis for the Republicans' theory that Hill had fantasized that Clarence Thomas had harassed her.

But Kothe, on questioning from Senator Arlen Specter, repudiated his own use of that very word. In fact, Kothe said, he was unhappy now about this verbal choice in his initial statement and had been careful not to repeat it.

Senator Specter persisted. "Well, Professor Kothe, was there anything that you could point to in Professor Hill's conduct which would lead you in a—either an evidentiary or a feeling way to that conclusion of fantasy?"

"No," Kothe said. "I think perhaps my selection of words there was probably unfortunate. I've never seen Anita Hill in a situation where she wasn't a decent person, a dignified person, a jovial person. I've never seen her in a situation where actually you would say she was fantasizing in that sense. I almost regret that I had used that in my first reaction."

That left Doggett as the pillar of the only remaining explanation the Republicans could come up with for Hill's testimony.

After being admonished by Chairman Biden to be brief, the black lawyer proceeded to give the committee his life's history and goals in a 2,800-word statement that emphasized his own struggles to overcome discrimination. All over the country, people falling asleep in front of their television sets were jolted awake by this tall, quick-tongued young lawyer.

Specter asked Doggett to read a section from his original affidavit to the committee in which he had said that based on a brief conversation with Hill at a going-away party he had the "feeling" that "she was somewhat unstable and that in my case, she had fantasized about my being interested in her romantically."

Continuing with his affidavit, Doggett read:

It was my opinion at the time and is my opinion now that Ms. Hill's fantasies about my sexual interest in her were an indication of the fact that she was having a problem with being rejected by men she was attracted to. Her statements and actions in my presence during the time when she alleges that Clarence Thomas harassed her were totally inconsistent with her current descriptions and are, in my opinion, yet another example of her ability to fabricate the idea that someone was interested in her when, in fact, no such interest existed.

Doggett also recounted the story about how he had come across Hill while he was out jogging and they had talked about getting together for dinner.

Even when I was jogging by her house and she said "Hi, John" and we had a conversation and she raised the issue of "Well, since we are neighbors, why don't we have dinner?" I tried to make it very clear that although I respected her as a person and as a fellow alumnus of Yale Law School and as somebody I thought was very decent, the only relationship I was interested in was a professional relationship. And as I stated in my affidavit, she said: "Well, what would be a good time?" I was in my jogging clothes, and so obviously I don't have a calendar with me. And I said: "Well, I will check my calendar, and I will get back to you." And I checked my calendar, and I said: "It looks like Tuesday will work. You get back to me if that will work, and let's talk about a place." Later on, after that dinner agreement arrangement fell through, she gave me a call and said: "What happened?" I said: "What do you mean what happened? I never heard from you." She said: "Well, I never heard from you." And apparently, we both had expected the other person to call to confirm.

At the end of that "I never heard from you," if I was interested in her, the logical response would have been: Well, since we didn't get together this time, let's do it again. There was no response, and there was a very awkward pregnant pause, and the conversation ended. And I never saw Anita Hill again until that going-away party, where she dropped that bombshell on me.

Although Specter congratulated Doggett on his "powerful" testimony, his theories and his presentation were too much for Biden. Through the first two weeks of hearings in September and then these three excruciating days of additional hearings, the chairman had taken pains to be fair. Although he had voted against Thomas, reluctantly, he had always maintained a carefully neutral tone with the witnesses. He was so determined to be cordial to all that sometimes he appeared to have no opinion of his own about anything. Now, however, Chairman Biden spoke up. Perhaps it was the lateness of the hour and the accumulation of the hearings' myriad aggravations, mishaps, frivolities, and disasters, but Doggett was more than he could take.

"Mr. Doggett, I don't doubt what you said. But I—I kind of find it equally bizarre that you would be so shocked," said a suddenly animated Biden. To the committee chairman, the behavior that Doggett ascribed to Hill was entirely imaginable in himself or anyone else.

"I know some men—maybe I'm just accustomed to being—when I was younger, being turned down more than you were," Biden said, glaring down at the witness from his central position among the senators. "But some men sit and say, 'Gees, I wonder if she's just bashful. That's why she did that. That was the reason for the pregnant pause,' or 'I wonder if she really wants me to call her back. She didn't say "Don't call me again." She didn't say "I don't want to hear from you again."' Maybe—and then you see her a little while later at a party, and she's leaving town. And you walk up to her and you say, 'You know, can I talk to you?' and she says, 'Yeah.' And you walk over to a corner of the party and say, 'You know, you really shouldn't let guys down like that. You led me to believe that you wanted to go out with me. You shouldn't do that to women—or to men.'

"And if she turned around and said, 'You're fantasizing. How could you ever think that? What an outrageous? You must be demented. You must be crazy?' I don't think that's how normal people function," Biden declared.

The committee chairman was so wound up he would hardly let the loquacious Doggett get a word in edgewise.

"How one can draw the conclusion from that kind of exchange that this is a woman who is fantasizing, this is a woman who must have a problem because she's turned—are you a psychiatrist?" Biden asked abruptly.

"Senator, I'm trying to follow your question"— Doggett sputtered.

"No. Are you a psychiatrist?" Biden insisted.

—"but I may have to ask you to restate it," Doggett continued.

Biden wanted an answer. "No. My question is: Are you a psychiatrist?"

"Absolutely not," Doggett replied finally.

"Are you a psychologist?" Biden pursued the idea.

"Absolutely not," Doggett conceded.

"Well, how from that kind of exchange can you draw the conclusion that she obviously has a serious problem?"

Biden was getting worked up. "You told her—you've told her, her comments were totally uncalled for and completely unfounded. Balderdash!" Biden exclaimed.

Biden asked whether there were other instances where Hill had accused him of leading her on. There were none, Doggett eventually conceded. Biden was so hot that Thurmond had to step in and demand that Doggett be allowed to answer. But Biden would not quit.

"There is someplace in there where you say that this must mean she's used to—this is a complex from being rejected by men. You say the fact—you believe, 'Ms. Hill's fantasies about my sexual interest in her were an indication of the fact she was having a problem with being rejected by men she was being attracted to.'

"It seems to me," said Biden to the general merriment of the exhausted audience that had remained in the Caucus Room even though the hour was now past midnight, "that is a true leap in faith or ego, one of the two."

Then there came the following exchange:

DOGGETT: Would you like for me to respond to your—to your question, sir?

BIDEN: I'd like you to say anything you want. I mean, I truly would because I'm having trouble understanding this one, and I won't say any more.

DOGGETT: I understand that.

THURMOND: And take your time, and say what you please.

DOGGETT: Thank you, sir.

BIDEN: As long as you want.

DOGGETT: I appreciate your concern.

BIDEN: My confusion, not concern.

DOGGETT: I assumed you were concerned, also.

BIDEN: No, I'm not concerned.

DOGGETT: I appreciate your confusion. I will do what I can to try to clarify it. A, I clearly reacted to this event differently than you would, and I respect our differences in opinions. B, there were a number of occasions where Gil Hardy and others, who were black Yale Law School graduates, made an attempt to bring together those of us who were in town, including people like me who were not practicing law and who were not involved in the political process, so that we could have social fellowship, and we had parties and other get-togethers.

I observed from a distance—and I'm not a psychiatrist—I'm not an expert—I'm just a man—Anita Hill attempting to be friendly with men, engage them in conversation, initiate conversation, elongate conversations and people talking with her and eventually going away.

BIDEN: Can you name any of those men for us, for the record?

DOGGETT: Sir, eight—almost nine years have gone by. If she had filed a sexual harassment charge—
BIDEN: No, that's not the issue.

Doggett conceded he could remember no names.

By the time Biden was through with Doggett, there seemed little reason left to take the fantasy theory seriously, if there ever had been. Indeed, Dr. Satinover, the Connecticut psychiatrist, said in an interview that after watching Doggett's testimony he concluded there was little basis for his theory that Hill might be suffering from "erotomania."

But the Democrats were not finished with the Texas lawyer. They had had little to grasp onto in three days of hearings, and they were not ready to let go of this opportunity for cross-examination.

Senator Metzenbaum proceeded to ambush Doggett much as the Republicans had ambushed Hill. The senator read from another document, not Doggett's affidavit, but a transcript of a statement made under questioning by committee aides. According to this transcript, committee lawyers informed Doggett that several women had come forward to charge him with sexual harassment. These included a young woman who said that when she was nineteen, on her first day on the job in an office in which Doggett worked, he had confronted her in front of an elevator, kissed her on the mouth and told her she would enjoy working with him. The young woman said there were other similar instances of Doggett harassing her.

Doggett, outraged, denied knowing the woman or ever having behaved in such a manner. He said the facts she had presented were wrong.

"I did not do any of the things that she alleged, and, in fact, the first time any of these issues were raised was the day before I was supposed to come here, eight and a half years later. I knew when I put my information into the ring that I was saying: I am open season. For anybody to believe that on the first day of work for a woman working in the Xerox room, who is 19 years old, a 33-year-old black man would walk up to a 19-year-old white girl and kiss her on the mouth as the first thing that they did—whoever believes that really needs psychiatric care."

Asked how he knew she was white, Doggett said he had asked a friend about her.

When Biden returned to the room after a brief absence, he was chagrined to discovered what Metzenbaum was up to.

"I'm pissed off, sir," Doggett told him, and the chairman this time was sympathetic.

When Metzenbaum referred to other charges of harassment against Doggett, Biden stepped in and ruled the line of questioning out of order.

"Let the record show," Biden said, "and I am stating it—there is absolutely no evidence, none—no evidence in this record, no evidence before this committee that you did anything wrong with regard to anything—with regard to anything, none. I say that as the chairman of this committee. I think your judgment about women is not so hot. Whether or not people fanatasize or don't, you and I disagree in that."

Doggett had some friendly questioning from Republican senators. But then Senator Leahy wanted a crack at him.

LEAHY: Now, based on such minimal contacts with Professor Hill, how could you conclude that she had fantasies about your sexual interest in her? Or do you just feel that you have some kind of a natural irresistibility?

DOGGETT'S WIFE: He does.

DOGGETT: Well, my wife says I do.

LEAHY: Mmm-hmm.

DOGGETT: And I won't argue with her.

LEAHY: Well, Anita Hill apparently doesn't say you do, though, Mr. Doggett. She doesn't even remember you.

DOGGETT: No. She didn't say that, sir.

LEAHY: She said she barely remembers you. When I asked her to describe you, she had some difficulty and thought that you were tall.

DOGGETT: I looked at Anita Hill's face when you folks mentioned my name. She remembers me, Senator. I assure you of that.

Leahy is ordinarily very straight: He is a New Englander, not given to great public expression of humor. But he, too, was having a hard time staying in character with this witness.

LEAHY: You have a remarkable insight into her. You're able to watch her face and know—and mentioned your name. By golly, John Doggett's name gets mentioned, this woman is wow! It's—it triggered a bell? Is that what you're saying? I mean, I don't understand.

No other witnesses had been challenged so successfully by the Democrats, but it hardly mattered. It was the early hours of Monday morning by the time Doggett had finished. Most people had gone to bed. Many of those still awake thought that Doggett's testimony had trivialized the Republicans' case and cast a final ridiculous atmosphere over the proceedings that had taken place in the Senate Caucus Room.

Senator Arlen Specter, though, the sharp prosecutor and the Republican who had pushed hardest for Doggett's appearance, was pleased for some inexplicable reason. "Don't you think that went well?" he remarked to a couple in the committee's anteroom immediately after the conclusion of the hearings.

# Chapter 19

The Thomas-Hill episode was not the first sexual harassment scandal to beset the nation. The capital experienced the first such scandal back in the 1860s; the tempest reached phenomenal proportions and should have served as a stern warning to the federal government to regulate the behavior of its bosses, who were then all men.

In 1864, three years into the Civil War, the government in Washington had found itself short of manpower. With men disappearing into the army, women were hired in significant numbers for the first time; seventy were signed up to work in the Treasury Department, where the government was issuing the first federal currency in a drastic effort to finance the war.

The boss of the Treasury numbering room, a man named S.M. Clark, insisted that his women employees, who were paid half the wages of men, purchase their jobs with sexual favors. The episode was chronicled in letters written by Thomas Walter, the architect who had just finished overseeing the completion of his design for the grand new Capitol dome.

"Things are truly awful," Walter wrote about the goings-on at the

Treasury in a letter to his wife, whom he had dispatched to Pennsylvania until the danger of a Confederate invasion had passed. Clark had been such a sexual scoundrel that twenty women had testified in affidavits to a congressional subcommittee that "they could only get their places or hold them by yielding to [his] embraces," the architect reported. Moreover, these and other embraces had been so vigorous that the talk was that "between forty and fifty of the women employed in Mr. Clark's department are about to increase the population," Walter wrote. "The corruptions of this place are dreadful; I cannot understand how any body can like to live here; it is a perfect Sodom."

The affair was investigated and Clark was charged "with doing wrong in office" and "having a fine time" with the "girls" under his employ. History has not made clear the fate of this Clark, although it is known that he still had his job a good six months after Walter described these events to his wife.

What is known beyond a shadow of a doubt, is that the federal government—although certainly distracted by the myriad other events that followed the War Between the States—overlooked the issue of sexual harassment in its offices and workplaces well into the next century. Even by 1991, though, when laws and regulations had been established prohibiting the practice of sexual harassment, members of the Senate Judiciary Committee seemed at times to be as obtuse about the issue as people had been in Clark's day. And many members of the Senate as a whole also failed to "get it" until calls from angry women engulfed their offices. Anita Hill's story touched the raw nerves of millions of women who had endured the injuries and insults of living with harassment in a society in which men still possess most of the power and can use it for sexual purposes.

The fact that sexual harassment on the job was illegal had not yet sunk into the collective conscience of the male-dominated Senate.

In the early 1980s, when Hill said she was harassed, she would have had a much more difficult time proving her case than in 1991. The law on sexual harassment had been changing dramatically.

It was not until 1964 that the legal foundation for objecting to sexual harassment was laid down as part of the Civil Rights Act. Title VII of that act prohibits an employer from discriminating "against any individual with respect to his compensation, terms, conditions or privileges of employment, because of such individual's race, color, religion, sex, or national origin."

Women's groups began to publicize the issue of sexual harassment in the 1970s; but it was not until 1979 that the Office of Personnel Management issued a government-wide memorandum that defined sexual harassment and warned that such conduct was unacceptable. The warning had no legal teeth, though. Finally, the following year, the Equal Employment Opportunity Commission, under the chairmanship of Eleanor Holmes Norton, issued guidelines declaring it illegal to sexually harass someone on the job.

The EEOC rules made it clear that it was no longer legal to harass an employee by directly asking for sexual favors in exchange for a promotion or simply for job security. It also was no longer legal to harass an employee by making sexual advances or remarks that create an intimidating, hostile, or offensive work environment.

In simple English, this meant, for instance, that it was against the law for a boss to demand a kiss from his secretary or for a colleague to torture another with unwelcome sexual talk. Men could no longer demand sex as part of women's job security. Women were given the right to work in a place free of offensive sexual attacks and remarks.

The outgoing officials of the Carter administration had put the sexual harassment rules into effect by the week following Ronald Reagan's election as President. They had guessed that the Republicans coming into power would have a far more conservative approach to the rights of women in the workplace.

The transition team that President-elect Reagan installed to give the EEOC a going-over was headed by Jay Parker and included the young Clarence Thomas, then making his foray into the Republican administration. Parker, the veteran black conservative, was only too happy to recommend restrictions on the scope of the agency whose mandate was to prevent discrimination in the workplace. Thomas, his political protégé, was equally amenable to the project. It would give Thomas an early initiation to the legal theory of sexual harassment, an issue that he did not then know would become a major part of his life.

In a memorandum that Thomas wrote for Parker— along with the one that the White House had passed on to the Senate with Parker's name obscured—he attacked an important point in the agency's new guidelines. Recommending that the guidelines as a whole be reexamined, he emphasized that one rule in particular should be jettisoned, the rule governing an employer's liability for sexual harassment perpetrated by a supervisor. Under the original EEOC guidelines, an employer would be held strictly liable for the harassment of a worker by a superviser. Without that rule, it would be difficult for someone to bring a forceful lawsuit against a company for failing to keep the work environment free of sexual problems.

In the final report on the EEOC authored by the Reagan team, including Thomas, the new guidelines were severely critiqued. The report complained that the guidelines would undoubtedly lead "to a barrage of trivial complaints against employers around the nation." The report also argued that the EEOC was overreaching its mandate. "The elimination of personal slights and sexual advances which contribute to an 'intimidating, hostile or offensive working environment' is a goal impossible to reach. Expenditure of the EEOC's limited resources in pursuit of this goal is unwise," the report advised.

In the end, realizing that sexual harassment was a workplace reality, the Reagan administration did not scuttle the guidelines. The EEOC's rules soon became standard across the country and workers, mainly women, began filing complaints against their employers alleging sexual harassment. Gradually, the law regarding sexual harassment matured.

Back at the dawn of the Reagan era, Thomas also didn't know that he would one day be in charge of the EEOC. During the years he chaired the EEOC, Thomas's views on affirmative action grew more conservative, but his opinion about the need to protect workers against sexual harassment changed in the other direction. He began to recognize sexual harassment as a serious problem.

One EEOC lawyer hypothesized that Thomas, upon reflecting on the issue, drew a parallel between racial and sexual harassment. Another said that the reason for Thomas's changing his tune may have been the influence of his vice chairman, Ricky Silberman. This was not the first time that Thomas had changed his views radically on an issue; he was the same man who had swung from antiestablishment militancy to radical conservatism, from Catholicism to fundamentalism, from reading Malcolm X to reading Thomas Sowell.

What remained the outstanding mystery, though, was how it came to be that Anita Hill accused Thomas of repeatedly violating the same standards of conduct his agency was in charge of enforcing. If Hill's charges were true, could it have been possible that Thomas didn't realize that repeated talk about pornographic movies amounted to sexual harassment? Could Thomas have thought that sort of crude and inept conduct with which Hill charged him was appealing? In the early 1980s when Hill worked for Thomas, the sexual harassment standards were still new and the law behind them still in a fledgling stage. But even then, unwelcome sexual advances of any kind were considered unacceptable in the workplace.

If Hill had taken legal action back then, though, she would have had difficulty. A victim of sexual harassment needed a corroborating witness—someone who had observed the conduct—to legally prove a case. A woman's word alone, even if it was believed, was not sufficient to make a legal case.

It wasn't until mid-1983, when Hill had decided to leave the EEOC, that "verbal sexual abuse" was legally recognized as a form of sexual harassment in a federal court ruling. And it would not be until 1986 that the Supreme Court would confirm the EEOC guidelines.

By 1985, two years after Hill had quit working at the EEOC, Thomas had changed his opinion enough to go out of his way to bolster the law against sexual harassment—with the important exception of holding an employer automatically liable. Thomas's opportunity came when a case concerning sexual harassment was taken on appeal to the Supreme Court. The case had been decided in favor of a woman bank employee, Mechelle Vinson, by the U.S. Court of Appeals for the District of Columbia.

But three conservative judges on the appellate court at that time—including Robert Bork and Antonin Scalia—had issued a strong dissenting opinion. The conservative judges argued that harassment on the job did not violate antidiscrimination laws. Judge Bork belittled the idea of sexual harassment being made illegal, saying that the result would be employers being held liable for "sexual dalliances." It was then up to the Supreme Court to make the crucial decision about the legalities of sexual conduct in the workplace.

Thomas made an unusual trip to the office of the solicitor general, who was Charles Fried at that time, to argue that the Reagan administration should ignore the conservatives' dissent. Acting as EEOC chairman, Thomas wanted the government to file a strong brief in the

Supreme Court case in favor of upholding the law against sexual harassment, which the solicitor general did indeed.

After Hill's charges had exploded into the news, Fried summed up Thomas's attitude in a letter requested by Senator Danforth, who was looking for anything he could get to defend Thomas. "Chairman Thomas," Fried wrote, "came to my office personally and met with my staff and me. He made a strong and very persuasive argument that sexual harassment is properly considered a form of discrimination because as a practical matter it seriously interferes with equal opportunities for women in the workplace."

In June 1986, the Supreme Court upheld the EEOC guidelines in a unanimous ruling written by Chief Justice Rehnquist in the case of *Meritor Savings Bank* v. *Vinson*. This decision made history, guaranteeing the legal right of a woman—or a man—to work without being sexually tormented. The court's opinion held that sexual harassment does violate Title VII of the Civil Rights Act if it creates a hostile or offensive environment for the victim, regardless of whether it directly threatens the individual's job.

This case was based on charges of the most unsubtle kind of sexual harassment brought by Mechelle Vinson against Sidney Taylor, the manager of the branch of the Washington bank. Vinson worked for the bank for four years in the 1970s, climbing up the promotions ladder from teller to assistant branch manager. At first, Vinson testified, she refused Taylor's advances. Her problem with Taylor began when he took her to a Chinese restaurant and then insisted on driving her to a motel and having sex with her. Vinson testified that she had complied with Taylor's demands only for fear that her boss would fire her. After that, according to Vinson's testimony, Taylor made repeated demands for sexual favors. She was forced to have sex with him some forty or fifty times, usually at the bank, both during and after business hours. The sex took place in the bank vault, the storage area, and the basement.

In addition, Vinson testified that Taylor fondled her breasts and buttocks in front of other bank employees, followed her into the women's restroom and exposed himself to her. All these incidents were against her will, Vinson said in court, including one in which Taylor so brutally attacked her that she had to see a doctor for vaginal bleeding.

Taylor denied it all. He testified that he had never fondled Vinson, that he had never had sex with her and that she instead had made sexual advances to him, which he declined. Vinson had no witnesses to corroborate her charges. She also testified that she had not complained for fear of reprisals from Taylor. It was never disputed that Vinson received her promotions because of her good work as an employee.

The Supreme Court's task was not to decide the facts of the case— those had been ruled upon by the lower courts—but rather to decide the larger issues about sexual harassment. It rejected the employer's argument that Title VII prohibits only discrimination that causes tangible economic injury. The court held that employees have the right to work in an environment free from sexual intimidation, ridicule, and insult. A sexually hostile workplace, like a racially hostile one, was ruled to be illegal. The court also held that an employee's seeming compliance with harassment did not make it legal. The fundamental question, according to the court, is whether "the alleged sexual advances were unwelcome, not whether her actual participation . . . was voluntary."

Although the facts of this case were extraordinarily ugly, it was in many ways a classic. Vinson had won the case without any testimony from corroborating witnesses. Her word was sufficient even though her boss denied her charges. She endured the harassment for years for fear that her boss would retaliate. He held the power and she was therefore vulnerable. Even though the harassment was severe, it still took her a very long time to step forward publicly with her charges.

The Supreme Court decision was in keeping with what Clarence Thomas wanted. Without a doubt, it made sexual harassment in the workplace illegal. But it also refrained from establishing an employer's automatic responsibility for harassment. This was precisely the position Thomas had been advocating back in 1980 when he helped the Reagan administration attack the EEOC. The court had created no clear, overarching standard for making an employer or company liable for harassment in its workplaces or offices. Lawsuits against employers were not made easy.

Women's rights groups hope that another breakthrough may be consolidated in the future. They are watching the fate of an appellate court ruling handed down in 1991 that expanded the concept of sexual harassment.

The ruling stemmed from a lawsuit brought by a female agent at a California office of the Internal Revenue Service against a fellow, male agent. The woman, Kerry Ellison, brought sexual harassment charges against Sterling Gray, an older, married man who pestered her by asking for dates and then by sending her love letters.

Gray's messages to Ellison were gently amorous, not ugly or pornographic. "I cried over you all last night, and I'm totally drained today," one note read. "Some people seek the woman, I seek the child inside. With gentleness and deepest respect, Sterling," said another. However, Ellison felt the letters were frightening.

Ellison took her unusual case to court and it wound its way up to the U.S. Circuit Court of Appeals in San Francisco. The case depended on interpreting the letters from a woman's point of view. Traditionally, the law has used the standard of a "reasonable person" to judge cases, but it agreed with Ellison that a "reasonable woman" could interpret Gray's letters differently than a man.

By acknowledging this, the court recognized that women live with the threat of sexual violence and that unwelcome attention, although benign-seeming, could be frightening from a female perspective. The three-judge panel on the California court wrote that "a gender-conscious examination of sexual harassment will enable women to participate in the workplace on an equal footing."

Women are the principal victims of sexual harassment, although a much smaller percentage of men are similarly aggrieved. Surveys consistently report that about 40 percent of women workers have experienced sexual harassment. Pornographic pictures plastered around a workplace can amount to sexual harassment, as can a stream of lewd notes, or pinching or fondling. Victims can be over sixty years in age or under twenty; they can be professionals or blue-collar workers; they can be married, single or divorced. It is common for victims of sexual harassment to report psychological stress and related symptoms such as insomnia, depression, headaches, or nervousness.

Though workers victimized by sexual harassment now have ways to officially complain or to sue, the vast majority do not do so. According to a federal survey, only five percent of both the women and men who reported being harassed took formal action. Although most employees knew that they could file grievances or make formal complaints, few did. Half of the victims tried to ignore the harassment even though this did not stop it in most cases.

But if a woman did make a formal complaint to the Equal Opportunity Employment Commission, the chances were that she wouldn't be richly compensated, if at all. Recently, the EEOC was throwing out more than half of all the sexual harassment complaints it received because it found "no cause" for the case, according to Helen Norton of the Women's Legal Defense Fund. Norton said that the number of these rejections had jumped when the EEOC was chaired by Thomas, whom she called "the king of no-cause findings." If the EEOC finds merit in a case, it first tries to mediate between victim and employer to negotiate a settlement. Only then will the agency take the case to court. The only other option for someone complaining of sexual harassment is to hire a private lawyer.

In a few extraordinary cases, women have won large sums legally. In 1986, for example, an Ohio woman brought a case against an employer who insisted that she perform oral sex in order to keep her job. She won more than three million dollars. But until recently under federal law, women who took their cases to court could get only back wages and job reinstatement, and those are among the minority who are not afraid to act. Victims often feel that complaining is tantamount to committing professional suicide. In the end, a theft of one's sexual dignity can be more difficult to report than a theft of one's wallet.

After the Thomas-Hill hearings had concluded, women dominated the discussions of sexual harassment in the nation's media. Catharine MacKinnon, a University of Michigan law professor and one of the legal pioneers on the issue, appeared on *The Donahue Show* to air her opinions about the hearings and to offer her views on the origin of the infamous Coke can and other pornographic images.

"It seems to me that where Professor Hill has taken the credibility beating has been on the subject of pornography, the specifics of pornography that she mentioned. It seems to me that these things are regarded by people as somehow so incredible, so horrible, so extreme, so wild, so unbelievable, that people don't feel comfortable believing it, and also because a great many women, unlike a great many men, have not seen this pornography. They do not know in pornography that Coke cans are used to penetrate women. That's what the pubic hair is doing. It's a direct scenario out of pornography."

Specialists in sexual harassment were not the only women who were outraged; across the country, anger was building. No matter what the outcome of the Thomas nomination, sexual harassment had become an issue on the nation's political landscape, and would not disappear.

Few experts were prepared to explain how reality might look from the point of view of a harasser. One who showed professional sympathy for Clarence Thomas was Robert Williams, a Washington lawyer specializing in representing employers rather than victims. Writing in the *The National Law Journal* the day before Hill began her testimony before the Judiciary Committee, he said that the charges against Thomas could well become a permanent scar on his reputation.

> [I]t appears that the accusations already may have caused the judge irreparable damage. If he cannot refute them conclusively, he is likely to face suspicion for the remainder of his career. . . . The controversy . . . dramatically illustrates a practical reality all too familiar to private employers that have been dealing with the charges of sexual harassment for years: Regardless of where the law places the burden of proof, unless the accused can prove affirmatively that the alleged harassment never occurred, he is likely to be viewed ever after as a man of suspect morals and questionable judgment. Yet to prove affirmatively that harassment did not occur may be practically impossible. Because harassment allegations usually involve private conduct, the accused often has no way to rebut the charges but through his own sworn denial.

But after the Judiciary Committee finished its final three days of hearings, Williams was critical of the bungling he had seen and the committee's failure to keep the episode as confidential as possible. When it came to dealing with sexual harassment, the Senate had performed miserably, Williams said in an interview.

> Hill's sexual harassment charge was typical of those we see in the workplace. Employers have learned how to handle these things better than the committee. The fundamental point that employers are drilled on is that you must take these things seriously and investigate them in the appropriate forum. The Judiciary Committee didn't do this systematic, step-by-step

investigation that employers would have to do. They waited until the whole thing was exposed in the press and then they did their investigating in front of the whole country. It was an inappropriate forum.

The Judiciary Committee's handling of the hearings had fueled public disgust with the entire Senate. Individual senators anxiously consulted polls to gauge the feelings of their constituents about this suddenly volatile issue.

The one hundred members of the Senate had yet to vote on Clarence Thomas's confirmation. They had to make up their minds about the extraordinary spectacle they had just witnessed.

The nomination hearings had been confusing to everyone. While Clarence Thomas had been making his prime-time case with the aid of the Republicans, Anita Hill's lawyers were struggling; they couldn't believe the casual nature of the proceedings, the freedom with which their opponents were ripping into their witness. In the middle of the hearings, one of them had turned to a colleague and said, "I'm having a hard time taking this all in, getting my arms around this. There's no jury!"

Perhaps the Hill team had been in too much turmoil at the outset of the hearings to absorb Chairman Biden's initial words about what was going to happen:

> Those watching these proceedings will see witnesses being sworn and testifying pursuant to subpoena. But I want to emphasize that this is not a trial, this is not a courtroom. And at the end of our proceedings there will be no formal verdict of guilt or innocence, nor any finding of civil liability.

Because this is not a trial, the proceedings will not be conducted the way
in which a sexual harassment trial would be handled in a court of law. For
example, on the advice of the nonpartisan Senate legal counsel, the rules
of evidence that apply in courtrooms will not apply here today. Thus,
evidence and questions that would not be permitted in a court of law must,
under Senate rules, be allowed here.

Had it been a trial in a civil court, where the burden of proof is less
than that in a criminal court, Hill might well have won on a sexual
harassment charge. She was a good witness who seemed to have no
motive to lie and whose testimony was partially corroborated. Most of
the Republicans' attacks on her character would never have been
permitted into evidence.

Thomas, on the other hand, was a man whose sincerity had already
been thrown into question during the first round of hearings. His
replies to the senators had not seemed entirely honest, particularly his
denial of ever having discussed *Roe* v. *Wade*. In the second round,
Thomas had refused to answer relevant questions and refused to
cooperate by watching Hill's testimony.

But the Hill camp never understood that the Senate Caucus Room,
for all its formal grandeur, was no courtroom. The hearings were part
of a political process, not a judicial one.

"What they knew about politics you could put in a small thimble,"
commented one Senate staffer about Hill's legal advisers.

The lawyers had recommended to Hill and her supporting witnesses
that they refrain from public relations activities: they were not to
respond in the press or on television to the charges being lodged
against Professor Hill. The lawyers were governed by their feeling that
if the hearings had been a trial, this sort of conduct would have been
unseemly and perhaps prohibited. The lawyers themselves shied away
from reporters. So the Hill supporters had no Senator Danforth to
rush to the microphones at every break.

By Washington standards, this lack of an aggressive effort to explain
Hill and polish her image was a major miscalculation. A belief that the
cause was right, or legally compelling, was not sufficient to win the
tough Capitol games that were being played. The hastily prepared Hill
team had not sorted this out beforehand. In addition, Anita Hill had
taken an earnest stance that her purpose was not to derail the nomina-

tion, but to tell her story. In that sense, she succeeded in her mission.

But even within the looser rules of the Washington political game, the second round of hearings had not been played properly. The Democrats had played by one set of rules, the Republicans by another. The Democrats wanted to be fair; the Republicans wanted to win, at any cost, a reversal of the Bork hearings. Chairman Biden had called for fairness in his opening statement. In retrospect, Biden had been optimistic, even naive, given that he was a seasoned politician who knew the tricks of Washington.

"Achieving fairness, in the atmosphere in which these hearings are being held, may be the most difficult task I have ever undertaken in my close to nineteen years in the United States Senate," the chairman had said.

Toward that end, Biden had announced his personal ruling that there would be no questions allowed about "the private conduct, out-of-the-workplace relationships, and intimate lives and practices of Judge Thomas, Professor Hill, and any other witness that comes before us.

"The committee is not here to put Judge Thomas or Professor Hill on trial. I hope my colleagues will bear in mind that the best way to do our job is to ask questions that are nonjudgmental and openended and attempt to avoid questions that badger and harass any witness."

This noble sentiment made fairness the emphasis of the hearings rather than finding out the truth about what had happened between Hill and Thomas. If the Democrats could not ask Thomas whether he had continued to be an avid consumer of pornography after he graduated from law school, how could they establish the plausibility of his describing obscene movies to Anita Hill? Thomas had made it clear at the outset that he would not answer such questions, but the spectacle of his refusing to do so could have changed the tenor of the hearings.

There was another way of investigating this crucial issue, had the committee wanted to do it. Two owners of video stores in the Washington area later indicated to journalists that they had rented pornographic movies to Thomas in recent years. But the store owners produced no records to prove the rental transactions, so newspapers refrained from publishing the unsubstantiated stories. One of the owners hinted that if he were to be subpoenaed he could supply records. The Judiciary Committee, with its power to subpoena witnesses and documents, could have gotten to the bottom of these stories.

Once the second round of the hearings was underway, Chairman Biden failed to enforce his own fairness doctrine. He didn't rein in the Republicans, allowing them to run roughshod over the inquiry into Hill's charges. Biden had vowed to his staff that he would rise to defend Hill if the Republicans became too vicious. But it was not until Doggett offered his outrageous version of Hill's psychological state in the final hours of the hearings that the chairman acted forcefully.

Despite his fairness edict, Biden had skewed the hearings in Thomas's favor from the start by offering Clarence Thomas the choice of testifying first or last, before or after Hill. Late the night before the hearings the White House had demanded that its man go both first and last, and Biden agreed. This gave Thomas the chance to rebut Hill's charges before she formally made them and the additional chance to rebut the charges later. In the end, Thomas had three separate opportunities to make his case and a monopoly of the television hours when the most viewers were watching.

In Washington, where the politics of this scheduling was understood, many liberals were appalled at the way Biden and the other Democrats on the committee had handled the arrangements.

"There were a number of people around town the first day who concluded that the Democrats had been taken for a ride on the scheduling," said a political consultant close to Senator Kennedy. "A number of us screamed and yelled and the response came back there was a very strong feeling of the chairman and the Democrats that they had to give the impression of fairness."

The Democrats had approached the hearings timidly for several reasons. The most obvious was that they did not want to get embroiled in what might appear to be personal attacks on a black man. The Democrats were, after all, members of the party that pledged to support minorities. In addition, Thomas was the accused, and therefore deserved some consideration. Another important factor was the overall confusion that the Republicans used to their advantage. Claiming that the sexual harassment charges had been leaked at the eleventh hour, they were able to cast Hill as a pawn in a plot devised by Thomas's enemies: they made Clarence Thomas into the victim rather than Anita Hill. The truth, of course, was that Hill had come forward much earlier, and had been ignored by the committee.

Senator Hatch along with Senator Danforth had intimidated the committee Democrats by ranting about a suspected "leaker"; any Democrat who appeared too zealous in Hill's defense automatically risked suspicion. The Democrats on the committee had their own conflicts of interest. They had all known about Hill's charges, and had done nothing; to champion Hill's case now would be to demonstrate how wrong they had been earlier. Biden in particular, and the Democrats generally, had an interest in an inconclusive outcome. This caution on the part of the senators leached down to the level of the staff, where the real work of the Senate was done.

The net result was that no senator in the Caucus Room defended Anita Hill. The role of judge was acted by Biden, that of the jury by the committee, and that of the prosecutor by the combination of Specter and Hatch.

Despite the anguish and the theatrics, the sincerity and the deviousness on display, the extraordinarily intense three days of hearings about Anita Hill's charges did not significantly change the minds of Americans. At the conclusion, polls showed that people still tended to believe Thomas rather than Hill by a two-to-one ratio.

A telling exception to the trend was recorded in a survey of one hundred state and federal judges conducted for *The National Law Journal*. The judges believed Hill rather than Thomas by a two-to-one ratio in a reversal of the opinion of the general population.

The explanations for the general public's attitude toward Hill were numerous. Forces were acting against her case that had nothing to do with the facts. The polls measuring public opinion were taken when Thomas's striking testimony was still fresh in people's minds.

In addition, from the outset Republicans and other conservatives were inclined to disbelieve her simply because they wanted to believe Thomas. His nomination had become a partisan cause. Another factor was the tendency of the male half of the population to see in Anita Hill everything they thought was wrong with modern, aggressive, rights-mongering women. Many men thought the charges were unimportant even if they were true.

"Clarence Thomas didn't do anything wrong that any American male hasn't done," said a Colorado machinist, voicing a typical opinion to a newspaper reporter.

Blacks on the whole can be counted upon to support liberal causes. But in the case of Hill versus Thomas, they were divided; they had been in disagreement about Clarence Thomas from the start. Once the NAACP made a stand on the nomination, the organization had diminished some of the support for Thomas in the black community. But a majority of blacks had continued to favor Thomas when the first round of hearings began. Hill's charges increased Thomas's standing in the black community because, as Thomas pointed out, they fed into the stereotype of the sexually hyperactive black male; this caused a backlash in his favor. The fact that Hill was black did not make a difference here. Many blacks felt that Hill should have kept her mouth shut rather than attacking a fellow black so publicly and so prominently in an all-white forum.

"I do not think that a black woman under any circumstances should report any kind of sexual issue to the white man, unless it's rape or something like that," said Shahrazad Ali, author of *The Blackman's Guide to Understanding the Blackwoman.*

"I don't think white feminists will be permitted to define the parameters of black male-female relationships anymore," said Robert Woodson, president of the National Center for Neighborhood Enterprise in Washington. "That's for African-Americans to decide."

"In the quiet and resolute spirit she might very well have learned from Sunday school, Hill confronted and ultimately breached a series of taboos in the black community that have survived both slavery and the post-segregation life she and Clarence Thomas share," wrote newspaper editor Rosemary L. Bray in the *The New York Times Magazine.* "Anita Hill put her private business in the street, and she downgraded a black man to a room filled with white men who might alter his fate—surely a large enough betrayal for her to be read out of the race."

Hill had as much a right as Thomas to complain about being stereotyped, though; she had to deal with fourteen white male senators who, not surprisingly, evidenced little understanding of her situation. They had not experienced the feeling of being powerless and vulnerable in American society. They had little basis on which to comprehend how a woman might silently accommodate a tormentor.

Many ordinary Americans could not make sense of the idea that Hill had remained on cordial terms with a boss such as the one she described. She had explained that she felt it had been necessary for her professional advancement. Hill and her friends were professional women, whose demeanor and values were quite different from those of many of the average Americans judging her. From their point of view, Hill could have acted differently. She could have quit her job with Thomas or at least not complained about behavior that women have always endured. A class tension—the six pack versus the wine bottle— was working against Hill, as well.

Hill's case was also damaged by the widespread perception that she was solely responsible for the last-minute nature of her charges. Most people did not know how she had tried to get the committee to pay attention to her story back in September. A less moribund Democratic voice in the hearings might have pointed out that Hill's charges had nothing to do with Thomas's personal life, but with what she claimed had happened on the job, in the same agency dedicated to enforcing the laws against sexual harassment.

The White House was able to trump the initial outpouring of feminist support for Anita Hill with the racism card that Thomas played so well.

"In our society racism is a much more powerful weapon than sexism," said Kate Michelman, the leader of the National Abortion Rights Action League. "Sexism has not achieved the level of abhorrence that racism has. You can be sexist and still achieve a Supreme Court seat, but not a racist. If he had called someone a 'nigger' he would be gone, he would not be on the court. But it was different because it involved a man taking advantage of a woman because of her sex."

In part, Michelman conceded, this was due to a difference in approach between the civil rights and the women's rights movements.

"Martin Luther King focused on the horror of discrimination in racism. He didn't repudiate the white race in doing so. Some people believe that the feminist movement began with an angry repudiation of the important role women held as wife and mother. It had a negative impact, the idea that those roles were no longer valuable. Racism and sexism as concepts have evolved differently. The White House was able to tap into the antifeminist views held in society. And if you pit racism against sexism, racism will always win out because rasicm is unacceptable and sexism is still acceptable."

One day remained between the end of the hearings and the final vote by the Senate on what had become the most bizarre confirmation battle in the history of the Supreme Court. Though the hearings were over, the politicking did not stop.

Senator Danforth held a last press conference, and in his desperation to see Thomas through to the Supreme Court he persisted in promulgating the fantasy theory even though its basis had been thoroughly discredited. He was one of the few Republicans willing to mention "erotomania" in public.

Senator Danforth also released the affidavit from John Burke, the lawyer who had been a partner in Hill's former law firm, stating that she had been asked to leave the firm. As Danforth was well aware, the reason for Hill's departure was much disputed. Three other former partners in the firm of Wald, Harkrader & Ross challenged Burke's statement. One of them, Donald Green, came forward immediately with an affidavit stating that the firm had *not* asked her to leave.

Danforth released the Burke affidavit even though the Judiciary Committee had refused to subpoena Hill's personnel records, deeming it an invasion of her privacy. Hill had not volunteered them, either. Those records would have shown a mixed evaluation typical of the usually critical review of a new lawyer's work.

When the records were eventually dug out of storage in the suburbs of Washington, they did offer an interesting explanation for the controversy over Hill's employment at the law firm. Green summed this up in a letter to Senator Biden written after the hearings and the vote: the records did not show that Hill had ever worked directly for Burke, as he had stated in his affidavit. Green said the records did show, however, that *another* black woman lawyer had worked for Burke, had received an unsatisfactory evaluation for her first year at the firm, and had been asked to find another job. Green's letter made it appear that Burke had confused the two black women.

When Hill arrived home in Norman, Oklahoma, she made a brief statement to reporters in response to the counterattacks that had been made on her reputation.

"It was suggested that I had fantasies, that I was a spurned woman and that I had a martyr complex. I will not dignify those theories, except to assure everyone that I am not imagining the conduct to which I testified. I have been deeply hurt and offended by the nature of the attacks on my character. I had nothing to gain by subjecting myself to the process. In fact, I had more to gain by remaining silent. The personal attacks on me without an iota of evidence were particularly reprehensible, and I felt it necessary to come forward to address those attacks."

Hill's lawyers had advised her not to hold a full-blown press conference, so she did not respond to the many questions on the lips of the journalists. Her lawyers, continuing to act as if they were in a courtroom, did not want any appearance that she was trying to influence the opinion of the Senate or the country.

Those on the Thomas side were not so bashful. The staff of Pat Robertson, the evangelist, organized telephone banks to make thousands of calls to Senate offices urging confirmation. Members of Paul Weyrich's Library Court coalition, the far-right groups that Thomas had stroked so carefully, concentrated on lobbying senators who could make the difference in a close vote on Thomas, senators such as DeConcini of the Judiciary Committee and David Boren of Oklahoma, another conservative Democrat. Weyrich had fears that Senator Boren, who had declared himself a Thomas supporter, might switch his vote because of Hill's Oklahoma connection. Since Library Court had six affiliates in Oklahoma, it was able to put considerable pressure on the senator not to change his mind.

The morning of Tuesday, October 15, the day of the vote, Richard Shelby, the Alabama Democrat, was on national television bright and early. He appeared on NBC's *Today* show to announce his vote in favor of Thomas, rather than waiting to proclaim his decision on the Senate floor in keeping with the usual protocol. Shelby's leap onto the Thomas bandwagon was a sign of the politics to come.

Normally, Shelby would have followed the lead of the senior senator from Alabama, Howell Heflin, who as a committee member had already voted against Thomas. Shelby had become so identified with Heflin that some people liked to call him "Sheflin." Like Heflin, Shelby had voted against the nomination of Robert Bork four years earlier. But this time Shelby was going to cut his own trail. He was up for reelection for the first time the following year, and he could afford to alienate neither the state's conservatives nor its blacks, who both supported Thomas.

The man Shelby had to pay most attention to in the black community was Joe Reed. Shelby would not have taken the Senate seat away from Republican Jeremiah Denton in 1986 without the support of Reed, the kingpin of black Alabama Democrats, who had decided not to oppose Thomas after his meeting with the nominee in Washington that summer. Reed was worrying about his power base at Alabama State University. He still wanted the help of both Clarence Thomas on the Supreme Court and the Republicans in the White House. As the day progressed, it became clear that Thomas held the support of enough Southern Democrats to provide the margin of victory. The race card had turned out to be an ace.

Of course, the black vote was not the only reason Thomas would attract eleven Democratic supporters; their votes were the basis of the mathematics that gave Thomas the confirmation from a Senate dominated by Democrats.

Charles S. Robb, for instance, the Virginia Democrat whose original political identity was based on his first marriage to Lyndon Johnson's daughter, told a reporter that he was influenced in his decision to vote for Thomas by his own personal problems.

Senator Robb had been accused of having an adulterous affair with a Virginia beauty queen, Tai Collins, as well as attending wild beach parties with people suspected of drug trafficking. He denied having slept with Collins, but admitted to having accepted "a back rub" from her in a hotel room. He said he had nothing to do with drugs.

These accusations, Robb told a reporter on the day of the vote, "gave me an understanding of allegations that were untrue and unprovable." Indeed, too many senators had all too much reason to sympathize with people accused of wrongdoing. The moral problems of these senators inhibited the institution from challenging a nominee on questions of character.

The Senate exhibited a fundamental lack of ethics during the Thomas hearings: John Danforth, Arlen Specter, Orrin Hatch, and Alan Simpson attacked Hill with any weapon available, no matter how unfair or ludicrous. The tone had been set at the start by President

Bush, who started the nomination with a questionable claim about the qualifications of Thomas and helped end it by approving of the tactics used against Hill.

Senator Kennedy epitomized the Senate's problems with its members' personal morality, but having picked himself up a bit at the end of the hearings, he had plenty to say about political ethics. Stepping out of his fog of personal embarrassment, he made a powerful speech on the Senate floor. Senators came and went from the floor in a steady stream throughout the day to air their convictions and their anger about the saga of the Thomas nomination. They spoke at their antique wooden desks, which fan out in neat lines in the high-ceilinged chamber. Kennedy said:

> The most distressing aspect of the hearings was the eagerness with which many of Judge Thomas's supporters resorted to innuendos and scurrilous attacks on Professor Hill for her testimony about her charges of deeply offensive and humiliating actions by Judge Thomas. They have charged that Professor Hill's allegations were an effort to play on racial fears and racial stereotypes. But the issue here is sexual oppression, not racial oppression . . . I reject the notion that racism is relevant to this controversy. It involves an Afro-American man and an Afro-American woman, and it ultimately involves the character of America itself.
>
> The struggle for racial justice in its truest sense was meant to wipe out all forms of oppression. No one, least of all Judge Thomas, is entitled to invoke one form of oppression to excuse another. The deliberate, provocative use of a term like lynching is not only wrong in fact, it is a gross misuse of America's most tragic—most historic tragedy and pain to buy a political advantage.
>
> The Senate today is not passing judgment solely on Judge Thomas or Professor Hill. The Senate is making a fundamental statement about our values and our conscience. Make no mistake about it. We in the Senate are also passing judgment on ourselves. Are we an old boys' club, insensitive at best and perhaps something worse? Will we strain to concoct any excuse to impose any burden? To tolerate any unsubstantiated attack on a woman in order to rationalize a vote for this nomination? Will we refuse to heed the rights and claims of the majority of Americans who are women, but who are so much a minority in this chamber? What kind of Senate are we?
>
> Because if we cannot listen and respond to this woman, as credible as she is, with the significant corroboration she offers, then what message are we

sending to women across America? What American woman in the future
will dare to come forward? There is no proof that Anita Hill has perjured
herself, and shame on anyone who suggests that she has.

There is no proof . . . that any advocacy groups made Anita Hill say what
she said, or made up a story for her to repeat. . . . There is . . . no proof
at all that Anita Hill is fantasizing these charges or is mentally unbalanced.
. . . The treatment of Anita Hill is what every woman fears who thinks of
lifting the veil and revealing her sexual harassment.

His speech drew an immediate retort from Senator Specter, just the
kind of rhetorical knife in the back that had kept Kennedy mute
throughout most of the hearings.

"We do not need characterizations like shame in this chamber from
the senator from Massachusetts."

Senator Orrin Hatch also had a nasty retort. "Anybody who believes
that," he said about Kennedy's criticism of the perjury charge, "I
know a bridge up in Massachusetts that I'll be happy to sell to them."
It was a bald reference to Kennedy's car accident at Chappaquiddick
Island in 1969 in which a young woman drowned.

Another reason Thomas won the vote of one out of every five
Democratic senators was the party's weak leadership on the issue.
When some key senators went to George Mitchell, the majority leader,
and asked him to rally the party against Thomas, he refused even
though he himself opposed Thomas, according to Senate insiders.
Thus even members of the party leadership like Senator Robb, the
chairman of the Democratic Senatorial Campaign Committee, and
Senator Alan Dixon of Illinois, the party's chief deputy whip, felt free
to vote for Thomas.

In an interview after the vote, Senator Mitchell said he had worked
hard to persuade his fellow Democrats to vote against Thomas. He
maintained that the era when the majority leader could twist arms to
produce votes was a thing of the past.

"The days are long since gone when I can say to a senator this is a
party issue and therefore you must vote with us," Mitchell said.

But Senator Mitchell's critics believe that he could have easily
delivered a vote against Thomas; he twisted arms effectively several
months later on a major tax bill.

If the Republicans had remained essentially unified, losing only two of their forty-three votes on the confirmation, why hadn't the Democrats? The Democrats may have believed that they would lose in the long run, anyway.

Senator Mitchell thought, correctly, that as long as a conservative Republican was in the White House, the nominees to the Supreme Court would all probably be as right-wing as Thomas. In the end, what would be the difference if Thomas lost and another ultraconservative was nominated? Looking at the larger picture, the majority leader thought the best way to balance the Supreme Court was to elect a Democrat to the White House. The most cynical of the Democrats thought that Thomas's conservative vote on the court might stir up support for the Democrats in the coming presidential election—particularly if *Roe* v. *Wade* was overturned in the meantime.

Senator Alan Dixon of Illinois, one of the Democrats who voted for Thomas, gave a speech explaining his vote that was typical of the many lukewarm endorsements Thomas received that day from Democrats and Republicans alike. Few senators, other than the nominee's die-hard supporters, said outright that they believed Thomas. Most admitted they were not certain of the truth, although many felt that it was only fair to give the benefit of the doubt to the accused.

In his speech, Dixon said:

> Last Friday the Judiciary Committee began what became three long days of public hearings. For those three days the nation became riveted on the testimony of Judge Thomas, Professor Hill, and the other witnesses and transfixed on an issue—workplace sexual harassment. I condemn in the strongest way, as I have throughout my career, any type of sexual harassment. The last week has been a kind of national tragedy. But if the result is that the country becomes more sensitive to sexual harassment, then the dark clouds will have had a valuable silver lining.
>
> Today's vote is not a referendum on sexual harassment. If it were, I would hope and expect that the vote here in the Senate would be unanimous against it. Today's vote is also not a referendum on the nomination process. If it were, I think the vote would be unanimous that the process has swung out of control and that it reflects poorly on the Senate. What today's vote is about is whether Judge Clarence Thomas deserves appointment to the United States Supreme Court.
>
> Part of that calculation now involves the question of whether Judge Thomas sexually harassed Professor Anita Hill when they worked together

CAPITOL GAMES

at the Education Department and the Equal Employment Opportunity Commission. The Judiciary Committee tried its best over the weekend to get to the truth of this matter. The unfortunate fact is, however, that Senate hearings are ill suited to determine the true facts in situations like this one.

Like most Americans, I spent a lot of time watching the hearings. I spent a lot of my career as a trial lawyer, and I've seen a lot of witnesses. What I saw last weekend was two convincing witnesses. Professor Hill's testimony was moving and credible. Judge Thomas's denial was forceful and equally credible.

So what should the Senate do? Make no mistake. In the view of this senator at least, a charge of sexual harassment, if proven, disqualifies any nominee for a position on the United States Supreme Court. If Professor Hill had been credible, and Judge Thomas had not, the Senate's decision would be simple. If Judge Thomas had been credible, and Professor Hill had not, the Senate's choice would be equally clear. Since both were credible, however, and since it is impossible to get to the bottom of this matter, I think we have to fall back on our legal system and its presumption of innocence for those accused . . . That isn't a legal loophole, it is a basic, essential right—a right of every American. If we're not to become a country where being charged is equivalent to being found guilty, we must preserve and we must protect that presumption.

In this case, that means that Judge Thomas is entitled to a presumption of innocence. Since the Judiciary Committee hearing did not overcome that presumption, that means Professor Hill's allegations cannot be used to justify a vote against Judge Thomas. A decision on this nomination cannot be made on sexual harassment grounds. Instead it must be made on the issues that have been before the Senate for the past one hundred days and more.

Senator Dixon went on to say he was casting his vote for Thomas. That decision was to prove the biggest mistake of his political career.

The anguish caused by the nomination imbroglio was expressed by another conservative Democrat. Like Dixon, Senator James Exon of Nebraska had announced his intention to vote for Thomas before he had heard of Anita Hill, and had also asked for the delay to hear the charges.

After carefully listening to both Thomas and Hill, this one member of the eventual jury of one hundred feels both appear believable, but one, seemingly, is lying under oath, a criminal offense of perjury. Unfortu-

nately, after the hearing, it is difficult, if not impossible, for me to determine what the facts or the truth are. I suspect that this might be the
opinion of many who listened to the recently concluded hearings.

The President has said as recently as Sunday that the charges against the
nominee are ridiculous and the process is ridiculous. This from the man
who from the beginning started the process with ridiculous statements that
his nominee was selected strictly on the basis of the best-qualified individual in all of America, and that the decision was devoid of any and all
political or racial considerations.

Ridiculous statements in all of this began with the President. Is it any
wonder that the nation is embroiled in this bitter controversy over ridiculous statements and conclusions magnified by the President's latest pro-
nouncements from the golf course? You will forgive me if I employ my
constitutional rights to criticize King George.

Those whom I customarily turn to for advice on such important matters
are deeply divided. My constituents, my family, my closest friends, and
even my staff are unbelievably split. Emotions are running amok, and from
every direction, more so than I can recall previously from over twenty years
of public service. The boat of discussion and decision-making has been so
violently rocked that the rudder has been out of the water so often it is
difficult to steer any sound course to a sound determination. . . .

Unfortunately, in my view, the hearings of the past few days have not
produced any overall conclusive facts or definitive truths on the charges by
Hill or the firm denials by Thomas. The key and central issue here, though,
is not what is in the best interests of either of the two antagonists. . . .

We must concentrate now on the all-encompassing issue as to whether
or not Clarence Thomas should be confirmed to a lifetime appointment to
the highest court in the land. On October 4, I supported the nomination
on the floor on the basis of my knowledge at that time. Among other
things, I stated that I felt Judge Thomas met the test of judicial temperament. Notwithstanding my appreciation of the nominee's rage at the allegations, I was surprised and disappointed at many of his statements. They
were not made in a fit of instantaneous anger, but rather, well-thought out
and premeditated remarks. . . .

On the other hand, I have not been particularly impressed with the
reasons advanced by Professor Hill as to how she could have brought
herself to follow Judge Thomas so faithfully and so long in her career,
given the sordid remarks allegedly made to her. I can understand her
reluctance to make a formal complaint at the time, and her not telling any
or all of the vast array of Thomas-supporting witnesses who seemed to be

saying in testimony that she should have confided in them. . . . Yet I cannot readily understand why a person with her talents would not have conveniently found for herself a more satisfying position and superior, quietly if that were her wishes. . . .

In conclusion, let me say I have deliberated over this position and studied it for hours and hours and for days. There have been swings pro and con as I watched the hearings for solid conclusions that never materialized. . . .

Notwithstanding my reservations as to the nominee, I intend to vote for confirmation, but without enthusiasm. It is my hope that, if confirmed, Judge Thomas will be a better justice because of this ordeal. It is my belief that he will not turn out to be the doctrinaire ideologue on the court that he is projected to be. . . . Time will tell.

Republicans breathed a sigh of relief. It had not been immediately clear from his speech which way Exon was heading. They knew that Thomas had lost some of his Democratic support, but if Exon and Dixon and Shelby were sticking with them, they were in good shape. As the day wore on the Republican vote counters grew confident, thinking that Thomas had a comfortable margin of votes. They were a little too confident.

Typical of the twists and turns the Thomas nomination had taken, the most articulate response to the lukewarm logic of these conservative Democrats came from another conservative Democrat, Robert Byrd, who had served thirty-three years in the Senate and was now silver-haired and seventy-three years old. As a young man Byrd had been an avid member of the Ku Klux Klan, and had filibustered the 1964 Civil Rights Act with a fourteen-hour speech. Senator Byrd had been prepared to vote for Thomas when the Hill charges surfaced publicly. A true believer in a conservative Supreme Court who hailed from the conservative state of West Virginia, he had no political reason to vote against Thomas. But as he said so eloquently that day, he believed Anita Hill, and thought that Clarence Thomas had engaged in "stonewalling and blatant intimidation." Byrd had been deeply offended by Thomas's criticism of the Senate to which he had devoted most of his life. He was even more offended by the argument that the benefit of the doubt should go to Thomas. In a confirmation, that benefit should go to the country, he insisted.

I believe Anita Hill. . . . I watched her on that screen intensely and I
replayed her appearance and her statement. I did not see on that face the
knotted brow of satanic revenge. I did not see a face that was contorted
with hate. I did not hear a voice that was tremulous with passion. . . .

I saw an individual who did not flinch, who showed no nervousness,
who spoke calmly throughout, dispassionately and who answered difficult
questions. . . . I thought that Anita Hill was thoughtful, reflective and
truthful. . . .

Granted, let's say then, that there may have been a few inconsistencies,
granted for the sake of those that think there were. That doesn't mean that
she was lying. . . . Perhaps longer hearings would have given her the
opportunity and the committee the opportunity to clarify whatever seeming inconsistencies there might have been to the satisfaction of those who
held them.

She was a reluctant witness. There are those who say, "Well, why didn't
she come forward in the previous confirmation hearings?" She wasn't
contacted in the previous hearings. They will contend, "Why did she wait
ten years?" The fact that she waited ten years does not negate the truth of
her assertion. . . .

She explained that she had spoken to other individuals early on, '81, '82,
'83, '87, and those same persons came forward later and corroborated the
fact that she had talked about this early on. Well, why didn't she file a
claim? She stated her reasons. She said that perhaps she used poor judgment. How many in this chamber have not used poor judgment? Who can
stand in this chamber and say, "I have never used poor judgment"? And
at the age of twenty-five one can understand that an individual might be
more vulnerable to failing to use good judgment. . . .

They talk about fantasies. The dean of Oral Roberts University explained that perhaps the use of the word—he had regretted the use of the
word "fantasy." He had regretted the use of it. It was just something that
came out at the moment. . . .

Then they talk about a conspiracy, special interest groups got to her,
or that she invented this, it's just something that she made up, a woman
spurned, a woman scorned. I don't believe that any reasonable man
could carefully look at that woman's face or listen to what she had to say
and in the whole context of the circumstances and believe that she was
inventing this story. . . . Truth is a powerful thing and sometimes it's a
strange thing.

To those who wish to think of a confirmation hearing as a court case, as
having the surroundings and carrying the environment of a trial, one may

[here he paused] see things, perhaps differently. This is not a court case. This is a confirmation hearing.

Senator Byrd had never lost an election since he was first went to the state legislature in 1946. He was famous for protecting his electoral mandate by bringing home pork-barrel projects to his state in outrageous quantity. As he once said, "There are only four things people believe in in West Virginia—God Almighty; Sears, Roebuck; Carter's Little Liver Pills; and Robert C. Byrd." He was the only senator brave enough to say about Clarence Thomas what many others were thinking. He continued:

Mr. President, what are my other reasons? Aside from believing Anita Hill, I was offended by Judge Thomas's stonewalling the committee. He said he wanted to come back before the committee and clear his name. But he didn't even listen to the principal witness, the only witness against him. He said he couldn't listen to it. He was tired of lies. What kind of judicial temperament does that demonstrate? . . .

By refusing to watch her testimony, he put up a wall between himself and the committee. How could the committee question him? How could the committee learn the truth if the accused refused even to hear the charges? What does this say about the conduct of a judge? . . . A man whose primary function in his professional life is to listen to the evidence, to listen to both sides, whether plaintiff or defendant in a civil case, or prosecutor and the accused in a criminal case.

I have substantial doubts after this episode about the judicial temperament of Judge Thomas, doubts that I did not have prior to this weekend's hearing. How can we have confidence, if he is confirmed, that he will be an objective judge, willing to decide cases based on the evidence presented, if the one case that has mattered most to him in his lifetime, he shut his eyes and closed his ears and closed his mind and didn't even bother to watch the sworn testimony of Anita Hill? . . .

Another reason why I shall vote against Judge Thomas, he not only effectively stonewalled the committee, he just in the main made his speeches before the committee. . . .

I, frankly, was offended by his injection of racism into these hearings. It was a diversionary tactic intended to divert both the committee's and the American public's attention away from the issue at hand, the issue being which one is telling the truth. . . .

Instead of focusing on the charges and attempting to be helpful to the committee—of course he was embittered by the leak and he could have so stated, but he indicted the whole committee and he indicted the Senate and he indicted the process. . . . The process is a constitutional one that was determined by our forefathers, who sat in Philadelphia in 1787. . . .

It is because of the process that Judge Thomas was given his day to clear his name. . . .

He tried to shift the ground, and I think it was blatant intimidation, and I'm sorry to say I think it worked. I sat there and I wondered, who is going to ask him some tough questions. Are they afraid of it? He said to Senator Metzenbaum—I believe it was—"God is my judge. You're not my judge, Senator." Well, of course, God is my judge. I'm not God. But I do have a vote, and I have a responsibility to make a determination as to how I shall vote. And that kind of talk, that kind of arrogance, will never get my vote. . . .

I'm very sorry that the matter of race was injected here, not in the effort to clear one's name but in the effort to shift the ground. And so, instead of making an effort to clear his name in the minds of the committee members and in the minds of other senators who were not on the committee, he shifted the blame to the process and to race prejudice. I think it was preposterous. A black American woman was making the charge against a black American male. Where is the racism? Nonsense. Nonsense.

Now I will get to my last stated reason for voting against Judge Thomas. I've heard it said, "Well, you should give the benefit of the doubt—if you have a doubt about this, and it's obvious that nobody can really say with certitude as to which one is telling the truth, the whole truth, and nothing but the truth, so help him or her God—then we should give the benefit to Judge Thomas. He's the nominee."

Now, Mr. President, [addressing the presiding officer of the Senate] of all the excuses for voting for Judge Thomas, I think that is the weakest one I've heard. When are senators going to learn that this proceeding was not being made in a court of law? This was not a civil case, it was not a criminal case, where there are various standards of doubt, beyond a reasonable doubt, so on and so on. This is a confirmation process. We're talking about someone who was nominated for one of the most powerful positions in this country. Some would say, "Well, he'll only be one of nine men." Suppose it's a divided court, four to four. That one man will make the difference. Suppose it's a divided court and he doesn't show up for some reason—he doesn't act on the matter. That tie is in essence a decision in some cases. And his decision will affect millions of Americans—black, white, minorities, the majority, women, men, children, in all aspects of living—social security, workmen's compensation, whatever it might be that might get to the Supreme Court of the United States. That one man in that instance will have more power than one hundred senators—more power in that instance than the president of the United States.

This is not a justice of the peace. This is a man who is being nominated to go on the highest court of the land. Give him the benefit of the doubt? He has no particular right to this seat. No individual has a particular right to a Supreme Court seat.

Such an honor of sitting on the Supreme Court of the United States should be reserved for only those who are most qualified and those whose temperament and character best reflect judicial and personal commitments to excellence. A credible charge of the type that has been leveled at Judge Thomas is enough, in my view, to mandate that we ought to look for a more exemplary nominee.

If we're going to give the benefit of the doubt, let's give it to the court. Let's give it to the country. . . .

If there's a cloud of doubt, this is the last chance. He's not running for the United States Senate, where there'd be another chance in six years. He's not running for the House of Representatives, where there'll be another chance in two years. He's not even running; he's been nominated to the Supreme Court of the United States, and if he is not rejected, which I predict he will not be rejected—I think too many have made up their minds. I think too many have been swayed by this argument about the benefit of the doubt. This is the last clear chance, to use a bit of legal terminology. This is it. You'll live with this decision the next thirty years. . . .

Perhaps we need to clean up the process if we can, but the process, quote, end quote, "is a constitutional process," and it has done us well for over two centuries. And as far as I'm concerned the benefit of the doubt, shall go to the court and to my children and to my grandchildren and to my country."

Byrd had been Senate majority leader when the nomination of Robert Bork was defeated. After this speech several senators lamented that if Senator Byrd was still in charge, Thomas would not have been confirmed.

One of the most interesting votes that day was that of Republican Nancy Landon Kassebaum of Kansas. As an already announced supporter of Thomas and one of the two women in the Senate, Kassebaum, a broadcasting executive and divorced mother of four children, was on the spot. She was a moderate who had gone her own way in the past, voting against President Bush's nomination of John Tower as secretary of defense, for example.

Kassebaum began her Senate floor speech by taking both Thomas and her fellow Republicans to task. She said that Thomas's "high-tech lynching" had no validity and that there was "no evidence in the record before us to support any claim that Professor Hill is mentally unstable, is inclined to wild fantasy, or is part of a decade-long conspiracy to get Clarence Thomas. What I do find in this record is much less comforting than these easy and highly speculative theories."

It seemed that she was preparing to vote against Thomas, but then Kassebaum took another turn. She refused, she said, to look at this issue though a woman's eyes.

> Three weeks ago I spoke in support of Judge Thomas's confirmation. In all that has come to light since then, I find no compelling basis to overturn that judgment. In fact, I believe it would be manifestly unfair for the Senate to destroy a Supreme Court nominee on the basis of evidence that finally boils down to the testimony of one person, however creditable, against his flat, unequivocal, and equally creditable denial.
>
> Throughout my years here I have taken pride in the fact that I am a United States senator, not a woman senator. When some of my male colleagues have suggested that I know nothing about national defense issues because I am a woman, I have been offended.
>
> In the same vein, I have to assume that many of my male colleagues are offended by the notion that they cannot begin to understand the seriousness of sexual harassment or the anguish of its victims. On the question before us, some women suggest that I should judge this nomination not as a senator but as a woman, one of only two in the Senate. I reject that suggestion.
>
> The issue before me is whether, with all of the ambiguity surrounding this matter, the allegation by Professor Hill was substantiated to the point that I should change my previous view. Mr. President, I have reached the conclusion that it has not and I therefore will vote to confirm Judge Thomas.

Clarence Thomas, for his part, was doing his best to ignore the United States Senate and the rest of Washington. He and his wife had managed to literally shut out the outside world, closing the kitchen blinds, turning on their "Christian praise" music and holding hands with friends as they read the Bible together for hours. At times, Thomas went outside to shoot basketball hoops with an old friend from St. Louis as they awaited the vote.

If the result of the vote was preordained, there remained considerable drama in the decisions of individual senators. Joseph Lieberman, a Democrat from Connecticut, had been inclined to vote for Thomas from their first meeting in July. Lieberman, like Thomas a Yale Law School graduate, had been impressed by the force of his personality and his seeming sincerity.

But Senator Lieberman was deeply troubled by the harassment charges, and according to Republican lobbyists, his wife was particularly upset. He had watched the hearings over the weekend, despite the injunction of his Jewish faith not to work on the Sabbath. As the vote approached he went over confirmation documents. He slept poorly. As he was being driven to Capitol Hill Tuesday morning, the phone in his car rang with a call from the President. His driver steered slowly around Washington while they talked. In his office he began to draft a statement in favor of Thomas, but he threw it out. Finally, just half an hour before the evening vote, he made up his mind to vote against Thomas. Hill, and her panel of witnesses, had been too credible.

Senator Danforth was deeply disappointed when Lieberman told him of his decision, stopping by Danforth's desk on the Senate floor a few minutes after the voting had started. The senators were voting one by one, and observers filled the galleries above the Senate chamber. Danforth had been counting on Lieberman, but he knew he had enough votes anyway, just barely enough. Vice President Quayle was presiding over the Senate for the vote so that in the event of a tie he could cast the final vote for Thomas. Despite the impending victory, there was no glee in the Thomas camp. The whole experience of the past week had been too painful.

Senator Danforth, in his last day of speeches about Clarence Thomas, recalled the joy he and Thomas had shared on July 1 on the occasion of the nomination.

   But joy has long since left both Clarence Thomas and Jack Danforth
   and the many friends of Clarence Thomas. There is no joy in these proceed-

ings and no matter how the vote turns out, no joy is possible. The joy that
we experienced three and a half months ago has turned to pain and the best
that can be said is that in approximately another hour, there will be a
feeling of relief at the determination one way or another.

Danforth's answer to Byrd, and those who thought like him, was
that the Senate should not defeat Thomas based on proceedings that
had flown out of control.

No one, no human being ever should have to go through what Clarence
Thomas has gone through for the last hundred-plus days and particularly
for the last ten days. It is not right. It is terribly, terribly wrong. It is not
true that the ends justify the means. It is not true that any strategy is
permissible in order to win a political point. It is not true that in order to
further a political agenda, it is all right to destroy a human being. That is
not what our country is all about. We have developed a legal system in
America to protect individuals. It is not worth any political objective to
destroy an individual, and that is what was attempted with respect to the
Thomas nomination.

Clarence Thomas will survive because he is an enormously strong person
of very deep religious faith. But many people could not have endured this.
Many people's lives literally would be in jeopardy if forced to endure the
kind of thing that Clarence Thomas went through. We must get our acts
together. We, meaning the Senate and the various interest groups and the
staff people, here in the Senate, cannot permit ourselves to go through this
again. It is wrong, and the one healthy thing that's happening is that the
American people are speaking out and they are saying that it is wrong.

Senator Danforth also made a prediction, one that would seem
lacking in prophetic accuracy as Thomas's initial opinions began to
trickle out of the Supreme Court the following year.

Clarence Thomas is going to surprise many people on the United States
Supreme Court. He is going to be a good and competent and decent and
fair justice. He is going to be the people's justice on the United States
Supreme Court.

The Senate voted to approve Clarence Thomas, by 52 to 48 votes.
This was a victory tarnished by more negative votes than any success-

ful nominee had ever received. Thomas would carry with him to the court the unresolved charges of sexual harassment and a cloud of unanswered questions as to whether he had committed perjury during the confirmation process.

The celebration that night at the Thomases' house was small. About fifteen people were there. Some "whoopin' and hollerin' " was going on, as Ricky Silberman from the EEOC put it, but the main feeling was relief and exhaustion. Danforth came briefly, as did some of the other Republican senators. Thomas's son Jamal was not there. He had been sent by his father to a military academy in Virginia for a year of post–high-school training. Boyden Gray came, as did Kenneth Duberstein and his wife.

Thomas stepped outside his house into the rainy night and gave a brief but statesmanlike speech. Standing next to his wife and Senator Strom Thurmond, and holding an umbrella, he thanked God for his survival and his success. He called for healing.

"I think that no matter how difficult or painful the process has been that this is a time for healing in our country, that we have to put these things behind us, that we have to go forward, and that we have to look for ways to solve problems that I think became apparent through this process, and certainly have been apparent in our country for some time.

"But this is more a time for healing, not a time for anger or for animus or animosity."

An hour after the confirmation, Senator Arlen Specter got his reward from the conservative movement. He had been asked to appear on Paul Weyrich's *Library Court Live*, a closed circuit television version of the Library Court meetings Thomas had attended earlier. The meetings were beamed to conservative groups across the country—to the heart of the far right, a place where Arlen Specter normally was reviled as a traitor to the Republican party. But that night he was the guest of honor, and he received a standing ovation for what he had done to Anita Hill. He boasted of his new conservative credentials by telling a little anecdote about what had happened as he left the Senate floor after the vote. A feminist leader, whose name he did not mention, told him, "I hope God strikes you dead."

Specter had won conservative support, but at the expense of alienating many of his supporters in the women's movement, who were a significant part of his electoral base. They had trusted the Pennsylvania senator because he was a moderate Republican who favored abortion rights.

Kate Michelman of the National Abortion Rights Action League, also from Pennsylvania, said later that she could no longer trust Specter despite the good working relationship they had in the past.

"He sold his soul to the devil trying to make up for his Robert Bork vote by trying to become the darling of the right wing on Thomas," Michelman said. "I can't even look at him. I can't trust him."

Arlen Specter was not the only politician who would feel the ire of women. The hearings' combustible mix of race, sex, and the Supreme Court had resulted in a national soap opera with enduring ramifications. Incumbents would fall and unknowns would win in coming elections in a country whose politics would be forever changed.

# Epilogue

Once Clarence Thomas had been elevated to the Supreme Court, life did not return to normal.

Back in Pin Point, Georgia, the people among whom Thomas had spent the years of his poverty-stricken childhood were bursting with pride. Many were wearing new T-shirts boasting that the tiny community under the live oaks was "The Home of Clarence Thomas." The shirts were illustrated with a romanticized sketch of the defunct crab factory in the marsh where the new Supreme Court justice's mother and sister had labored for nickels picking crabs.

Isaac Martin, the loyal second cousin of Thomas, was hard at work fixing up Pin Point's dilapidated, one-room community center. "They used to ignore us," Martin said of the world's attitude toward Pin Point. "Now we're starting to get tourists through here and so we've got to look good."

For his part, Thomas continued to isolate himself from the world that had treated him so harshly. According to a friend, he no longer read the newspapers that the liberals had used to attack him so furiously. Thomas and his wife bought a five-acre lot in suburban Virginia a full hour away, to get as far from Washington as they could.

One exception to this isolation was a very unjudicial appearance in *People* magazine in November. Official Washington and the decorous Supreme Court were astonished by a kind of fundamentalist version of a Hollywood picture layout of the Thomases at home. One photograph showed them stretched out on a carpet in their living room. Accompanying the photographs was a long interview with Virginia Thomas about their difficult experiences. "In my heart," Mrs. Thomas said, confiding to the magazine her opinion of Anita Hill, "I always believed she was probably someone in love with my husband and never got what she wanted."

Under a photograph of the two of them drinking coffee in their kitchen was a quotation from Virginia Thomas threatening the liberal organizations that inevitably would be appearing before her husband at the Supreme Court.

"Clarence will give everyone a fair day in court," she said. "But I feel he doesn't owe any of the groups who opposed him anything."

Exactly one month after he was confirmed, Supreme Court Justice Clarence Thomas paid a return visit to Paul Weyrich's *Library Court Live*. He thanked the group and its affiliates across the country—whose members were engaged in trying to overturn *Roe* v. *Wade* and influence other cases he would soon hear as a justice—for their help on his behalf during the confirmation process. He also answered personal questions.

In Lone Tree, Oklahoma, the reporters had stopped swarming down the dirt roads looking for anyone related to Anita Hill. But her family hadn't forgotten the events in far-away Washington that had invaded all their lives.

At a Sunday service at the Lone Tree Baptist Church, a simple clapboard building in a prairie field, an older brother of Anita Hill gave a sermon about the power of a woman. Preaching to a few dozen relatives and neighbors, the Reverend Winston Hill described how the biblical prophetess Deborah had faith in God and thus gave victory to the Israelites over an enemy army possessing iron chariots.

"In the end, everything will work out all right—providing you have faith," Hill sermonized. Then, he concluded, "What I mean is that a woman from Lone Tree is not an insignificant creature."

Hill herself had returned to her teaching life at the Norman campus of the University of Oklahoma, but not without some final travail. On her flight from Washington, she changed planes in Dallas. In the airport, strangers recognized her and hurled insults at her. "Little wench," shouted a young man. "Shame. Shame," added a woman who shook a reproving finger at Hill. Protected by a tight entourage of family and friends, Hill made it back to the friendly atmosphere of her home state.

On the door of her office at the law school, Hill taped up a new cartoon. It depicted two dinosaurs in a primeval setting backdropped by volcanoes. One dinosaur is saying to the other: "Don't worry about me. I'm a survivor."

The city council of Norman honored its returned law professor by giving Hill its annual human rights award. "The issue of sexual harassment has been raised to a higher level, which should benefit us all," said Tom McAuliffe, head of the city's human rights commission.

The council meeting to decide if the award should go to Hill attracted a huge crowd by Norman's standards, almost one hundred people. There hadn't been such a fuss at the city council since dog owners, aggravated by a leash regulation, had tried to make a point by backing a rule that would have forced cat owners to similarly restrain their felines.

As welcoming as Norman generally was, Anita Hill was shocked for a long while by what had happened in the capital. She spent long hours rehashing the events of Washington with Shirley Wiegand, her friend and colleague. Wiegand summed up their thoughts in a scathing "open letter" that she fired off to the Senate Judiciary Committee:

> These are the questions and concerns we have:
> When Anita and I first began to discuss her obligation to tell the truth about Clarence Thomas, we knew there would be repercussions. We knew her life would be disrupted and that some would not take her concerns seriously. In fact, my concern as early as August was that you senators would not care about whether she had been sexually harassed. Nevertheless, when she was asked, she had to tell the truth. Thus, when we learned that we would be travelling to Washington, we were neither nervous nor upset. We had "The Truth." We thought that Anita would tell you the truth and then she could come home. Little did we know that the truth would not be relevant.
> As I watched the hearings on October 11, I was very proud of Anita.

When one of you asked that Anita's colleagues suggest ways in which to improve the hearing process, I assiduously began making notes. Oh, I jotted down things like "no media," "follow the rules of evidence," "arrange for private hearings," etc. You see, I still believed at that moment that you were seriously interested! But as the hearings unfolded, I came to see that you were not.

What I saw was that certain senators were engaging in an inquisition and the rest of you were allowing it. Senators Specter and Hatch and Simpson participated in the vicious attack on an innocent woman, backed up by countless unknown participants behind the scenes, and the rest of you stood by and watched. Anita had no advocate at the hearing. I have read of the hearings being compared to a gang rape—precisely.

That leaves Anita and me with the real question, one which we have tried to answer and cannot: how can each of you, and particularly the three senators mentioned above, look at yourselves in the mirror? How can you justify what you did? Anita and I both grew up in farm families, she in Oklahoma, I in Wisconsin. Our parents trained us to be honest and to live our lives with integrity. We learned to "do unto others as you would have others do unto you." Our real question is this: how can you live with yourselves? Is it the political process that has so corrupted you? Or was there no integrity even before politics engulfed you?

I cannot believe that any one of you does not believe Anita Hill. I will not review all of the testimony; that was your job. But to listen to her and to accuse her of fantasy or, worse, perjury, reflects something other than a search for truth.

Prior to Anita deciding to come forward, she and I discussed whether we should trust the "process." . . . But once she decided to do so, I fully supported her decision. The process failed her. . . . As long as you care more about your political future than about the life of an innocent, honest woman; as long as you care more about your television profile than about the truth; as long as you care more about political expediency than about the sexual harassment of thousands of women, the process cannot be fixed.

In the past couple of weeks, I have been with Anita when strangers have hissed at her . . . when they have called her horrible names. She has been forced to install an elaborate security system in her home to protect her from the strangers who have threatened her. I have been the subject of tabloid smear campaigns, originating I am sure in Washington. I have received hate letters because I support my friend and colleague. Do you care?

Senators, I have lost all faith in your system. I have lost all faith in each

one of you. . . . You will be pleased to know that when we saw what was
happening in Washington, Anita and I packed up the truth and brought
it home with us. It made us happy to be at peace with ourselves.

Hill's thoughts had been incorporated in Wiegand's letter, which
amounted to the strongest statement issued on Hill's behalf after the
hearings, though it was not made public. Hill made a few public
appearances in the months following her go-round with the Judiciary
Committee, but she did not capitalize on her instant fame, or notoriety. In the eyes of conservatives and believers in Justice Thomas, Hill
was the epitome of all that had gone wrong, an error in the process,
an unfair blemish on the reputation of an upstanding man; in the eyes
of liberals and believers in women's rights, Hill was an emblem of the
future, a beacon in the murk of a political system founded on chauvinism, run by men and oblivious to basic human decency.

A group of women state legislators from around the country, who
had gathered at a sexual harassment conference in California, went
wild when Hill appeared before them. They stood on their chairs, they
banged their tables, they twirled hundreds of peach-colored napkins
and chanted the name of the Oklahoma law professor turned champion.

In her speech to them, Hill let go more than usual, comparing
sexual harassment to a beast in the workplace. "The reality is that this
powerful beast is used to reinforce a sense of inequality to keep women
in their place, notwithstanding our increasing numbers in the workplace," Hill said with a note of feminism that inspired her fans. She
talked about the hundreds and hundreds of letters she had received
from women. Many of the writers recounted their own tales of sexual
harassment, including some who had remained silent for as long as six
decades. She talked about how hard it could be for victims of sexual
harassment to step forward. First they had to overcome their feelings
of self-doubt and guilt, as well as fears of their bosses.

The case of Hill versus Thomas was not fading from the public
conscience. In fact, a new phrase sprang up—"the Anita Hill effect."
The accumulated anger of women would translate into a new force in
politics, one that would threaten male incumbents and make easier the
passage of legislation against workplace discrimination.

The most immediate and obvious result of the hearings was a surge in the number of sexual harassment complaints being filed. The Equal Employment Opportunity Commission reported that in the three-month period following the Hill-Thomas hearings, its offices nation-wide received 1,244 complaints of sexual harassment. In comparison, during the same months the year before, the agency recorded 728 complaints. The vast majority of the complaints were filed by women.

Businesses everywhere were worrying about the issue. Many were calling the EEOC and asking for help with training programs. The idea behind the programs was to educate confused workers as to the difference between camaraderie and abusive behavior. Men, in particu-lar, were going to have to learn the difference between complimenting women and humiliating them; the fine line between asking women out and threatening them; between making humorous conversation and falling into lewd conduct; between being romantic and being obscene.

And more complaints and lawsuits were certain because shortly after the hearings ended, the Democrats in the Senate and the hardline conservatives in the White House ended the bitter battle they had been waging for nearly two years over civil rights legislation. As a final compromise, the legislation made it easier for minorities and women to sue their companies for workplace discrimination. It also gave the victims of sexual discrimination the right to sue for limited damages. Previously victims of sexual harassment, for instance, could only win back pay. Now they could sue for up to $300,000 in damages.

The Civil Rights Act of 1991, which President Bush signed into law in November, pulled together in the end many of the major figures in the Thomas nomination. A catalyst for the compromise was wide-spread dread of another round of fighting and explosive debate about an issue involving race and sex. The closing fiasco of the Thomas nomination hearings had been enough. The White House also owed a favor to Senator Jack Danforth, who had so loyally backed Thomas, and who had also fervently believed in the civil rights legislation.

This was similar to the legislation which C. Boyden Gray, the White House counsel, had been so vehemently opposed to when he encoun-tered Clarence Thomas during the Pennsylvania Avenue footrace. It was Thomas's agreement about the evils of what the White House derogatorily called "the quota bill" that had sparked Gray's interest in the man from Pin Point as a possible Supreme Court nominee.

The final negotiations that led to enactment of the civil rights bill began the same day that Thomas had his victory party on the White House lawn. Afterwards, President Bush retreated into the White House to meet privately with some of the key players, including Senator Danforth and Senator Arlen Specter who, wearing his moderate-Republican hat, had also been pushing for the legislation. Danforth and Specter warned the President that he could expect political backlash from the hearings, particularly on the part of women, and that signing the civil rights bill would help.

Senator Danforth had slipped back easily into his role as the widely respected purveyor of political morality and brokered the deal between the White House and the Democrats led by Senator Ted Kennedy, who had slipped back just as easily into his role as the liberal advocate of the oppressed. Gray remained as hardline as ever, trying to roll back affirmative action policies even as Bush was signing the bill.

Senator Kennedy, who had been the original sponsor of the legislation and chief negotiator for the Democrats, was able to carry news of a "victory" for civil rights home to Massachusetts, where he had planned to come clean in public about his personal problems. He did so in a speech at the Institute of Politics at Harvard's Kennedy School of Government, which was named in honor of his assassinated brother. The senator's miserable performance at the Hill-Thomas hearings had given him impetus to discuss his failings publicly.

"My views on issues have made some people angry over the years—and frankly, I accept that as the price of fighting hard for my beliefs," Kennedy said. "But I am painfully aware that the criticism directed at me in recent months involves far more than honest disagreement with my positions, or the usual criticism from the far right. It also involves the disappointment of friends and many others who rely on me to fight the good fight.

"To them I say: I recognize my own shortcomings—the faults in the conduct of my private life. I realize that I alone am responsible for them, and I am the one who must confront them. Today, more than ever before, I believe that each of us as individuals must not only struggle to make a better world, but to make ourselves better, too."

The whole story of the Thomas nomination might have ended differently if Kennedy had tried to turn over a new leaf earlier, if he had spoken during the events as he did in retrospect.

"Some of the anger of recent days," he said in his Massachusetts speech, "the powerful public reaction to the final phase of the Thomas hearings, reflects the pain of a new idea still being born—the idea of a society where sex discrimination is ended, and sexual harassment is unacceptable—the idea of an America where the majority who are women are truly and finally equal citizens."

A few months later, Kennedy announced his engagement to remarry, his fiancée a 38-year-old Washington lawyer named Victoria Reggie. The hope was that she would help anchor him to a more sober lifestyle.

Of the leading members of the Senate Judiciary Committee, Kennedy fared the worst in a poll taken about senatorial conduct at the hearings. In an opinion survey, the Gallup Organization found that only a sparse 22 percent of the people polled gave Kennedy a favorable rating for his performance. He might have done that well if he had skipped the hearings entirely. His popularity also took a general dive in Massachusetts.

In the Gallup poll, Senator Simpson merited a mere 41 percent favorable rating for his buffoonish behavior and Senator Specter scraped by with a 48 percent favorable rating for his inquisition of Hill.

Senator Biden, although criticized roundly in Washington for the political mess into which the hearings degenerated, came out well—at least in comparison to his colleagues. He won a 63 percent approval rating in the poll. His efforts as committee chairman to be fair, while producing disastrous results, had left more Americans pleased than furious. Biden himself, though, was unhappy with the job he and his committee had done.

The committee as a whole, as an entity comprised of fourteen senators, was not highly rated in the poll. One out of two Americans questioned said that the whole episode had eroded their faith in the Senate and its workings. But Chairman Biden was planning to rally the committee and hold hearings on reforming the process. His hope was that these hearings would be far more decorous than the Thomas nomination hearings.

In the meantime, George Mitchell, the Senate majority leader, reported the rather self-serving results of a senatorial task force that had looked into the nomination and confirmation process. The report, which Mitchell summarized on the Senate floor, complained that critics on all sides had wrongly lambasted the Senate Judiciary Committee.

"Critics bemoan the nature, the extent, or the scope of the questioning in Senate confirmation hearings." Mitchell said. "But these critics should keep in mind that they have no idea what questions—what political or ideological considerations—are brought to bear in the executive branch's review of potential candidates for a position. That is a process conducted entirely in private. It is insulated from public scrutiny. It is wholly unbalanced to hyperanalyze the process that the Senate uses to consider nominees, while uttering not a word about the process the president uses to consider and reject many possible candidates for each nomination.

"The wisdom of the open nature of the Senate hearings was widely questioned during the Judiciary Committee's consideration of the charges of sexual harassment against Judge Thomas last fall. After being criticized for conducting its investigation of the charges in confidence before the public disclosure of the allegations, the committee was then criticized even more for conducting its subsequent hearings on these matters in public."

An aggravated President Bush had some choice words of criticism for the committee that had so dragged out the confirmation of his Supreme Court nominee. Labeling the hearings a "circus and travesty," he argued that the Judiciary Committee should straighten out its act. He said his judicial nominees should be speedily confirmed in a process lasting forty-five days rather than two or even three months. The committee's handling of Thomas, the President averred, had been akin to "a burlesque show."

Senator Simpson tried to be more conciliatory when he addressed a group of professional women meeting on Capitol Hill shortly after the hearings. He pointed out to the women, many of whom were incensed about the part the Wyoming senator had played in trying to vilify Hill, that at least he had the courage "to show up" in front of them. He complained that women's groups had "savaged" him for his role.

"I don't seek your pity," he told the women. "But I certainly hope we can raise the level of discourse and debate even though we may want to flatten each other's brains."

Of the committee members, Senator Specter faced the most serious political problems in the aftermath of the hearings. Shortly after Thomas's confirmation, the senator's office was on the telephone to the office of the National Organization for Women, asking for information on sexual harassment. The senator and his aides needed to do some careful studying of the issue, which was going to have an effect on his unpredictable political future. He was up for reelection in 1992.

His performance at the hearings would help him among conservatives leery about his stand in favor of abortion rights and still angry about his previous vote against Bork. His zealous work on behalf of Thomas's confirmation was a big plus with Pennsylvania's right wing, important for his tough primary fight in April 1992. But he also faced the prospect of women's ire translating into ballots for his Democratic opponent the following November. His accusation during the hearings that Hill had committed perjury would rankle forever in the minds of women.

In early 1992, Senator Alan Dixon, a two-term incumbent in Illinois, suffered an awesome political defeat in a primary election that, in normal times, he could have won handily. Dixon was one of the Democrats who had deserted his party to vote for Thomas's confirmation. It turned out to be a vote that mattered more than he could have guessed. Dixon was beaten by an unknown, a black woman lawyer named Carol Moseley Braun, with an obscure political position as Cook County recorder of deeds. Braun had entered the race after Dixon's vote to confirm Thomas and had won not only black support but votes from women of both races. The Dixon upset sent shivers through the political spines of incumbents like Specter. And it gave a boost to the political hopes of women running for election.

For instance, in California, a state with two Senate seats open in 1992, women were hoping to win both. Two strong women candidates—Dianne Feinstein, the former San Francisco mayor, and Barbara Boxer, currently a U.S. representative—were both using pro-Hill–anti-Thomas sentiment to the maximum. Their male Democratic opponents were reduced to arguing that they had better feminist credentials than the women candidates.

Feinstein's fund-raising letter went right to the point: "Dear Friend, I will never forget the weekend of October 11. It was sad and painful to all of us who care about the role of women in our society. The sense of rage I felt as I watched what they did to Anita Hill has not subsided with the passage of time. I am sure you feel the same."

Representative Boxer made a campaign staple of her account of how she and other congresswomen marched to the Senate to demand that the vote on Thomas be delayed so that Hill's allegations could be considered. Boxer was also using and reusing the provocative statement: "If there had been only one woman on the Judiciary Committee, things would have been different."

Both women were hoping the Hill effect would work for them. They were not alone. As contributions to their campaigns increased dramatically after the hearings, so did the amount of money being donated to other women candidates and to women's organizations.

The women at Emily's List, an organization that raises money for female Democratic candidates, watched happily as a wave of donations hit their office. Contributions to Emily's List—the name comes from the initials of Early Money Is Like Yeast—rose by more than 50 percent in the two months following the hearings. The organization raised $1.5 million in 1990, which it divvied up between fourteen women candidates. The women at Emily's List were hoping to take in twice that amount in 1992 and give it to women early enough to make a difference in their campaigns.

A significant fact about the new money coming into Emily's List was that much of it was being donated by women who had not been known as political activists. The hearings had engaged a whole new group of women who had previously not been paying much attention to politics. Although national polls taken immediately after the hearings showed that more women believed Thomas than Hill, those who sided with the Oklahoma law professor were more apt to be politically energized.

Other women's groups—like the Fund for the Feminist Majority, the National Women's Political Caucus and the Women's Campaign Fund—also reported fund-raising booms. One anonymous person decided on a more direct way of expressing an opinion. On a sidewalk across the street from the Supreme Court, a message appeared in blue paint, in a cursive and feminine style: ANITA TOLD THE TRUTH.

Clarence Thomas's initial opinions as a Supreme Court justice, though by no means conclusive, indicated that he might not be the judicial moderate that his defender, Senator Danforth, had promised. Indeed, in his early opinions Thomas showed himself to be every bit as extreme as the much-maligned citizens groups had said he would be. Paul Weyrich's New Right coalition, Library Court, was pleased with its handiwork, while those liberals who had taken a risk on Thomas were dismayed.

It will be years before a full profile of Thomas's judicial philosophy can be drawn. But at the outset of his term, Thomas seemed to be aligning himself with the extreme conservative views of Justice Antonin Scalia.

The new justice's opinion in one case in particular worried court watchers. Justice Thomas shocked the nation and won a rebuke from the court's conservative majority with a dissent concerning the treatment of prisoners. His dissent was made from the court's decision on a lawsuit brought by a state penitentiary prisoner in Louisiana who had been beaten by guards. The beating was retribution for an argument the inmate, Keith Hudson, had with a prison guard. While the handcuffed and shackled Hudson was held by one guard, another punched him in the mouth, eyes, chest, and stomach. Their supervisor watched the beating, warning the guards "not to have too much fun." The beating loosened Hudson's teeth, cracked his dental plate, and caused small bruises and swelling on his face, mouth and lip.

Seven of the justices, including conservatives William H. Rehnquist and Anthony Kennedy, voted to approve a monetary award. But Thomas, using arguments sketched by Scalia in oral arguments, wrote that the inmate was not entitled to the $800 in damages awarded him by a federal magistrate for violation of his constitutional rights. Thomas said the beating did not violate the Eighth Amendment to the Constitution's ban on cruel and unusual punishment because Hudson's injuries, which did not require hospitalization, were not serious enough.

"In my view," Justice Thomas wrote, "a use of force that causes only insignificant harm to a prisoner may be immoral, it may be tortuous, it may be criminal, and it may even be remedial under other provisions of the Federal Constitution, but it is not 'cruel and unusual punishment.'" He said that the majority's decision was "yet another manifestation of the pervasive view that the federal Constitution must address all ills in our society."

Thomas's opinion seemed to suggest that the Eighth Amendment should not be applied at all to what he called "prisoner grievances."

He seemed a different man from the one who had told the Senate
Judiciary Committee, when he was up for confirmation, that he used
to watch prisoners from his appellate court office and "say to myself
almost every day, there but for the grace of God go I."

The dissent earned Thomas a headline description on *The New
York Times* editorial page as "The Youngest, Cruelest Justice." *The
Washington Post* editorial page, which had stuck up for Thomas
through the bitter end of the hearings, called the opinion written by
the new justice "mind-boggling." Justice Sandra Day O'Connor, who
wrote the majority opinion, took Thomas to task for suggesting that
the court evaluate the beating the same way it would complaints about
other facets of prison life:

"To deny, as the dissent does, the difference between punching a
prisoner in the face and serving him unappetizing food is to ignore the
concepts of dignity, civilized standards, humanity and decency that
animate the Eighth Amendment."

Thomas was equally cold regarding prisoners on death row, even
those who might not belong there. When a witness whose testimony
had convicted Justin Lee May of murder in Texas recanted shortly
before May was to be executed, Thomas voted with Scalia and Rehnquist to allow the state to execute him anyway, without any hearing.
Fortunately for May, the three justices were outvoted. Later, Thomas
and four other justices refused to stay the execution of another Texas
prisoner who also had produced compelling new evidence of his innocence, even though the high court had agreed to hear his appeal. At
the very last minute, a Texas court stayed the execution so the appeal
could be heard.

Thomas also voted against hearing the appeal of Haitian refugees
about to be forceably repatriated. In another case, he wrote an opinion
rejecting the Bush administration's view that organizers attempting to
unionize a grocery store had the right of access to a lot where the
workers parked their cars.

He agreed in a unanimous decision that a 1972 statute outlawing sex
discrimination in schools allowed a Georgia high school student forced
to have sex with a teacher to sue the school system. But in this case,
he joined with Scalia and Rehnquist in saying that the holding should
have been much more limited than what the majority of the high
court's justices decided.

But Clarence Thomas also served notice that his vote could not always be predicted. An exception to the early pattern was a vote in April 1992 in a case involving child pornography. The newest justice provided the crucial fifth vote to support the claim by Keith Jacobson, a retired career military man, that he had been entrapped by a Postal Service undercover sting operation in which he was repeatedly sent offers to buy pornographic pictures of young boys through the mail before he finally made a purchase.

And in February 1992, Thomas finally issued a controversial decision pertaining to a case he had heard while still on the Court of Appeals. This was the decision in an affirmative action case that *The Legal Times* had suggested he had delayed ruling on in order to avoid controversy during his confirmation hearings. The decision overturned the Federal Communications Commission's policy of giving preferences to women in granting radio and television broadcast licenses, saying that the policy discriminated illegally against men. The decision, had it been known the previous summer when it was first drafted, might well have made Thomas's confirmation more difficult.

The raw emotions and political angers that had been raised by the imbroglio of the Thomas confirmation did not quiet quickly.

Phyllis Berry Myers, one of the EEOC women who testified for Thomas, landed a job with Paul Weyrich doing a new version of *Library Court Live* aimed at black voters. For months she could not go to the grocery store or walk down a sidewalk without people coming up to congratulate her.

Senator Brock Adams, a Democrat from Washington State, announced he would not seek reelection in 1992 after *The Seattle Times* reported that eight women had signed statements charging him with sexual harassment over the years. Senator Adams had voted against Thomas.

Joe Reed, the black Alabama Democrat who had refused to oppose Thomas, got just what he wanted from the Bush administration. The White House ordered the Justice Department to reverse its position against historically black colleges. This would protect Reed's power base.

Benjamin Hooks announced that he would retire as executive director of the NAACP effective April 1, 1993.

The Senate, outraged by the embarrassment into which it had fallen during the Hill-Thomas hearings, did not try to evaluate its own performance. It did not berate itself for failing to ascertain and prove the truth in this extraordinary case. Instead, it authorized an investigation into who had leaked the substance of Hill's charges and ruined what would have been an otherwise relatively uneventful and untroubling confirmation process. The purpose of the investigation was to find out who had betrayed the Senate, who had provided the disclosures about Hill that were first printed by *Newsday* and aired by National Public Radio.

Peter Fleming, a New York lawyer, received the appointment as special independent counsel in charge of the investigation. Fleming began questioning Senate staffers, senators, and people in citizens' groups across Washington. He also went after me. Citing the First Amendment privileges of a journalist, I refused a request by Fleming in January 1992 to appear voluntarily to discuss the article I had written breaking the news of Anita Hill's allegations. In response, Fleming sent a subpoena.

"Greetings," the offical document said. Not since I received notices from my draft board had that word seemed so chilling. "Pursuant to lawful authority, YOU ARE HEREBY COMMANDED to appear before the Office of Temporary Special Counsel of the Senate of the United States, on February 13, 1992, at 10 o'clock."

I agreed to appear in order to verify that I had written the article in question and that it was accurate to the best of my knowledge. I also would testify to the accuracy of subsequent public statements I had made about it. But I would do nothing more, under the conviction that I was protected by the First Amendment, which forbids Congress from passing any law abridging the freedom of the press. I made it clear I would not supply any information that might, even remotely, help lead Fleming to my source, or sources.

Flanked by lawyers I appeared as ordered, as did Anthony Marro, *Newsday*'s editor. *Newsday* had been ordered to produce notes and other documents associated with the article I had written. Marro provided Fleming with copies of my article, but refused to hand over any other documents. In a cubbyhole of a room in one of the Senate office buildings, I spent four hours closeted with Fleming and three assistants. Two lawyers advised me as Fleming interrogated me about my article and I repeatedly refused to answer any questions about the origin of my information.

At the outset of the session, I read Fleming a statement explaining what my conduct would be.

> I respectfully decline to answer the Special Independent Counsel's questions here today because they are posed for the explicit purpose of seeking the identity of my sources. I do so not only as an assertion of my rights under the First Amendment, but also of those of my readers, and of the American people. They had a need and a right to know that serious allegations had been made against a nominee to the Supreme Court. It was my job to tell them. It is they whom I was trying to serve in writing my story. It is the readers of *Newsday* and the many other newspapers that carried my story whose rights are being hauled up before the Senate today. No matter what is done as a result of today's events, it will not succeed in forcing me to reveal my sources; because if it did, I might never again be able to tell my readers what their government does not want them to know.

Nina Totenberg, the National Public Radio reporter who had the first broadcast interview with Hill, went through a similar process later in the month.

We both knew that we could go to jail if the Senate voted to hold us in contempt for refusing to cooperate with its investigator. But that outcome seemed unlikely. The subpoenas had raised a hue and cry in the media. In editorials, columns, articles, and news broadcasts, newspapers, radio, and television lambasted the Senate. The message was that the Senate, having been embarrassed by the disclosures of sexual harassment charges it had neglected, now was ignoring the Constitution in order to investigate a matter in which there was no evidence that any law had been broken.

But Fleming persisted. In March he subpoenaed my telephone records, both at the office and at home. Totenberg received a similar document. This invasion of our privacy raised even more of an outcry. When Fleming asked the Senate Rules Committee to order us to cooperate, the committee balked. Wendell Ford, a Kentucky Democrat and chairman of the committee, issued a statement setting an historic precedent.

"The traditions of the Senate regarding the press and the First Amendment require us to carefully balance the competing demands presented by this case," Ford said. "Through the years Congress has exercised a policy of restraint in this area, and I believe this tradition must be continued. And that is why we have denied the Special Independent Counsel's requests today."

The hunt for my source, or sources, was over. But the controversial investigation had served to remind voters of the Senate's bungling of the hearings. It had reinforced the negative views about Congress that were being buttressed by almost daily reports of check-bouncing by House members and drug dealing by employees of the House post office.

The Senate, while spending vast amounts of money to investigate the so-called leaks, had made no effort to investigate who had lied under oath to the Judiciary Committee, Hill or Thomas. The Republicans had no appetite for investigating the alleged conspiracy that they said had been concocted to sabotage their nominee to the Supreme Court.

# Bibliographical Note

The primary sources for the material in this book come from our own reporting. Timothy Phelps covered every aspect of the Clarence Thomas story for *Newsday*, from the nomination through the confirmation three and a half months later. Helen Winternitz traveled to Pin Point, Georgia, and Norman and Lone Tree, Oklahoma, where she interviewed family and friends of both Clarence Thomas and Anita Hill. In Washington, we and three research assistants interviewed over a hundred more people, many of whom wanted to remain anonymous.

Neither Clarence Thomas nor Anita Hill agreed to be interviewed for the book, although close friends of both provided us invaluable insights and anecdotes about them. Most of the key senators on the Judiciary Committee refused to be interviewed, reflecting the embarrassment of the spectacle they presented to the public as well as the anxiety caused by the investigation into the sources for my reporting. Many of their staff members were helpful, though, and for that we are grateful. The same is true of the White House, where many of the key figures decided to duck rather than speak. Thanks, however, to several officials there who must go unnamed, we were able to put together that side of the saga as well.

The description of Thomas's emerging philosophy was garnered from reading hundreds of speeches that he delivered during the 1980s.

We supplemented our own work with articles from various news organizations, including *The New York Times, Newsday, The Washington Post, The Boston Globe, The Wall Street Journal, The Los Angeles Times, The Washington Times,* the *Legal Times, The National Law Journal* and the Associated Press. News magazines also were useful, including *Newsweek,* in particular, as well as *Time,* and *U.S. News & World Report. The American Lawyer* published a profile of Charles Ogletree in December 1991.

The reporting of *Washington Post* reporter Juan Williams was helpful, especially his profile of Clarence Thomas published in *The Atlantic* in February 1987. Also consulted were: a profile of Thurgood Marshall in *The Washington Post Magazine* on January 7, 1990; profiles of Clarence Thomas in the St. Louis *Post-Dispatch* on July 7, 1991, and the *Legal Times* on December 31, 1984; a valuable interview with Clarence Thomas in *Reason* in November 1987; and a profile of Virginia Thomas in *The Washington Post* on September 10, 1991.

*Essence* Magazine provided useful material on the black reaction to the Hill hearings in its January 1992 edition. *The New York Review of Books* published an insightful article in January 1992, on George Bush's twists and turns on the race issue.

Important historical background was provided by Ethan Broner in *Battle for Justice: How the Bork Nomination Shook America:* W.W. Norton & Co, New York, 1989, and Henry J. Abraham in *Freedom and the Court: Civil Rights and Liberties in the United States:* Oxford University Press, New York, 1988.

*Congressional Quarterly's Guide to the U.S. Supreme Court,* by Elder Witt: Congressional Quarterly, Washington, 1990, provided historical detail on the court and its decisions. *The National Law Journal's* annual Supreme Court reviews were another helpful source of information. The background on the Warren Court in this book was enriched by numerous personal conversations between members of that court and coauthor Phelps.

*Simple Justice,* by Richard Kluger: Vintage Books, New York,

1977, provides a thoroughly researched and well told history of the Supreme Court's *Brown* v. *Board of Education* decision outlawing school desegregation.

*Politics in America 1992*, Congressional Quarterly's guide to the members of Congress, provided detail for the political and personal biographies of the senators.

Other books that provided background included *The Brethren: Inside the Supreme Court*, by Bob Woodward and Scott Armstrong: Simon & Schuster, New York, 1979; *Packing the Courts: The Conservative Campaign to Rewrite the Constitution*, by Herman Schwartz: Charles Scribner's Sons, New York, 1988; *Order & Law; Arguing the Reagan Revolution—A Firsthand Account*, by Charles Fried: Simon & Schuster, New York, 1991; *The New Right v. The Constitution*, by Stephen Macedo: Cato Institute, Washington 1987; and God *Save This Honorable Court*, Laurence H. Tribe: Random House, New York, 1985.

We also consulted *Reflections of an Affirmative Action Baby*, by Stephen L. Carter: Basic Books, New York, 1991; *The Content of Our Character: A New Vision of Race in America*, by Shelby Steele: St. Martin's Press, New York, 1990; *The Economics and Politics of Race*, by Thomas Sowell: William Morrow and Company, New York, 1983.

Pertinent books about women's perspectives were *Sexual Harassment of Working Women*, by Catherine A. MacKinnon: Yale University Press, New Haven and London, 1979, and *Backlash*, by Susan Faludi: Crown Publishers, New York, 1991.

Books that provided historical background on Georgia and Oklahoma included *Drums and Shadows: Survival Studies among the Georgia Coastal Negroes*, by the Georgia Writers' Project: University of Georgia Press, Athens, Georgia, 1940; *The Savannah*, by Thomas L. Stokes: University of Georgia Press, 1982; and *Morris Historical Highlights: A History of Morris, Oklahoma*, by Steven B. Guy: Heritage House Publishing, Marceline, Missouri.

# Index

ABC-TV, iv-v, 71, 267–68
abortion:
  gag rule and, 19, 159
  illegal, 27, 191
  pro-choice views on, 10, 18–20, 110,
    138, 159, 164, 180, 188, 194–95,
    202, 208
  pro-life views on, 10–11, 16, 18–20, 66,
    69, 116, 128, 130–31, 159
  Thomas and, 10–11, 18–20, 23–24, 51,
    62, 66, 135, 136, 138, 163, 170,
    179–80, 191–95, 197, 205
  *see also Roe* v. *Wade*
Adams, Brock, 430
Adams, Floyd, 37–38
affirmative action, 25, 28, 81, 107,
  118
  criticism of, 55, 56, 81, 83, 103, 132,
    137, 139, 157, 168
  Thomas as beneficiary of, 45, 49–50,
    204
  Thomas's opposition to, 2–3, 23, 45,
    49–50, 77, 84, 85, 87, 95–96, 105,
    113, 121, 135, 201–4, 239, 382

  Thomas's support of, 97, 99, 100–101,
    106, 204
AFL-CIO, 79, 138
African-American Freedom Alliance, 133
Agency for International Development
  (AID), 279–80
AIDS, 131, 335
Alabama Democratic Caucus, 144–46
Alabama State University, 144, 400
Ali, Shahrazad, 396
Alliance for Justice, 25–27, 62, 73,
  123–24, 133, 136, 138, 210, 228
Alvarez, J. C., 369
Amend, Deborah, 71
American Association of Retired Persons
  (AARP), 118, 120, 135–36, 201
American Bar Association (ABA), 4, 317
  Thomas rated by, 140–41
American Civil Liberties Union (ACLU),
  29
American Enterprise Institute, 16
American Federation of State, County
  and Municipal Employees
  (AFSCME), 138

*American Lawyer*, 295
American Life Lobby, 128
American Public Welfare Association, 356
*American Spectator*, 20
American University, 356
Amherst College, 174
Anderson, Christine "Tina," 34, 35, 39, 40, 102, 112
Anderson, Myers, 33–44, 54, 55, 59–60, 168, 177
    business zeal of, 34–35, 36, 39–40, 145
    death of, 40, 102
    Thomas influenced by, 44, 49, 60, 88, 102, 112, 114, 145
    values of, 35–39, 44, 54, 94, 112
Anna Maria College, 48
Anti-Defamation League, 67
anti-Semitism, 66–67, 300
apartheid, 46, 67–68, 83–84, 89–90, 305, 359
*Arizona* v. *Fulminante*, 159
Arnett, Peter, 276
Arnold, Fortas and Porter, 153
Aron, Nan, 25–26, 73, 136–37
Ashcroft, John, 54
Associated Press, 231, 276
Association of American Law Schools, 286
*Atlantic, The*, 41, 53, 202
Attorney's Office, U.S., 63

Bailey, F. Lee, 345
Baldwin, Donald, 208
*Baltimore Sun, The*, 6, 7
Bamberger, Clinton, 305
Bamford, Richard H., 119
Baptist Church, 23, 32, 54, 59, 70, 128
Barnes, Fred, 142
Basie, Count, 250
Bauer, Gary L., 130, 132–33, 180
*Behind the Green Door* (film), 52
Bell, William M., 90, 91
Bennett, William, 128–29
*Benton* v. *Maryland*, 151
Biden, Joseph, 143, 169–70, 174–81, 186–89, 424
    background and career of, 187–88

conciliatory manner of, 169, 175–76, 178, 187, 189, 208
Doggett questioned by, 372–75
ethical questions avoided by, 189, 212–13
Hill questioned by, 313–16
Judiciary Committee chairmanship of, 26, 120, 169–70, 197, 198, 206, 209, 210, 211–14, 218–19, 221–25, 239, 263, 274–75, 290, 292, 299, 302–3, 306–7, 313–16, 346–47, 391–95, 398
plagiarism charges against, 142, 187–88
on Thomas, 221–23, 224–25
Thomas questioned by, 174, 175–81, 182, 192, 347, 351
Bill of Rights, 151
birth control, 128, 152
Black, Elizabeth, 156
Black, Hugo, 152, 154, 156, 206, 207
*Blackman's Guide to Understanding the Blackwoman, The* (Ali), 396
Blackmun, Harry A., 154, 155, 156, 158, 161, 163, 165, 174
Black Muslims, 23, 66–67
Black Panthers, 45
Black Power, 41, 48, 154–55
Bob Jones University, 95
Bolick, Clint, 7–8, 12, 74, 75, 297
Boren, David, 399
Bork, Robert H., 26–27, 70, 74, 109, 120, 129, 130, 136–37, 138, 153, 198, 357, 359, 383
    judicial qualifications of, 126, 141
    Senate Judiciary Committee
        confirmation hearings of, 179, 181, 183, 187, 202, 257, 287
    Senate rejection of, 12, 21, 27, 63, 73, 124, 126–27, 132–33, 142, 157, 171, 202, 215, 222, 264, 271, 290, 317, 399–400, 410
    Specter and, 202, 290, 317
    Ted Kennedy and, 27, 80, 124, 134, 183, 359
*Boston Globe, The*, 62–63, 188–89
Boxer, Barbara, 426, 427
boycotts, 36, 209
Bozell, Brent, 143
Brandeis, Louis Dembitz, 207

*Branzburg* v. *Hayes*, 201
Braun, Carol Moseley, 426
Bray, Rosemary L., 396
Brennan, William J., Jr., 2, 11–12, 61,
    151, 152, 155, 156, 157, 158–59
Brown, Floyd, 141–43
Brown, Hank, 173, 199, 288, 302
Brown, Judie, 128
*Brown* v. *Board of Education*, 23, 33,
    152
    Marshall and, 112, 150, 162–63
    Thomas's opposition to, 112–13
Brudney, Jim, 174–75, 186, 210, 327–28,
    345, 346
Budget Committee, Senate, 265
Burger, Warren Earl, 150, 154–57, 160
Burke, John, 365, 398
Bush, Barbara, 13
Bush, Dorothy Walker, 13
Bush, George, v, 11, 60, 275
    civil rights record of, 2, 5, 139–40, 190
    court-packing efforts of, 165
    Thomas confirmation celebrated by,
        v–vi
    Thomas supported by, 4, 12–16, 28,
        70, 101, 119–20, 138–40, 163, 205,
        243–44, 287–88, 300, 305, 328,
        400–401, 425
    vice-presidency of, 1, 103, 140
Bush, Jamie, 361
Bush, Prescott, 1
Bush administration, 141, 287–88, 429
    black officials in, 29, 70
    congressional relations of, 2
    Thomas nomination and, v–vii, 62–80,
        135–36, 181
business regulations, 2, 87, 110, 111, 177,
    178
Byrd, Robert, 406–10, 413

Cable News Network (CNN), 190, 244,
    276
Calabresi, Guido, 206–7
Caldwell, Barry, 363
California, University of, at Berkeley, 82
Cardozo, Benjamin Nathan, 207
Carr, John W., 356, 358
Carswell, G. Harrold, 141, 155–56

Carter, Jimmy, 81, 84, 94, 287, 381
Carter, Stephen L., 239
*Carter* v. *Sedgwick County, Kansas*, 342,
    349–50
Cato Institute, 26, 112, 114
Center for Ecology and Social Justice, 25
Central Intelligence Agency (CIA), 178,
    322
Chamber of Commerce, 23, 71, 106, 115,
    304
charismatic movement, v, 65, 116, 134
charitable groups, private, 83, 259
*Charlotte Observer, The*, 278, 280, 297
Chavez, Linda, 266
Cherokee Indians, 251
Chicago, University of, 132
child care issues, 130, 335
Christian Coalition, 133–34
Chrysler Corporation, 77
Churchill, Winston, 22
church/state separation, 69, 131, 155, 201
Citizens' Committee to Confirm Clarence
    Thomas, 133
civil liberties, 2, 150, 151
civil rights:
    Hill's views on, 247, 254–55, 256, 258,
        348
    media coverage of, 6
    race-specific vs. social approaches to,
        168
    "separate but equal" doctrine and,
        144–45
    Thomas's views on, 2–4, 14–15, 18, 20,
        23, 45, 49–50, 62, 66, 76, 77, 84, 85,
        87–89, 94–106, 110, 112–13, 121,
        135, 144–45, 184, 201–4, 209, 214
Civil Rights Act (1964), 42, 84, 94, 113,
    140, 155, 406
    Title VII of, 380–81, 384, 385
Civil Rights Act (1991), 422–23
Civil Rights Commission, 90
civil rights legislation, 23, 42, 73, 76, 79,
    264, 422–23
    Democratic support of, 2, 5, 124, 359
    Republican opposition to, 2, 5, 28,
        103–4, 139–40, 422
civil rights movement, 23, 25, 26, 28–30,
    36, 44, 60, 62, 209

criticism of, 55–56, 88, 121, 133,
  136–37, 139–40, 173
militant demonstrations in, 45–46
Thomas as beneficiary of, 45, 49–50,
  73, 76, 77, 88, 173, 204
Thomas's criticism of, 88, 104, 121,
  133, 173
women's rights movement vs., 397–98
civil rights organizations, 4, 6, 12
Thomas at odds with, 28–30, 66,
  75–79, 94–95, 99, 100, 103–4, 106,
  121, 144, 168, 173, 262
  see also specific organizations
Civil War, U.S., 111, 251, 379–80
Claremont College, 9
Clarence Thomas Sourcebook, 184
Clark, S. M., 379–80
Clark, Susan, 251–53
Clark, Tom, 150
Clark College, 87–88
class-action lawsuits, 95, 96, 118
Coalition for Traditional Values, 131
Coalition of Black Trade Unionists, 209
Coalitions for America, 194
Cochran, Thad, 182, 209
Coleman, Lovida, 52–53
Collins, Tai, 400
Comanche Indians, 259
Compton, Dorothy, 270
Concerned Women for America, 131
Congress, U.S., 155, 170–71, 200
Bush administration and, 2
public liaison with, 170–71
Thomas and, 106–7, 117–21
  see also House of Representatives,
  U.S.; Senate, U.S.
Congressional Black Caucus, 66, 75, 205,
  209
Connor, Eugene "Bull," 133
conservative movement, 1–5, 7, 25, 165
blacks in, 82–86, 90–91, 119
extremist and radical elements in, 109,
  127–34, 143, 205, 209–10
religious elements in, 127–28, 131,
  133–34
Constitution, U.S., 21, 26, 50, 110–11,
  127, 151–52, 186, 191, 222
First Amendment to, 159, 201, 431–32

Fifth Amendment to, 151, 164
Eighth Amendment to, 428–29
Fourteenth Amendment to, 151, 152,
  179
constitutional law, 200–201, 220,
  222
Corr, William, 126, 175, 186
Court of Appeals for the District of
  Columbia Circuit, U.S., 71
Thomas as judge on, vii, 3, 4, 7, 18,
  63, 65, 123, 129, 171, 188, 223–24,
  255, 274, 301, 430
Thomas's nomination and confirmation
  for, 120–21, 123, 129, 171, 188, 190,
  201, 211
Court of Appeals for the San Francisco
  Circuit, U.S., 386
Cranston, Alan, 142, 189, 264–65
criminal rights, 159, 207
Crown Theater, 52
Cuban American Research, 25
Cult Awareness Network, 116
Cutler, Lloyd, 286–87

Dallas Cowboys, 104
Dallas Times Herald, The, 66
Dana College, 234
Danforth, John C. "Jack," 209, 224, 395,
  400
background and political career of, 5,
  53, 57, 62, 81, 136, 139, 270–71
hearings attended by, 167–69, 172,
  181, 299, 302
moral reputation of, 6, 271, 423
political views of, 2, 5–6, 139, 270,
  422–23
Thomas as assistant attorney general
  to, 5, 53–55, 57, 206, 242, 271
Thomas as legislative aide to, 57, 81,
  82, 243
Thomas supported by, iii, 5–6, 15, 62,
  72–73, 136, 137, 143, 182, 239–40,
  242–43, 268–75, 289–90, 291, 319,
  384, 392, 398, 412–13
death penalty, 25, 155, 158, 160, 164,
  188, 201, 270
death squads, 83
Declaration of Independence, 20, 110–11

DeConcini, Dennis, vi, 135, 214–15, 221, 224, 241, 265, 333, 399
*Deep Throat* (film), 52
Deets, Horace, 136
Defense Department, U.S., 262
Deitz, Park, 361
Delaware, University of, 187
Del Bianco, Mark, 254, 255
Delta Sigma Theta sorority, 145
Demarest, David F., Jr., 71
Democratic party, 5, 59, 62, 100
    Hill's affiliation with, 247, 254–55, 256
    in South, 72, 74, 137, 144–46, 219
Democratic Senatorial Campaign Committee, 295, 402
Denton, Jeremiah, 400
*Devil in Miss Jones, The* (film), 52
Devillier Communications, 287
Disler, Mark, 304
Dixon, Alan, 402–4, 426
Doak, Shrum, Harris, Sherman, Donilon, 287
Doggett, John, III, 370–77
    sexual fantasy ascribed to Hill by, vi, 319–21, 361, 371–77, 394, 398
Dole, Robert J., 218–19, 274
*Donahue Show, The*, 387
Donilon, Tom, 239
Douglas, Elsie, 163
Douglas, William O., 152, 156, 199
Doyle, James, 207–8
drug abuse, 168, 300
Duberstein, Kenneth, 205, 288, 290, 299, 332, 414
    Thomas prepared by, 22–23, 70, 72, 123, 143, 168–69, 172, 178, 184, 197
Dukakis, Michael, 28, 141, 287
Dukes, Hazel, 30, 75
Duke University, 77

Eagle Forum, 130–31
economic rights, 178, 222–23
*Economics and Politics of Race, The* (Sowell), 56–57
EDP Enterprises, 209
Education Department, U.S.:
    Hill at, 86, 89, 91, 235, 254–55, 308–9, 325, 348

Reagan and, 309
    Thomas as Assistant Secretary of Civil Rights in, 86–91, 144–45, 200, 235, 254–55, 308–9
Education Fund, 25
Eisenhower, Dwight D., 1, 11, 61, 156
elections:
    of 1964, 109
    of 1970, 139–40
    of 1972, 187
    of 1976, 57
    of 1980, 81, 381
    of 1984, 103, 121
    of 1988, 28, 141
Ellison, Kerry, 386
Emerson, Thomas, 192
Emily's List, 287, 427
enterprise zones, 103
environmental issues, 25, 163, 164–65, 177, 220
Environmental Protection Agency (EPA), 57
Episcopal Church, 11, 23, 49, 65–66, 116, 129
Equal Employment Opportunity Commission (EEOC), 82, 86, 90–91, 94, 181–82, 271
    bureaucratic disarray of, 93, 101, 118, 119–21
    controversy and criticism surrounding Thomas at, 94–102, 106, 118–21, 125, 135–36, 171, 201
    delayed and lapsed cases at, 93, 119–21, 136
    Hill at, 91, 102, 227, 230, 233, 235–36, 255, 267–69, 309–11, 325, 336–37, 348
    lawsuits filed by, 94, 100, 118, 121
    mandate of, 7–8, 94, 95
    pension rights issue and, 118–20, 135–36
    sexual harassment cases filed at, since hearings, 421–22
    sexual harassment policies of, 84, 381–84, 387
    telephone logs of, 268, 269, 311, 325–27

Thomas as chairman of, 2, 7–8, 22, 23,
    64, 66, 68, 69, 91, 93–107, 109–22,
    125, 126, 127, 129, 135–36, 147,
    171, 176, 183, 188–89, 194–95, 201,
    203–4, 213, 230, 233, 235–36, 255,
    256, 267–69, 274, 277, 278, 289,
    297, 309–11, 336–37, 382–84
Thomas's critique of guidelines of, 84,
    381–82, 385
Wright as director of public affairs at,
    277, 278, 280–84, 297, 354–55
    see also job discrimination
Equal Rights Amendment (ERA),
    130–31
erotomania, 361–62, 375, 398
Ethics Committee, Senate, 215, 265, 333
Exon, James, 261, 262, 404–6
Exon, Patricia, 261
Exorcist, The (Blatty), 343–44, 348, 349,
    350

Fabrizio, Tony, 141–42
family-planning clinics, 19, 159
Family Research Council, 130
Farrakhan, Louis, 66–67
Federal Bureau of Investigation (FBI),
    63–64, 83, 211, 213–14, 229, 290
    Hill questioned by, 215–19, 221, 233,
        235, 245, 318, 339
    report issued by, 243, 271–72, 273,
        303, 304, 349
    Thomas questioned by, 63–64, 217–18,
        235, 241, 268–69, 300, 334
Federal Communications Commission
    (FCC), 6, 223, 430
Federal Home Loan Bank Board, 215
Federalist Society, 111–12, 114
Feinstein, Dianne, 426–27
feminism, see women's rights movement
Fiers, Alan, 322
Fitch, Nancy, 370
Fitzgerald, Ella, 250
Fitzwater, Marlin, vi, 141, 287
Fleming, Peter, 431–32
Ford, Gerald R., 156
Ford, Wendell, 432–33
Ford Foundation, 7
Fortas, Abe, 153–54, 156

Fountainhead, The (Rand), 117
Foxman, Abraham, 67
Framble, Abraham, 33
Frank, John P., 286, 295, 306
Frankfurter, Felix, 156, 207
Franklin, John Hope, 77–78, 208
Freedom of Information Act (1966), 147
Friday, Thomas, 4
Fried, Charles, 383–84
Friedman, Milton, 55
Friends of the FBI, 83
Fuller, Jack, 40
fundamentalism, 128, 382
Fund for the Feminist Majority, 427
Furman v. Georgia, 155, 201
Future Homemakers of America, 252

Gallup Organization, 424
Garcia v. San Antonio, 165
Gardner, Warner W., 286
Garza, Emilio M., 8
Gates, William, 178
gay rights, 128, 131
General Accounting Office (GAO), 93,
    101
General Electric, 48
Georgetown University Law Center, 285
Gibson, William F., 79
Gilette, Mark, 237, 258
Ginsburg, Douglas H., 63
Goldberg, Arthur, 153, 154, 156
Goldstein, Barry, 121
Goldwater, Barry, 1, 9–10, 109–10, 140
Gomperts, John, 134–35
Graham, Annie, 31–32, 33, 34, 39
Grant, Harriet, 211–13, 218, 280
Gray, Clayland Boyden, 1–5, 8–9, 12–13,
    15–16, 70–71, 111, 131–32, 139, 287,
    288, 414, 422–23
Gray, Sterling, 386
Green, Donald H., 294–95, 321–22, 365,
    398
Greene, Harold H., 119
Grey, Jerome, 145
Griggs v. Duke Power Co., 155, 200, 201
Griswold, Erwin N., 198–99, 201, 206
Griswold v. Connecticut, 152, 192
Grove City College v. Bell, 200

Hall, Fawn, 350
Hamer, Fannie Lou, 173
Hampe, Carl, 245, 291
Handitrans, 259
Hardnett, Sukari, 364
Hardy, Gil, 86, 374
Harlan, John M. (justice 1877–1911), 199
Harlan, John M. (justice 1955–1971),
    154, 199, 207
Harris, Thad, 36
Hart, B. Sam, 90
Harvard Law School, 286, 294
Harvard University, 142, 198, 261
    Kennedy School of Government at,
    423
Harvie, Christopher J., 126, 175
Hatch, Orrin G., 11, 182, 186, 192, 234,
    240–41, 269, 280, 297, 302–4,
    357–58, 395, 400, 402, 420
    background and political career of, 335
    Thomas questioned by, 334–44, 348
Haynsworth, Clement, Jr., 155–56, 295
Hazard, Geoffrey, 254
Heartland Coalition for the Confirmation
    of Judge Clarence Thomas, 209
Heflin, Howell, 144, 190, 215, 219–21,
    280, 292, 399–400
    Hill questioned by, 322–25
    Thomas questioned by, 215, 332–34,
    347, 349–51
Heidepriem, Nikki, 295–96
Height, Dorothy, 173
Helms, Jesse, 139, 280
Henderson, Wade, 29–30, 75–76, 77,
    78–79, 137
Heritage Foundation, 20, 112, 114, 127,
    180, 186
Hill, Albert, 247–50, 255–56, 296, 313
Hill, Anita Faye, 210–19, 223
    academic excellence of, 250, 251,
    252–54, 258–59, 338
    aloofness ascribed to, 336, 369
    attacks on character and credibility of,
    vi, 239–40, 243, 245, 265, 267–69,
    288, 289, 312, 317, 319–20, 336–46,
    352–54, 357–58, 365–66, 369–70,
    392, 394–95, 398–99, 400–402, 420
    black criticism of, 396

childhood and adolescence of, 248–53
civil rights views of, 247, 254–55, 256,
    258, 348
commercial code law specialty of, 259,
    286, 342
in continued contact with Thomas,
    235–36, 239–40, 241, 255, 256, 268,
    269, 309, 311, 325–27, 397, 405–6
delay in examining evidence of,
    123–26, 186, 210–14, 218–19, 221,
    244–45, 316, 397
demeanor of, 89, 235, 244, 251, 252,
    307–8, 328
Democratic affiliation of, 247, 254–55,
    256
disputed law firm dismissal of, 314,
    321–22, 365, 398
early ambitions of, 251, 254
early education of, 251–53, 323–24
Education Department job of, 86, 89,
    91, 235, 254–55, 308–9, 325, 348
EEOC, job at, 91, 102, 227, 230, 233,
    235, 255, 267–69, 309–11, 325,
    336–37, 348; promotion at, 337;
    salary at, 337
fantasies ascribed to, 269, 319–21,
    323–24, 358, 359, 361–62, 371–77,
    398, 407
feminist support for, 239, 295–96, 304,
    387–88, 397–98
friends confided in by, 102, 124,
    174–75, 210, 212, 233, 237, 255,
    311, 319, 321, 356–59, 407
humor of, 252, 259–60
inconsistency seen in statements of,
    317, 327–28, 338–39, 345, 407
initial press contacts with, 230–31,
    245
intelligence of, 252, 258, 259, 338,
    348
law firm joined by, 254, 289, 294, 314,
    321–22, 365, 398
as law professor, iv, vii, 102, 123–24,
    210, 211–12, 216, 230, 238, 256–60,
    293, 310, 318–19, 348, 418–19
legal education of, 86, 124, 174, 239,
    253–54, 348, 357
legal publications of, 259

legal team assembled for hearings,
    285–87, 294–96, 304–7, 313, 354,
    366–67, 391–92, 399
lifestyle and social life of, 89, 253, 254,
    257–58, 308, 310, 317, 320
media coverage of, iv, 233–34, 236,
    238–39, 240, 244–45, 247, 293–94
motivation question and, 216, 238,
    244, 323–24, 327–28, 347, 392
National Public Radio (NPR)
    interview of, 237, 240, 432
opportunity to testify sought by, 303,
    305, 307
physical appearance of, 244, 252, 308
political and feminist alliances lacked
    by, 216, 244, 305, 388
political reticence of, 257, 348
polygraph test of, 217, 360–61, 367
praise by friends and colleagues of,
    237–39, 244, 247, 252–53, 254, 258,
    259
privacy and anonymity guarded by,
    210, 212–13, 216–17, 230–32, 302,
    305–6
public manner of, 244–45, 308
public opinion on, 395–97, 419,
    426–27
public relations efforts on behalf of,
    286–87, 295–96, 360–61, 392–93
public statements of, 238–39, 244–45,
    261, 262, 266, 268, 288, 398–99, 421
reluctance to step forward by, 146,
    210–11, 214–16, 219, 227, 230–32,
    235–36, 267
rural poverty background of, 248–51,
    267
scholarships and awards of, 253–54
sexual harassment complaint not filed
    by, 236, 243, 263, 312, 318–19,
    356–57, 407
sincerity and honesty seen in, 238,
    239, 245, 248, 254, 288
social activism of, 258–59
strength and determination of, 252,
    258, 329
student counseling by, 253, 256, 259
student prominence and activism of,
    252–54

students and colleagues as critical of,
    248, 269, 336, 352–53, 365
supporters of, 261–64, 266–67, 275,
    285–87, 294–96, 305–7, 329
Thomas charged with sexual
    harassment by, iv, 69, 102, 123–26,
    174–75, 186, 210–11, 213, 217, 221,
    229–31, 233–36, 257, 264–65, 301,
    308–12, 314–16, 340–42, 356–59,
    382–84
Thomas's job recommendations for,
    269, 311
Thomas's overtures to, 217, 308–11,
    314–15, 319, 322, 325
Thomas's retaliation feared by, 236,
    268, 310–11, 312, 318–19, 326
women's rights as viewed by, 216, 247,
    252, 253, 255, 256, 258–59, 348,
    352–53
Hill, Dolores, 251
Hill, Eddie, 251
Hill, Erma, 247–50, 255–56, 296, 313
Hill, Winston, 249–51, 296, 418
Hilson, Louise, 287, 295
Hilton, Steve, 181, 319
Hoerchner, Susan, 212, 213, 356, 365
Hogan, Cynthia, 279–83, 284–85
Holmes, Oliver Wendell, 111–12, 161,
    207, 220–21
Holt, Diane, 311, 369
Holy Cross College, 45–49, 52, 63, 208
    Black Student Union at, 46–49
homosexuality, 90, 131, 257, 297, 354–55
Hooks, Benjamin L., 6, 8, 12, 15, 28–30,
    66, 73–79, 137, 208–9, 430
Hoover, Herbert, 78–79
Hoover, J. Edgar, 83
Horton, Willie, 28, 136, 140, 141–42
House, Toni, vii
House of Representatives, U.S., 263,
    264
    check-bouncing scandal in, 433
Hudson, Keith, 428
Hughes, Charles Evans, 199
Hughes, Johnny, 207

Immaculate Conception Seminary, 43–44
Institute for Justice, 7

integration, 44
  forced, 87, 99, 113
  school, 85, 113, 144–45, 201, 251, 252
Internal Revenue Service (IRS), 64, 386
Iran-Contra scandal, 113, 172, 227
Iraq, 275

Jackson, Alphonso, 209
Jackson, Jesse, 141
Jackson, Robert H., 162–63, 199
Jacob, John E., 74
Jacobson, Keith, 430
Jaffa, Harry, 109–10
Jarvis, Sonia, 296
Jipping, Tom, 3–4, 72, 129–30, 132, 134,
  181–82, 194–95
job discrimination, 2, 7–8, 139–40
  age-related, 7–8, 94, 118–21, 201–2
  disability-related, 7–8, 94
  EEOC lawsuits against, 94, 100, 118,
    121
  race-related, 7–8, 94, 97, 105, 120–21
  sex-related, 7–8, 84, 94, 97, 105,
    120–21, 183, 185, 200, 208, 242,
    379–90
  Supreme Court decisions on, 103, 105,
    155, 200, 383–85
John Birch Society, 26
Johnson, Lester, 43, 48, 50, 76, 197–98, 289
Johnson, Lyndon B., 198, 400
  Supreme Court nominations of, 4, 151,
    153–54
Johnston, J. Bennett, 215
Jones, Edith, 4
Jones, Robb M., iii
Jordan, Emma, 285–86, 305–6
Jourdain, Rose, 362–64, 368
Judaism, 67
Judiciary Committee, Senate, 9–10, 11,
  21, 26, 165, 359
  Biden's chairmanship of, 26, 120,
    169–70, 197, 198, 206, 209, 210,
    211–14, 218–19, 221–25, 239, 263,
    274–75, 290, 292, 299, 302–3, 307,
    313–16, 346–47, 391–95, 398
  criticism of, 388–89, 419–21, 424–25
  Democratic majority on, 74, 169, 172,
    173, 186, 204–5

hearings process of, 21, 61, 126–27
leaks suspected in, 234, 240, 241,
  271–72, 293, 303, 304, 331, 333,
  394–95, 431
male membership of, 124, 168, 396–97
members of, 135–36, 142, 144, 169,
  186–87
procedural difficulties of, 302–4, 307
questionable moral authority of, 27–28,
  124–25, 265
Republican minority on, 169, 172, 187,
  202
sexual harassment issue initially
  ignored by, 124–26, 186, 217,
  218–19, 221, 225, 231, 233, 234,
  240, 245, 266, 285, 380, 395, 397
staff aides of, 169, 184, 186, 191,
  204–5, 216, 278–79, 280
subcommittees of, 186–87
subpoena power of, 285, 368, 393–94
swing vote of, 190, 194
Thomas's appellate court confirmation
  hearings in, 120–21, 171, 188, 190,
  201
Thomas's excoriation of, 331–32
see also Thomas Supreme Court
  confirmation hearings
Justice Department, U.S., 4, 68, 89, 98–
  99, 103, 154, 162, 190, 294, 353, 430
  civil rights policies of, 105, 106,
    162–63
  Thomas supported by, vi, 24, 66,
    70–72, 170

Kassebaum, Nancy Landon, 242, 410–11
Kaufman, Ron, 71
Keating, Charles H., 215, 241, 265
Keating Five, 215, 265
Kemp, Evan, 8–9
Kennebunkport, Maine, 4, 9, 12–16, 101,
  141, 171, 300
Kennedy, Anthony M., 157, 164, 165,
  220, 428
Kennedy, Edward M. "Ted," 2, 27–28,
  80, 142, 146, 175, 186, 189, 215,
  241, 287, 292, 293, 303, 306, 394
  Bork opposed by, 27, 80, 124, 134,
    183, 359

civil rights sponsored by, 2, 124, 359,
    423
personal indiscretions and reputation
    of, 28, 125, 142, 183, 264, 265,
    359–60, 401, 402, 423–24
on Senate ethics, 401–2
Thomas questioned by, 183, 184–86,
    191
Kennedy, Flo, 21
Kennedy, John F., 156
Kennedy, Robert F., 46
*Keyes* v. *Denver*, 201
King, Martin Luther, Jr., 66, 140, 173,
    397
    assassination of, 44, 45, 46
    federal holiday in honor of, 116
King, Roy C., 251, 252
Kingston Group, 128
Kirkland, Lane, 138
Klain, Ronald A., 9–10, 221
Klein, Freida, 387
Knight-Ridder Newspapers, 297
Knop, Opal, 116
Kohl, Herb, 302, 358
Kothe, Charles A., 269, 320–21, 370–71
Kreiter, Nancy, 120–21
Kristol, Bill, 3, 71–72, 288, 365
Ku Klux Klan, 406

Labor Department, U.S., 13, 71, 304
labor movement, 25, 27, 79–80, 103, 106,
    134, 138, 203–4
LaHaye, Beverly, 131
L'Amour, Louis, 22
Laster, Gail, 126, 146
Law, Elizabeth, 209
Law, W. W., 36, 60
Leadership Conference on Civil Rights,
    73–74, 133, 138, 228, 234
Leahy, Patrick J., 11, 171, 280, 292, 293,
    376–77
    Hill questioned by, 318–19, 326–27
    Thomas questioned by, 191–95,
        200–201, 346–49
Lear, Norman, 27
*Legal Times,* the, 104, 223–24, 228, 430
Lehrman, Lewis E., 20, 180, 185–86
*Lemon* v. *Kurtzman,* 155, 201

Letterer, Lisa, 296
Liberman, Lee, 3, 8, 12, 70, 74, 111,
    131–32, 182, 288
libertarianism, 1, 7, 26, 132, 176, 182,
    220
*Liberty,* 70
Library Court, 128–30, 181, 194, 399,
    414, 428
*Library Court Live,* 414, 418, 430
Lichtman, Judy, 239
Lieberman, Joseph, 261, 412
*Life,* 153–54
Lifespring, 115–16
Lincoln Institute, 83–84, 117
*Lincoln Review,* 64–65, 67–68, 82,
    83–84, 89–90, 117
Lincoln Savings and Loan Association,
    265
Lincoln University, 54
lobbying groups, 71
    conservative, 3, 10, 75, 78, 115,
        127–31, 181–82, 209–10
    liberal, 17–21, 22, 24–27, 30, 62, 69,
        73–74, 78, 134–38, 147, 181, 228,
        271
    for women's rights, 262, 263
Lockheed, 77
Lone Tree, Okla., 248–51, 255–56, 418
Lone Tree Baptist Church, 249, 256, 418
Long Dong Silver, 314, 341–43, 344,
    349–50
Los Angeles Raiders, 104
*Los Angeles Times, The,* 65–66, 231, 236
Lowery, Joseph, 74
Lucas, William, 190
Lucy, William, 209
Luttig, Michael, 71–72, 341

McCarthy, Joseph R., 61, 171, 344, 351
McClure, Frederick D., 24, 70, 72,
    168–69, 172
McDowell, Bobbie, 145
Macedo, Stephen, 176, 182
McGovern, George, 54
Mackey, John P., 71–72, 209
MacKinnon, Catharine, 387
Malcolm X, 14, 45, 46, 47, 382
Manhattan Project, 7

Manion, Daniel, 26
March on Washington (1963), 140
Marriott Hotel (Washington, D.C.), 306
Marro, Anthony, 431
Marshall, Cecilia Suyat, 154
Marshall, Thurgood, 1–6, 13, 14, 15, 29,
    33, 60, 66, 110, 112, 150–52, 158,
    161–63, 199
  civil rights advocacy of, 2, 4, 73, 112,
    150–51, 161–63, 173
  deteriorating health of, 2, 150, 162
  LBJ's nomination of, 4–5, 150
  radical black criticism of, 154–55
  retirement of, 1–2, 3, 4, 8, 11, 130,
    150, 160, 162
  Thomas's attacks on, 28, 73, 173
Martin, Emma Mae Thomas, 31, 33, 34,
    58–59, 145, 198
  welfare dependency of, 58–59, 85, 169,
    191
Martin, Isaac, 417
May, Justin Lee, 429
Meese, Ed, 82, 85, 90, 105–7, 125
Meet the Press, 10–11
Meritor Savings Bank v. Vinson, 383–85
Methodist Church, 23, 116
Metzenbaum, Howard, 124, 125–26, 146,
    175, 186, 188, 234, 287, 293, 346,
    351, 375–76
  background and career of, 191
  Thomas questioned by, 190–91
Metzger, Leigh Ann, 70, 71, 131
Michelman, Kate, 18–19, 21, 24, 62, 353,
    397–98, 415
Mikulski, Barbara, 242, 266–67, 287
Miller v. California, 201
Milton Academy, 69
minimum wage, 65, 85, 165, 220
Minor, Paul K., 360
Miranda v. Arizona, 295
Miranowski, Jerry, 254
Mitchell, George J., 218–19, 241–42, 263,
    264, 274, 293, 402–3, 424–25
Moral Majority, 127
Morris, Okla., 248, 251–53
Morris High School, 252
Morris Junior High School, 251–52
Moynihan, Daniel Patrick, 261–62, 263

Myers, Phyllis Berry, 282, 283, 317, 370,
    430

Nader, Ralph, 228
Napolitano, Janet, 286–87, 295
Nation, 64–65
National Abortion Rights Action League
    (NARAL), 18, 20, 22, 23, 138,
    295–96, 397, 415
National Association for the
    Advancement of Colored People
    (NAACP), 35, 36, 43, 53, 71, 121,
    140, 173
  Bush's criticism of, 140
  founding of, 56
  Hooks's leadership of, 6, 12, 28–30,
    66, 73–79, 137, 208–9, 430
  Legal Defense Fund of, 121, 184, 254
  Savannah office of, 35, 36, 43, 60, 94
  Thomas's nomination and, 6, 8, 12,
    28–30, 62, 66, 68, 73–80, 121, 135,
    137, 294, 396
National Bar Association (NBA), 76
National Center for Neighborhood
    Enterprise, 209, 396
National Coalition on Black Voter
    Participation, 296
National Enquirer, 257
National Honor Society, 252
National Law Enforcement Council, 208
National Law Journal, 295, 388, 395
National Organization for Women
    (NOW), 20–21, 208, 426
National Public Radio (NPR), 237, 240,
    431, 432
National Republican Congressional
    Committee, 143
National Right to Life Committee, 128
National Sheriffs Association, 208
National Troopers Coalition, 207
National Urban League, 74–75, 99, 173
National Women's Political Caucus, 427
Native Americans, 251, 259
Native Son (Wright), 43
natural law, 176–78, 186, 187
  Thomas and, 110–12, 176–78, 180,
    186, 187, 220–21, 310
NBC-TV, 399

Neas, Ralph, 73, 74, 234
New Deal, 79, 110, 156
Newman, Constance, 182
New Orleans Police Department, 99
New Right, 109–10, 127–31, 335, 428
*Newsday*, 64, 67–68, 126, 227, 230, 231, 282
  circulation of, 210, 234
  Hill's allegations reported by, iv, 227, 233–34, 236, 239, 240, 266, 307, 431–32
*Newsweek*, 90
*New Yorker, The*, 42
*New York Herald Tribune, The*, 7
*New York Times, The*, iv, 78, 155, 201, 239, 298, 429
*New York Times Magazine, The*, 396
*New York Times* v. *United States*, 201
*Nightline*, iv-v, 71, 267–68
Nixon, Pat, 156
Nixon, Richard M., 6, 46, 141, 153, 155, 198
  Supreme Court nominations of, 141, 154, 155–56
Norman, Okla., 237–39, 256–59, 293–94, 327, 398, 418–19
North, Oliver, 14, 109, 113, 350
North Carolina, University of, 277–78
Norton, Eleanor Holmes, 381
Norton, Helen, 387

Oberly, Johnna, 259
O'Connor, Sandra Day, 157, 158, 159, 165, 220, 429
Office of Personnel Management, 182, 381
Office of Temporary Special Council, Senate, 431–33
Ogletree, Charles, 286, 294–95, 304–7, 360–61
Oklahoma State University, 253, 323–24
  Women's Council of, 253
Oklahoma University Law School
  Black Law Student Association of, 259
  Hill as law professor at, iv, vii, 102, 123–24, 210, 211–12, 216, 230, 237–38, 256–60, 293, 310, 318–19
  President's Advisory Committee on Minority Affairs of, 259

  Thomas invited to speak at, 239–40, 256, 268
Okmulgee, Okla., 252
Oral Roberts University, 310, 352, 353, 407
  O. W. Colburn School of Law at, 102, 248, 255, 269, 318–19, 320–21
Osage Indians, 259
*Othello* (Shakespeare), 355
Oxford University, 174

Pacific Research Institute, 176
Palm Beach, Fla., 125, 142, 183, 360
Palmer, John E., 209
Paoletta, Mark, 70–71
Parker, Jay, 82–84
  as foreign agent of South Africa, 68, 82–84, 89–90, 116–17, 146
  Thomas and, 82–84, 89–90, 116–17, 146, 381–82
Parker, John J., 78–79
Parks, Rosa, 173, 209
Parsons, Arch, 6–7, 12, 74
Paul, Joel, 356, 357, 358
Payne, Pervis Tyrone, 160–61
Peck, Gregory, 27
Peck, Jeff, 307
Peed, Carl, 208
*Penry* v. *Lynaugh*, 164
*Pentagon Papers*, 155, 201
*People*, 418
People for the American Way, 27, 78, 126, 133, 134, 147, 188, 271, 272
Pepper, Hamilton & Scheetz, 294, 321
Perry, Michael, 158
Persian Gulf War, 11, 70, 276
Phelps, Timothy M., 146, 227–38
  confidential sources of, 227–28, 229, 232–33, 431–33
  Hill's charges first reported by, 227–28, 233–34, 307, 431–32
Pin Point, Ga., 13, 18, 31–33, 57–59, 72, 78, 169, 172, 417
*Plessy* v. *Ferguson*, 162–63
poll taxes, 79
pornography, iii, 51–53, 217, 314–15, 322, 340–42, 346–47, 383, 386, 387–88, 393–94, 430

Powell, Lewis F., Jr., 63, 154, 156, 157, 199
press, freedom of, 159, 431–32
prisoner rights, 158, 159–61, 164, 428–29
privacy rights, 152, 179, 192, 222, 310
property rights, 110, 111, 161, 164–65, 176, 177–78, 182, 220
Pryor, David H., 120

Quayle, J. Danforth, 3, 5–6, 71, 91, 412
Quinn, Frank, 101
quotas, racial, 2–3, 4, 14, 28, 77, 84, 95, 96, 105, 118, 203–4, 348

racism, 23, 36, 42–44, 45–46, 67–68, 73, 79, 95, 150, 167, 202–3
  elitism and, 47, 55, 56
  sexism vs., 397–98
  stereotypes based on, 29, 41, 49, 339–43, 396
  see also apartheid
Ralston-Purina Company, 224, 270
Rand, Ayn, 22, 109, 117
rape, 28, 117, 128, 217, 258, 386
Raspberry, William, 168
Rauh, Joseph L., 209, 228
Reagan, Nancy, 172
Reagan, Ronald, 4–5, 22, 60, 81, 90, 134, 180, 325, 381
  governorship of, 82
  racial bias ascribed to, 95
  second term of, 25, 103–4, 121
  Supreme Court nominations of, 10, 25, 127, 156–57
Reagan administration, 57, 130, 172, 294
  black officials in, 68, 82, 86, 90–91, 95, 381–82
  civil rights policies of, 81, 90–91, 94–107, 381–83
  conservative agenda of, 25, 81–82, 85, 87, 90–91, 94–107, 156–57
  federal judiciary agenda of, 25, 105, 156–57
  Thomas and, 81–91, 103–6, 114, 118, 121, 381–84
  Thomas's policies adapted to, 103–6, 114, 118, 121
Reason, 183

Reed, Joe, 144–45, 146, 400, 430
Rehnquist, Nan, iii-vi
Rehnquist, William H., iii-vi, 26, 150, 154, 156–65, 220, 428, 429
Republican National Committee, 182
Republican Party
  conservative wing of, 2–4, 25, 26, 81–95
  Thomas's affiliation with, 54, 55
Resnick, Judith, 285–86
Reynolds, Osborne M., Jr., 238
Reynolds, William Bradford, 98–100, 103, 106–7, 294
Riley, Melissa, 280
Robb, Charles S., 400, 402
Roberts, Michele, 286
Roberts, Owen, 79
Robertson, Pat, v-vi, 133–34, 320–21, 399
Robinson, Walter, 188–89
Roe v. Wade, 18–20, 179, 191–95, 200, 201, 228, 403, 418
  opposition to, 18–20, 136, 164
  passage of, 10, 51, 155, 193–94
  Thomas questioned on, 51, 192–95, 392
Roman Catholic Church, 59, 128, 129
  Thomas and, v, 11, 14, 23, 37–49, 55, 65, 89, 136, 170, 208, 382
Roosevelt, Eleanor, 260
Roosevelt, Franklin D., 156
Rose, Charlie, 279
Ross, Susan Deller, 286, 306
Ruff, Charles, 360
Rules Committee, Senate, 306, 328–29, 432–33
Russell Senate Office Building, 290
  Senate Caucus Room in, 167, 169, 171, 175, 183, 198, 200, 204, 299, 306, 308, 392
Rust v. Sullivan, 159

St. Alban's Church, 270
St. Benedict the Moor school, 37–38
St. John Vianney Minor Seminary, 42–43
St. Louis Post-Dispatch, The, 81
Saltonstall, Thomas, 189
Sasser, Jim, 265–66

Satinover, Jeffrey, 361–62, 375
Savannah, Ga., 32–37, 43, 60, 78, 94, 289
savings and loan industry, 77
    scandal in, 142, 215, 241, 265
Scalia, Antonin, 26, 132, 145, 157–58,
    160, 164, 165, 220, 383, 428, 429
Schlafly, Phyllis, 130–31
Schneider, William, 16
school busing, 23, 81, 85, 90, 113, 134,
    155, 201, 202
Schroeder, Patricia, 264
Schwartz, Mark, 278–79
Scott-Davis, Algenita, 76
Seattle Times, The, 436
segregation, 4, 14, 23, 30, 33, 36, 38,
    40–42, 47, 55, 79, 89, 107, 140
    legal justification of, 162
    psychological effects of, 112–13
    of schools, 89
Seidman, Ricki, 124, 146, 175, 210–11
Self, Leisha, 216, 257–58
Selmon, Dewey, 237
Semerad, Kate, 279–80
Senate, U.S., 5, 19, 57, 91, 140, 430–31
    advise and consent mandate of, 127,
        266
    Democratic majority in, 26, 74, 264,
        271, 400
    leaks investigated by, 430–31, 433
    male domination of, 241–42, 380, 401
    old-boys'-club atmosphere in, 241–42,
        401
    postponement of confirmation vote in,
        234, 241, 262–76, 285, 287
    public communication with members
        of, 134, 170–71, 262
    speeches on nomination in, 401–13
    Thomas confirmed by, iv, vi, 399–414
    women in, 242, 411
    see also specific Senate committees
sexual harassment
    appellate court decisions on, 383,
        385–86
    Judiciary Committee's failure to
        comprehend importance of, 124,
        239–42, 262, 264–65, 266–67, 275,
        380, 397
    disbelief of victims of, 267, 387

    EEOC guidelines on, 84, 381–84
    grievances filed on, 386
    historic instances of, 379–80, 383–86,
        387
    laws on, 84, 94, 241, 267, 284, 318,
        352, 380–86, 397
    legal cases brought on, 384–86, 387
    liability of employers and, 84, 380–81,
        382, 385
    men as victims of, 386
    Meritor decision on, 383–85
    stress caused by, 310, 386
    surveys on, 387
    Thomas's views on, 381–84, 485
    views of conservative women on,
        130–31
Shakespeare, William, 355
Shaw, Gaylord, 231, 233
Shelby, Richard, 144, 399–400
Sheldon, Louis, 131
Sherman, Wendy, 287, 295, 306
Shoemaker, Jane, 280
Silberman, Larry, 274
Silberman, Ricky, 101, 105, 114–15,
    181–82, 267, 274, 296–97, 382,
    414
Simmons, Althea, 121
Simon, Paul, 219, 234, 241, 293
Simon, William E., 113–14
Simpson, Alan, 191, 234, 240, 245,
    267–68, 275–76, 297, 303–4, 400,
    420, 424, 425
    Thomas questioned by, 351–55
Singleton, Harry, 50–51, 325
Siraco, John, 47
Slaughter, Louise, 264
slavery, 23, 34, 35, 110, 111, 112–13,
    144, 151, 177, 251
Smith, Dorrance C., 71
Smith, Jo Ann, 258–59
Smith, Judy, 63, 65, 68, 70, 182
Smith, William Kennedy, 28, 125
Souter, David, 4, 22, 70, 72, 129, 159,
    164, 171, 172, 194, 220, 222
    opposition to, 264, 359
South Africa
    apartheid in, 46, 67–68, 83–84, 89–90,
        305, 359

black homelands proposed for, 83–84,
    89–90
sanctions against, 65, 116–17
Thomas's connections to, 82–84,
    89–90, 116–17, 146, 305
Southern Christian Leadership
    Conference (SCLC), 74, 173
Sowell, Thomas, 55–57, 82, 96, 184–85,
    382
Specter, Arlen, iv-v, 192, 262–63, 280,
    424, 425–26
    Bork hearings and, 202, 291, 317, 415,
        426
    Doggett questioned by, 371–72
    election challenge faced by, iv, 202,
        317, 345, 426
    Hill accused of perjury by, 344–46,
        358, 402, 426
    Hill questioned by, iv, 277, 290–91,
        316–18, 319–21, 325–26, 327–28,
        334, 344–466
    objections to questioning by, 345–46,
        414–15, 426
    political views of, 202, 290–91, 346
    prosecutorial skills of, 202, 290,
        316–18, 322, 328, 345, 377, 395
    strategic use of, 316–17
    television appearances of, iv-v, 263, 414
    Thomas questioned by, 202–4, 214,
        223, 241, 344
Stanford University, Hoover Institute of,
    55
Stanton Group, 128
states rights, 111, 151, 165
Stevens, John Paul, 156, 158, 161, 163,
    165
Stevenson, Adlai, 153
Stewart, Carlton, 317
Stillwater, Okla., 252–53
Stone, Harlan Fiske, iii-iv, 199
Stotts, Carl, 103, 105
Sununu, John, 3–4, 5, 9, 143
Supreme Court, Alabama, 219
Supreme Court, U.S.:
    ABA rating of nominees for, 140–41
    activism in, 161, 176, 182
    adherence to precedent in (stare
        decisis), 161
    Burger era in, 154–57, 160
    civil rights decisions of, 2, 23, 76, 103,
        105, 106, 111, 112–13, 150–53, 155,
        162–63, 202, 223
    conservative drift of, 1, 10, 11, 25, 26,
        127, 147, 150, 154, 156–65, 220
    death penalty decisions of, 155, 158,
        160, 201
    first woman appointed to, 157
    intrusion of politics into, 126, 132–33,
        153–57, 161–62
    job discrimination decisions of, 103,
        105, 155, 200, 383–85
    LBJ's nominations to, 4, 151, 153–54
    legal ideal vs. reality of, 149
    lifetime tenure of justices in, 69, 156
    Meritor decision of, 383–85
    Nixon's nominations to, 141, 154,
        155–56
    precedents overruled in, 152, 159,
        160–63, 180–81
    public opinion on decisions of, 159,
        161
    Reagan's nominations to, 10, 25,
        156–57
    Rehnquist era in, 26, 150, 156–65
    selection process for, 61–62, 69
    Thomas's ambitions for seat on, 81, 115
    Thomas's criticism of, 112–13, 152,
        203
    Thomas's initial opinions in, 413,
        427–30
    Thomas's qualifications for, 135,
        140–41, 171, 184, 199–201, 214,
        220–21, 243, 401
    Warren era in, 1–2, 11–12, 150–55,
        156, 158, 159, 164
    working atmosphere in, 163
Supreme Court Watch, 224
Suthard, Bob, 207
Swank, David, 245
Swann v. Charlotte-Mecklenburg, 155,
    201
Sweeney, Al, 281
Syracuse University Law School, 187

Talkin, Pam, 290
Taylor, Sidney, 384–85

Temple University, 370
Terry, Henry Cornelius, 49, 51–52
Thomas, Clarence
 ABA qualifications rating of, 140–41
 abortion issue and, 10–11, 18–20,
  23–24, 51, 62, 65–66, 135, 136, 138,
  163, 170, 179–80, 191–95, 197, 205,
  392
 academic excellence of, 43, 47, 49, 207
 advertisements on behalf of, 133, 134,
  141–43
 alienation and independence of, 23, 33,
  41, 42, 43, 47, 50, 51, 104
 ambitions of, 2, 42, 47, 48, 54, 81,
  114–15
 anger and bitterness of, 23, 43, 44, 46,
  50, 55, 99, 104, 106, 114, 145, 289,
  291, 300–302, 331–33, 343
 antidiscrimination work of, 23, 46, 49,
  50, 75, 96–98, 121, 183, 203–4
 antisocial qualities of, 47–48, 101–2,
  104
 as assistant attorney general, 5, 53–55,
  57, 206, 242, 271
 big business and, 118
 birth of, 3, 13, 22, 31, 58
 black criticism of, 59–60, 66, 75–80,
  86–87, 89, 99, 100, 116, 120–21,
  135–38, 209, 294, 396
 black self-help espoused by, 3, 4, 60,
  67, 77, 87–88, 112, 139
 black support of, 74, 75, 78, 79, 133,
  135–36, 139, 182, 368–70, 396
 "black work" eschewed by, 85–86, 91,
  103
 Catholic training of, v, 11, 14, 23,
  37–49, 55, 65, 89, 136, 170, 208, 382
 childhood and adolescence of, v, 3,
  13–14, 31–34, 36–49, 58, 60, 88,
  172–73
 childhood poverty of, 13–14, 24,
  31–33, 55, 136, 168, 172–73, 205
 civil rights as viewed by, 2–4, 14–15,
  18, 20, 23, 45, 49–50, 62, 66, 76, 77,
  84, 85, 87–89, 94–106, 110, 112–14,
  121, 134–35, 145, 184, 201–4, 209,
  214
 college education of, 45–49, 63

 conjecture on withdrawal of, from
  nomination, 175, 287, 291, 302,
  327–28
 conservative political views of, iv, 2, 3,
  4, 7–8, 14–15, 16, 18–20, 22, 23, 28,
  29, 50–51, 54–57, 59–60, 64–66, 72,
  85, 94, 103–6, 109–15, 147, 152,
  220–21, 223, 255, 288, 382
 conservative sartorial style of, 88–89,
  94, 170
 contradictory policy reversals of, 90,
  97–98, 100–101, 104, 106, 176–81,
  184–86, 190–91, 192, 220
 on Court of Appeals, vii, 3, 4, 7, 18,
  63, 65, 123, 129, 171, 188, 223–24,
  255, 274, 301, 430
 dates with employees sought by, 217,
  281–82, 308–11, 314–15, 319, 322
 debating skills of, 46–47, 86–87, 197
 dignity and respect sought by, 43, 49,
  301–2, 332–33
 divorce of, 9, 17, 68–69, 86, 115, 301
 draft deferment of, 63
 early jobs of, 5, 47, 50, 53–55, 57, 81
 at Education Department, 86–91,
  144–45, 200, 235, 254–55, 308–9
 as EEOC chairman, 2, 7–9, 22, 23, 64,
  66, 68, 69, 91, 93–107, 109–22, 125,
  126, 127, 129, 135–36, 147, 171,
  176, 183, 188–89, 194–95, 201,
  203–4, 213, 230, 233, 235–36, 255,
  256, 267–69, 274, 277, 278, 290,
  297, 309–11, 336–37, 382–84
 employee relations of, 89, 101–2, 278,
  280–84, 290, 297, 308–11, 334,
  336–37, 347
 father of, v, 31, 114
 financial improprieties of, 188–89
 financial status of, 22, 54, 57, 59, 64,
  86, 102
 grandparents' rearing of, 14, 34–43,
  59–60, 88, 102, 112, 173, 174
 Hill's charges denied by, 218, 240,
  241, 243, 268–69, 272, 299–302, 322,
  331, 334–36, 343–44, 348
 Hill testimony ignored by, 332–34,
  392, 408
 humor of, 23, 48, 52

as ideologue, 171

intellect of, 42, 60, 199–200, 206–7

investigation into past of, 17–21, 24,
   29–30, 62–69, 123–26, 147, 171,
   175–95, 210–11, 272, 300–301

judicial improprieties of, 65, 130,
   143–46, 224

legal education of, 5, 49–55, 57, 86,
   187, 192–95, 200–201, 204, 206–7,
   320

legal practice and writings of, 4, 5, 17,
   18, 53–54, 57, 65, 84, 117, 140, 176,
   184, 220

marijuana use of, 46, 63–64, 67

marriages of, see Thomas, Kathy
   Grace Ambush; Thomas, Virginia
   Lamp

media coverage of, iii, iv-v, vii, 10–11,
   13–16, 18, 24, 41, 62–69, 71, 78, 81,
   85–86, 104, 123, 168, 418, 429

moderate to radical swing of, 109–15,
   117, 127, 220, 382

natural law theory espoused by,
   110–12, 176–78, 180, 186, 187,
   220–21, 310

opportunism seen in, 60, 119, 121, 220

opposition to nomination of, 6, 16,
   18–25, 27–29, 62–70, 73–80, 123–24,
   134–38, 147, 192–93, 198–200, 209,
   219–25

perjury question and, 241, 323

personality of, 47, 54, 60, 101–2, 104,
   129–30, 176, 301, 304, 337–38

personal lobbying campaign of, 72–73,
   75–76, 80, 130, 143–46, 399

philosophical development of, 14,
   44–47, 54–55, 94, 105, 109–14,
   127–29, 176–80, 206–7

physical appearance of, 41, 46, 47, 48,
   55, 94, 114, 289

political and financial support of, iii,
   v-vi, 3–4, 6–9, 21–24, 29, 57, 58, 62,
   70–75, 78, 80, 129–34, 135–36,
   138–44, 167–69, 181–83, 186,
   206–10, 304, 399–401

pornography as penchant of, iii, 51–52,
   217, 314–15, 322, 340–42, 346–47,
   366, 383, 387–88, 393–94

public opinion polls on, 74, 139, 170,
   297–98, 395–96, 427

public relations efforts on behalf of,
   70–76, 78, 133–34, 138–39, 141–43,
   181–83, 398, 399

race factor in nomination of, 3, 4, 6–8,
   10, 12, 13–16, 27, 28–30, 72–80,
   140, 143–46, 168, 201–3, 205,
   397–98, 408

racial discrimination experienced by,
   41–44, 53, 55, 114, 168, 202, 289

racist sexual stereotyping as viewed by,
   339–41

rapid professional and political rise of,
   57, 86

reading tastes of, 22, 42–43

religious affiliations of, v, 11, 14,
   22–23, 37–44, 54–55, 65–66, 116,
   129, 134, 382

Republican Party joined by, 54, 55,
   85

ridicule and ostracism of, 43, 86–87,
   99, 104

sadness and outrage of, 268, 274,
   301–2

seminary training of, 14, 23, 42–44,
   55, 168

Senate confirmation of, iv, v, vi,
   399–414

sexual harassment as viewed by,
   381–84, 385

sexual language used by, 51–52, 217,
   233, 281–82, 308–10, 314–16

social and professional awkwardness of,
   84, 94, 101–2, 115, 145, 337–38

specific issues avoided by, 76, 179,
   183, 192–95, 197–98

speeches of, 20, 40–41, 60, 66–67, 84,
   87–88, 94, 97–98, 109–15, 117, 125,
   126, 127, 147, 176, 177, 180, 182,
   184–85, 220–21, 272

sports enthusiasms of, 47, 57, 63, 104

student loans of, 22, 54, 57

student militancy of, 14, 44–46, 48–49,
   55, 94

support by female colleagues of,
   289–90, 296

tax problems of, 64, 102

understanding of constitutional law
  lacked by, 200–201
vindication sought by, 273–74, 301–2,
  331–34, 408
youthful studiousness of, 33, 42–43,
  47, 50, 53
Thomas, Jamal Adeen, 17, 23, 51, 291,
  414
childhood and adolescence of, 9, 54,
  81, 88, 102, 116, 169
Thomas's custody of, 9, 88, 102
Thomas, Kathy Grace Ambush, 9, 17, 23,
  48, 49, 50, 51, 54, 68–69, 81, 86, 102
Thomas, Myers, 31, 34, 36–40, 42, 58,
  59, 169, 172–73
Thomas, Virginia "Ginny" Lamp, iii, iv,
  vi, 65, 71–72, 130, 334
background and education of, 23,
  115–16
Chamber of Commerce job of, 23, 71,
  107, 115, 304
conservatism of, 107, 115
hearings attended by, 169, 198, 299,
  307, 336
Labor Department job of, 13, 71
Thomas's marriage to, 23, 115, 116,
  145–46, 152, 311
Thomas's relationship with, 13, 23,
  107, 115–16, 274, 411–12, 417–18
Thomas Supreme Court confirmation
  hearings (first round), 167–95,
  197–210, 220–25
abortion issue raised in, 179–80,
  191–95, 205, 392
affirmative action issue raised in, 201–4
civil rights issues avoided in, 201–2,
  204, 208
collusion of officials in, 182, 266
favorable vote expected in, 171–72,
  214–15
personal and ethical issues avoided in,
  189
strategic preparation and rehearsal of
  Thomas for, 21–24, 64, 70–72, 78,
  123, 130–34, 163, 168, 170, 171,
  172, 177, 184, 197–98, 205, 286
television coverage of, 170, 181, 187,
  197–98, 201–2

Thomas family members at, 169, 178,
  183, 191, 198
Thomas's credibility in, 178–81,
  192–95, 234–35, 392
Thomas's demeanor in, 169–70, 176,
  180, 193, 197
Thomas's grasp of constitutional law
  examined in, 200–201
Thomas's legal philosophy examined
  in, 175–78, 180, 200–221, 299
Thomas's opening statement in,
  172–74
Thomas's speeches examined in,
  176–77, 180, 182, 184–85, 220
Thomas's testimony in, 175–86,
  190–95, 200–205, 211, 220–21, 392
tie vote in, 224, 228, 231
witnesses opposing Thomas in,
  198–200, 208–9
witnesses supporting Thomas in, 198,
  206–9
Thomas Supreme Court confirmation
  hearings (second round), 299–329,
  331–78, 393–95
affidavits supporting Hill in, 362–65,
  367–68
affidavits supporting Thomas in,
  352–54, 361–62, 365–66
Coke can/pubic hair testimony in,
  309–10, 314–15, 316, 318, 325, 336,
  341, 343, 344, 387–88
conspiracy theory raised in, 342–44,
  351, 357–58, 365, 394–95, 402, 433
dating requests discussed in, 308–9,
  310, 314–15, 319
Exorcist cited in, 343–44, 348–50
Hill accused of perjury in, 344–46,
  358, 402, 426
Hill family members at, 296, 313–14
Hill's demeanor in, 308, 315–16, 328,
  407
Hill's law firm experience discussed in,
  314, 321–22, 365, 398
Hill's motivation questioned in,
  323–24, 327–28, 347
Hill's opening statement in, 296,
  308–12, 388
leaks decried in, 302, 331, 333

Long Dong Silver discussed in, 314,
  341–43, 344, 349–50
lynching allusions in, 302, 332,
  339–40, 411
national fascination with, 300, 312, 338
political jockeying at conclusion of,
  398–413
pornography discussed in, 314, 322,
  335, 340–43, 344, 346–47, 349–50,
  366, 387–88
racist sexual stereotypes dicussed in,
  339–41, 396
Republican vs. Democratic strategies
  in, 289–93, 304, 338, 353–54,
  393–95
sexual fantasy theory raised in, 320–21,
  323–24, 359, 361–62, 407
strategic preparation of Hill for,
  294–96
television coverage of, 300, 307, 333,
  338, 345, 346, 371, 394
Thomas family members at, 299, 307
Thomas's demeanor in, 299, 336
Thomas's denial of Hill's charges in,
  299–302, 322–23, 334–36, 343–44,
  394
Thomas's victimized posture in,
  300–302, 304, 331–34, 344, 350–51
varieties of sexual acts referred to in,
  310, 315, 316, 335, 340
witnesses supporting Hill in, 356–58
witnesses supporting Thomas in,
  368–77
Thompson, Diane, 287
Thornberry, Homer, 153
Thornburgh, Richard, 3, 4, 5, 8–10, 13
Thurmond, Strom, 26, 73, 80, 106–7,
  167, 169, 219, 240, 264, 275, 280,
  283, 290, 303–4, 316, 321, 370, 373,
  414
Time, 70
Today, 399
Totenberg, Nina, 432
Tower, John, 262, 411
Transkei, 83–84
Treasury Department, U.S., 379–80
Truro Episcopal Church, 65–66, 116, 134
Tulsa, Okla., 255, 311, 352

Uniform Guidelines on Employee
  Selection Procedure, 97, 103
United Auto Workers, 138
United Nations, 7, 153, 154

Venda, 89–90
victim's rights, 160–61
Vietnam War, 46, 63, 83, 155, 171, 276
  opposition to, 44, 45, 48, 188
Vinson, Mechelle, 383, 384–85
Virginia, University of, 111

Wald, Harkrader & Ross, 254, 289, 294,
  314, 321–22, 365, 398
Wall Street Journal, The, 68–69, 188
Walter, Thomas, 379–80
Warren, Earl, 1–2, 11–12, 112, 150–55,
  156, 158, 159, 164
Washington, Booker T., 46, 77
Washington, Craig, 29
Washington Court Hotel, 78
Washington Post, The, iv, 63, 64, 85–86,
  116, 155, 168, 236, 240, 296,
  297–98, 429
Watergate scandal, 154, 171
Watt, James, 100
Webber, Michael, 67
welfare system, 81, 83, 87, 88, 134, 169,
  180
  Thomas's criticism of, 85, 145, 262
Wellington, Harry, 51
Wells, Ellen M., 356–57, 358
Weyrich, Paul, 127–29, 194–95, 335, 399,
  414, 428, 430
White, Byron R., vi, 156, 158, 164
White House Bulletin, 16
White House Office of Public Liaison, 70
White House Working Group on the
  Family, 180–81
Wiegand, Shirley, 216, 237–38, 256–57,
  305–6, 419–21
Wilkins, Roy, 173
Williams, Armstrong, 269
Williams, Juan, 202
Williams, Leola, v, 31–34, 39, 42, 58,
  114, 169, 178, 289, 301
  hearings attended by, 169, 178, 183,
  198

marriages of, 31, 34
menial labor of, 32, 39, 58, 173
as nursing assistant, 58, 289
Williams, Robert, 388–89
Williams, Sam, 34–35, 59–60
Wilson, Margaret Bush, 53–54
Winston-Salem *Chronicle*, The, 278
Women Employed, 120–21
Women for Judge Thomas, 78
Women's Campaign Fund, 427
Women's Legal Defense Fund, 78, 239,
   387
Women's Resource Center, 258–59
women's rights movement, 19, 20–21, 25,
   26, 62, 69, 80, 84, 120–21, 136,
   179–80, 216, 258–59, 266
   civil rights movement vs., 397–98
   lobbyists for, 20–21, 208, 262, 263
   opposition to, 56–57, 115, 128, 130–31,
      397–98
   sexual harassment issue raised by, 381,
      385–86, 387–88
Woods, Harriett, 271
Woodson, Robert, 209, 396
Wooten, Terry L., 280–81, 283–84,
   321–22
World Anti-Communist League, 83

Wright, Angela, 101, 277–85, 290,
   353–55, 362–64
   EEOC position of, 277, 278, 280–84,
      297, 354–55
   employment history of, 279–80, 297,
      354–55, 368
   media attention to, 312–13
   subpoena issued to, 285, 368
   Thomas's firing of, 101, 278, 282–83,
      297, 354–55
   written statement of, 367–68
Wright, Richard, 42–43

Yale Law School, 26, 206, 271
   Hill's education at, 86, 124, 174, 239,
      253–54, 348, 357
   Thomas's education at, 5, 49–55, 57,
      86, 187, 192–95, 200–201, 204,
      206–7, 320
Yale University, 270
Yard, Molly, 208
Young, Whitney, 173
Young Americans for Freedom, 83

Zimbalist, Efrem, Jr., 83
Zschau, Ed, 265
Zuckerman, Jeffrey, 105, 109